HISTORICAL DICTIONARIES OF AFRICA

Edited by Jon Woronoff

1. *Cameroon,* by Victor T. Le Vine and Roger P. Nye. 1974. *Out of print. See No. 48.*
2. *The Congo,* 2nd ed., by Virginia Thompson and Richard Adloff. 1984. *Out of print. See No. 69.*
3. *Swaziland,* by John J. Grotpeter. 1975.
4. *The Gambia,* 2nd ed., by Harry A. Gailey. 1987. *Out of print. See No. 79.*
5. *Botswana,* by Richard P. Stevens. 1975. *Out of print. See No. 70.*
6. *Somalia,* by Margaret F. Castagno. 1975. *Out of print. See No. 87.*
7. *Benin (Dahomey),* 2nd ed., by Samuel Decalo. 1987. *Out of print. See No. 61.*
8. *Burundi,* by Warren Weinstein. 1976. *Out of print. See No. 73.*
9. *Togo,* 3rd ed., by Samuel Decalo. 1996.
10. *Lesotho,* by Gordon Haliburton. 1977. *Out of print. See No. 90.*
11. *Mali,* 3rd ed., by Pascal James Imperato. 1996.
12. *Sierra Leone,* by Cyril Patrick Foray. 1977.
13. *Chad,* 3rd ed., by Samuel Decalo. 1997.
14. *Upper Volta,* by Daniel Miles McFarland. 1978.
15. *Tanzania,* by Laura S. Kurtz. 1978.
16. *Guinea,* 3rd ed., by Thomas O'Toole with Ibrahima Bah-Lalya. 1995. *Out of print. See No. 94.*
17. *Sudan,* by John Voll. 1978. *Out of print. See No. 53.*
18. *Rhodesia/Zimbabwe,* by R. Kent Rasmussen. 1979. *Out of print. See No. 46.*
19. *Zambia,* 2nd ed., by John J. Grotpeter, Brian V. Siegel, and James R. Pletcher. 1998.
20. *Niger,* 3rd ed., by Samuel Decalo. 1997.
21. *Equatorial Guinea,* 3rd ed., by Max Liniger-Goumaz. 2000.
22. *Guinea-Bissau,* 3rd ed., by Richard Lobban and Peter Mendy. 1997.
23. *Senegal,* by Lucie G. Colvin. 1981. *Out of print. See No. 65.*
24. *Morocco,* by William Spencer. 1980. *Out of print. See No. 71.*
25. *Malawi,* by Cynthia A. Crosby. 1980. *Out of print. See No. 84.*
26. *Angola,* by Phyllis Martin. 1980. *Out of print. See No. 92.*
27. *The Central African Republic,* by Pierre Kalck. 1980. *Out of print. See No. 51.*
28. *Algeria,* by Alf Andrew Heggoy. 1981. *Out of print. See No. 66.*
29. *Kenya,* by Bethwell A. Ogot. 1981. *Out of print. See No. 77.*
30. *Gabon,* by David E. Gardinier. 1981. *Out of print. See No. 58.*
31. *Mauritania,* by Alfred G. Gerteiny. 1981. *Out of print. See No. 68.*

32. *Ethiopia,* by Chris Prouty and Eugene Rosenfeld. 1981. *Out of print. See No. 91.*
33. *Libya,* 3rd ed., by Ronald Bruce St John. 1998.
34. *Mauritius,* by Lindsay Riviere. 1982. *Out of print. See No. 49.*
35. *Western Sahara,* by Tony Hodges. 1982. *Out of print. See No. 55.*
36. *Egypt,* by Joan Wucher King. 1984. *Out of print. See No. 89.*
37. *South Africa,* by Christopher Saunders. 1983. *Out of print. See No. 78.*
38. *Liberia,* by D. Elwood Dunn and Svend E. Holsoe. 1985. *Out of print. See No. 83.*
39. *Ghana,* by Daniel Miles McFarland. 1985. *Out of print. See No. 63.*
40. *Nigeria,* 2nd ed., by Anthony Oyewole and John Lucas. 2000.
41. *Côte d'Ivoire (The Ivory Coast),* 2nd ed., by Robert J. Mundt. 1995.
42. *Cape Verde,* 2nd ed., by Richard Lobban and Marilyn Halter. 1988. *Out of print. See No. 62.*
43. *Zaire,* by F. Scott Bobb. 1988. *Out of print. See No. 76.*
44. *Botswana,* 2nd ed., by Fred Morton, Andrew Murray, and Jeff Ramsay. 1989. *Out of print. See No. 70.*
45. *Tunisia,* 2nd ed., by Kenneth J. Perkins. 1997.
46. *Zimbabwe,* 2nd ed., by Steven C. Rubert and R. Kent Rasmussen. 1990. *Out of print. See No. 86.*
47. *Mozambique,* by Mario Azevedo. 1991. *Out of print. See No. 88.*
48. *Cameroon,* 2nd ed., by Mark W. DeLancey and H. Mbella Mokeba. 1990.
49. *Mauritius,* 2nd ed., by Sydney Selvon. 1991.
50. *Madagascar,* by Maureen Covell. 1995. *Out of print. See No. 98.*
51. *The Central African Republic,* 2nd ed., by Pierre Kalck; translated by Thomas O'Toole. 1992. *Out of print. See No. 93.*
52. *Angola,* 2nd ed., by Susan H. Broadhead. 1992. *Out of print. See No. 92.*
53. *Sudan,* 2nd ed., by Carolyn Fluehr-Lobban, Richard A. Lobban Jr., and John Obert Voll. 1992. *Out of print. See No. 85.*
54. *Malawi,* 2nd ed., by Cynthia A. Crosby. 1993. *Out of print. See No. 84.*
55. *Western Sahara,* 2nd ed., by Anthony Pazzanita and Tony Hodges. 1994. *Out of print. See No. 96.*
56. *Ethiopia and Eritrea,* 2nd ed., by Chris Prouty and Eugene Rosenfeld. 1994. *Out of print. See No. 91.*
57. *Namibia,* by John J. Grotpeter. 1994.
58. *Gabon,* 2nd ed., by David E. Gardinier. 1994.
59. *Comoro Islands,* by Martin Ottenheimer and Harriet Ottenheimer. 1994.
60. *Rwanda,* by Learthen Dorsey. 1994.
61. *Benin,* 3rd ed., by Samuel Decalo. 1995.
62. *Republic of Cape Verde,* 3rd ed., by Richard Lobban and Marlene Lopes. 1995.

63. *Ghana,* 2nd ed., by David Owusu-Ansah and Daniel Miles McFarland. 1995. *Out of print. See No. 97.*
64. *Uganda,* by M. Louise Pirouet. 1995.
65. *Senegal,* 2nd ed., by Andrew F. Clark and Lucie Colvin Phillips. 1994.
66. *Algeria,* 2nd ed., by Phillip Chiviges Naylor and Alf Andrew Heggoy. 1994.
67. *Egypt,* 2nd ed., by Arthur Goldschmidt Jr. 1994. *Out of print. See No. 89.*
68. *Mauritania,* 2nd ed., by Anthony G. Pazzanita. 1996.
69. *Congo,* 3rd ed., by Samuel Decalo, Virginia Thompson, and Richard Adloff. 1996.
70. *Botswana,* 3rd ed., by Jeff Ramsay, Barry Morton, and Fred Morton. 1996.
71. *Morocco,* 2nd ed., by Thomas K. Park. 1996.
72. *Tanzania,* 2nd ed., by Thomas P. Ofcansky and Rodger Yeager. 1997.
73. *Burundi,* 2nd ed., by Ellen K. Eggers. 1997.
74. *Burkina Faso,* 2nd ed., by Daniel Miles McFarland and Lawrence Rupley. 1998.
75. *Eritrea,* by Tom Killion. 1998.
76. *Democratic Republic of the Congo (Zaire)*, by F. Scott Bobb. 1999. (Revised edition of *Historical Dictionary of Zaire*, No. 43)
77. *Kenya,* 2nd ed., by Robert M. Maxon and Thomas P. Ofcansky. 2000.
78. *South Africa,* 2nd ed., by Christopher Saunders and Nicholas Southey. 2000.
79. *The Gambia,* 3rd ed., by Arnold Hughes and Harry A. Gailey. 2000.
80. *Swaziland,* 2nd ed., by Alan R. Booth. 2000.
81. *Republic of Cameroon,* 3rd ed., by Mark W. DeLancey and Mark Dike DeLancey. 2000.
82. *Djibouti,* by Daoud A. Alwan and Yohanis Mibrathu. 2000.
83. *Liberia,* 2nd ed., by D. Elwood Dunn, Amos J. Beyan, and Carl Patrick Burrowes. 2001.
84. *Malawi,* 3rd ed., by Owen J. Kalinga and Cynthia A. Crosby. 2001.
85. *Sudan,* 3rd ed., by Richard A. Lobban Jr., Robert S. Kramer, and Carolyn Fluehr-Lobban. 2002.
86. *Zimbabwe,* 3rd ed., by Steven C. Rubert and R. Kent Rasmussen. 2001.
87. *Somalia,* 2nd ed., by Mohamed Haji Mukhtar. 2002.
88. *Mozambique,* 2nd ed., by Mario Azevedo, Emmanuel Nnadozie, and Tomé Mbuia João. 2003.
89. *Egypt,* 3rd ed., by Arthur Goldschmidt Jr. and Robert Johnston. 2003.
90. *Lesotho,* by Scott Rosenberg, Richard Weisfelder, and Michelle Frisbie-Fulton. 2004.
91. *Ethiopia, New Edition,* by David H. Shinn and Thomas P. Ofcansky. 2004.
92. *Angola, New Edition,* by W. Martin James. 2004.

93. *Central African Republic,* 3rd ed., by Pierre Kalck, translated by Xavier-Samuel Kalck, 2005.
94. *Guinea,* 4th ed., by Thomas O'Toole with Janice E. Baker, 2005.
95. *Morocco,* 2nd ed., by Thomas K. Park and Aomar Boum, 2005.
96. *Western Sahara,* 3rd ed., by Anthony G. Pazzanita, 2005.
97. *Ghana,* 3rd ed., by David Owusu-Ansah, 2005.
98. *Madagascar,* 2nd ed., by Philip M. Allen and Maureen Covell, 2005.
99. *Sierra Leone,* New Edition, by C. Magbaily Fyle, 2006.

Historical Dictionary of Sierra Leone

New Edition

C. Magbaily Fyle

Historical Dictionaries of Africa, No. 99

The Scarecrow Press, Inc.
Lanham, Maryland • Toronto • Oxford
2006

SCARECROW PRESS, INC.

Published in the United States of America
by Scarecrow Press, Inc.
A wholly owned subsidiary of
The Rowman & Littlefield Publishing Group, Inc.
4501 Forbes Boulevard, Suite 200, Lanham, Maryland 20706
www.scarecrowpress.com

PO Box 317
Oxford
OX2 9RU, UK

British Library Cataloguing in Publication Information Available

Library of Congress Cataloging-in-Publication Data

Fyle, C. Magbaily, 1944–
Historical dictionary of Sierra Leone / C. Magbaily Fyle.
p. cm. — (Historical dictionaries of Africa ; no. 99)
Rev. ed. of: Historical dictionary of Sierra Leone / Cyril P. Foray. 1977.
Includes bibliographical references.
ISBN-10: 0-8108-5339-6 (hardcover : alk. paper)
ISBN-13: 978-0-8108-5339-3
1. Sierra Leone—History—Dictionaries. I. Foray, Cyril P., 1934– Historical dictionary of Sierra Leone. II. Title. III. Series: African historical dictionaries ; no. 99.
DT516.5.F868 2005
966.4'003—dc22

2005014693

♾™ The paper used in this publication meets the minimum requirements of American National Standard for Information Sciences—Permanence of Paper for Printed Library Materials, ANSI/NISO Z39.48-1992.
Manufactured in the United States of America.

Contents

Editor's Foreword

Sierra Leone is another African country that has had more than its share of troubles. Many of these were not even its fault. There were more than enough causes of friction; the country began as a colony, West Africa, like neighboring Liberia, to receive liberated Africans and freed slaves and evolved into a British protectorate that reached much farther inland and included a variety of ethnic groups, some in conflict with others. Still, Sierra Leone got off to a reasonable start politically and economically, despite differences within the elite, punctuated by military intervention. The worst troubles, however, resulted from the spread of Liberia's civil wars into its neighbor, Sierra Leone. It took intervention by an African military force dominated by Nigeria to sort that out and to restore a tenuous peace. Now Sierra Leone has another chance, and with considerable effort and luck may fulfill some of its earlier promise. That is, at any rate, what the Sierra Leoneans and their friends hope.

Much of this historical review of the country will be complicated and inexplicable to outsiders. Indeed, many Sierra Leoneans cannot grasp what has happened either. The causes and explanations—at least some of them—only become clearer with a rather long view, such as that provided by this *Historical Dictionary of Sierra Leone.* It traces the history of the region from earlier times through colonial rule and into independence, through somewhat happier times into troubled times, and finally until the present. The course of events can be followed most simply through the chronology, and the explanations begin to fall into place with the introduction. But the core of the book is a compilation of several hundred entries in the dictionary concerning crucial events, ethnic groups, movements, political parties, and especially persons—persons whose actions and influence strongly impacted events. This study includes a bibliography, listing many sources that can shed further light on specific aspects and features of the country and its history.

This is the second historical dictionary on Sierra Leone, the first having been written by Cyril Patrick Foray and published in 1977. That is more than 25 years ago, an exceptionally long time for books in this series. But it would have been hard to know exactly what was going on in Sierra Leone for the past decade or so. And it would have been even harder to find someone who could present it cogently. This meant it was necessary to wait until the right author could be found, ultimately in the person of C. Magbaily Fyle. Dr. Fyle knows Sierra Leone far better than most, having been born and educated in the country, having taught history at Fourah Bay College, and having also served as dean of the Faculty of Arts and university public orator. In addition, Dr. Fyle was a member of many boards and was a nonexecutive director of the Central Bank of Sierra Leone. Since 1991, C. Magbaily Fyle has been a professor in the African American and African Studies Department of Ohio State University.

However, it takes more than knowing; it is also necessary to convey this information, something he has been doing for decades as the author of numerous articles and eight books, including *The History of Sierra Leone: A Concise Introduction*. This entirely new volume brings the story up to date for the many readers who want to know what happened and begin to understand why.

Jon Woronoff
Series Editor

Acronyms and Abbreviations

AFRC	Armed Forces Revolutionary Council
AMA	American Missionary Association
AME	African Methodist Episcopal
APC	All Peoples Congress
CAST	Consolidated African Selection Trust
CDF	Colonial Development Fund; also Civil Defense Force
CMS	Church Missionary Society
DCP	Democratic Center Party
DELCO	Sierra Leone Development Company
DICORWAF	Diamond Corporation of West Africa
ECOMOG	Economic Community Cease-Fire Monitoring Group
ECOWAS	Economic Community of West African States
EUB	Evangelical United Brethren
FBC	Fourah Bay College
FSSG	Freetown Secondary School for Girls
GDO	Government Diamond Office
IBTI	International Bank for Trade and Industry
IMF	International Monetary Fund
KPM	Kono Progressive Movement
LURD	Liberians United for Reconciliation and Democracy
MBHS	Methodist Boys High School
NARECOM	National Rehabilitation Committee
NCBWA	National Congress of British West Africa
NDB	National Development Bank
NDMC	National Diamond Mining Company
NPFL	National Patriotic Front of Liberia
NPRC	National Provisional Ruling Council
NRC	National Reformation Council
NUP	National Unity Party

OBBA	Old Bo Boys Association
OBE	Order of the British Empire
PDP	People's Democratic Party
PEPU	Protectorate Educational Progressive Union
PNP	People's National Party
PPP	People's Progressive Party
RUF	Revolutionary United Front
SIEROMCO	Sierra Leone Ore and Metal Company
SLBS	Sierra Leone Broadcasting Service
SLIM	Sierra Leone Independence Movement
SLPIM	Sierra Leone Progressive Independence Movement
SLPMB	Sierra Leone Produce Marketing Board
SLPP	Sierra Leone People's Party
SLST	Sierra Leone Selection Trust
SOS	Sierra Leone Organization Society
TRC	Truth and Reconciliation Commission
UBC	United Brethren in Christ
UDP	United Democratic Party
ULIMO	United Liberation Movement for Democracy in Liberia
UN	United Nations
UNIA	United Negro Improvement Association
UNPP	United National Peoples Party
UPP	United Progressive Party
WASU	West African Students Union

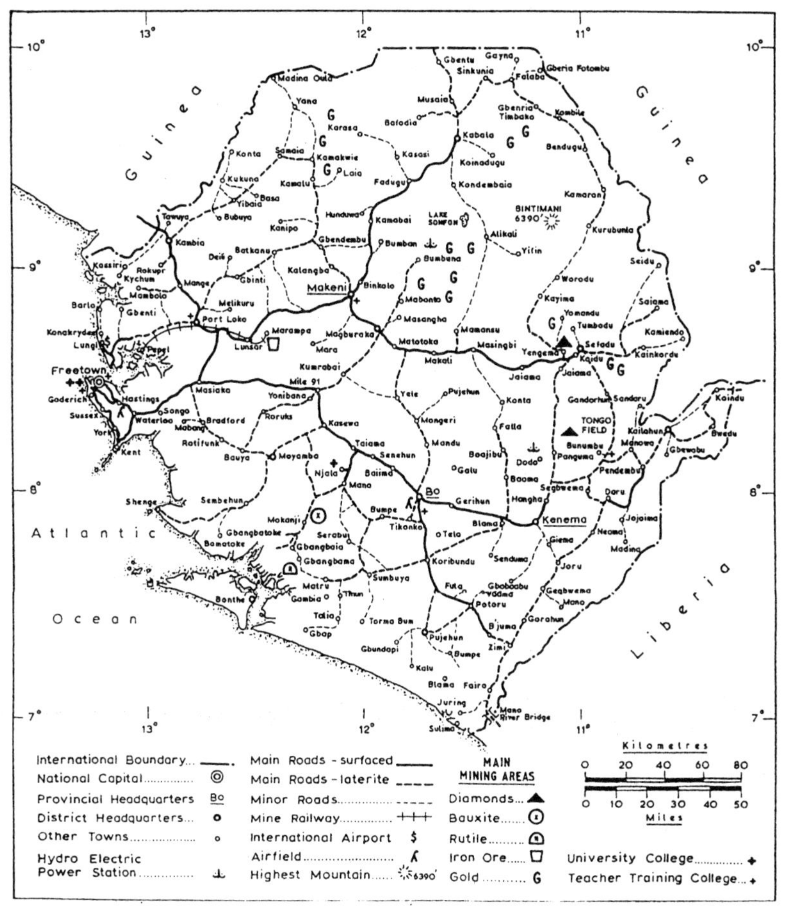

A General Map of Sierra Leone

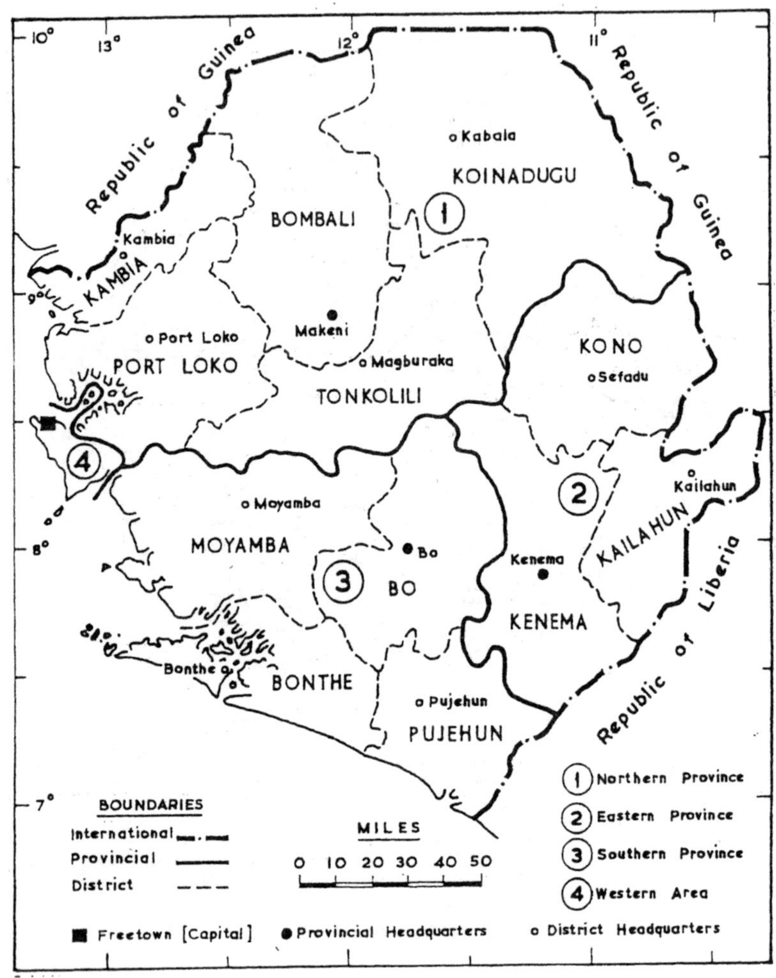

Administrative Divisions in Sierra Leone

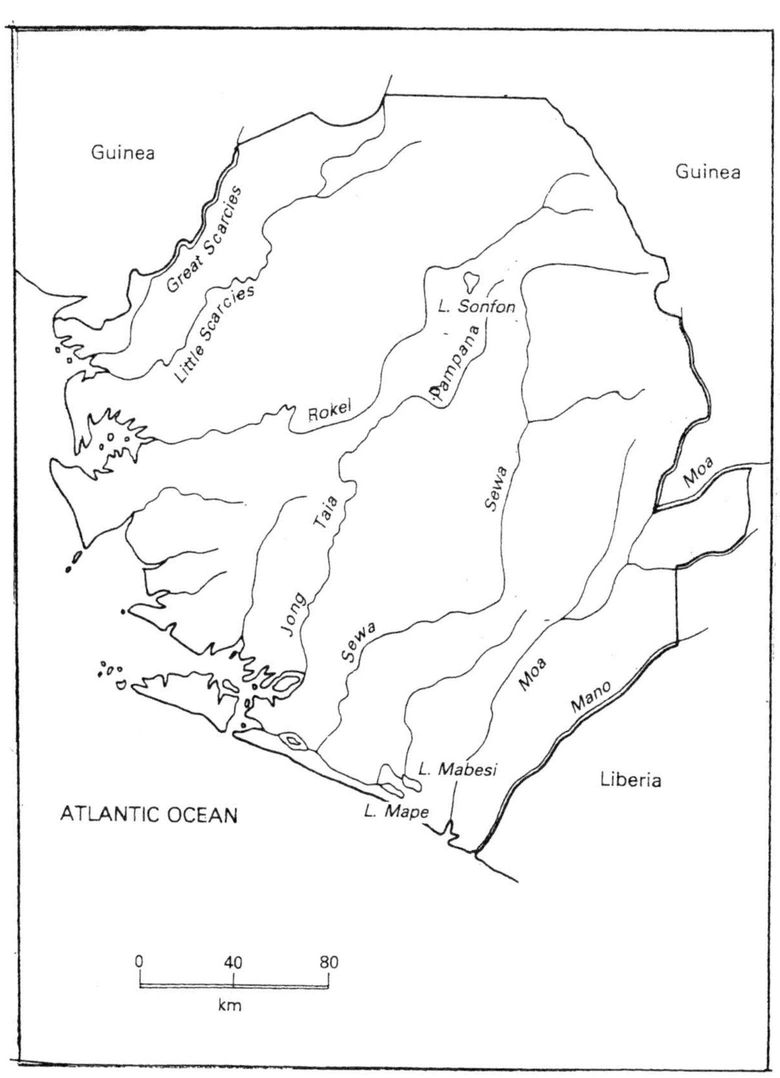

Major Rivers in Sierra Leone

Chronology

Pre-15th century Coastal Sierra Leone occupied by the Bulom, Krim, Baga, Kissi, Gola, and Nalou. Limba found in the northern interior.

1460–1500 Portuguese ship captains use the term *Serra lyoa* (meaning lion mountains) to refer to the coastal area around Sierra Leone.

15th–16th centuries Temne advance from Futa Jalon region to occupy north-central Sierra Leone as far as the peninsula area of present-day Freetown.

1545–1565 Invasion of a Mande group called the Mani starting from the eastern area of the Liberia/Sierra Leone border.

1560–1605 Farma Tami, leader of a Mani subgroup, named head of the Sape confederacy around Koya, comprised of primarily Mandinka, Temne, and Baga peoples.

1684 English trader, Thomas Corker, comes to Sherbro territory and begins working for the Royal African Company. He was the progenitor of the Caulker family.

1727 Futa Jalon jihad begins, leading to the conquest of parts of Yalunka and Limba territory in northern Sierra Leone.

1780 Falaba is founded as a defensible fortress for resisting the Futa Jalon jihadists. Falaba became the center of the Solima Yalunka Kingdom.

1787 Some 411 freed blacks and their white friends from England land in Sierra Leone peninsula; brought there by British humanitarians with government support to found a "Province of Freedom." New settlement called Granville Town.

1789 King Tom, on whose territory Granville Town was planted, burns down the settlement because its leader refuses to recognize King Tom's suzerainty.

1791 The Sierra Leone Company, consisting of British philanthropists and businessmen, refounds the destroyed Granville Town and renamed it Freetown.

1792 Some 1,190 freed blacks from Nova Scotia, mostly former slaves in the American colonies, brought to Freetown.

1799 Nova Scotian repatriates in Freetown rebel against the Sierra Leone Company on taxation and representation.

1800 New group of freed blacks, the Maroons, from Jamaica via Nova Scotia, land in Freetown; helped the Company against the settler rebellion. War breaks out between the Sierra Leone colony and neighboring Temne, led by Bai Farma, King Tom's overlord, trying to reestablish his control over the peninsula.

1808 Colony population grows to estimated 2,000.

1808–1816 British Navy begins landing more than 6,000 slaves in Freetown, captured on board ships in West African waters.

1811 Census of Freetown puts population at 1,900.

1815 Establishment of Bunduka clan domination at Mafonda in the Sanda Temne area, displacing the Limba people there.

1816 John McCormack, an Irishman, begins shipping timber from Sierra Leone to England. Brima Konkoura Sankoh became *alimamy* (ruler) at Saindugu in Temne country, marking Soso ascendance among the Temne around Port Loko.

1819 British governor of the colony, Charles Macarthy, negotiates the rest of the Sierra Leone peninsula from Temne rulers and starts founding new villages with British names around the Freetown colony.

1820s Loko leader, Gumbu Smart, whose father, of the same name, had won the town of Rokon from the Masimera Temne, clashes with the Temne, leading to war. Mediated by Krio traders with Colonial government assistance.

1827 Fourah Bay College established by the Church Missionary Society to train local teachers and missionaries.

1840s Sattang Lahai, a Soso leader, becomes ruler of Rowulah in the Temne-controlled state of Magbema.

1842 Mende Mission founded on Sherbro Island by American missionaries with former slaves freed from America. Led by Sengbe Pieh, these slaves had rebelled on board the *Amistad* and had been captured and then released after a famous court case and sent back to Sierra Leone.

1845 Church Missionary Society (CMS) grammar school founded, the first secondary school in West Africa. (The name of the school was, and still is, the Grammar School.)

1849 A school for females, later named the Annie Walsh Memorial School, opens. This was the first secondary school for females in West Africa.

1857 Alimamy Rassin becomes *alimamy* of Mafonda in what later became the Sanda Tenraran chiefdom.

1860s Sewa becomes *manga* (ruler) of the Solima Yalunka state centered in (on) Falaba. What became the prominent trading center of Rotifunk fell under the rulership of the Loko warrior, Sori Kessebeh, acquired as a prize from R. C. B. Caulker, ruler of the Sherbro state centered on Bumpe.

1870s–1880s Kissi state centered on Luawa coalesces under Kai Londo.

1872 Edward Blyden visits Islamic university led by Foday Tarawaly at the Soso town of Gbile in northeastern Sierra Leone.

1873–1874 Suluku becomes *gbaku* (ruler) of Biriwa Limba state.

1879 First degrees of University of Durham, England, conferred on students who had finished Fourah Bay College.

1882 Madam Yoko of Senehun becomes ruler of the Kpaa Mende state with British Support. United Brethren in Christ Mission take over Mende Mission from American Missionary Association (AMA).

1884 Sofas conquer northern Sierra Leone. The sofas were soldiers of Mandinka empire builder, Samori Turay. Falaba, capital of Solima Yalunka kingdom, destroyed in the process.

1888 Rebellion against Samori's rule in northern Sierra Leone as far south as Biriwa Limba.

1889 Nyagua becomes *mahin* (ruler) of Upper Mende state based on Panguma. Samori's forces led by Kemoko Bilali reconquered northern Sierra Leone. Rapid British advance into the Sierra Leone interior led to a clash at Waima in Konoland between two wings of British forces, each thinking the other to be a contingent of Samori's sofas. The two British military leaders of both wings killed in the clash.

1895 Start of construction of Sierra Leone Railway which was to remain the dominant mode of hauling goods and transportation until it was phased out in the 1970s.

1896 **31 August:** Britain declares a "protectorate" over the interior of the Sierra Leone colony, adding this on to the colony. Boundaries demarcated with France and Liberia.

1898 **February:** Start of northern resistance to British protectorate led by Loko leader, Bai Bure. **April 27:** Coordinated, though unsuccessful, southern resistance against British rule launched. **November:** Bai Bure captured by British forces signaling the collapse of the resistance.

1905 AMA school at Rotifunk becomes a secondary school.

1906 Death of Alimamy Suluku, *gbaku* of Biriwa Limba. The British then split up former Biriwa Limba state into Biriwa Limba chiefdom and Saffroko Limba chiefdom. Bo School set up by the British for training of sons of paramount chiefs to mold them into loyal servants of the colonial government.

1919 Njala Agricultural and Teacher Training College opens. Started by colonial government. Railway workers strike turns into rioting in Freetown. Krios are blamed for the riots and the City Council, considered a Krio government, is charged compensation.

1922 Committee of Educated Aborigines (CEA) formed by educated protectorate leaders.

1924 Bunumbu Teachers' College set up initially by Methodist Missionary Society. New constitution proposed for the Sierra Leone colony, giving three paramount chiefs seats in the Legislative Council.

1926 Railway workers strike for wages; many are dismissed. Iron ore discovered at Marampa, Northern Province.

1928 **January 1:** Domestic slavery abolished by the British in Sierra Leone.

1930 Sierra Leone Development Company (DELCO), a British company, starts mining iron ore.

1931 Haidara revolt against colonial rule around Kambia; British colonial forces put down the rebellion. Diamonds first identified in Kono District.

1932 Sierra Leone Selection Trust, a subsidiary of the British Consolidated African Selection Trust (CAST), set up to mine diamonds.

1933 Bunumbu Teachers college renamed Union College, Bunumbu.

1937 "Native Administration" system, patterned after Lord Lugard's indirect rule system in northern Nigeria, is introduced into the Sierra Leone Protectorate.

1938 Wallace Johnson starts the West African Youth League in Freetown, mobilizing workers in new trade unions against the colonial government.

1939 As World War II begins, emergency powers are used to incarcerate Wallace Johnson.

1946 Protectorate Assembly set up by colonial government, including paramount chiefs and leading (Western trained) protectorate leaders, to advise colonial governor. Protectorate Educational Progressive Union (PEPU) formed by protectorate elite but including mostly paramount chiefs. District Councils inaugurated, to include paramount chiefs and other "enlightened" protectorate people in each district. Under the leadership of Dr. Milton Margai, Sierra Leone People's Party (SLPP) is formed from a merger of smaller, mainly protectorate organizations including PEPU and Sierra Leone Organization Society.

1947 New constitution proposed for the colony, which gives the majority of seats in Legislative Council to the majority population of the protectorate.

1949 Sierra Leone Produce Marketing Board formed by colonial government, intended to "stabilize" prices paid to local farmers for produce.

1950 National Council of Sierra Leone (NCSL) formed as a Krio based political party led by Dr. Bankole Bright.

1951 After much wrangling between Krios who oppose the constitution and the protectorate leadership, amended version of the new constitution is implemented. New elections held and won by the SLPP.

1955 Pithere Kamara led rebellion in the north against local government officials who are seen as stooges of the colonial government. Trade Union strikes led by Marcus Grant degenerate into rioting and looting: put down by the colonial government military.

1956 Kono Progressive Movement merges with Sierra Leone Independence Movement to emerge as Sierra Leone Progressive Independence Movement (SLPIM) led by Paramount Chief Tamba Mbriwa. United Progressive Party, a predominantly Krio party, is formed and led by C. B. Rogers-Wright.

1957 Universal adult suffrage is introduced. General elections are won by SLPP. New government is formed with Milton Margai as prime minister.

1958 Breakaway faction from SLPP led by Albert Margai, Siaka Stevens, S. T. Navo, and others form the People's National Party (PNP).

1960 United Front, a coalition of all political forces, led by Milton Margai, formed. At independence conference in London, Siaka Stevens refuses to sign documents agreeing to independence. Stevens returned to Sierra Leone to found Elections Before Independence Movement, later converted to a political party, the All People's Congress (APC).

1961 **April 27:** Independence Day for Sierra Leone.

1962 General elections won by the SLPP. The APC emerges as the most organized opposition.

1964 **March:** Njala University College opened. **April 28:** Death of Prime Minister Milton Margai. His brother, Albert Margai, is appointed as new prime minister. **August 4:** Sierra Leone currency, the Leone, is established.

1967 General elections. The APC wins by a narrow margin. Brigadier John Lansana, head of the military, seizes control of government immediately after swearing in of the new APC prime minister, Siaka Stevens. Lansana is ousted a few days later by junior military officers who invite Andrew Juxon-Smith, a senior officer on leave, to return and head a provisional government, the National Reformation Council (NRC).

1968 NRC is overthrown by warrant officers of the army. John Bangura, a formerly dismissed senior officer, invited to head the army. Bangura turned over government to the APC, led by Siaka Stevens.

1969 University of Sierra Leone set up, comprising Fourah Bay College and Njala University College.

1971 **April 19:** Sierra Leone becomes a republic with Siaka Stevens as executive president.

1972 University of Sierra Leone Act passed by Parliament formalizing university structure.

1973 Mano River Union formed initially between Liberia and Sierra Leone.

1974 National census puts population of Sierra Leone at 3.5 million.

1975 Sierra Leone Development Company (DELCO) declares bankruptcy, ending iron ore mining in Marampa.

1977 Widespread antigovernment protests start with student demonstrations at the university colleges.

1978 By a new constitution, Sierra Leone becomes a one-party state with Siaka Stevens' APC as the sole party.

1985 Army chief, Major-General Joseph Saidu Momoh, becomes president upon Siaka Stevens' retirement from that office.

1991 **March 23:** First report of civil war on eastern frontier with Liberia with rebels led by former corporal Foday Sankoh. **September:**

New constitution provides for a return to multiparty politics and a cabinet comprised of nonmembers of Parliament.

1992 **April 29:** Military coup d'état ousts government of Joseph Momoh. New military junta, the National Provisional Ruling Council (NPRC) led by Captain Valentine Strasser, assumes office.

1995 **August 15–17:** Constitutional Conference called by NPRC government of Valentine Strasser.

1996 **January 16:** Strasser is deposed by other military officers led by Julius Maada Bio who becomes the new head of state. **February 12:** Second Constitutional Conference called by NPRC government of Julium Maada Bio. Delegates, particularly female leaders, insist on return to parliamentary democracy. **February 26:** General elections. Indecisive presidential poll. **March 15:** Presidential runoff elections between Tejan Kabbah (SLPP) and John Karefa Smart (UNPP). Ahmad Tejan Kabbah becomes new president. **November 30:** Abidjan Accord—peace agreement between Sierra Leone government and the RUF signed in Abidjan.

1997 **May 25:** Military officers led by Johnny Paul Koroma oust Tejan Kabba's government. Revolutionary United Front (RUF) invited to join new Armed Forces Ruling Council (AFRC) government. Rebels move into Freetown. Civil Defense Forces formed comprising Kamajors, Tamaboros, Kapras, and Donso. Retired Captain Sam Hinga Norman leads forces. **July 5:** Army soldiers and RUF forces styled the "Peoples Army" capture Mano River Bridge in a clash with Kamajor forces. Hundreds of Kamajor reportedly killed. **23 October:** Economic Community of West African States (ECOWAS) six-month peace plan for Sierra Leone known as the Conakry Accord.

1998 Reported in January that AFRC forces capture diamond rich Tong Fields and other strategic positions in Kenema District from Kamajor. **February:** Forces of the Economic Community Cease-Fire Monitoring Group (ECOMOG) led by Nigeria expel rebels and AFRC from Freetown and restore Tejan Kabba's government. **March:** Tejan Kabba triumphantly returns to Freetown from exile in Guinea. **September 4:** Indictment in Freetown Magistrate's Court of RUF leader, Corporal Foday Saybana Sankoh.

1999 **January 6:** RUF and rebels of former army led by Johnny Paul Koroma storm Freetown and control most of the capital for a short time before being driven out by ECOMOG troops. Over 5,000 dead in Freetown, which is partly burned and heavily damaged. **April:** National Commission for Democracy and Human Rights organizes a National Consultative Conference on the Peace Process in Sierra Leone. Women were very vocal in the call for a return to democratic rule. **April 9:** statement by RUF leader Foday Sankoh to the National Consultative Conference on the Peace Process. **April 17:** Cease-fire agreement is signed in Lomé, Togo between Tejan Kabba government, Foday Sankoh leading RUF rebels, and Johnny Paul Koroma, leader of rump of AFRC. **July 7:** Lomé Peace Accord is signed setting up government of cooperation led by Tejan Kabba and including RUF leader Foday Sankoh and Johnny Paul Koroma. **November:** United Nations peacekeeping troops begin arriving in Freetown. RUF rebels oppose this.

2000 **February 3:** Anticorruption Act is passed. **April/May:** UN troops are abducted by rebels. **May 8:** Twenty are killed when Foday Sankoh's supporters open fire on large propeace demonstration in Freetown. Foday Sankoh is captured and imprisoned. Some 800 British troops arrive in Freetown to assist UN efforts. **August 11:** British soldiers are taken hostage by Johnny Paul Koroma's West Side Boys. British offensive rescues British hostages.

2001 **May:** Disarmament of rebels begins.

2002 **January 16:** War is declared over. United Nations and Sierra Leone Government sign agreement to set up war crimes tribunal for Sierra Leone, incorporating the statutes under which the Special Court for Sierra Leone will operate. **April 2:** Nomination day for general elections. **May 14:** General elections. SLPP led by Tejan Kabba wins huge victory. **July:** British troops leave Sierra Leone. **December:** UN-backed war crimes court set up.

2003 **April 14:** Truth and Reconciliation Commission starts sitting in Freetown.

Introduction

The state of Sierra Leone has a long and complex history, dominated more recently by the civil war that raged for a decade in that country. Nonetheless, the country's contribution to the colonial history of West Africa, despite its small size, is marked, particularly in the states of Nigeria, Ghana, and the Gambia.

LAND AND PEOPLE

Sierra Leone is situated on the southern part of the western bulge of the African continent. It has a land area of 73,326 square kilometers and an estimated population of four million. The landscape is dominated by a low-lying plain close to the coast, rising north-eastward into highlands, with the Bintumane peak (6,390 feet) being the highest. The peninsula on the coast is also lined with high peaks, which led the first Portuguese ship captains who visited there to call these mountains "*sera lyoa*" since they were shaped like lions. Numerous rivers, flowing northeasterly to southwesterly, are voluminous in the wet season; annual rainfall averages about 115 inches, most of it falling in July and August. Volumes are much less in the dry season.

About 70 percent of the population of Sierra Leone is engaged in agriculture, mostly autosubsistence farms. The dominant food crop is rice, cultivated by more than 80 percent of all farmers. Sierra Leone farmers acquired a reputation for developing the techniques of rice farming, and they exported these to North America during the era of the Atlantic slave trade, providing the states of Georgia and North Carolina with major economic activity. There is also extensive farming of export crops such as coffee and cacao. Mining was profitable at one time; however, 10 years of civil war have decimated government revenues from mining, particularly for rutile, diamonds, and gold. The **Sierra Rutile** Company, an American enterprise, is about to recommence mining at Mobimbi in southern Sierra Leone, while the government is making strenuous moves to establish control over the gold and diamond mines.

Administratively, Sierra Leone is divided into four units. These are the Western Area, comprising the capital, **Freetown**, and surrounding settlements, and the Southern, Eastern, and Northern Provinces. Each of these provinces is made up of districts headed by district officers. Districts are further subdivided into 184 chiefdoms headed by the paramount chiefs who resemble the indigenous authority that existed before colonial rule began in the early 20th century. There is a city council in Freetown and in the **Sherbro** District, while Town Councils take care of local government issues in the provincial headquarters towns of **Bo**, Kenema, and Makeni.

Sierra Leone has altogether 16 ethnic groups. The largest of these are the **Temne**, found in the north central part of the country, and the **Mende**, who are predominant in the southern and eastern regions. Together, Temne and Mende make up about 60 percent of the total population.

EARLY HISTORY

Earliest evidence from archeological and linguistic studies place a pre-fifth century provenance to a few particularly smaller ethnic groups of today. The **Kissi**, now straddling the common eastern borders between Sierra Leone and neighboring Guinea and Liberia are, along with the **Gola**, among the oldest inhabitants.

Their culture involved the use of steatite fertility figurines called ***nomoli*** that were buried in rice fields. These predate the 15th century. To the northeast lived the ethnic **Limba**, whose traditions and material culture indicate that they inhabited the mountainous regions around the Wara Wara mountains well before the 15th century. Closer to the coast were groups such as the Bullom, Nalou, Baga, Krim, speaking languages that indicate linguistic longevity.

The southern and eastern parts of Sierra Leone were injected with a strong ethnolinguistic influence in the form of a major invasion of a Mande people referred to as the Mani. The term *Mande* represents a group of languages and cultures that are closely similar, both emanating from the Mande (sometimes called Mali) empire of the 12th to 14th centuries. When that empire broke up, groups of Mande peoples moved in different directions, and one of these groups, the Mani, eventually settled outside the eastern borders of Sierra Leone. In the mid-15th century, they sent invading parties deep into the Sierra Leone area, invaders who stayed and ruled the areas over which they took control. Mande domination and interaction with the original inhabitants gave rise to new ethnic groups.

On the southern coastal area, Mande and Bulom ethnic groups interacted to give rise to the Sherbro, named after Serabola, a leader of a Mani party that had invaded that area. One Mani group moved into northeastern Sierra Leone and stayed there, becoming known over time as the Landogo, or more popularly ethnic **Loko**. Farma Tami, another Mani leader, set up a confederacy among Temne around present-day Port Loko and was still recognized as a Mani leader at the beginning of the 17th century. The main Mani incursion into Sierra Leone was much later—by the 18th century—in the form of successive waves of Mani movement into eastern Sierra Leone. This main Mani group, still referred to in this way by the Bullom, came to be known as the Mende.

Successive waves of Mande invasion from different directions also influenced the ethnic makeup of Sierra Leone. Thus the Koranko, a group linguistically almost identical with **Mandinka**, a language from heartland Mande, came to dominate the northeast, settling among and blending with many of the eastern Temne peoples. On the northwestern front, the Soso gradually expanded from southern Guinea littoral to establish towns and villages in northern Sierra Leone, influencing an ethnic Limba subgroup called the Tonko Limba.

In 1727, a major political and religious revolution took place in Futa Jalon just north of Sierra Leone, when Fula Islamic leaders organized to overthrow the governments of the **Yalunka** peoples who had been their rulers. The Fula became dominant and spread their idea of Islamic conversion into areas of northern Sierra Leone among some Limba and other Yalunka peoples. The Yalunka of this area, identified as the Solima Yalunka, later threw off Fula control and the resultant conflict led to the emergence of the Solima Yalunka state centered on Falaba in northern Sierra Leone.

INDIGENOUS POLITICAL ORGANIZATION

Political systems in the Sierra Leone area were fairly similar in structure even though they varied considerably in size, from relatively larger states such as the Solima Yalunka, the Biriwa Limba and the Sherbro states, to small "stateless" societies where polities comprised one large settlement and surrounding villages.

In the Solima Yalunka state, for example, *khori* (provinces), which constituted the state, were ruled in internal matters by their various *bangkolamangana* (village heads). Specific rights of appeal, inter-*khori* relations, and declarations of war and similar matters were reserved for the supreme ruler at the capital. Large areas of **Koranko** territory were part of the Solima Yalunka state by the late 18th to early 19th centuries, but only insofar as these Yalunka could exercise a dominant influence and obtain regular tribute. The Solima Yalunka capital at Falaba and consequently capital of the state was destroyed by the ***sofa*** forces of the Mandinka empire-builder, **Samori Turay [Toure]**.

Many states in the Sierra Leone interior in this same period were run along similar lines. There was another large state among the Biriwa Limba peoples led by **Alimamy Suluku** later in the 19th century. By the middle of that century, there were much smaller stateless entities among the Temne and Koranko peoples, but among the latter these small states were linked in some form of psychopolitical network centered on Morifindugu, their point of dispersal deeper into the Sierra Leone region. Although the ruler of Morifindugu, **Marlay Bockari**, in the second half of the 19th century did not rule over all of these Koranko polities, they all often fell back on Morifindugu in times of difficulty.

By the second half of the 19th century, there were, broadly speaking, two types of Mende states. One was based on the personality of a strong leader such as **Kai Londo** of Luawa, **Nyagua** of Panguma, **Mendegla** of Joru, and **Makavoray** of Tikonko. The territory under control of such leaders could expand or diminish, based on the king's prowess. In the second type of Mende state, the leader was basically a first among equals, with heads of segments of the state. Such states such as the Sherbro, Gallinas, Bumpe, and Kpaa Mende tended to have relatively fixed borders.

In all of these units, however, walled towns surrounded by open *fakai* (farm settlements) were grouped into larger units, a number of which constituted the state. An example of this was the Sherbro state, strong and powerful in the 18th century, ruled by the Bai Sherbro on Sherbro Island. By the end of the 19th century, however, the Sherbro state had begun to decline, influenced by the Mende, and the Bai Sherbro no longer commanded the same authority he once wielded.

Succession to high office followed broad patterns although there were slight variations. Succession was based on demonstration of some outstanding quality of leadership in war or religion or on the power to convince others. Among the Mende, rulers succeeded even if they did not belong to "ruling families," although members of such ruling families had more opportunities to acquire the necessary leadership qualities. In some other areas, such as the Koranko and Limba territories, candidates for high office had to both demonstrate leadership qualities *and* belong to a ruling family.

Most ruling houses were male-oriented and male-dominated, but among the Sherbro, for example, households headed by females were common, and women also ruled towns and villages. The celebrated **Madam Yoko** of Senehun in the Kpaa Mende state has aroused much interest since she had come to rule a larger state by the 1880s. Subsequently, the complicity of the British, who were already close by and were moving to establish dominance in the near interior, clouded the issue of the traditional legitimacy of Madam Yoko to rule the Kpaa Mende state.

INTERNAL COMMERCIAL ORGANIZATION AND CONFLICTS

Patterns of exchange included the use of locally produced goods as well as items from distant centers. Labor was exchanged for goods, as was expertise. Yalunka blacksmiths traveled to Koranko states on contract. Later, Koranko smiths made regular visits to Mende country. Locally manufactured goods such as cloth, soap, and hoes were extensively traded. Certain goods were traded over long distances involving traveling largely on foot for weeks at a time. These goods included gold, cattle, and cotton. Gold was traded from Boure in the Upper Niger River area to a number of trading centers in the Sierra Leone interior. Cotton from Sankaran in present-day Guinea found its way into Limba country where it was sold in exchange for cattle from Futa Jalon. **Kono** cloth was highly valued as far as Suluku's Biriwa Limba state, while Sankaran cloth was famous in distant Freetown. Internal market centers developed in the interior as a consequence at the towns of Katimbo in Biriwa Limba, Koindu in Kissi country, Falaba in the Solima Yalunka kingdom, and at other centers. Indigenous currency systems emerged as well among groups such as the Kissi and Mende, in the form of locally made cloth, for example.

This trade was largely unaffected by wars, despite the strong belief to the contrary by the colonial rulers at the coastal colony. Centers of strong political authority became areas of protection for trade routes. Wars were sometimes fought, as among the ethnic Temne in the 18th and 19th centuries for control of important trading areas such as the headwaters of navigable rivers. Sometimes rulers in the interior, such as **Sattan Lahai** in Kambia on the Great Scarcies River in the northwest, deliberately blocked trade routes to secure some political advantage. Neither such action nor political wars had any strong impact on trade. Such stoppages, when they did occur, were temporary, and alternative routes were quickly developed in areas where such trade interdictions were likely to last a long time. In 1877, for example, the Limba of Yagala destroyed the way station at Kabala on the important Kabala-Bumban-Port Loko trade route. The ruler of Kabala, Boltamba, quickly teamed up with Suluku of Biriwa Limba to establish an alternative route. What often created alarm was that those at one end of a particular route, the Krio traders of Kambia, for example, who were affected by Sattan Lahai's activities, made a major issue out of the whole matter. This caught the attention and interest of the Sierra Leone colony authorities who benefited from this trade.

The economic difficulties of the 1870s and 1880s were readily blamed on interior wars, and not on the world trade depression that prevailed at the time. In fact, the volume of exported trade goods from the coast increased during this period, although the value declined. In 1875, a war waged by Mende professional warriors spilled over into "British Sherbro." The governor of the colony at the time, Samuel Rowe, was determined to teach the Mende a lesson for violating "British territory." He led an expedition to the Bagru region in Sherbro country, entered into an agreement with the Mende to never again hire out warriors, and fined them 10,000 bushels of rice because, he said, "the country is one immense rice farm."

FOUNDING OF THE BRITISH COLONY OF SIERRA LEONE

The European presence on the coastal area of Sierra Leone dates from the mid-15th century. The earliest Europeans to visit this coast were the Portuguese, whose ship captains first used the term *serra lyoa* in reference to the mountainous coastal peninsula that is part of present-day Sierra Leone. This term survived, corrupted over the centuries to "Sierra Leone." Other Europeans followed as the fresh water closest to the coastal peninsula became a favorite stopping point for vessels. As the Atlantic slave trade became the dominant element of commerce on the coast, the British became the most prominent Europeans on the Sierra Leone coast. British traders started residing on the coast and marrying into local families, which led to the emergence of prominent mixed race families on the Sierra Leone coast including the Caulker, Cleveland, Rogers, and Tucker families.

The most important impact of British presence on the coast was the founding of the colony of Sierra Leone. British who were strongly opposed to the slave trade and slavery, managed to secure a court ruling in 1772 in England that slavery was not part of English law. This at once released a number of domestic slaves in England, largely from the homes of absentee British plantation owners in the Caribbean. These freed slaves in England, poor and destitute, were becoming a social problem, and such humanitarians as William Wilberforce and Granville Sharp eventually convinced the British government to support a plan that would remove these freed blacks to somewhere in Africa. The Sierra Leone peninsula was selected on the suggestion of Dr. Henry Smeathman, a botanist who had visited that area. Thus, in 1787, some 400 blacks and their white girlfriends were repatriated to the peninsula and were settled on land negotiated from the local Temne rulers.

This was initially not a British colony. It was a self-governing entity called the Province of Freedom, equipped with an idealistic constitution drafted by Granville Sharp and with a government run by the settlers themselves. The first settlement failed, however, as this Granville Town was burned down in 1879 by the local Temne suzerain, King Jimmy. It was refounded in 1791 with those of the early settlers who could be pulled together. This time, it was directed by a Sierra Leone Company chartered in England and including bankers and entrepreneurs eager to make it a profitable venture. Its population was soon replenished in

1791 by the Nova Scotians, former slaves who had fought with the British in the American Revolution on promise of their freedom. When the British lost the war, the blacks were taken to Nova Scotia. Eventually, they were brought to Sierra Leone with British government support. The Sierra Leone Company appointed Lieutenant John Clarkson as the first governor and renamed the settlement Freetown.

Another group of freed blacks from Jamaica traveled via Nova Scotia to the Sierra Leone colony in 1800. These were the Maroons, originally ethnic Asante from Ghana who had been enslaved and had fought their way to freedom in Jamaica. The Maroons helped the Sierra Leone Company administration put down a rebellion of the Nova Scotians against the government. In 1808, the British government took control of the tiny Sierra Leone colony from the company because it was useful as a station for British antislave trade efforts. The British navy was intercepting British and other ships that were still participating in the outlawed Atlantic slave trade. Condemned vessels and their human cargo could only be taken to Britain at great expense, and the Sierra Leone colony became known for trying the ship captains and releasing the captured slaves.

These captured slaves who were released in Freetown came to be known as recaptives or liberated Africans. Their numbers grew rapidly; and by 1850, more than 40,000 of them had been landed, swelling the population of the colony. Recaptive villages carrying British place names were founded outside Freetown, with names such as York, Kent, Wellington, Waterloo, Goderich, and so on. Many of the recaptives were of Yoruba origin, a result of civil wars in Yorubaland in present-day Nigeria.

Largely through trade, the recaptives became prosperous, overcoming the attitude of superiority of the former settlers. They bought property in Freetown, intermarried with the settlers, and generally adopted Christianity and Western ways. By the late 19th century, settlers and recaptives were fusing into one ethnicity that came to be known as **Krio** (often called Creole). Krio culture came to involve a blend of African, mostly Yoruba, culture and the Westernized values of the settlers, coupled with missionary and Victorian values drummed into the colony inhabitants by a persistent colonial government. Under British tutelage, institutions of Western education and Western Christianity were established in Freetown. The **Church Missionary Society (CMS)** set up the grammar school in 1815, the Female Institution, later called the **Annie Walsh School for Girls**, in 1849 and Fourah Bay College in 1827. These became the premier institutions for higher education not only in Sierra Leone, but in the entire West Africa region. Krios followed up their early introduction to Western education by assuming positions of prominence all over the Gold Coast (Ghana), Nigeria, and the Gambia; all of these area became British colonies.

COLONY AND INTERIOR RELATIONS

Relations between the tiny colony and the vast interior behind it inevitably developed, dominated by trade. The colony needed supplies, largely from the interior, and so encouraged trade. One early newspaper, *The Royal Gazette and Sierra Leone Advertiser* founded in 1808, dwelled extensively on relations with the interior and commented on sites with commercial possibilities such as areas where gold abounded. Traders coming from the far interior were well treated by the colony rulers, and their visits were widely publicized.

In order to promote good relations with rulers in the interior, successive visits into the interior were organized or encouraged by the colonial government. In 1822, for example, the Scottish explorer, Gordon Laing (1793–1826) went as far as Falaba; Cooper Thompson, a CMS linguist, went to Timbo, the capital of Futa Jalon in 1841. Winwood Read, the eccentric traveler and author, reached Boure on the headwaters of the Niger River in 1870. William Budge was sent to Kpaa Mende country in 1879. These trips paralleled others by African officials, such as **Edward Blyden**.

Krio traders, too, advanced into the interior, gravitating particularly to the headwaters of navigable rivers to trade. By the mid-19th century, many Krio traders had settled in such centers such as Port Loko, Kambia, Mofwe, Senehun, and Mattru. In these centers, Krio elements settled and interacted with other ethnic groups, taking wives locally and joining major institutions, such as the ***Poro***. In Kambia, by the 1880s, the Krio traders had elected for themselves a "king of the Creoles," an influential trader named Thomas Johnson.

The British government was often called upon by these Krio traders to mediate disruptions that threatened to affect trade. Such British involvement, motivated also by the desire to stimulate trade, occasionally led to British attacks on parts of the interior or to treaties with local rulers such as those in Port Loko in 1836 and in Futa Jalon in 1873, which were designed to end local wars and keep the peace. By the late 19th century, the British set up a department for handling relations with the Interior. It began as a one person department when **Thomas G. Lawson** was appointed "Native Interpreter and Government Messenger" in 1852. When Lawson retired in 1888 the department became known as the Aborigines Department and later, in 1891, as the Native Affairs Department headed by **J. C. E. Parkes**.

CONQUEST AND THE ESTABLISHMENT OF COLONIAL RULE IN THE PROTECTORATE

These patterns of contact represented British influence in the interior of Sierra Leone outside the small colony. But by the 1880s, competition between the European powers for territory in Africa ushered in an era of rampant imperialism. Britain followed up its initial moves with further treaties to secure commitment of interior areas toward Britain, and, in some cases, military expeditions followed. Finally, in 1896, after negotiations with the French who were similarly involved in neighboring Guinea, the British declared a "protectorate" over the vast interior of the colony. The protectorate and the colony now became the British territory of Sierra Leone.

Local rulers who watched this drama unfold soon came to realize that this was more than the "treaties of friendship" and missions sent into their territory from the colony. These rulers were quickly ordered to start paying taxes to the colony government and found that they were losing suzerainty to British officials who were now being sent into the interior as district commissioners. Some Temne and Mende rulers protested in petitions to the British against specific aspects of this new dispensation. Most importantly, they protested against the new house tax, which, as they expressed it, meant to them that they no longer owned their own houses. Failing redress, widespread rebellion erupted in 1898 in the north led by a famous ruler and warrior, Bai Bure, and in the south coordinated by a coalition of Mende leaders using the Poro society as the medium. With superior resources, the British quelled both rebellions by the end of the year.

The first few years of colonial rule in the protectorate were marked by British concern with maintaining law and order. The entire protectorate was divided into districts that were subdivided into chiefdoms. Chiefdoms generally represented former petty states, and their new rulers, called paramount chiefs, represented traditional political authority. But where chiefdoms were large, they were broken up to reduce the following of any paramount chief and thus his potential for resistance to government control. A system of servile labor common in the interior was labeled slavery by the British, and so the British claimed that they abolished slavery in 1928.

To collect revenue for the colony, the British first built a railway to the heartland of the palm belt in the extreme east of the protectorate. The railway thus aided the collection of produce that grew naturally in the rain forest—palm products and rubber. But the railway also increased mobility between Freetown and the interior so that Western goods and colonial influence could more readily penetrate the interior.

As collection of naturally growing produce dwindled, the British encouraged plantations for coffee and cocoa. However, this program did not flourish until after World War II. As exports of this produce increased, the British set up the **Sierra Leone Produce Marketing Board (SLPMB)** to regulate prices paid to farmers of the produce and to shelter these farmers from fluctuating world prices. In actuality, until the protectorate gained independence in 1961, the price of these commodities kept rising, and the revenue that was collected through the SLPMB was invested in Britain and never made its way to Sierra Leone, even after independence. Before coffee and cocoa became profitable, prospecting for minerals was the main means of increasing revenue. Gold, platinum, chrome, iron ore, and diamonds were initially identified, but iron ore and diamonds soon became the most important. Deposits of iron ore at Marampa proved viable, and a British-based company, the **Sierra Leone Development Company (DELCO)**, was set up to mine the ore with a lease of 99 years. DELCO built a 52-mile railway largely with colonial government loans. By 1940, iron ore had become dominant in the export sector, but diamonds had been discovered. In 1934. the **Sierra Leone Selection Trust (SLST)**, a subsidiary of De Beers, was set up to mine the precious mineral. The company's 99-year lease included the whole of Sierra Leone. In 1955, the lease was restricted, and private licenses were granted to individuals to do surface mining. This brought thousands of Sierra Leoneans and **Lebanese** into the Eastern Province diamond areas of Kenema and Kono and led to the growth of new thriving towns such as Yengema and Koidu. By the time of independence in 1961, diamonds contributed some 60 percent of Sierra Leone's mineral export earnings, whereas mining as a whole contributed 86.7 percent of export earnings.

Mining, particularly of diamonds, had an adverse effect on agriculture, as many people were attracted away from agriculture to the get rich quick mining lure of diamonds in particular. The production of basic foodstuff, such as rice, declined, because mining provided jobs with wages higher than in any other sector of the economy. It also provided a strong economic impulse, as quick wealth gained from both licensed and illicit mining began to circulate in the economy.

The colonial government introduced paved roads, pipe-borne water and electricity, modern hospitals, Western education, a banking system, and similar accouterments of a Western capitalist economy. A secondary school was established at Bo for the sons of chiefs, with the intention of making them into pliable colonial servants. Other high schools and a couple of teachers' colleges were set up in the interior, and these became the nucleus for the training of the urban westernized elite that was to ultimately assume political control at the end of the colonial rule. But the curriculum and colonial policy was to alienate these people from their own culture and traditions, as they were studiously taught that their own traditions were at best inferior, at worst barbaric, and not worth the attention or interest of "progressive" and "educated" Sierra Leoneans. This created a situation wherein this new elite had no interest in looking to solutions for improvement from inside their own societies, but proudly accepted any sense of direction derived from British or Western sources.

Local industry was also actively discouraged as the British were only interested in extracting raw materials. **Dr. John Abayomi-Cole**, a local entrepreneur, was banned from producing tobacco, brandy, soap, and sugar in the early 20th century. When a British businessman, D. B. Curry, started making chocolates, the British Cadbury company flooded the market with cheap chocolates to put him out of business. The colonial government gave a big subsidy to Freetown Cold Storage Company to aid its business, chiefly bottling Coca Cola, but the Government denied any subsidy to a local company, the Freetown Mineral Waters Company, forcing this company to close down. By 1949, the government gave small loans to support some industries such as soap making, timber sawing, but these proved too little, too late.

POLITICAL CHANGE AND INDEPENDENCE

After World War II, the British began to make constitutional amendments that were to represent a gradual devolution of political power into the hands of the urban elite. Representative institutions had been largely absent during the long period of rule of the colony, that is Freetown and the Western Area. Municipal government was set up for which only those who owned houses had the vote. A **Legislative Council** of the most senior colonial officials advised the governor, who was free to ignore their advice. An attempt to elect two local representatives to the Legislative Council in 1863 was quickly abandoned as the two who were elected were not those whom the colonial government intended. In the protectorate, **District Councils** were only set up in 1946 to advise the colonial governor and to assist in providing some necessary services. Similarly, a **Protectorate Assembly** was installed in the same year including paramount chiefs and other Western-educated protectorate citizens, to discuss matters affecting the protectorate. But these were appointive institutions, and the District Council elections were not held until 1956.

The 1947 constitution, implemented in 1951, was intended to pave the way for responsible government. It gave the majority in a newly constituted Legislative Council to the more numerous protectorate people, an issue hotly contested by the Krios who felt that their earlier access to Westernization placed them in a better position to rule Sierra Leone.

The British proceeded to introduce the new constitution, and political parties were quickly formed to contest elections on the new dispensation. Krio elements formed the **National Council of Sierra Leone**, pursuing a partisan stance against the new constitution. The party most representative of the entire country was formed from a merger of three segments: the **Sierra Leone Organization Society** formed in 1946 of Western trained protectorate leaders; the second was what had earlier been a benefit society, the **Protectorate Educational Progressive Union (PEPU)**, dominated by paramount chiefs, but including others of the Western trained elite; and the third group, the Krio based People's Party, founded by Rev. E. N. Jones, a Krio man who had adopted an indigenous name, Lamina Sankoh. The party formed from this merger was the **Sierra Leone People's Party (SLPP)**.

In the ensuing elections in 1951, the SLPP won and formed a new "government" headed by its leader, **Dr. Milton Margai**. Some African members of the Executive Council were given responsibilities for ministries in 1953 and, in 1954, Milton Margai was appointed chief minister. By the next elections in 1957, new parties had been formed, including such as the United Progressive Party, a predominantly Krio party led by **C. B. Rogers-Wright**, and the **Sierra Leone Progressive Independence Movement (SLPIM)**, which involved a combination of a Kono Progressive Movement and a Sierra Leone Independence Movement started by **Edward Blyden**. But the SLPP remained dominant and easily won the 1957 elections. After the elections, a breakaway group from the SLPP formed the **People's National Party (PNP)** led by **Albert Margai**, brother of Milton Margai. The prime minister was, however, able to bring all opposition factions together in a United Front, which went to London for constitutional talks leading to independence set for April 27, 1961. At this conference, **Siaka Stevens** refused to sign the documents agreeing to the new constitution. He returned to Freetown and set up an Elections Before Independence Movement, which was quickly transformed into the **All People's Congress (APC)** party. In the post-independence elections, the APC emerged as the leading opposition to the SLPP, winning a third of the contested seats.

POSTINDEPENDENCE POLITICS

Milton Margai died in 1964, and the governor general appointed his brother Albert to succeed him. Prominent members of the SLPP cabinet opposed this move, and the new prime minister immediately dropped them from his cabinet. That proved very costly to him as these men were all influential individuals. **S. T. Matturi** was an ethnic Kono leader, **J. Karefa-Smart** was a prominent Temne/Loko, Y. D. Sesay was Loko, and **M. S. Mustapha** was part of the strong **Muslim** Krio group of Freetown. Their constituencies were therefore alienated. Albert Margai had ambitions of turning the country into a one-party republic. He proposed this idea, and it was passed by Parliament; however, it needed a postelection Parliament to ratify it. Many Sierra Leoneans opposed this move, and this substantially increased opposition to Margai's rule.

However, Albert Margai did not attempt to alter the constitution in order to get his policy adopted. He was struggling with a postindependence economy that was bound to suffer because of dependence on Western global domination. He was accused of corruption by enemies he had already made because of his political ambitions. His policies benefited the APC, and in the 1967 elections Margai lost by a narrow margin. His party and government officials attempted to manipulate the election results, but the governor general appointed Siaka Stevens, the leader of the APC, as prime minister. Immediately after the swearing in ceremony, the commander of the armed forces, Brigadier David Lansana seized control of the government, put the governor general and Siaka Stevens under house arrest, and declared martial law. Lansana was overthrown a few days later by junior army officers in the army who then invited **Andrew Juxon-Smith**, a senior officer who was on study leave in Britain, to lead a military government. Juxon-Smith led a National Reformation Council (NRC) for one year before being himself overthrown by other junior officers in 1968. **John Bangura**, who had been retired from the army by Albert Margai, was recalled from exile in Guinea by these soldiers and he returned to hand over the reins of office to Siaka Stevens.

THE ERA OF SIAKA STEVENS

Siaka Stevens' rule lasted from 1968–1975. The economy underwent a gradual and continuous decline during his tenure, although there were some important improvements, such as in road networks. Corruption was obvious, marked by probes such as **Vouchergate** and Squandergate, which only ended in the firing of some public servants. Siaka Stevens entrenched himself in office through a series of measures. He played down ethnicity considerably and used this policy to reduce dependence on any of the two major ethnic groups—Temne and Mende—in his government. Whenever there were threats to his rule, he responded by incorporating the leaders of these pressure groups, such as the labor and teachers' unions, into his government. He also lavishly provided for the top brass in the army, giving them opportunities for corruption in prefinanced contracts; also, up to a hundred 50 kg. sacks of imported rice went monthly to each senior officer above the rank of captain. The army was not provided with arms on a regular basis, thus it was difficult to organize a coup d'état. Whenever there was a civil disturbance, the government depended on a paramilitary force created by Stevens called the Internal Security Unit, later the Special Security Division (SSD). This unit was used to strike terror into the populace, particularly during general elections.

In 1977, students of Fourah Bay College staged a demonstration during university convocation, leveling accusations of corruption against Siaka Stevens, who was also chancellor of the university. The APC retaliated by sending party stalwarts to attack the college two days later. However, the protest spread throughout the country and proved difficult for the government to quell. When the protests died down, Stevens used them as an excuse to call early elections that same year. These elections were rigged, and the new Parliament passed laws making Sierra Leone a one-party state in 1978. Stevens had, much earlier, in 1971, gotten the Parliament to declare Sierra Leone a republic with himself as executive president.

The economic decline under Stevens became severe in the 1980s, with massive budget deficits and a rapid slide in the value of the local currency, the Leone, accompanied by huge oil bills and an increasing dependency on external sources of funding, including the International Monetary Fund (IMF). The conditions imposed by the latter brought continued low wages, a rapid rise in the cost of consumer goods as government subsidies were lifted on essential goods, and a consequent growing impoverishment of the population. Social services such as education declined since teachers were not receiving even their meager salaries and went on prolonged strikes. An adequate supply of electrical energy became a rarity as prolonged power cuts became the norm. Lame policies of enforcement of government regulations meant a general deterioration of controls. The result was popular dissatisfaction manifested in strikes and unrest.

Old and in failing health, Siaka Stevens decided to retire from the presidency but not before he got Parliament to amend the constitution so that he could appoint his handpicked force commander, Brigadier **J. S. Momoh** as the new presidential candidate. In an obviously rigged election in October 1985, Momoh, the sole candidate, was overwhelmingly elected president.

Momoh's six years in office, from 1986 to 1992, marked a more rapid decline in the economy. It became clear that Stevens had selected Momoh because he wanted a weak leader to succeed him. Momoh seemed incapable of making any firm decisions on any issue. He became heavily dependent on close friends such as A. K. Turay who became minister of state in the president's office, and on father figures such as paramount chief **Alimamy Dura**, a prominent Limba politician. These interests coalesced in the formation of the Akutay Friendly Society, a Limba movement to which the president belonged. Akutay became a dominant player in the political arena, and sometimes cabinet meetings were actually held in the Limba language. A prominent Afro-Lebanese businessman Jamil Sahid Mohamed, who had had a lot of political clout under Siaka Stevens, was quietly removed from the scene, but the Lebanese continued to play a prominent role in the local economy, particularly in controlling diamond dealing and smuggling and retail trade.

A broad appeal for democratization followed the collapse in the early 1990s of the Soviet Union and the insistence by the United States and the IMF that financial assistance be tied to evidence of democratization. This influenced forces in Sierra Leone as the economy continued to decline and people became increasingly weary of the incumbent government. A radical newspaper, the *New Shaft*, took up this call, leading a petition-signing drive. This was followed by a conference by the Sierra Leone Bar Association in which a demand for democracy dominated the proceedings. Students of the **University of Sierra Leone**, both at **Njala University College** and Fourah Bay College, began to incite demonstrations.

President Momoh bowed to these pressures and convened a national Constitutional Review Commission in September 1990 that held sittings throughout the country. The commission ultimately recommended a new constitution, restoring multiparty politics. The president accepted the commission's report and after a new constitution was written took steps to get it through Parliament; this was followed by a referendum in which voters approved the new constitution. This constitution provided for the appointment of cabinet ministers from outside Parliament, and sitting members had to give up their parliamentary seats if they were appointed cabinet ministers. Newly appointed ministers had to be approved by Parliament. The intense political realignments and political activity that followed coincided with the start of the rebel war.

THE REBEL WAR

Evidence that is coming to light from the **Truth and Reconciliation Commission**, which began its work in Freetown in April 2003, is revealing more of the background to the start of the civil war. Its origins seem to have come from two main sources—from disenchanted Sierra Leoneans determined to change the system and from neighboring Liberia's **Charles Taylor**, hostile because Sierra Leone had agreed to be used as a base for operations of the **Economic Community Cease-Fire Monitoring Group (ECOMOG)**, which was against his interest in Liberia. The group of disenchanted Sierra Leoneans is said to have included some big names such as **John Karefa-Smart** and Lebanese interests such as Kasim Basma. Others, such as Cleo Hanciles, were among the young militants who had been dismissed from teaching positions or studentships at Fourah Bay College following a student demonstration there. Some of these young militants had gone through Ghana to Libya where they had been trained and, in the process, had developed contacts with Charles Taylor and another disgruntled former military officer in Sierra Leone, **Foday Sankoh**.

A coalition of all these interests came together, organized by Charles Taylor and bent on seeking revenge on Sierra Leone and profiting from Sierra Leone's diamonds. As one newspaper in Sierra Leone, *The New Citizen* (April 22, 2003), reported from evidence from the Truth and Reconciliation Commission, "The first armed incursion into Sierra Leone in the Bomaru area was carried out by elements of Charles Taylor's [National Patriotic Front of Liberia] NPFL and not by Foday Sankoh's **Revolutionary United Front (RUF)**." At Taylor's urging, the dissidents involved formed the RUF, led by Foday Sankoh. As the war intensified, the leadership ranks of the RUF came to be dominated by Foday Sankoh, guided by Charles Taylor and his concept of conducting a rebel war. This put Sankoh at odds with some of the more idealistic and Western educated elements, some of whom left the movement while others, such as Abu Kanu and Rashid Mansaray were summarily executed by Foday Sankoh. Sankoh became supreme. It was reported that at Pendembu around the eastern Sierra Leone border, Charles Taylor had declared Sankoh governor of Sierra Leone by April 1991.

The Sierra Leone army was utterly incapable of confronting the rebels. Bloated in the upper echelons by luxury, a lack of military activity, and no weapons, they were unable to defend the country. The Momoh government quickly responded by introducing hoodlums into the army, giving them a rough-and-ready training, and sending them to the war front. These new soldiers often fled before the advancing enemy.

As the war intensified, President Momoh reorganized his cabinet, dropping ministers whose loyalties were questioned. The APC party also threw out 10 leading figures, some of them ministers, for similar reasons. In the political turmoil of this situation and the growing civil war, the president could not make up his mind which constitution—the new one or the old one—to adhere to, and so he ended up using both. New parties were soon formed by those who left the APC party, and their leaders began to severely criticize the president under whom they had served as cabinet ministers a few months earlier.

In the first few months of 1992, the war seemed less threatening. It became clear that monies being appropriated for military operations were proving too burdensome for the weak Sierra Leone economy. Moreover, these allocations were diverted to individual interests so that soldiers on the war front were not receiving their wages. However, these soldiers were now armed, and a few of their leaders, young officers in their twenties below the rank of captain, decided to travel to Freetown and demand their wages. Information, not clearly confirmed, points to a coup plot having been hatched by these officers who were ostensibly coming to protest for wages. The protest resulted in the April 29 coup d'état in which these officers took control of the government and set up a new ruling military junta called the National Provisional Ruling Council (NPRC) led by Captain **Valentine Strasser**. These junior officers who were leading the government were so young that Freetown developed a new slogan for NPRC—*na pikin de rule contri* (it is children who are ruling the country).

NPRC RULE

The NPRC government was initially welcomed by the Freetown community in general. It launched an apparent war on corruption with commissions of inquiry and a campaign against lack of discipline in government service. But the government soon incurred the suspicion of the people when it passed decrees giving senior military officers powers of search without warrant and Decree 6 effectively implementing press censorship. The Senior Officers Special Military Tribunals Decree of 1992 was intended to try those opposed to the state. Under this decree, 26 alleged coup plotters were speedily tried, condemned to death, and executed in December 1992. This created much disenchantment with the military government, and the world press, which the Freetown population clung to avidly, even doubted whether there was a putsch. Some foreign governments including Italy and Britain announced suspension of aid. The military government tried to amend its policies by repealing the decrees for search without warrant and press censorship.

However, the continued civil war, which was now getting worse, did not help the junta's position. The army seemed incapable of successfully prosecuting the war. Localized groupings were being encouraged to organize for their own defense, leading to what were termed Civil Defense Forces. One group of traditional hunters called **Kamajor** organized by 1992 in an unofficial civil defense force at the southern town of Bo, relied on a mixture of indigenous medicine, religion, and force to fend off rebel attacks. The war appeared to be spreading as a result of RUF propaganda aimed at mobilization of disenchanted, unemployed youth in the interior, tired of government failure to address their needs. Many were forcibly drafted into RUF ranks, including children, both male and female, the latter more so as mistresses of the fighters.

Many of the Sierra Leone soldiers sent to the war front were unused to combat. Poorly paid and often not paid at all, many of them defected and became rebels, looting settlements in the interior. By the end of 1993, these new rebels, or "sobels" (soldier/ rebels) as they were called, had grown in number, with various groups of them operating in different parts of the interior. Some of these new rebel groups were civilian defense committees, armed by the military government, and these used the weapons so acquired to go on rampages. By mid-1994, it had become unclear who the rebel leader was, with leaders of various factions making that claim for themselves.

By 1995, pressures from civil society and the press began mounting again for a return to parliamentary democracy. This induced the military government to initiate moves toward a general election to elect a civilian government. Valentine Strasser's NPRC called for a constitutional conference in August 1995. The delegates demanded a return to democratic elections. On January 16, 1996, Strasser was removed in a coup and was replaced by his second in command, **Julius Maada Bio**. As the political movement toward the proposed elections quickened, Bio's government called another constitutional conference on February 12, 1996, a move that many saw as intended to derail the elections. The army had begun to support a plan of peace before elections. But the delegates at the February meeting overwhelmingly insisted on the elections as planned, rebuffing the army's position. Groups of women took to the streets of Freetown to demonstrate support for a return to a democratically elected government. The army acquiesced, and elections were held amidst general insecurity, particularly in the provinces where people resisted attempts by some military elements to stifle voting. The revived SLPP emerged victorious, and in April 1996 a new government led by **Ahmed Tejan Kabbah** was ushered in.

PRESIDENT KABBAH AND MILITARY INTERVENTION

President Kabbah began to address the issue of the war by diplomatic means and signed an accord with Foday Sankoh's RUF in November 1996. But certain groups, particularly in the army, remained disgruntled because they had lost power and influence. Kabbah had to address this problem as best he could. Faced with a regular army that he apparently believed he could not rely on, Kabbah proceeded to quickly arm the Kamajor, a group of traditional hunters mostly from the south and east of Sierra Leone who had loosely organized into local militia units and had assumed greater prominence as people grew wary of the army's response to the rebels. But the Kamajor was also seen as a southern Mende force, and this worried some segments of the population. Using IMF prescriptions also, Kabbah removed the monthly sack of rice benefit, which had remained a major subsidy of the government to each soldier.

Kabbah's reliance on the Kamajor and actions against the army came to be seen as an attempt by a Mende government to entrench itself by dependence on a Mende force at the expense of the regular army. The sack of rice factor fuelled the situation, since it was interpreted by the regular soldiers as disregard for the army.

The army was further disenchanted by the reliance that President Kabbah was beginning to place on the ECOMOG forces based in Sierra Leone. This force had been set up by the Economic Community of West African States (ECOWAS) but was dominated by Nigeria, which largely funded it. President Kabbah's personal security force now consisted mostly of Nigerian soldiers, and it was believed that Kabbah and the Nigerian President, Sani Abacha, had reached some sort of defense agreement. The army was beginning to feel marginalized.

There was a reported putsch by the end of 1996 in which the suspected leader, **Johnny Paul Koroma**, was arrested and imprisoned. Then, in May 1997 another attempt succeeded in ousting Kabba's government. The coup plotters from the army broke open the prison in Freetown and released all of the prisoners including Johnny Paul Koroma, who assumed leadership of the new military junta, the **Armed Forces Revolutionary Council (AFRC)**. Apparently out of fear of being subdued by ECOMOG forces, the AFRC invited the RUF to join them in a joint government in Freetown. This brought the RUF forces into the capital.

Members of the Kabbah government fled to neighboring Guinea. This coup was accompanied by widespread looting and destruction of government offices, which also involved the RUF force. This was particularly noticeable in the burning down of the Treasury and the Central Bank, which had been deeply involved in a major financial scandal. Private property and businesses were looted in Freetown. The more affluent in Freetown fled the capital for Guinea and, in crowded boats, for Banjul, the capital of Gambia.

The AFRC/RUF government lasted only a few months. In February 1998, ECOMOG forces, supported by the Kamajor, stormed Freetown and drove the AFRC/RUF junta from the capital. The dislodged rebel groups now started the civil war afresh in the provinces, with major atrocities such as hacking off limbs of civilians, which generated intense interest by international observers.

President Kabbah returned triumphantly to Freetown with the staunch support of international agencies that had been united against the AFRC/RUF ruling junta. The Freetown population was strongly supportive of President Kabbah, and, coupled with international goodwill, a massive crackdown was initiated on all who were believed to have helped install the junta or to have participated in its short-lived administration. Twenty-four soldiers were executed by firing squad after being found guilty before an obviously partisan court that did not allow for appeals. Death sentences were imposed on 26 civilians after public trials. On October 23, 1998, the death sentence was passed on Foday Sankoh, the RUF leader, after a trial for which he could find no defense lawyer in Freetown. Sankoh had been apprehended in Nigeria and was handed over to the Sierra Leone government. More than a thousand people were imprisoned, and many others fled and/or lost their jobs as punishment for having continued to work under the AFRC/RUF regime. An open witch hunt developed in which the Kamajor militia, led by Defense Minister **Hinga Norman**, seemed to have had unfettered sway in attacking suspects and sometimes executing them.

Meanwhile the civil war raged on. The country's economy was, of course, ruined. The RUF was in firm control of the diamondiferous Eastern Province. They were mining diamonds in the **Kono** and **Kenema** Districts, and much of the money from the sale of the diamonds was going through Charles Taylor in Liberia, who used some of it to provide arms for the rebels. As the international community moved to ban diamonds coming from Sierra Leone, there were reports of Al Qaeda involvement with Charles Taylor's government in Liberia to launder these diamonds. On the other hand, there was information from international press sources that money from natural resources such as diamonds was being funneled to foreign organizations such as the mercenary groups Sandline and Executive Outcomes in return for help in fighting the rebels.

These organizations, the Kamajor, and ECOMOG came to have dominant sway in determining the direction of events by the end of 1998. The Sandline/Executive Outcomes alliance was assisting in the war as well as training Kamajor fighters. It was a free feast for foreign Western interests in particular, as many companies competed for the spoils of war. And some were helping the RUF rebels, too. Many Western organizations were supplying arms to both sides in the war with an eye on diamond mining concessions, whichever side emerged victorious. Two British companies, Sky Air and Occidental, for example, were reported to have supplied nearly 400 tons of arms and ammunition to rebel forces, contrary to official British opposition to the war.

In this complex grab bag, the rebels who held most of the country were strengthened and began closing in on the capital, Freetown. Diplomatic maneuvers by President Kabbah were trivialized, particularly as the RUF leader, Foday Sankoh, was in prison and the hawks in the SLPP appeared keen to prosecute the war to the very end. On January 6, 1999, the RUF rebels and their *sobel* supporters, led by Johnny Paul Koroma, entered Freetown and took control of most of the capital. The ECOMOG forces fought back, holding out on the far west of Freetown for almost two weeks before they finally beat back the rebel advance out of Freetown. Residents of Freetown remembered those two weeks as a reign of terror when rape, murder, torture, and looting were the order of the day. This was led by the RUF and former military elements, supported by hoodlums capitalizing on the situation. The rebels broke into the prison and released all who had been condemned to death or held in custody. Huge sections of Freetown were set on fire as the rebels retreated.

It was some time before the situation calmed down in Freetown, as flagrant lack of discipline and disregard for law and order prevailed. Meanwhile, in the provinces the war continued, and ordinary citizens were subjected to widespread amputation of limbs. The RUF denied any responsibility for this, and it was blamed on a group called the West Side Boys, remnants of the former Sierra Leone army led by Johnny Paul Koroma.

Meanwhile diplomatic measures to end the war were being actively pursued. Following talks in Abidjan, Côte d'Ivoire, between the United Nations Special Representative for Sierra Leone and the RUF, a joint communiqué was issued on February 21, 1999, calling for a peace conference in Lomé, Togo, involving all parties to the conflict, including Foday Sankoh. A cease-fire agreement was hammered out on April 17, 1999, followed on July 7 by the **Lomé Peace Agreement** signed between the Kabbah government and the representatives of the RUF, led by Foday Sankoh and the West Side Boys, led by Johnny Paul Koroma.

The Lomé accord provided amnesty for those who had fought in the war. It laid down guidelines for a new national unity government headed by President Tejan Kabbah but including the rebel leaders Foday Sankoh and Johnny Paul Koroma. The agreement also provided for free and fair elections in which these former rebel leaders would participate. However, former members of the Sierra Leone army were dissatisfied with the Lomé agreement, and this led to meeting in Monrovia, the Liberian capital, in which Johnny Paul Koroma and Foday Sankoh sought Charles Taylor's intervention in settling the disagreements. When Koroma and Sankoh returned to Freetown early in October, they issued a joint statement indicating their cooperation and stating that the RUF/AFRC alliance would transform itself into a political movement.

Units from the United Nations peacekeeping forces began arriving in Sierra Leone in November 1999. The RUF expressed opposition to this force and, in fact, abducted some of the UN soldiers in April 2000. RUF representatives were increasingly restless about the implementation of the terms of the Lomé accord in the new government and complained of being marginalized. Finally, on May 8, 2000, a major demonstration was staged in Freetown in favor of a permanent peace. The demonstrators were apparently moving toward Foday Sankoh's residence when his supporters opened fire on the crowd, killing 20 of them. The next day, Foday Sankoh was captured and imprisoned.

The British government, which had been attentive to the postwar activities, sent a contingent of troops to assist the United Nations peacekeeping efforts. Eleven of these British soldiers were taken hostage by the West Side Boys, after which the British forces mounted an offensive against the West Side Boys, ostensibly to rescue these soldiers but apparently also to strike terror in the hearts of the rebels. This offensive and the continued presence of British troops visibly impressed the Freetown population, which began to feel more secure from rebel attacks. Finally, in May 2001, arrangements were made to begin disarming the rebels and reintegrating them into the larger society. Funding was provided from external sources to compensate those who turned in their weapons and to provide job training and implements for a fresh start for these former combatants.

As the ECOMOG and later the UN troops departed, some of the social effects of their presence were becoming apparent. Relatively well-paid soldiers being thrust into an impoverished population meant that many soldiers, with their vastly superior resources, preyed on the local population. This encouraged prostitution to an alarming degree and caused a staggering increase in the incidence of AIDS, which was blamed on UN soldiers from East and Central Africa where AIDS was more prevalent. In 2003, a special court sponsored by the UN indicted Foday Sankoh, Charles Taylor of Liberia, and a others for war crimes. A Truth and Reconciliation Commission also began hearings in Freetown in April 2003.

The Dictionary

– A –

ABAYOMI-COLE, JOHN AUGUSTUS (1848–1943). A prominent 19th-century figure in Freetown, John Augustus Abayomi-Cole was best known as a religious leader and herbalist. He started his own African church, the Gospel Mission Hall, where he encouraged various ethnic groups to come together and worship. This was unique for 19th-century **Freetown**.

Abayomi-Cole was born in Nigeria of Sierra Leone parentage. He attended the **Church Missionary Society (CMS)** Grammar School in Freetown, after which he accepted an appointment with the United Brethren Church (UBC) at Shenge in the **Bonthe** District. While with this mission, he went to the United States and was ordained as pastor in the American Wesleyan Methodist Church. His tenure as superintendent of the Maroon Chapel in Freetown, which began in 1887, was short-lived, and he moved to the hills of Leicester, near Freetown, where he farmed ginger, a crop then in demand in England, and later started his own church.

Abayomi-Cole was perhaps best known as an herbalist. He gained affiliation with the National Association of Medical herbalists in Great Britain. His writings indicate that he was interested in the useful medicines of Sierra Leone's several secret societies such as the **Poro** and the **Sande**. He made a lifelong study of remedial and medicinal herbs and used their healing properties to aid the sick. His keen interest in medical science made it possible for him to combine his knowledge of Western medicine with traditional herbal remedies.

Abayomi-Cole wrote regularly in the ***Sierra Leone Weekly News***, a leading West African newspaper, and also wrote a news summary in Arabic that was published in *Saturday Ho*, a magazine publication that appeared from 1891–1896. He also wrote a Mende grammar. But more importantly, he was known for his work in implementing practical applications in medicine and in industry. He distilled spirits (for which he was chased out of Sierra Leone in 1911), manufactured sugar from molasses, made soap, and extracted various foods from corn. He also ventured into the palm oil trade, as well as into growing such cash crops as cocoa, cassava, yams, corn, and other vegetables. In his later years, he enthusiastically founded an agricultural society in 1922. He had earlier founded the Sierra Leone Farmers Association and soon became president. Most of his pursuits were not looked upon favorably in the 19th century Freetown, due somewhat to the British disdain for such an avocation. Today, Abayomi-Cole is remembered in Sierra Leone as one of the pioneers of indigenous technical knowledge and independence in food production.

ABRAHAM, ARTHUR (1945–). Perhaps the foremost historian of the **Mende** of Sierra Leone, Arthur Abraham was born at Daru in the Kailahun District. Abraham took a history degree at **Fourah Bay College** in 1967 and a master of arts at the **University of Sierra Leone**. He obtained his Ph.D. from Birmingham University in England in 1974 and joined Fourah Bay College's history department. His career at Fourah Bay was interrupted when, in 1977, he went to teach at Cuttington College in Liberia for two years. On his return to Sierra Leone, he went into rice marketing with the Ben Kanu Company and did consultancy work. He returned to Fourah Bay College in 1991 as Director of the Institute of African Studies and rose to the rank of Professor of African Studies. In 1992, Abraham was appointed secretary of state for education by **Valentine Strasser** and later also served in the trade ministry. One of the refugees of the rebel invasion of Freetown in 1999, Arthur Abraham is now professor of history at the University of Virginia in the United States. He has written several books on Sierra Leone, particularly on the Mende, his most recent being *An Introduction to the Pre-Colonial History of the Mende of Sierra Leone*, published in 2003.

AKAR, JOHN (1927–1975). John Akar was best known in Sierra Leone as an advocate of making the Sierra Leone Broadcast Service more reflective of indigenous culture and also for starting the Sierra Leone National Dance Troupe.

Akar was born in Rotifunk, Bumpe Chiefdom, in the present Moyamba District where he attended the Evangelical United Brethren (EUB) School and later the Albert Academy secondary school in Freetown. He studied drama, dance, and journalism in Britain, the United States, France, and the West Indies. In 1957 he was appointed head of programs for the Sierra Leone Broadcasting Service and in 1960 became director of broadcasting. He brought a distinctive indigenous character to broadcasting in a country just emerging from colonial rule and absorbed with English culture as a standard of accomplishment. He founded the National Dance Troupe and used it to encourage Sierra Leoneans to be proud of their rich cultural heritage. He led the troupe on many successful performances around the world. The troupe was voted the best dance ensemble at the New York World's Fair in 1964 and performed in many Western capitals in Europe in the 1960s.

John Akar left the service of the Sierra Leone Government in 1971 shortly after he had served for two years as Sierra Leone's ambassador to the United States. He died in 1975 in the West Indies.

AKIBO-BETTS, ALFRED (1944–). Alfred Akibo-Betts became a prominent politician in **Freetown**, serving chiefly under the government of **Siaka Stevens** and later under other administrations. He was elected chairman of the Freetown Committee of Management, the equivalent of mayor of Freetown.

He was born in Freetown and attended the **Sierra Leone Grammar School**. He seemed destined for a career in politics, briefly gaining some recognition as an activist with the **Sierra Leone People's Party** government by 1967; however, he switched to the **All People's Congress** when it seemed clear that the APC would win the 1967 elections. Akibo-Betts was prominent in the APC youth movement and earned a reputation as well for thuggery. He was appointed as a deputy minister in Siaka Stevens' government by 1980. For a brief period in 1981, President **Siaka Stevens** assumed the portfolio of finance and appointed Alfred Akibo-Betts as deputy minister of finance. In this capacity, Akibo-Betts effectively ran the finance ministry for that period and developed a reputation for courage and forthrightness in revenue collection. He also became well known in connection with the unearthing of the "**Vouchergate**" and "Squandergate" scandals in which civil servants were exposed for having misappropriated large sums of government funds.

Akibo-Betts fell from grace with Siaka Stevens, and when he attempted to present himself as a candidate for elections in 1982, he was severely manhandled by thugs. When President **Joseph Momoh** took office in 1986, he appointed Akibo-Betts chairman of the Freetown Committee of Management. The Freetown City Council had been dissolved, and there was apparently no intention of holding municipal elections. During his tenure, he again became known for his rough handed methods in attempting to clean up the city of Freetown.

When Julius Maada Bio became head of state after a palace coup, which removed Valentine Strasser in 1996, Alfred Akibo-Betts was appointed minister of marine resources.

ALBERT ACADEMY BOYS SCHOOL. The Albert Academy was founded by the United Brethren in Christ Church (UBC) on October 4, 1904, and was located at Garrison House, in **Freetown**. The academy was named in memory of Rev. Ira E. Albert, a former UBC missionary; Rev. Albert's family provided most of the funds for the building that eventually became the present-day location of the Albert Academy on Berry Street in Freetown. This building was completed in 1907.

The earliest prospectus of the Albert Academy declared its intent to provide advanced training to students who were preparing to teach, preach, or engage in other mission work. From the onset, Albert Academy's curriculum emphasized a practical educational and strong industrial bias. Science was introduced in the curriculum and continued to be emphasized for many years. Pupils were drawn from both the colony and the protectorate. However, Albert Academy received a much higher proportion of protectorate pupils than other schools in Freetown. For a period in the 1920s and 1930s, Albert Academy was the major source for training teachers for the protectorate. It is still today one of the leading secondary schools in Freetown.

ALL PEOPLE'S CONGRESS (APC). The All People's Congress party was formed in 1960, one year before independence. To some degree, it represented the views of the leadership of the **People's Na-**

tional Party (PNP), whose primary leader, **Albert Margai**, had joined the United Front coalition formed by his brother, Prime Minister **Milton Margai**, and eventually was named to a cabinet position. **Siaka Stevens**, who founded the APC, had also been part of the leadership of the PNP but was not in Parliament at the time and so could not be rewarded with a cabinet position as demanded by the constitution. Merging into the United Front, then, was not an attractive option to him. After the constitutional talks in Britain that Siaka Stevens also attended, he refused to sign some of the documents sealing the agreement for independence. On his return to Sierra Leone, he immediately formed an Elections Before Independence Movement, a former platform of the PNP. Two months later, the movement was transformed into the All People's Congress with Siaka Stevens as its leader.

The APC began to score striking successes in local elections in **Freetown**, making the SLPP government somewhat jittery. Being more of a radical party with obvious leanings to a non-Western trained leadership and the masses, the SLPP government began to fear that the APC would disrupt the independence celebrations. Prime Minister Milton Margai therefore declared a state of emergency before the celebrations and sent the majority of the APC leadership, including Siaka Stevens, into detention. On his release, Siaka Stevens declared his party was law abiding. General elections were held in 1962 and the APC and its supporters won a third of the contested seats to become the opposition party in Parliament. The APC sustained its wave of popularity by winning Freetown municipality elections in the next couple of years and its leader, Siaka Stevens, was made mayor of Freetown.

When general elections were again held in 1967, the APC won a majority of seats, the first political party to score this success in the newly independent Africa. But the head of the army, who had been installed by the **SLPP** Prime Minister, intervened and there followed a year's military interregnum before the APC was reinstated as the new government in 1968. The APC government under Siaka Stevens went on to declare Sierra Leone a republic in 1971 and introduced a one-party state in 1978, making the APC the only recognized party in the country. A new constitution in 1991 brought back multiparty democracy and a military government followed the next year. The APC lost the general elections called by that military government in 1996 and became an opposition party. The party seemed to be in disarray for a few years thereafter but in municipal elections in Freetown in 2004, the APC seemed to have bounced back, winning most of the seats.

AMARA, ALIMAMY (c. 1805–1900). Alimamy Amara was a liberated African of **Yoruba** origin who was apprenticed as a youth to Alfa Musa Ojay, also of Yoruba origin, at Grassfields just outside Freetown. Ojay taught his new subject Arabic and converted him to **Islam**, giving him the name Amara. In the 1830s, Amara moved from Grassfields to Fula Town where he later became, an alimamy or head of the Fula Town community, one of the town's most prominent citizens. He pursued higher studies in Islam at Dinguiray (the present Republic of Guinea) where he studied with a famous Fulbe teacher. On his return to Fula Town, he became an acknowledged leader and, in 1875, he was recognized as alimamy or head of the Fula Town community. The colonial government acknowledged his position, and at a reception in 1886, Governor James Hay congratulated Alimamy Amara "for his intelligent administration and for the good example he set for his people." He often helped the colonial government address and resolve problems and was one of the leaders in assembling a meeting to elect an Aku king in 1891.

Amara's duties as alimamy involved spiritual leadership, since the alimamy was responsible for calling together the faithful to celebrate the **Muslim** holy days and festivals. There was sometimes disagreement among Muslim communities about the proper day on which to celebrate a major feast, depending on the sighting of the moon. Because the Islamic calendar had no fixed days for such observances, the community listened to the decisions of the alimamy. In 1887, for example, when one such dispute arose, Alimamy Amara pronounced that "He who controls the moon made it appear on the 22nd" and that pronouncement decided the date on which his own Muslim community celebrated the festival. Little is known of Amara by the end of the 19th century.

ANNIE WALSH MEMORIAL SCHOOL. The **CMS** started this school in 1845, then called the Female Institution, as a counterpart to the existing grammar school. What eventually became a secondary school for girls in the colony of Sierra Leone began as a Female Institution in the mountain village of Regent. Both British colony Sierra Leonean traditions were disposed toward little interest in higher education for women. In January 1849, the CMS sent out a Miss Julia Sass to start an institution for females in Freetown. She undertook to transform the Female Institution into the Annie Walsh Memorial School, named after the daughter of one of their missionary families, Rev. and Mrs. Walsh, who provided the building for the start of the school. Initially, there were three pupils, joined a few months later by three more. The curriculum included instruction in household chores, Bible training, and schoolroom teaching. By 1861 there were 30 pupils of whom 20 were boarders maintained by the CMS and other European interests. In July 1865, the school moved to a new building, which it has occupied to the present day. The curriculum was then modified to encompass secondary education in earnest. The Annie Walsh Memorial School sustained for many years the reputation as the leading secondary school for girls in Freetown. That reputation has since dissipated because such schools located in the east end of Freetown no longer attract the best students.

ANTHONY, FRANK S. (1910–). Frank Anthony was among the earliest protectorate people to receive a Western education and became one of the leaders of the movement leading to independence in Sierra Leone. He attended the **Albert Academy** secondary school and **Fourah Bay College**, and later Hampton Institute and Cornell University in the United States. Upon his return to Sierra Leone, he taught at the Bunumbu Teachers College starting in 1944 and later became principal of the Taiama Secondary School and Leona Secondary at **Bo**.

It was inevitable in the early days of the protectorate that protectorate Western trained people would take up leadership roles in the move to independence. Frank Anthony was no exception. He was one of the leading figures in the formation of the protectorate Teachers Union, and the **Sierra Leone Organization Society**. In the general elections of 1967, he was elected to Parliament an independent candidate representing Pujehun West constituency. The **Sierra Leone People's Party (SLPP)** lost the elections that year and hoped to declare victory by persuading **Frank Anthony** and three other independent candidate winners to declare for the party. These four men stood their ground and thus prevented the SLPP from claiming victory. After the military rule of the NRC, Anthony was appointed minister of agriculture and natural resources in 1968 and resident minister, Eastern Province, in 1969. He remained loyal to the SLPP until that party withdrew from the 1973 elections.

ARMED FORCES REVOLUTIONARY COUNCIL (AFRC). The AFRC came into being following a military coup on May 25, 1997, that ousted President **Ahmed Tejan Kabbah's** government, which was accused of marginalizing the army. The coup leaders freed one of their number, **Johnny Paul Koroma**, who had been imprisoned for plotting to overthrow the government. Koroma assumed leadership of the AFRC and they allied with the RUF rebels and the AFRC announced its government a few days later, with Koroma as chairman and **Foday Sankoh**, then in captivity in Nigeria, as vice chairman. The following eight-month rule was a stormy one, punctuated by tremendous international pressure to negotiate a peaceful settlement for the return of the Kabbah government. Pressures for a peaceful settlement failed, and the **Economic Community Cease-Fire Monitoring Group (ECOMOG)** launched an offensive in February 1998 that drove the **Armed Forces Revolutionary Council** (AFRC) and their Revolutionary United Front (RUF) allies from **Freetown** and restored the Kabbah government. The AFRC moved to the interior of the country and continued the civil war.

After the conclusion of the civil war and the general amnesty that was proclaimed, the AFRC transformed itself into a political party in the year 2000 and fielded a candidate, **Alimamy Pallo Bangura**, who ran unsuccessfully for president in the 2002 presidential elections.

ASANA BEYA (c. 1914–1987). Asana Beya distinguished himself in combat during World War II, receiving the British Distinguished Conduct Medal, for which he was honorably remembered at the time of his death in 1987.

Born in Rotifunk in the Maforki Chiefdom, he enlisted in the colonial army a few years before the start of World War II. At the outbreak of the war, his battalion was posted to the Southeast Asian (Burmese) war front. Beya's leadership qualities and courage were quickly recognized, and the European leader of the battalion recommended his promotion to the rank of lance corporal and by 1944, he had advanced to the rank of sergeant.

It was during an engagement when his platoon was attacked by a Japanese force on December 23, 1944, that Beya valiantly proved his mettle. According to the *Regimental History*, "when it became apparent that the enemy were on the point of overrunning his [Beya's] position, he seized an LMG and advanced toward the enemy, disregarding the heavy fire directed against him.... killed six of the enemy before the remainder turned and fled. His leadership was an inspiration to all around him and it was largely due to his courage, initiative and resolution that the attack was finally beaten off . . . Sgt. Beya was awarded an immediate DCM."

When Asana Beya died in 1987, the president of Sierra Leone, Major-General **J. S. Momoh**, who had himself been head of the Sierra Leone army, accorded Beya full military honors.

– B –

BA FODAY MANSARAY (c. 1750–1818). Ba Foday Mansaray was a Limba leader who founded a political unit in Wara Wara District, based in the town of Bafodea, which is named after him. He was born about the middle of the 18th century. His father, Papay Ndayin, had earlier in the century led migrants of the Mansaray clan (ethnic **Mandinka**) from the north into Wara Wara Limba country in the present Koinadugu District. After Ndayin had settled at Kayinbon, a town occupied by the Kamara, an ethnic **Limba** clan, Ndayin was given Binti, the daughter of Temeta, the Kayinbon chief, as his wife. She became Ba Foday's mother, and thus Ba Foday was born of a Mansaray and Kamara union.

Upon the death of his father, Ba Foday became ruler of Kayinbon, which put the Mandinka Mansaray clan in the ascendancy there. Ba Foday then convinced his Mansaray and Limba kinsmen to move away from Kayinbon, which was in a hilly area, and to establish a new town in a well-watered valley. Participating family units, whether Kamara, Mansaray, or Konte (another Mandinka group) from about 15 neighboring Wara Wara Limba towns and villages built houses for themselves in the new town. The town, ruled by Ba Foday, was named Ba Fodaya (today called Bafodea) after the ruler and became the capital of the towns and villages that had participated in its construction.

Ba Foday then consolidated his rule, from this new base, and expanded it to include what is now the former chiefdom of Kamuke, now part of Wara Wara Yagala. It also included sections of what is today the Kasunko chiefdom. By the end of the 18th century, Ba Foday was himself appointing the heads of the towns under his control, although these appointees continued to be selected from among the towns' ruling families.

During his rule, Ba Foday successfully resisted attempts by the Fula of Futa Jalon (north of Wara Wara, in the Republic of Guinea) to subdue the Wara Wara people. Earlier, in 1727–1728 the **Fula** had successfully launched a jihad (holy war waged in the name of Islam) in Futa Jalon, and wanted to extend the jihad to neighboring countries. By the second decade of the 19th century, however, Ba Foday had repelled the Fula army from his Kamuke province. However, the war took its toll and Ba Foday died soon afterward, probably about 1818.

Though Wara Wara country, centered on the town of Bafodea, temporarily came under the control of Futa Jalon soon after Ba Foday's death, this great Limba leader had nevertheless succeeded in consolidating a polity that was to survive into the colonial period, when it was split up into a number of chiefdoms. He also secured the rulership of this state for his descendants.

BAILOR, MAX A. B. (1929–). A prominent educator who received his early education at **Albert Academy School** in **Freetown**, Bailor went on to Otterbein College in the United States where he obtained an M.A. in education. He was, successively, a teacher and then principal of the Albert Academy School and subsequently amassed an impressive list of activities in education, as a member of the West African Exams Council, member and president of the **Milton Margai** Teachers College Council, and member and vice chairman of the Court of the University of Sierra Leone. He also served on the Sierra Leone Law Reform Commission and was director of the National Petroleum Company. In 1888, he was appointed chief electoral commissioner, a position he held until 1991.

BALANJI. This is a xylophone-type musical instrument very popular among most ethnic groups in Sierra Leone. It originated with the **Mande** peoples, but as Mande elements were integrated into different communities in Sierra Leone, so was the balanji. It is the major musical instrument of the *yeliba*, the minstrel historians and entertainers in traditional society. The balanji has an upper and lower frame to allow room for the calabash resonators under the wooden slats. The slats are tied onto the upper frame and the lower frame rests on the ground. The two frames are connected by vertical sticks at the corners. Between the frames, the calabashes are organized in a zigzag fashion underneath the slats. Slats and calabashes, varying from 14 to 20 in number, are graded in size to give different sounds. The player strikes the slats with a pair of mallets with leather heads. The balanji can be played by an individual or by a group.

BAMBAFARA (c. 1835–1921). Bambafara was ruler of the Koranko of Nieni from the late 18th century until his death in 1921. The son of Yirimusukali of the Koroma clan who ruled Nieni before him, Bambafara was born in Yifin, then the seat of Nieni Koranko country. As a young warrior, he was captured by **Suluku**, the Biriwa Limba ruler and spent a number of years in Bumban, Suluku's capital. After his release some time in the 1870s, Bambafara became ruler of Nieni. He consolidated his rule over the Nieni polity by installing his own trusted lieutenants as heads of provinces, among them a prominent warrior named Sayo Demba of the Thoronka clan, as ruler of Kaliang neighboring Nieni to the west, and another leading warrior, Banda Karifa, who was recognized as ruler of Wuli, another province of Nieni. Bambafara exerted a strong influence over the Kono people of Sando and the Koranko of Sambaia, now in the Tonkolili District. As the dominant figure in this extensive area, he was renowned for helping his subjects, earning the name of *Konkifaga*, or hunger killer. His territory came under the sweep of the **Mandinka** empire-builder, **Samori Toure** 1890s, whereupon Bambafara moved his capital to a more defensible mountain position called Kintibalia, thus providing a safe haven for his Koranko people and for his Kono allies.

As Samori's **sofa** lessened, the British protectorate emerged. Early in 1895, the British convinced Bambafara to move his capital from Kintibalia to a newly built town named Kruto, about six kilometers away. Bambafara was initially recognized by the British as paramount chief of Nieni, Kaliang, Wuli, and Sambaia—the areas over which he had ruled before the sofa invasion. By 1899, however, this large chiefdom was broken up by the British, and Wuli, Sambaia, and Kaliang became separate chiefdoms. Bambafara continued as paramount chief of Nieni, and his authority was habitually invoked by the British colonial administration in the settlement of disputes in many neighboring **Koranko** and **Temne** chiefdoms.

BALLANTA-TAYLOR, NICHOLAS JULIUS GEORGE (1893–1962). Nicholas Julius George Ballanta-Taylor was a musicologist, organist, and composer, who devoted his career to bringing African rhythms into Western forms of music.

He was born in **Freetown** and educated at the local **CMS Grammar School** and at **Fourah Bay College**. At that time, music was not taught at either institution so Nicholas, as was the tradition in Freetown, learned music privately and ultimately earned a bachelor of music degree in 1925 from Durham University in England as an external candidate.

While he was in government service in the Gambia in 1914, Nicholas observed that a Bambara flutist produced a note between B-natural and B-flat, a note that he could not match on his harmonium. This prompted a search into the nature of African music, which took him to many parts of West and Central Africa, the United States, and Europe. In the 1920s in the United States, he studied the affinity between African American and African music. Aided by funds from the Peabody Institute, Ballanta studied piano with John Orth, and composition under Yacehia of the Boston Conservatory. He graduated from the Institute of Musical Art in New York in 1924. Working at Penn Normal, Industrial, and Agricultural School at St. Helena, South Carolina, Nicholas was acclaimed a genius in recording and transcribing spirituals and having them published. He conducted many of his own compositions at Symphony Hall in Boston, and one of his compositions was played at a student recital in New York in 1923.

From 1924–1926 he toured Africa, collecting specimens of musical forms. In 1925, he won the prestigious John Guggenheim Memorial Foundation Fellowship to conduct scientific studies on his musical conception. Through a second grant in 1927, he did theoretical work on musical scales in Germany and conducted additional field work in Africa. His manuscript The Aesthetics of African Music, which included 350 musical examples, is unique in this field.

Ballanta returned to Sierra Leone in 1933 and taught music, played the organ, and wrote and produced three operas, *Afiwa*, *Boima*, and *Effuah*, in addition to a concert overture.

Ballanta worked at a time when, in addition to prejudice about African studies, little was known about African music. His original research was therefore only fully appreciated after his death. In 1926, he was quoted in an interview asserting that the basic principle of jazz—its rhythm—was African but that the harmony and synchronization was not. He commented extensively about African music in journals such as *West Africa* in the 1930s, helping to dispel myths about the subject.

BANDAJUMA. The capital town of the Sowa chiefdom in the Pujehun District, sometimes written as Bandasuma in old records, it had a prominent female ruler in Madam Nyaloh in the 1880s. At the declaration of the protectorate, various chiefdoms around Bandajuma were grouped together into what was called the Bandajuma District. Bandajuma was one of the centers of major resistance during the 1898 rebellion. Thirty people were executed there at the end of the resistance.

BANGURA, ALIMAMY PALLO (c. 1955–). Pallo Bangura was a lecturer in political science at **Fourah Bay College** in the 1980s. When the NPRC military government was formed after the coup d'état of 1992, Pallo Bangura was appointed Sierra Leone's permanent representative to the United Nations. When the **Armed Forces Revolutionary Council** government of **Johnny Paul Koroma** came to power in 1997, Pallo Bangura was named foreign minister. He played a leading role in negotiations between the AFRC/RUF and the government of President **Kabbah** after the AFRC was deposed by the **ECOMOG** forces. In the short-lived unity government that was set up after the Lomé Peace Accord was signed in 1999, Pallo Bangura served as minister of energy and power. By the year 2000, the **RUF** had become a political party, and Pallo Bangura became its secretary-general. In the presidential elections of 2002, Pallo Bangura was the RUF Party's presidential candidate, since Foday Sankoh, the RUF Party leader was still in prison.

BANGURA, JOHN (1930–1971). John Bangura, a career officer, became head of the Sierra Leone army but ended up being executed for treason. He was born on March 8, 1930, at Kalangba to ethnic **Loko** parents. He attended local schools at Bagbema, Binkolo, and Koyiema in **Bo**, and later joined the army, obtaining his training at the prestigious Sandhurst military academy in England. Back in Sierra Leone, he rose to the rank of colonel before being implicated in a charge of mutiny in 1967 and detained by the **Albert Margai** government. He was released a few months later and was posted to a diplomatic position with the Sierra Leone embassy in the United States. In the military interregnum that followed, John Bangura went to Guinea where the opponents of the military had congregated. When junior ranks in the army overthrew the military junta in 1968, they chose Bangura as their leader of the new government. Subsequently, Bangura handed over the reins of government to **Siaka Stevens** and the **All People's Congress (APC)** who had won the elections a year earlier before the military takeover. He remained head of the army for another two years before he was arrested for treason, allegedly plotting a coup d'état in March 1971. He was tried and executed the same year.

BANGURA, THAIMU (1942–1999). Political leader and founder of the People's Democratic Party—Sorbeh—in the run up to the 1996 general elections, Thaimu Bangura was born in Madina Sanda in the Bombali District on October 23, 1942. He was educated at **Fourah Bay College**, where he took the diploma in economic studies and later qualified as a lawyer in Temple Inn in the United Kingdom. He had served as deputy forwarding manager for the Sierra Leone National Shipping Agencies and in the Sierra Leone civil service before going to England for further studies. After his return he was state counsel in the Law Officers Department before contesting the general elections for the Bombali Central constituency in 1977. The challenge was successful, Thaimu Bangura was appointed to the cabinet where he served first as minister of information and later in the Social Welfare Department. From 1982 to 1991, Thaimu was in Parliament without a cabinet position and became very active as leader of the Backbenchers Association. Then, as general elections approached in 1996, Thaimu formed his political party, the People's Democratic Party, popularly called ""Sorbeh."' He was a presidential candidate in the elections under his Sorbeh banner but lost to **Tejan-Kabbah**. In the political bargaining that followed the elections, Thaimu Bangura was appointed minister of finance and later to minister of works, labour and energy, and power in 1998. He died a year later.

BANKOLE-BRIGHT, HERBERT CHRISTIAN (c. 1883–1958). Herbert Christian Bankole-Bright was known more as a politician and journalist than as a medical practitioner, the vocation for which he had trained. His controversial political career has left a legacy in Sierra Leone history.

Nigerian by birth, he was schooled at the Wesleyan (later Methodist) Boys High School in **Freetown** and at the University of Edinburgh, where he qualified in medicine. While in Britain, he was engaged in political activism as a vocal member of the West African Students Union (WASU), a training ground for future politicians in British West Africa. He returned to Freetown and set up private practice. However, politics beckoned and he became one of the founders of the National Congress of British West Africa (NCBWA), a lobbying body of West African professionals in colonial British West Africa. In 1924, together with Ernest Beoku-Betts, he was elected to the Legislative Council where he championed workers rights and supported the 1926 Railway Workers strike.

However, Bankole-Bright lost the confidence of his supporters when he supported the colonial administration in passing three bills meant to destroy the West African Youth League, which had become a thorn in the flesh of the British in Sierra Leone. This position angered his supporters, and he was dismissed as vice president of the local branch of the NCBWA and was forced to resign his seat in the Legislative Council.

In 1951, Bankole-Bright was again elected a member of the **Legislative Council**, but he was now leader of a **Krio** political party, the **National Council of Sierra Leone**, and so became leader of the opposition. There again, he moved himself into the political wilderness by opposing the predominance of people from the protectorate in the new Sierra Leone politics following the Stevenson Constitution of 1947. Throughout all of this, Bankole-Bright remained vocal as proprietor and editor of two newspapers, the *Evening Despatch* and the *Aurora*. He died in 1958.

BANTA. An ethnic group, no longer in existence, that inhabited the southern parts of **Mende** country prior to the Mende "invasion" of the Sierra Leone interior. Today, two chiefdoms, Upper and Lower Banta in the Moyamba District, are named after the Banta, although these are now predominantly Mende chiefdoms.

The Banta are generally believed to be an offshoot of the Temne, which became isolated from the main Temne of north central Sierra Leone. One tradition holds that probably in the early 18th century, this Temne group conquered an area between the Jong River and the sea and there created a Banta polity known as Mabanta, centered on Gbangbatoke (present Upper Banta chiefdom). This polity, quite secluded from the main areas of Temne country, is believed to have at one point controlled the Yoni Temne country to their north. The location of Banta country led to much interaction with the neighboring **Sherbro** from where it is believed that the **Poro** society originated from the center of Yoni in Sherbro territory and was taken to what became Yoni Temne territory. This evidence could strengthen the idea of links between Banta, Sherbro, and Yoni, which gave the Banta dialect a peculiar uniqueness from the mainstream Temne.

Banta religion included powerful river spirits, and the Banta, upon reaching old age, were believed to mysteriously transform themselves into elephants. Every elephant shot, would utter a Banta word before dying, the traditions recall. The Banta were unsuccessful in resisting the incoming Mende and survived only in small numbers, their dialect of Temne remaining largely a memory in former Banta territory situated around Gbangbatoke.

BANYA, SAMA (1931–). A prominent medical doctor and political leader in Sierra Leone, Sama Banya was born on June 10, 1931, in the Kailahun District. He attended the **Bo** Government and the **Prince of Wales** secondary schools and later Bristol University and the London Medical School where he qualified as a doctor. He was appointed medical officer in the Sierra Leone government in 1963. He went in to private practice in Kenema in 1968 and was founder and proprietor of the Nongowa Clinic and Emma Thompson Nursing Home, a 40-bed facility that opened on April 15, 1972.

In 1978, Sama Banya was elected to Parliament for the Kailahun South constituency under the one-party state and was appointed resident minister for the Eastern Province. He was a member of Parliament until 1986 when **Siaka Stevens** left office. He held several portfolios including that of minister of finance. In 1985 when he was minister of the interior, he was dropped from the cabinet when, according to his own testimony, he refused to support the constitutional amendment that would make it possible for Major-General **Joseph Saidu Momoh** to become president. In 1998, Sama Banya was appointed minister of foreign affairs and international cooperation in the government of president **Tejan-Kabbah**. Sama Banya also served on a number of government boards including the University Court, the National Sports Council and the National Advisory Committee of Bunumbu College. Banya has not been a government minister since 2001; he is now a regular columnist in the *Salone Times*, a newspaper that favors the **Sierra Leone People's Party (SLPP)**.

BARCLAYS BANK OF SIERRA LEONE. Throughout most of the 20th century, Barclays Bank of Sierra Leone was one of the two or three leading banks in Sierra Leone. It was incorporated in 1917 as a branch of Barclays Bank in England to serve the British colony. In 1971, it became the Barclays Bank of Sierra Leone, establishing a separate identity from its parent body. It had branches in the major towns in the provinces and was a pillar of the Sierra Leone economy. Because of the ravages of the rebel war, the bank closed at the end of the century, and its physical assets were taken over by the Sierra Leone government to form the Rokel Bank, a government parastatal institution.

BARLATT, SAMUEL JOSIAH SIGISMUND (1867–1940). A lawyer, Samuel Josiah Sigismund Barlatt came from a prominent family, his father having been mayor of **Freetown** before the son assumed that position in the troubled years of 1918–1920.

He was born in Freetown and was schooled at the **CMS Grammar School** and at **Fourah Bay College**, where he received a bachelor of arts degree and a licentiate in theology. He later studied law in England and was called to the bar at Gray's Inn. He also earned a master's degree from Durham University. Barlatt returned to Sierra Leone in 1910 to set up in private law practice. He was often called upon by the colonial government to act as police magistrate. His family connections helped him to be elected mayor of Freetown in 1918, and during his tenure a major influenza pandemic, the 1919 Syrian **riots**, and the Elder Dempster Lines seamen's strike of 1920 all occurred. He was noted for physically helping during the pandemic and for bringing peace during the two strikes. Although he was regarded as too conservative by the Freetown community of the time, he participated actively in the work of the National Congress of British West Africa, which was definitely not pro-British. He was a member of the Fourah Bay College Council and was a prominent churchman.

BARRIE, BAILOR. A **Fula** trader and businessman in Sierra Leone, Bailor Barrie's name became a byword for wealth in Sierra Leone throughout the 1970s and 1980s. He reportedly dabbled in the diamond business where he amassed his wealth and then established businesses in Freetown, notably M. B. Barrie Motors at the east end of **Freetown**. He was reportedly very kind to his ethnic Fula people and helped to set many of them up to start business as cab drivers or shop owners. He died in a road accident in the 1980s.

BENKA-COKER, SALAKO A. (1900–1965). Salako Benka-Coker was the first Sierra Leonean to hold the position of chief justice in that country on the eve of independence. He was educated at the **CMS Grammar School** and at **Fourah Bay College**, where he obtained a B.A. in 1916. After teaching briefly and working as a mercantile clerk for two years, he went to England and studied law and was called to the Bar in Middle Temple in January 1926.

At the beginning of his career as a lawyer, Salako Benka-Coker was in private practice in Bathurst (now Banjul), the Gambia, for nine years before returning to Sierra Leone. He continued private practice in Sierra Leone for another eight years before accepting appointment as Crown Counsel in 1943. He held this position for a decade and became acting attorney-general in 1953, serving intermittently until 1956. In 1957, he was named acting puisne [younger or junior] judge, and acting chief justice in 1959. He occupied that position in a substantive capacity in 1960. While he was chief justice, he acted as governor general on a number of occasions.

Salako Benka-Coker is also well known for his support of the Boy Scouts movement, having served as commissioner of boy scouts in the Gambia while he practiced law there. He was also vice chairman of the Sierra Leone Sports Council, and in 1962, he was honored with the degree of doctor of civil laws by Durham University, his alma mater.

BEOKU-BETTS, SIR ERNEST SAMUEL (1895–1957). Ernest Samuel Beoku-Betts was among the leading jurists in the colony of Sierra Leone in the first half of the 20th century. He was prominent in local politics and succeeded in maintaining the respect of the colonial government, which conferred a knighthood on him in 1957.

He was born March 15, 1895, to a well-to-do merchant in Freetown. He attended the Leopold Educational Institute, **Fourah Bay College** and later Durham University and University of London. He was called to the bar in 1917. At some point during this period, he added the name '"Beoku"' to compound his family name, in recognition of his parents' birthplace, the town of Abeokuta in Nigeria. He set up a thriving private law practice in Freetown but also took a keen interest in civic affairs, serving first as a member of the Freetown City Council and then as mayor from 1925 to 1926. The 1924 colonial constitution for Sierra Leone increased the membership of the Legislative Council, providing for three elected members in the colony. Ernest Beoku-Betts was one of those elected in 1924 to fill the three seats. In the Legislative Council, he championed the rights of workers and of Africans in the colonial service, earning the disapprobation of the governor of the colony. He was openly supportive of the railway workers strike of 1926, which infuriated the governor. He and Bankole-Bright (they were referred to as the "double Bs"), dominated local politics in Freetown in the 1920s and 1930s.

In 1937, Beoku-Betts abandoned politics for the bench and was appointed police magistrate. Later, he acquired a string of firsts, as puisne judge in 1945, first Sierra Leonean West African Court of Appeals judge, and first Sierra Leonean vice president of the Legislative Council in 1953. A knighthood was conferred on him in 1957, the year that he died.

BEREWA, SOLOMON (1944–). Successively holding the positions of attorney general and then vice president of the Republic of Sierra Leone in the immediate aftermath of the rebel war, Solomon Berewa was a force to be reckoned with in the post–civil war politics of Sierra Leone.

He was educated at the Albert Academy secondary school and received a bachelor of arts degree from **Fourah Bay College** in 1963. He taught at his alma mater for a year and then joined the Sierra Leone Government service in the Cooperative Department. He then studied in Great Britain where he received a certificate in accounting and became a lawyer in 1973. He then returned to Sierra Leone where he became state counsel in the Law Officers Department in the same year. In 1981, Solomon left government service and joined a private law firm. He taught criminal procedure in the Sierra Leone Law School part time. Berewa was appointed attorney-general and minister of justice in April 1996 and presided over the treason trials that were held following the rebel occupation of Freetown in 1997–1998. After the SLPP won the elections of 2002, Berewa became vice president of the Republic of Sierra Leone.

BILALI (c. 1820–1888). Also known as Mori Lamina, Bilali was ruler of Tonko **Limba** in the 1870s and 1880s. His father, Mori Shaka, was one of the Soso rulers of Kukuna, in what is now the Kambia District. His mother was a Koranko of servile status. He was brought up in the warrior tradition and became a great warrior, feared by the neighboring Tonko Limba. When Mori Shaka died, he left the knowledge of the use of his war charms with Bilali, even though he had many other sons. Since Mori Shaka had left many debts, his other sons proposed to pay them off by selling off some of the 200 slaves Shaka had left behind. The head slaves, of whom Bilali was one, told the creditors that they were willing to work off the debt by farming and by trading with canoes. But the creditors drove them away, scorning any settlement with slaves. Apparently jealous of Bilali's prowess, his brothers attempted to execute their plan of payment by selling some slaves, including Bilali's two sons. Bilali and the other head slaves redeemed those who were sold. Later, Bilali also redeemed his sister and some of his other children who had also been sold by his brothers.

By this time, Bilali had decided that he had to escape from Kukuna. Together with the slaves supporting him, he fled Kukuna in 1836 after negotiating for protection with the ruler of Tonko Limba. His brothers pursued him, but he defeated them in combat. He then marched on in triumph to Tonko Limba, where he built a town called Kolunkuray on land given to him by the Bombo Lahai, ruler of Tonko Limba. Bilali later expanded the area under his authority by building more towns around Kolunkuray. He then moved his headquarters to Liminaya.

From the time of his escape from Kukuna in 1836 onward, Bilali's brothers, who later became the rulers of Kukuna, never gave up the idea of recapturing him. They formed coalitions for this purpose, including the Soso of the Morea state centered on Forecaria (now in Guinea), as well as the Soso of Kambia under **Sattan Lahai**. With help from the Tonko Limba, Bilali successfully resisted all attacks. The constant campaigns against Bilali ultimately pauperized the Kukuna rulers, but Bilali continued to thrive as more and more slaves rallied to his cause. By the 1870s, Bilali had entered into diplomatic relations with neighboring Koranko and Loko rulers in order to strengthen his power. By this time he was regarded as an important independent ruler in his own right. He was also one of the rulers who accorded protection to trade caravans that traveled to the Sierra Leone colony from the interior. Bilali died some time in the 1880s after successfully defending his freedom for many years.

BIO, JULIUS MAADA (c. 1963–). Maada Bio, who ultimately became one of the heads of state of Sierra Leone, was one of the soldiers on the frontline of the Sierra Leone army who staged the coup d'état that ousted President Joseph Saidu Momoh in 1992. He became chief secretary of state and deputy chairman of the NPRC in

1993 when **S. A. J. Musa** was removed from that position. He was also head of defense and was therefore in charge of the army. On January, 15, 1996, Maada Bio replaced Captain Valentine Strasser in a palace coup and became the new head of state. He concluded elections in April of that same year and handed over the reins of government to the newly elected president, **Ahmed Tejan Kabbah**. He then left Sierra Leone for the United States.

BLYDEN, EDWARD WILMOT (1832–1912). Edward Blyden was a controversial public figure both in Liberia and in Sierra Leone, which became his home in his later life. Blyden is best remembered as the father of Pan-Africanism, which he advocated through his writings and public appearances.

Edward Blyden was born in the Virgin Islands of Ibo slave parentage. At the age of eighteen, this gifted student attempted to enroll at a theological college in the United States but was rejected because he was black. After experiencing many instances of racism in America, Blyden immigrated to Liberia in 1851 and started afresh. In Liberia, he attained prominence in public service, became a professor of classics, president of Liberia College, ambassador to Great Britain, minister of the interior, and secretary of state. In 1885, he made an unsuccessful bid for the presidency of Liberia.

During this period, Blyden had spent a brief time in Sierra Leone, serving as government agent to the interior in 1871. He led two official expeditions to Falaba and Futa Jalon in the interior of Sierra Leone and the reports that he wrote still serve as major historical sources.

After he failed to win the presidency in Liberia in 1885, Blyden returned to Sierra Leone where he remained for the rest of his life. He stimulated controversy and lively debate in Freetown by his opposition to an indiscriminate emulation of Western culture.

The publication of his book *Christianity, Islam and the Negro Race*, motivated some of the Krio of Freetown to become more pro-African.

Blyden is best remembered for his contribution to Pan-Africanism. He actively defended African and black civilization in his writings. He expressed a belief in an independent West African nation and encouraged British colonial efforts to move toward this. He advanced the idea of the African personality and a distinctive culture equal to but different from European culture. He called for an independent West African University run solely by Africans, teaching African languages, cultures, and values. Blyden took an active interest in Islam, regarding Muslim Africans as more authentic than Christian ones. He learned to read Arabic and maintained close relations for many years with the Muslim community in Freetown, serving as director of Mohammedan education in Sierra Leone.

Although Edward Blyden died in 1912, his legacy remains as part of black intellectual discourse as the father of Pan-Africanism.

BLYDEN, EDWARD WILMOT, III (c. 1918–). Edward Wilmot Blyden III was the grandson of the Pan-Africanist of the same name and was the founder of the political party called the Sierra Leone Independence Movement in the political competition preceding independence in Sierra Leone. He was born in Freetown and attended the Wesleyan Boys High School and **Fourah Bay College** before going to the United States to study at Lincoln University, later receiving a Ph.D. from Harvard University. He served at Fourah Bay College in the early 1950s as head of the Extra-Mural Studies Department, and in 1957 he formed the Sierra Leone Independence Movement, a political party that had a brief existence before merging with the Kono Progressive Movement of **Tamba Songo Mbriwa**.

Blyden then moved to Nigeria, where he taught at the University of Nigeria at Nsukka before returning to Sierra Leone in 1967 as director of the Institute of African Studies at the University of Sierra Leone. He also served as University Public Orator before he was appointed ambassador to the USSR in 1974. Blyden lives in retirement in Freetown.

BO. Bo is the second largest town in Sierra Leone. It is located in central Sierra Leone in the Kakua chiefdom and in the district named after the town. During the colonial period, Bo town was the center of administration of the entire protectorate, and the seat of the chief commissioner of the protectorate was at Bo. The dominant ethnic group Bo is Mende. Bo is more cosmopolitan than most towns in Sierra Leone, with religious persuasion divided among Christians, **Muslims**, and followers of traditional religion; the categories are not always mutually exclusive.

BO GOVERNMENT SCHOOL. Bo Government School was founded in 1906 principally for the sons and nominees of traditional rulers or chiefs in the Sierra Leone protectorate. The objective was to prepare these would be chiefs for effective government of their chiefdoms. Students were not expected to seek employment after completing their education but were to return to their chiefdoms. Run by the colonial government, the school started in September 1906 with 83 pupils. The curriculum included the normal academic curriculum augmented by special and practical training in farming, carpentry, bridge building, road making, and land surveying. From the beginning, pupils were taught that manual labor was as important as learning the three "Rs." The students were expected to pay fees to be borne by their chiefdoms. In 1913, the chiefs complained about the high fees, and the colonial government removed the requirement for a refund of the fees if the products of the school sought employment in government service. The school's status was elevated with the introduction of the Junior Cambridge Certificate examinations in 1937. In 1941, a Senior Cambridge class was added and the school achieved full secondary status. Bo school became the most prominent school in the provinces and attracted pupils from Freetown. Its alumni association, the Old Bo Boys Association (OBBA), became a strong lobbying force in politics particularly and in Sierra Leone generally.

BOKARI, ALIMAMY KANDEH. Alimamy Kandeh Bokari was, in the 1860s and 1870s, ruler of the Soso state of Morea, currently divided between the Republics of Guinea and Sierra Leone. During this period, he figured prominently in political disputes between neighboring African parties and also the British and the French. Morea was a major trading area, with competing African rulers and systems vying for dominance equally with the British from Sierra Leone and the French from Guinea. When the ruler of Morea died in 1865, Bokari contested the rulership militarily but lost to a French-backed candidate, Maligi Gbele. However, in 1866, Bokari prevailed and Maligi Gbele was executed. The French and then the British acknowledged Bokari as ruler of Morea. The British and the French were now heavily involved in this contested area as part of the Scramble for Africa, and Bokari learned to play one European power against the other, much in the tradition of the Mandinka conqueror, **Samori Toure**.

Bokari sought and obtained British support against French pressure on him, and the British governor in Sierra Leone visited him in the 1870s. But French pressure was relentless and, as the British gave in, Bokari fled south to the British side of the divide. He continued to play a significant role in local politics on the Sierra Leone side of the territory until his death.

BOKARI BOMBOLAI (c. 1835–1900). Bokari Bombolai was a prominent political figure in Koya Temne country where he became the *Bai Kompa* (ruler) in 1890. Koya was close to the **Freetown** colony, and Bokari Bombolai had previously worked and been imprisoned in Freetown. Bokari contested the rulership of Koya for several years against William Lawson, son of the influential government interpreter in Freetown who had strong colony backing for his claim. Bokari ultimately prevailed when Lawson's father retired from government service and the British decided that Bokari's stature merited his accession to the rulership in order to maintain peace in the region. Bokari Bombolai was thus confirmed as the *Bai Kompa* by the British in 1890.

The British established control over Koya and other regions in the area in 1896 and imposed a tax on houses. This led to resistance by local rulers in which the Bai Kompa Bokari was implicated. He successfully evaded capture by the British and tried to sue for peace by paying some tax in 1898. He was, however, deposed by the British and died shortly after the resistance was suppressed.

BOCKARIE, SAM (MASKITA) (c. 1960–2003). During the civil war in Sierra Leone, Sam Maskita Bockari became well known as a ruthless leader of the **Revolutionary United Front (RUF).** A Kissi by ethnicity, Sam Bockarie was born in the village of Gbadiwulo in the Kissi Tongi chiefdom of the Kailahun District. His father, Bockari Gbandawa, had at one time been court chairman (an appointive position to the local court) in Kissi Tongi. Sam spent part of his young adult life as a barber in the diamond mining Kono District.

Bockarie rose to prominence as the leading RUF commander under **Foday Sankoh**. He acquired the pseudonym "Maskita" (mosquito) both for his lean appearance and for his persistent harassment of the enemy in war. By 1997, Sam Bockarie became the virtual leader of the RUF forces after Foday Sankoh was detained in Nigeria. When the RUF was invited to join an **Armed Forces Revolutionary Council (AFRC)** government under **Johnny Paul Koroma**, Sam Bockarie was prominent in that short-lived government (1997–1998). After the AFRC/RUF government was ousted, Sam Bockarie returned to the war front and continued leading the RUF forces and speaking for the RUF throughout 1998 and the first half of 1999. During this time Foday Sankoh was in prison in **Freetown** and Bockarie was in close contact with **Charles Taylor** in Liberia and was viewed as Taylor's strongman.

As the RUF moved toward a peace accord with the Sierra Leone government, Bockarie, who opposed the peace process, fell out with the propeace RUF leaders and was deposed. He removed to Liberia and became chief of security under Charles Taylor. When the United Nations outlawed the RUF presence in Liberia, Taylor was reportedly forced to temporarily send Bockarie out of the country, sending him first to the Congo to fight for President Laurent Kabila and also to Angola with Jonas Savimbi. Bockarie returned to Liberia in June 2001 and continued to work for Charles Taylor, transporting arms to Liberia from Burkina Faso. On March 10, 2003, Sam Bockarie was indicted for war crimes by the UN-backed Special Court in Freetown. On May 6, Bockarie was reported killed by Charles Taylor who by then viewed him as a threat.

BONTHE. An island in the extreme southeastern coastal area of Sierra Leone, Bonthe came to constitute a district, with its chief town on the island. Bonthe has a long history of trade and contact with Europeans, documented since the 15th century. Some of the dominant families, such as the Caulkers, Clevelands, and Tuckers of Bonthe are products of marriages between early European traders in the area and African women. Bonthe Island had one of the earliest municipal administrations in Sierra Leone, similar to **Freetown**, the capital. It therefore has an equally long history of Western education of its inhabitants. It is also recorded in oral traditions that the Poro, a secret society in Sierra Leone, originated from Yoni in the Bonthe Island. Bonthe was originally home to some of the oldest ethnic groups in Sierra Leone, such as the Bullom. Today, it is ethnically dominated by the Sherbro, themselves a mixture of Bullom and Mani peoples.

BREWA, LUSENI ALFRED MORLU (1924–). Luseni Alfred Morlu Brewa, a lawyer and politician, assumed a prominent position in Sierra Leone's political history when in the 1967 elections he was one of four candidates who won their seats as independent candidates and refused to be wooed to cross over and join the **Albert Margai** government, which had narrowly lost the elections.

He was born in Taiama in the Kori chiefdom of the Moyamba District. His early education was at the Bo Government School and the **Prince of Wales School** and later at Northwestern University and the University of Chicago in the United States. He qualified in law at Lincoln's Inn in England in 1959. After a brief period in private practice on his return home, Luseni Brewa stood for Parliamentary election in 1962 as an independent candidate for Moyamba North constituency and won. He was reelected in the hotly contested elections of 1967. The **Sierra Leone People's Party** (SLPP), seen as a party dominated by the eastern and southern peoples of Sierra Leone, lost the election by a narrow majority and sought to woo Luseni Brewa and three other candidates who hailed from the south to cross over and declare for the SLPP so that that party could declare victory. Luseni Brewa stood firm, however, and the SLPP was unable to declare victory. Instead, the head of the army, David Lansana, an appointee of the SLPP government, assumed the reins of government.

Throughout the 1970s, Luseni Brewa served in various ministerial posts in the APC government that followed a one-year military rule.

BULLOM. The Bullom ethnic group represents perhaps the oldest residents of the area of present-day Sierra Leone. They were progressively pushed toward the coast by successive waves of migrants from the north. As they reached the coast, the Bullom were literally divided into two groups by the incoming Temne. Very few Bullom people survive with a distinct ethnic identity today, having been largely absorbed by other groups. The northern Bullom along the coastal areas of northern Sierra Leone are culturally dominated by the Temne to the point where, today, many of them do not identify themselves as Bullom. To the south, the Bullom came to be dominated by the Mani invaders in the 15th century, giving rise to the Sherbro ethnic group. Today, there is a chiefdom, the Kafu Bullom chiefdom in the Port Loko District, which carries the toponomy. The Loko

Masama chiefdom in the same district also represents Bullom strongholds where the emergent Loko and Temne ethnic groups, eventually assimilated the Bullom.

BUNDU, ABASS (c. 1946–). Abass Bundu was a prominent politician in the 1980s and 1990s who later formed a political party that was in contention in the 1996 general elections for which he contested the presidency. He was born in Gbinti of **Fula/Temne** parentage and received secondary education in Freetown. He qualified as a lawyer in England and took the Ph.D. from Cambridge University. He then joined the Commonwealth Secretariat for about a decade before returning to Sierra Leone and entering politics. He was returned to Parliament unopposed in 1982 and was appointed minister of agriculture in the **Siaka Stevens** government. After he was dropped from the cabinet Siaka Stevens supported Bundu's nomination and appointment as secretary of the **Economic Community of West African States (ECOWAS)**. When the **NPRC** removed the government of President **Joseph Saidu Momoh**, Bundu returned home to become minister of foreign affairs in the military government of **Valentine Strasser**. When the NPRC organized elections for a new government, Bundu formed his own political party, the **People's Progressive Party (PPP)**, and contested the 1996 elections for the position of president.

Bundu lost the election and his party failed to win the required 5 percent of the total votes cast to qualify its leader for a place in Parliament. Bundu remained active in politics, becoming a major force in an Alliance for Peace and Democracy in Sierra Leone, an organization operating from London. He became active in supporting the military government of **Johnny Paul Koroma** and this set him on a collision course with President Tejan Kabbah after the **Sierra Leone People's Party (SLPP)** government was reinstated. Bundu has continued to live outside Sierra Leone since then.

BUNGIE, ALIMAMY (1870–1935). Alimamy Bungie was a flamboyant, generous, and successful carpenter who left an indelible mark on the upper echelons of **Freetown** society in the early 20th century. His family name was Lumpkin, and he was christened William Rainy, names given to him by his grandfather, Henry Lumpkin, the first nominated African member of the Sierra Leone **Legislative Council**. He never attended secondary school, and his father apprenticed him to a master carpenter, where he learned the trade. Lumpkin, who later changed his name to Alimamy Bungie, ranged around a great deal in his youth. He spent some time in Sherbro country, joining a brass band and doing some journalism there, and later went to the Congo where Krio entrepreneurs were wont to go and seek their fortunes in those days.

When he returned to Freetown, Alimamy Bungie set up a carpenter's shop in Kissy Street which soon became a thriving business. He was especially known for making coffins for the rich and poor alike, and if his customer was short of funds, he would advance credit. During the influenza epidemic of 1918, he supplied some coffins free to needy bereaved families. His funeral administration, supplying hearse and coffin and even providing wake keepers for the bereaved, became well known in Freetown, so well known, in fact, that a **Krio** proverb developed around it: "*luk we yu de shek lek da feda na Bungi as*" (you quiver such as the feather on Bungie's hearse). This was in reference to Bungie's hearse, rumbling along the rocky streets of Freetown with a loosely positioned bunch of feathers at the top.

Bungie's flamboyance was also well known. He was liberal with the invitations to his annual *awujoh* or feast at the recreation grounds in Freetown. When the Prince of Wales visited Freetown in 1925, Bungie made sure that he would be recognized. He painted his popular store, which had moved to the center of Freetown, completely black. He hired a brass band on the ready, and as the royal procession passed in front of his shop, the band struck up "God Save the King," forcing the procession to come to a halt. Bungie was mentioned in the well-known book, *Journey without Maps*, written in 1935 by the eccentric British journalist, Graham Greene.

After his death in 1935, a life-sized painting of him was placed in the Freetown city hall, named Wilberforce Memorial Hall, a fitting tribute to the popular Alimamy Bungie.

BUNUMBU UNION COLLEGE. This was the first institution of higher education in the Provinces of Sierra Leone and was originally intended to train teachers. It was started by the Methodist Mission in Sierra Leone in 1924 at the town of Bunumbu in the Peje West chiefdom. Starting with six students, enrollment increased to twelve by 1925. It was renamed Union College in 1933 when it was transferred to a new site in Bununbu, and the other missions in Sierra Leone (the **CMS** and the United Brethren Church) united to maintain the institution.

Union College Bunumbu trained a strong group of protectorate teachers, many of whom went on to further education, some becoming prominent political leaders in Sierra Leone. Bunumbu College became a polytechnic at the beginning of the 21st century, providing higher education up to degree level.

BUREH, BAI (c. 1840–1908). Bai Bureh was more commonly known as Kebalai in the region where he lived and worked. When he became ruler of Kasseh, a small territory on the left bank of the Scarcies River, he took the **Temne** rulership title of "bai" and the name of Bureh. He is nationally recognized as the leader of the 1898 rebellion in northern Sierra Leone against the imposition of colonial rule by the British.

Bai Bureh was born in the village of Rothenki, near the town of Makeni in the Northern Province. His father was a **Loko** ruler and sent him to the Loko training school for warriors at Gbendembu-Gowahun. It was there that the name "Kebalai," meaning "basket never full," referring to a warrior who could incessantly massacre the enemy, came to be applied to this masterly fighter.

Before becoming ruler of Kasseh, Kebalai had been embroiled in a long drawn out struggle between Soso rulers on the border of the present Sierra Leone and Guinea, a conflict the British continuously tried to end to facilitate trade to their colony in Sierra Leone. After he became Bai Bureh in the 1880s, his position was recognized by the British in Sierra Leone, who sometimes called on him for assistance; for example, in 1892, he helped quell a Soso resistance at a center called Tambi. However, Bai Bureh also occasionally fell afoul of the British while pursuing his own political designs so that the British governor in the 1890s labeled him as a "recalcitrant" who failed to acknowledge British authority.

After the British protectorate was declared over the Sierra Leone interior in 1896, a house tax was imposed, which many of the rulers and their people opposed, in addition to imposing the new laws the British were trying to implement. The British reaction was a forceful show of authority, including arresting, deposing, and brutalizing some of the local rulers. Bai Bureh was believed to be one of the rulers staunchly opposed to the tax and thus faced inevitable confrontation with the British who determined to make an example of him. This led to a major war of resistance in 1898 between the British and a Bai Bureh–led coalition that lasted for 10 months. Bai Bureh was defeated by the British-led forces, which had superior resources and armaments and had also destroyed the food supplies and large sections of territory. Bai Bureh surrendered, was arrested, and was exiled to the Gold Coast. He was brought back in 1905 and reinstated as ruler of Kasseh where he died in 1908.

– C –

CALENDER, EBENEZER (1912–1985). Ebenezer Calender was one of the best-known musicians in Sierra Leone's history. His career lasted for almost half a century. He had his own special brand of music, the "maringa," and he wrote and composed his own songs and played a number of musical instruments, chief of which was the guitar.

Calender, as he was popularly known, was born in **Freetown** on November 12, 1912. After dropping out of school, he joined the Public Works Department in 1927 and trained as a carpenter. He used this job training to work at the United Africa Company as a cabinetmaker and as a coffin maker with the popular **Alimamy Bungie's** undertaker establishment. While he was at the latter, his interest in music emerged and he learned to play the guitar on his own homemade instrument. Pa Bungie would organize wake-keeping for some of his clients and would send his workers to sing at such events. Calender's singing began to become a regular routine on such occasions, and he also sang in the company of a popular flutist, called 'Never Tire'. They would perform after work on open fields and crowds would gather and give them money. Gradually, they began to get invitations to sing at parties, particularly at wedding feasts and other events.

Calender quickly made a name for himself and soon developed his own band. He learned to play other instruments—such as the mandolin, cornet, and trumpet, all of which became part of his band. By the 1940s, Calender had become established as a prominent musical figure in Freetown, and his band included local instruments, such as the "*bata*," a hand drum and the triangle, a metal frame played with a metal bar. He developed his own distinctive rhythm, the "maringa" music, a kind of calypso, for which he was popularly known. By the end of the 1940s, he had become known for popular songs such as "Fire, Fire," which was popularized internationally by the Ghanian musician, E. T. Mensah. Other songs such as "Double Decker Buses," (to commemorate the coming of that bus to Freetown), "Baby Lay You Powder Now," and "Who Stole the Chicken in the Pen" became household tunes. He composed and played more than 200 pieces, and a number of them were recorded by record labels, such as Decca.

Ebenezer Calender also helped popularize the radio when he joined the Sierra Leone Broadcasting Service in 1952 as a program officer. He had regular musical programs on the radio for many years, and near the latter part of his career he began to sing more of the Negro spirituals and the wake songs he had originally started with. He performed with the Sierra Leone National Dance Troupe at the Commonwealth Arts Festival in 1965 and 1966. In 1983, he was awarded the Certificate of Honor, a national award by the president of the republic, for his contribution to the development of indigenous music. When he died in 1985, musical groups from all over Freetown converged at his home at the foothills of Mount Aureol and sang many of his popular songs for more than 24 hours. Thousands watched his funeral procession as a final fitting tribute to Ebenezer Calender.

CARDEW, SIR FREDERIC (1839–1921). Sir Frederic Cardew was the British governor of Sierra Leone during whose tenure a protectorate was declared over a vast area that, added to the colony, became the area of present-day Sierra Leone. A former military officer, he became governor in 1894 and quickly toured most of the protectorate and protectorate negotiated the boundaries with the French and Liberian authorities. A British protectorate was declared over the interior of the colony in August 31, 1896.

It was also during Cardew's tenure that the **Sierra Leone railway** was planned; construction started in 1895, reaching its farthest limit in Pendembu in 1903. Cardew instituted a house tax to finance administration in the Sierra Leone colony. This led to major rebellions in 1898 that were quelled by the colonial administration. Cardew initially had good relations with the **Krio** leadership in Freetown, but when Samuel Lewis, the most prominent Krio lawyer, opposed his policies, Cardew turned against Krios and implemented policies to keep them from senior government positions, declaring that they were unfit for such positions.

Cardew made some effort to promote agriculture in Sierra Leone by establishing a botanical station and introducing small agricultural subsidies to farmers. He left Sierra Leone at the end of his tour of duty in 1900 and retired; he remained in private life until his death.

CASELY-HAYFORD, ADELAIDE (1868–1960). Adelaide Casely-Hayford is remembered as a cultural nationalist who labored tirelessly to emphasize African values in a colonial urban African setting that was stoutly opposed to such an emphasis. Born Adelaide Smith in **Freetown** on June 27, 1868, she spent much of her childhood and teenage years in England where her father had retired in 1872. Adelaide studied music at the Stuttgart Conservatory in Germany and returned to her homeland in Freetown when she was in her late twenties. After a few years in Freetown, Adelaide returned to England where, working with one of her sisters, she opened a boarding home for African bachelors. It was during this period that she met and married J. E. Casely-Hayford, a Gold Coast lawyer and a prominent Pan-Africanist who had jointly founded the National Congress of British West Africa (NCBWA).

Apparently influenced by her husband, Adelaide began familiarizing herself with the ideas of movements such as Marcus Garvey's Universal Negro Improvement Association (UNIA) that had developed in the United States. A Freetown branch of the UNIA had been organized and Adelaide joined its Ladies division, becoming its president. Her membership in this organization was short-lived, since her ideas about opening a girl's vocational institution were not well received within the organization. In 1920, the same year that she relinquished her membership of the Ladies Division, she visited the United States to familiarize herself with African American programs for industrial education and also to raise funds for her proposed vocational institution. Attired in her traditional African dress, she gave public lectures aimed at properly educating American audiences about Africa.

After her return to Freetown, she opened the Girl's Vocational School in October 1923, advocating the same ideas of cultural nationalism and Africanity that she had been developing. There were limitations on how far she could follow these principles. Because of hostility from the community, for instance, she had to back away from her desire that the 14 students who initially entered the school wear African attire. She did, however, develop a curriculum involving African history, folklore, songs, and artwork. Traditional dances and African games were prominent features on Africa Day, celebrated once a year when the students wore African dress.

Adelaide headed the school until her retirement in 1940 when the school was forced to close down. She was a gifted public speaker who advocated the need for a Congress Day to mark the founding of the National Congress of British West Africa (NCBWA), the most prominent nationalist movement in Africa at the time. She also called for the setting up of a national university with a professorship in the major African languages. She laid great emphasis on African art as Africa's contribution to global culture. These views were considerably ahead of her time and scant attention was paid to her advocacy. In spite of her overtly anticolonial posture, the British government decorated her with the Member of the British Empire (MBE) in 1950. In her later years, Adelaide wrote poetry and her memoirs, giving a lasting testimony to her contribution to society and the influences on her life.

CAULKER, RICHARD CANRAY BA (18?–1901). Canray Ba is the same as Richard, the latter name given to him when he attended a Western school. Different segments of the extended family of the Caulkers ruled parts of Sherbro Island and other smaller islands near the southern coast. Sometimes these segments had conflicts, being referred to here as factions.

Ruler of Bumpe territory (1864–1888) among the **Sherbro** people and later confirmed as paramount chief of the Bumpe chiefdom (1895–1898), Canray Ba was educated at the **CMS** Grammar School in **Freetown**, then the most prestigious secondary school. He became friendly with Gbenjei, ruler of the Kpaa **Mende** territory and married one of Gbenjei's daughters named Yogbo. Canray Ba took his new wife when she was still a minor, together with her brother, also a minor, named Bagi. When Yogbo reached adulthood, after going through the Bondo rites she assumed the name of Bora; her brother assumed the adult name of Kong after going through the necessary **Poro** ceremonies. Named after Kong and Bora, the territory around Senehun came to be called Kongbora, the name of a current chiefdom.

Canray Ba founded the settlement of Mobagi, named after Bagi, which was later called Senehun. This and other settlements increased the size of the neighboring Kpaa Mende state. After a major war between Caulker factions in Sherbro country, the governor of the Sierra Leone colony expended his peace efforts toward a treaty binding Canray Ba and other Caulker rulers to extend specific courtesies to the British. An earlier colonial treaty of 1825 extending British suzerainty over Caulker territory, had lain dormant but was revived in 1881, placing Canray Ba's territory under British control. Another major Caulker family dispute leading to warfare in 1888 spelled execution for some Caulker rulers, but Canray Ba was only sent into exile in the Gambia. On his return in 1895, he was reinstated as chief of Bumpe. After the 1898 uprising, the governor of Sierra Leone, Samuel Rowe, suspected that Canray Ba had been involved in the uprising and had him deposed. He was imprisoned in a town named Kwelu.

CAULKER, SOLOMON BROOKS (1911–1960). A well-known broadcaster who became vice principal of **Fourah Bay College**. Solomon Caulker was born in Mambo village in the Kagboro chiefdom on February 12, 1911. He went to school in Shenge primary school and the **Albert Academy** in **Freetown**, obtained a B.A. from Lebanon Valley College, Annville, Pennsylvania, in 1941, and a bachelor of divinity from Bonebrake Theological Seminary in Dayton, Ohio, in 1944. He became an ordained minister in the Evangelical United Brethren Church (EUB) in Sierra Leone and a lecturer at Fourah Bay College, where be became vice principal in 1958. He conducted a popular radio show in Sierra Leone named "Radio Forum." He died in a plane crash in Dakar, Senegal, on August 29, 1960.

CHALMERS REPORT. Following the 1898 rebellion in Sierra Leone, the colonial government appointed a commission of inquiry into the causes of the rebellion. David Chalmers, a retired judge in the colonial service, was sent to Freetown in 1898 to head the commission. Over a period of four months, Chalmers interviewed about 300 witnesses and wrote a lengthy report with a huge appendix of some 680 pages containing the evidence that the commission had collected. This has remained a main source of information about the 1898 rebellion.

The substance of the report was that the colonial authorities had overreached themselves by imposing an onerous tax on the people and had used brutal methods to collect the tax. Decisions surrounding the declaration of the protectorate in 1896 lessening the powers of the traditional rulers in the eyes of the people were cited as additional grievances. Chalmers recommended doing away with many of the methods that had been used to govern the protectorate. The colonial government, however, supported the actions that were condemned in the Chalmers report and rejected Chalmers' criticisms.

CHAYTOR, DANIEL E. H. (1931–). Daniel Chaytor was among the founding faculty of Njala University College and its first Sierra Leonean Dean of Basic Sciences. He rose to become vice chancellor of the University of Sierra Leone.

Born in **Freetown** on April 13, 1931, Daniel attended the **Prince of Wales School** and studied the sciences at universities in England where he earned the Ph.D. in zoology. He returned to Sierra Leone to teach at **Fourah Bay College** and responded to the call to start the Njala University College (NUC) as a new arm of the University of Sierra Leone in 1964. He was vice principal of NUC in 1968 before returning to Fourah Bay College in the following year. There he became professor of zoology and director of the newly founded Institute of Marine Biology and Oceanography of the **University of Sierra Leone**. Dan Chaytor is highly respected in his field and took a visiting position at Massachusetts Institute of Technology in the United States in 1969. He held a number of consultancies for United Nations Institutions in Liberia and other African countries. In 1993, he was appointed vice chancellor of the University of Sierra Leone.

CHENEY-COKER, SYL (1945–). Syl Cheney-Coker is an internationally known poet and novelist from Sierra Leone. He was born in **Freetown** and had his early schooling there before going to the United

States where he studied at the universities of Oregon and Wisconsin. In 1988, he was a visiting writer in the International Writing Program at the University of Iowa in the United States and has held several visiting appointments and fellowships in different countries. His poetry collections and novels reflect his cultural background in Sierra Leone. He has four collections of poetry, three of which—*Concerto for an Exile*; *The Graveyard Also Has Teeth*; and *The Blood in the Desert's Eyes*—were all published by Heinemann. His most recent novel, also published by Heinemann, *The Last Harmattan of Alusine Dunbar*, was based on a history of Sierra Leone and won him the prestigious Commonwealth Writers Prize for African Literature in 1996. He currently lives in Sierra Leone where he continues to write.

CINQUE, JOSEPH. *See* PIEH SENGBE.

CIVIL DEFENSE FORCES (CDF). *See* KAMAJOR.

COLERIDGE-TAYLOR, GEORGE (1932–). Diplomat, civil servant, and educator, George Coleridge-Taylor was born in Freetown July 4, 1932. He attended the **Prince of Wales secondary school**, **Fourah Bay College**, and the University of Durham where he studied philosophy; he later studied diplomacy at the Australian National University. He joined the Sierra Leone civil service as diplomatic officer in the Ministry of Foreign Affairs in 1962. He stayed on at that ministry, serving at Sierra Leone Missions in the United States and Nigeria and rising to the position of permanent secretary of the foreign ministry in December 1970. In 1975, he was assigned to the **Mano River Union** secretariat, where he became director of finance and administration. After a year, he took up a position as director of finance and administration of the West African Rice Development Association in Monrovia, Liberia, where he served until 1984. Upon returning to Sierra Leone he became permanent secretary of the Ministry of Mines for two years before embarking on a career teaching philosophy at Fourah Bay College.

Coleridge-Taylor has served on many boards and has designed training programs for diplomats in Sierra Leone. In 1998, he was appointed commissioner and acting chairman of the National Commission for Democracy and Human Rights.

COLLIER, GERSHON (1927–1994). Diplomat, chief justice of Sierra Leone, and educator, Gershon Collier was born in Freetown and educated at the **CMS Grammar School** and **Fourah Bay College** and studied law at the Middle Temple Inns of Court in London and at New York University. Gershon Collier was one of the supporters of **Albert Margai** when the latter left the **Sierra Leone People's Party** and formed the **People's National Party** in 1958. In fact, Collier was a member of that party's first executive committee. He became Sierra Leone's first ambassador and permanent representative to the United Nations in 1961, gaining valuable experience and contact with Third World leaders, such as Gamal Abdel Nasser of Egypt, who became godfather to one of Gershon's sons whom he named Gamal. He also served simultaneously as ambassador to the United States. In 1967, he became chief justice of Sierra Leone, handpicked by the prime minister, Sir Albert Margai. He left this position when Albert Margai lost the election in 1967 and a military government followed. Gershon Collier then moved to the United States in 1967 and took a teaching appointment at New York University. He remained in the United States and continued writing and teaching until his death on May 25, 1994.

CONTEH, ABDULAI. Lawyer and politician Abdulai Conteh was vice president of Sierra Leone in the 1880s. He was educated at London University, where he took the Ph.D. in law and returned to start private practice in Sierra Leone in 1975 and to teach law at **Fourah Bay College**. In 1977, he was elected to Parliament as an unopposed member for Kambia. He became a cabinet minister, holding various portfolios including foreign affairs and finance before he was removed by **Siaka Stevens** because of his opposition to naming **Joseph Saidu Momoh** as Stevens' successor. Conteh was again appointed minister by Momoh and became vice president. He fled the country in 1992 as a result of the military coup and new military junta led by **Valentine Strasser**. He has been in exile since then, and became chief justice of the Central American state of Belize.

CONTON, WILLIAM F. (1925–2003). William Farquah Conton was a public servant, educator, and writer, who also served as an international administrator and later as minister of education in the government of President **Joseph Saidu Momoh**.

He was born in Bathurst (now Banjul) the Gambia on September 5, 1925. After primary schooling in the Gambia and in French Guinea, (now the Republic of Guinea) Conton attended the **CMS Grammar School** in **Freetown**. He received his higher education in England where he read history at the University of Durham. On his return to Sierra Leone in 1947 he taught history at Fourah Bay College for six years before assuming the position of headmaster of Accra High School in the Gold Coast in 1953. He returned to Freetown in 1960 and became, successively, principal of **Bo Government School** and of the **Prince of Wales School** before being appointed chief education officer in 1963. He took early retirement from public service in Sierra Leone to assume a position with the United Nations in the Equal Opportunity Office in Paris in 1969. When Conton later returned to Sierra Leone, he served in various public bodies including the University Court and was later appointed minister of education in the government of President **Momoh**.

Conton was also a writer. One of the first group of modern African writers, his first novel, published in 1960, was entitled, *The African*. He also wrote a history text for schools in Africa and other short stories. He died in 2003.

CUMMINGS-JOHN, CONSTANCE (1918–). In an age when women were not considered candidates for political activity, Constance Cummings-John blazed the trail in establishing effective women's participation in the politics of independence in Sierra Leone.

She was born in and received her high school education in **Freetown** before going to England where she trained as a teacher at Whitelands College in Putney. While in London, she participated in the activities of the West African Students Union (WASU) and the League of Colored People, both centers of black political activism at the time. In 1936, she went to the United States to do a six-month course at Cornell University and experienced racism and sexism firsthand. In 1937, she married the lawyer Ethan Cummings-John and returned to Freetown. She was principal of the African Methodist Episcopal (AME) Girls Vocational School, which she helped transform, and she later founded the Roosevelt Secondary School for Girls in Freetown.

Her political career advanced when she joined forces with Wallace-Johnson to found the Sierra Leone chapter of the West African Youth

League. In the municipal elections in Freetown in November 1938, the League candidates swept the polls. Mrs. Cummings-John thus became a councilor, after receiving the highest number of votes cast for any constituency. Mrs. Cummings-John was very active in Sierra Leone politics in the 1950s as a member of the **Sierra Leone People's Party**. She also joined forces with such women stalwarts as **Ella Koblo Gulama** and Patience Richards to form a women's movement, which became a powerful voice for women's interests in Sierra Leone. She was nicknamed "Fatu" in **Freetown** for her drive to team up with women from the provinces in her political activity. In 1966, she became the first woman mayor of Freetown.

– D –

DALA MODU (c. 1770–1841). An important diplomat and trader in the Rokel River (Sierra Leone River) region for decades, Modu was influential in liaising and settling disputes between the British in Sierra Leone and ascended to the position of ruler of a section of Temne-Loko territory in the interior of Sierra Leone with ultimate British recognition. Modu was an ethnic Soso from Wonkafong, currently in Guinea, from where he moved, with the support of his father, to settle in **Freetown** in 1795. He learned English and the colony's currency, including weights and measures. This put him in a unique position to become an economic and political intermediary between local people from the interior and the British authorities in the colony.

When Nova Scotians rebelled against the colony rulers in 1800, Modu was instrumental in quelling the disturbance to the satisfaction of the British. In 1806, he was charged with slave trading. When called to a hearing, he appeared in a **Muslim** robe rather than Western dress. The British authorities saw this as defiance and expelled Modu from the colony. He moved a short distance away and settled at Bullom shore, continuing his services as broker between colony authorities and interior rulers and traders. Through these activities, he acquired wealth and prominence and also led to an expansion of the Soso presence in the **Bullom** Shore area. The British, too, sought to use Modu's influence, and on two occasions he was instrumental in British control over the Isles de Los and Matacong, two islands where the French had interests. He had strong trading links with prominent businessmen in the colony and became the principal broker for traders from the interior coming to trade in Freetown. In 1836, in return for successfully mediating in a war between the **Loko** and **Temne**, the British recognized his help by approving of his regency of Loko Masama, a territory he had literally ruled since 1829. In 1837, he also became ruler of the important trading town of Rokon, with British approval. Although some of the colony rulers were uncomfortable with him, they generally maintained good relations with Modu, giving him annual payments for his services. His funeral was attended by many local rulers, as well as by Europeans from the colony.

DEMBA, PA. Pa Demba was a head of a village close to the new colony of Sierra Leone, and his willingness to help the distressed settlers when the colony was attacked by the French is a good example of disinterested cooperation.

Little else is known of Pa Demba who ruled this village, which was located around the junction of modern Campbell Street and Pademba Road in **Freetown**. When the fledgling colony was attacked and destroyed by French warships in 1794, Pa Demba offered his village as refuge for a Nova Scotian schoolmistress from the colony as well as several of the distressed settlers. This gesture was all the more significant as the Koya Temne, who owned the land on which the colony was founded, had a long-standing threat against what they considered an upstart colony. This could have put Pa Demba in serious danger. In spite of these odds, Pa Demba provided succor for the distressed colonists. Pademba Road, passing through the former village of this generous ruler, is now a main artery in Freetown.

DEMOCRATIC CENTER PARTY (DCP). This party was formed by a veteran politician, **Abu A. Koroma**, to contest the 1996 general elections. The DCP leader polled 5 percent of the popular vote cast for the president and this entitled his party to three seats in Parliament.

DISTRICT COUNCILS. District Councils were formed in 1946 in each district to advise the government on matters in their districts and to act as an investigative arm for complaints against chiefs. The chairman of the District Council was the British district commissioner. Paramount chiefs sat as ex-officio members, and the "tribal authorities" chose one member from each chiefdom to represent nonchiefly interests. The paramount chief usually had a strong influence in the selection of this member. Since most of the paramount chiefs and their nominees were not literate, an ordinance of 1950 amended the membership to include three more literate members to be appointed by the district commissioner. In 1954, the chiefs were allowed to elect one of their members to become president of the council, and a few years later popular elections for members of the **District Councils** began.

District Councils provided social services such as road building and agricultural improvement, funded mostly from local resources. The councils were suspended in 1962 following the newly independent government's investigations into allegations of mismanagement and corruption. They were reinstated in 1965, but the military government of the **National Reformation Council** dissolved them in 1967. District Councils remained in limbo for the next 37 years until they were revived with popular elections in 2004.

DOVE-EDWIN COMMISSION OF INQUIRY (1967). Soon after seizing power in the coup d'état of 1967 and setting up a military junta, this **National Reformation Council** (**NRC**) government established a commission of inquiry to investigate the conduct of the recent elections, which were widely believed to have been rigged. The commissioner appointed was G. Dove-Edwin, an appeals court judge. The commission started sittings in June 1967 and submitted its four-volume report in September of the same year. After studying the report, the NRC issued a statement that concluded the elections "were rigged and corrupt."

DRESS REFORM SOCIETY. This was the brainchild of **Edward Wilmot Blyden**, who was active in Sierra Leone in the late 19th century in emphasizing African values as a means of salvation of the African. Blyden was joined by people such as **Joseph Claudius May**

and **A. E. Tuboku-Metzger**. Formed in the 1880s, the society sought to emphasize respect for African culture, manifested most significantly by adoption of African forms of dress in place of the European dress that had become so dominant in Freetown. Not only did the Dress Reform Society influence dress patterns, it also encouraged respect for African names, so that some leading figures in Freetown sought to change their names altogether to African names or to modify their Western names by compounding them with African ones. Thus resulted the Tuboku-Metzger, Aboko-Cole, **Beoku-Betts**, Awunor-**Renner**, **Bankole-Bright** names and others. While the movement was not all pervasive, it made a significant mark on a colony where the colonial authorities had succeeded in emphasizing western culture and condemning African values to the point where the majority of emergent educated **Freetown** inhabitants had come to believe that African values were inferior.

DUMBUYA, AHMED RAMADAN (1942–). Ahmed Dumbuya was interim leader of the **National Unity Party (NUP)** before he became minister of foreign affairs a second time. He attended the **Bo Government Secondary School** and **Fourah Bay College** and later to the United States for his higher studies, which culminated with a Ph.D. in political science from Washington State University. He returned to teach at his alma mater, Fourah Bay College, where he became head of the Political Science Department and dean of the Faculty of Economics and Social Studies. After one failed attempt to secure a seat in Parliament, Ahmed Dumbuya was appointed foreign minister in the government of President **Joseph Saidu Momoh** in 1990. He was part of the National Unity Party of John Karimu in the 1996 elections, and became a member of Parliament representing that party under the proportional representation system. When Karimu was appointed a cabinet minister in President **Kabbah's** government, Ahmed Dumbuya became interim leader of the NUP. He, too, was later appointed minister of foreign affairs by President Kabbah, and when he lost that position, he remained a member of Parliament representing the NUP.

DURA I, ALIMAMY (c. 1886–1946). In the troubled period accompanying the declaration of the protectorate in 1896, the paramount chieftaincy of Alimamy Dura I represents a successful attempt by one ruler to survive contentious claims to his position with the support of the colonial government.

Alimamy Dura was appointed in 1916 to fill the position of paramount chief of Saffroko Limba chiefdom in place of his father, Alimamy Omaru, the former ruler. Because of powerful rival claimants, Dura was put on a year's probation as paramount chief. Saffroko had been a province of the Biriwa **Limba** kingdom under **Alimamy Suluku** before the colonial period, and as long as Suluku lived, the Saffroko would not choose a new paramount chief on the urgings of the colonial government. Suluku lived until 1906, and this long period meant that there were several ambitious claimants to the new throne waiting in the wings. Alimamy Omaru was made the first paramount chief of Saffroko Limba in 1907, and the rumblings about contested authority, which had been muffled for the nine years of his rule, erupted during the rule of his son **Alimamy Dura**. Three major aspirants to the position began to make trouble for Alimamy Dura. One of them, Sorie Limba, had formerly held the powerful position of court messenger and claimed the chiefship on the grounds that he had played a significant role in securing autonomy for the chiefdom. The second, Lamina Suntu, said that Omaru had promised him the chiefship on his deathbed and threatened to put the chiefdom under a powerful curse if he did not receive it. The third man, Diko, was the chief of a section of the chiefdom called Kamasele.

The rival claimants would not give in even after the colonial government confirmed Dura's position. Section chief Diko refused to pay his tax and had to be arrested before he gave up the resistance. Sorie Limba put the chiefdom under a heavy curse that was dreaded by the local people and only refrained from further hostile acts when he was sentenced to six months' imprisonment. Lamina Suntu's was the most elaborate opposition. In December 1917, Suntu marched on Kabinkolo, the chiefdom headquarters town, with about 100 followers armed with sticks. The colonial government responded by banishing Suntu to Makeni a few miles from Kabinkolo.

During all this, Dura showed remarkable fortitude, reporting every incident of insubordination in scrupulous detail to the colonial authorities. He received moral support from the authorities and from neighboring paramount chiefs such as Pompoli of Biriwa Limba.

Some of his opponents even spurred other neighboring paramount chiefs to make trouble for Dura. For example, in January 1918, Bayo Yembe, paramount chief of Kalantuba chiefdom to the north of Safroko Limba, invaded Dura's chiefdom in an attempt to secure control of two sections. Dura remained calm in this extreme provocation, and the colonial government ordered Bayo Yembe to pay damages to Dura.

Dura remained a force for peace and progress in his chiefdom, urging his people to rebuild roads and cultivate rice. He also encouraged them to seek Western education in the local schools established by the American Wesleyan Mission. He died in 1946 and was succeeded by his son, Alimamy Dura II.

DURING, CHRIS (c. 1927–). Chris During was a popular comedian and singer whose name became a household word, especially in connection with the Sierra Leone Broadcasting Service (SLBS), where he worked throughout the 1960s through the 1980s.

During was born in the Gold Coast (now Ghana) in the late 1920s. His father, like many educated Sierra Leoneans of that period, had taken up colonial government service in the Gold Coast railway and During was raised in Sekondi and Takoradi in the Gold Coast. He came to Freetown with his parents and attended the **CMS Grammar School** in the 1940s. According to his own recollection, he was the first person to speak the Krio language on the Sierra Leone radio, in 1957, against the objections of the director of broadcasting, an Englishman named Leslie Perowne. This was at a time when the use of the Krio language in official matters was unacceptable to the Freetown middle class.

Chris During did special comedy shows at the SLBS and led a radio band called *Gee Bodi Wata*, with a popular song called "Ghost de Whistle." He and Salako-Maxwell became, by the 1970s, the major broadcasters in **Krio** in the SLBS. Now in retirement, he is still remembered for his shows.

DUSU SORI (c. 1840–1940). Dusu Sori ruled the Dembelia Musaia chiefdom in northeastern Sierra Leone from about 1881 to 1940, except for a short interval in the mid-1880s. He belonged to the Jawara clan, the predominant Yalunka clan in what is now the Dembelia

Musaia chiefdom in the Koinadugu district. He was born in Musaia, the chief town of Dembelia country. His mother, Dusu, was a Koranko, for Musaia was originally Koranko country before the Jawara Yalunka came there to settle in the late 17th century. Dusu Sori became ruler of Musaia territory in about 1881. When the *sofa* warriors of **Samori Toure**, the great Mandinka ruler and leader, took control of the Solima state in 1884, Dusu Sori was deposed. Another ruler, Hamadu, was installed in his place. But Hamadu disappeared in 1888; whether he was executed or fled is uncertain, and Dusu Sori was reinstated. Under Dusu Sori, Musaia became a rallying point for all Yalunka who had formerly belonged to the Solima state, as Falaba, their former capital, had been destroyed by the **sofa**.

As the British moved to establish a protectorate over the Sierra Leone hinterland in the 1890s, Dusu Sori became a spokesman for other Yalunka rulers in the area in dealings with the British about their appointments of paramount chiefs. From this advantageous standpoint, he was able to expand his own power. He included the Limba town of Largo and parts of the neighboring Folosaba **Yalunka** country within the area he claimed as being under his jurisdiction. The British confirmed his claims and made him paramount of the enlarged Dembelia Musaia chiefdom. This caused much dissatisfaction among the Folosaba and Wara Wara Limba people to whom Largo had belonged. However, with the backing of the colonial rulers, Dusu Sori continued to rule this large chiefdom for a very long time. Upon his death, the British district commissioner of Koinadugu described him as "the doyen of protectorate chiefs."

– E –

EASMON, M. C. F. (1890–1972). A distinguished doctor in the colonial medical service, McCormack Charles Farrell Easmon became a cultural nationalist and founded of the Sierra Leone National Museum.

M. C. F. Easmon was born in Accra in the Gold Coast where his father, a prominent Krio doctor, was working at the time. He was educated at the **CMS Grammar School** in Freetown and attended school in England where he did university work at Epsom College in

Surrey and qualified in Medicine at the medical school of St. Mary's Hospital in London. When Dr. Easmon returned to Sierra Leone in 1913, he was refused a post in the West African Medical Service because he was African. There were then two categories in the service: Europeans in the "colonial service" and Africans in the inferior "local service." Easmon was forced into the local service despite his excellent qualifications. He campaigned for years against this racism in the medical service, earning the antipathy of the British authorities, who called him the "Yellow Peril." He served as a medical officer in Cameroon during World War I. After the war, he returned to England and qualified in obstetrics and gynecology in 1925.

M. C. F. Easmon's career in the medical establishment took him to the protectorate for the next 20 years. While there, he became deeply interested in the culture and traditions of protectorate peoples. He published a series of pieces on **Madam Yoko**, on paramount chiefs, the famous Massaquoi Crown, and Sierra Leone's distinctive country cloth. He also wrote and published pieces on the early history of the **Freetown** colony.

The two segments of the colonial medical service were unified a year after Dr. Easmon retired from the medical service in 1945. He was later appointed temporary medical officer in 1949 and held that post for a few years. He served on several government boards and was also a director of the Central Bank of Sierra Leone. His chief interest by this time was in Sierra Leone's cultural heritage. In 1947, he became the first chairman of the Monuments and Relics Commission and presided over the official declaration of 20 national historic sites. As a member of an elitist organization called the Sierra Leone Society, he was instrumental in founding the Sierra Leone Museum in 1958 and became its first curator. While working hard to acquire and display artifacts of Sierra Leone's cultural heritage, he also labored to educate the general public on its value. He hosted a popular radio program called "Sierra Leone in Retrospect." He died in England in 1972.

EASMON, RAYMOND SARIF (1913–). A medical practitioner by profession, Raymond Sarif Easmon was best known in Sierra Leone as a playwright and political activist who was detained for his public expression of opposition to the Siaka Stevens government.

Easmon was educated at the **Prince of Wales School** in **Freetown** and studied medicine at Newcastle University in England. He worked briefly in the government service in Sierra Leone before setting up private practice. Throughout his practice, he wrote short stories and plays and a novel, *The Burnt-Out Marriage*, published in 1967. His published plays, *Dear Parent and Ogre* (1964) and *The New Patriots* (1965) were performed in Freetown and earned him the highest regard in elite Freetown society.

Raymond Sarif Easmon also took a keen interest in local politics. When the government of **Albert Margai** was overthrown, he served as chairman of the Civilian Rule Committee, under the one year military government of **Andrew Juxon-Smith**. While he welcomed the **Siaka Stevens** government, he became one of its most vocal critics when it became evident that the government was authoritarian and corrupt. He published scathing articles in public newspapers and for this opposition was arrested and detained under public emergency regulations in 1970. Released in 1971, he remained opposed to the government but was less vitriolic. He has kept a much lower profile in the ensuing years.

ECONOMIC COMMUNITY CEASE-FIRE MONITORING GROUP (ECOMOG). ECOMOG, as it is usually called, was formed in August 1990 by the regional economic union, the Economic Community of West African States (ECOWAS), in an attempt to mediate the bloody civil war in Liberia. On December 24, 1989, **Charles Taylor** and his National Patriotic Front of Liberia (NPFL) had invaded Liberia from the neighboring Ivory Coast. As the war became increasingly bloody and the UN personnel withdrew from Liberia, ECOMOG was set up, starting with 3,000 troops, mostly from Nigeria, but also from the Gambia, Ghana, Guinea, and Sierra Leone and later joined by Mali and Senegalese troops. The West African countries explained that their intervention was necessary in a conflict involving their own nationals in Liberia and the refugees fleeing Liberia into their countries. The ECOMOG mandate was to impose a cease-fire, help form an interim government, and hold elections. As NPFL attacks continued, ECOMOG was transformed from a peacekeeping to a peace-enforcing force, and by 1992 ECOMOG jets were flying over Liberia.

Charles Taylor's strong hostility toward ECOMOG was hardened further by the formation in 1991of the United Liberation Movement for Democracy in Liberia (ULIMO) by former soldiers of the Liberian army who had fled to Sierra Leone. Taylor began to turn his hostility on Sierra Leone with the emerging evidence of complicity between ECOMOG and the ULIMO especially since ULIMO attacks on NPFL positions increased. Some of ECOMOG activities against Taylor were beginning to involve Sierra Leone, and Taylor began to engineer a movement to invade Sierra Leone.

The civil war in Sierra Leone brought ECOMOG forces to Sierra Leone initially on a peace-keeping mission. The government of President Kabba, elected in 1994, made arrangements with Nigeria and Guinea that brought soldiers of those countries to Sierra Leone. Since Nigeria was the dominant force in ECOMOG, the two became almost indistinguishable. When the Kabba[h] government was ousted in a coup in 1997, ECOWAS received greater international support to use ECOMOG forces to remove the RUF military junta. ECOMOG successfully ousted the junta in February 1998 and virtually took control of military security in Sierra Leone until UN peacekeeping forces were deployed in the country.

EZZIDIO, JOHN (c. 1810–1872). A liberated African from Nupe in Nigeria, John Ezzidio became a wealthy merchant and saw public service in the colony of Sierra Leone, becoming mayor of Freetown and the only elected African member of Sierra Leone's Legislative Council in the 19th century.

Ezzidio was brought to Freetown after the British navy captured the slave ship on which he had been stowed to be taken to Brazil. Released in Freetown when he was in his teens, he began working for Billaud, a French merchant in the colony. It was Billaud who called him Isidore, which over the years came to be rendered as Ezzidio. He worked for other merchants and within 10 years of reaching Freetown, he had saved enough money to start his own business. By 1841, he had built his own house, a major achievement in the colony. Ezzidio soon entered into public life, first elected an alderman in the City Council and then, in 1845, as mayor of Freetown.

John Ezzidio was also active in church life in Freetown as a local preacher and class leader in the Wesleyan Methodist Mission in

Sierra Leone. He made such an impression on the British head of this mission, Rev. Thomas Dove, that Dove took Ezzidio to England on a visit. This made it possible for Ezzidio to expand his business by direct contact with British trading companies. By the 1850s, Ezzidio was regarded as the most successful merchant in the colony. In 1863, the British attempted the elective principle for Sierra Leone's **Legislative Council**. Ezzsidio beat the British candidate in elections for a coveted seat in the Legislative Council. Since the British Colonial rulers quickly abolished the elective principle, Ezzidio remained the only elected member to the Legislative Council until such elections were restored in 1924. Ezzidio was prominent in signing petitions to the British government; in 1947, for example, he was one of those who petitioned the Colonial Office for the removal of Governor Norman Macdonald from Sierra Leone.

Ezzidio's prominence in church life set him on a collision course with the British head of the Methodist Church, Rev. Benjamin Tregaskis, who appeared to have resented Ezzidio's influential role in the church. A bitter feud with Tregaskis took a toll on Ezzidio's health at a time when he also suffered significant losses in his business. He had labored to start the building of Wesley Church, but this feud left the venture unfinished and Ezzidio died in 1872.

– F –

FARMA TAMI (MID-16TH CENTURY). Farma Tami was the eponymous founder of the Temne regal title of Bai Farma. Historical sources indicate that Tami was one of the leaders among the Mani, a Mandinka group from the old Kingdom of Mali, who invaded the Sierra Leone interior in the mid-16th century. Tami is said to have led a group of his Mandinka warriors into Temne land, conquered the area, and became ruler among the Temne of the Port Loko area. Tami's successors were culturally absorbed and became Temne. The town of Robaga, which had been Tami's headquarters, became a holy place for the Temne. Successive Temne rulers in this area have retained the title of Farma, to which the Temne add their own title for a ruler, "obai."

FAWUNDU, FRANCIS (c. 1845–1920). Fawundu was ruler of Mano Gbonjeima, a polity that became the Mano Sakrim chiefdom under colonial rule. He was educated in mission schools and became a wealthy trader in the trading town of Mano. When his father, Sengbe Fawundu, ruler of Mano, died in 1892, the son was named his successor. When the British declared a protectorate in 1896 and instituted a house tax, Fawundu questioned the abrogation of their sovereign rights. In 1897, he was one of the leaders of a delegation to the colonial governor, opposing the house tax. His continued opposition to the house tax and his insistence on signing his correspondence as "king of Mano" drew the ire of the governor, who described him as "disrespectful and insubordinate." But Fawundu insisted on the title, claiming that the British had addressed him that way since before 1896. His determined refusal to accept colonial rule led to his deposition in January 1898. A few months later, the 1898 rebellion broke out and Fawundu, suspected of instigating the rebellion, was arrested and jailed. He was released in November 1898 and was reinstated a few months later, after "publicly submitting" to the governor's authority. Still regarded as a thorn on the government's side, Fawundu was again deposed in 1914 and died shortly thereafter.

FODAY TARAWALY (c. 1801–c. 1877). Foday Tarawaly was ruler of the town of Gbile (Billeh), a town on the Great Scarcies River close to Kambia. He was best known as an **Islamic** scholar who founded a center of Koranic learning that flourished from the mid-19th century until 1875. He was born in Morea Soso country in the Northern Rivers area of the present Republic of Guinea where he was also educated and earned a reputation as an erudite scholar. Some time in the 1820s, Foday left Morea with his older brother, Brima Kondito, and traveled to Dixing in the Kambia District of northwestern Sierra Leone. There they became the subjects of the Soso Sankoh family, which dominated the area. The Sankoh gave the village of Gbile to the brother, Brima Kondito but since Brima wished to travel farther south, he left Foday Tarawaly to rule Gbile.

Foday Tarawaly transformed Gbile into a thriving center for Islamic learning. His erudition and piety earned him the designation of "High Priest of the Morea." By the mid-19th century, Foday

Tarawaly's institution at Gbile had reached its apogee. Edward Wilmot Blyden visited Gbile in January of 1872 and recorded this description of the Islamic center:

> Opposite Kambia, on the northern bank of the Great Scarcies, is the Mohammedan town of Bileh, whose presiding genius, Fode [sic] Tarawally, enjoys great literary celebrity. Billeh is a sort of university town, devoted altogether to the cultivation of Mohammedan learning. On the 12th of January I visited it and made a small present to the literary chieftain. I found him . . . reading a manuscript . . . He received me with an easy grace and dignity and had all the gravity and reserve of a teacher. He addressed me occasionally in Arabic. . . . He not only seemed at home in the dogmas of his faith, but he discussed instructively some of the most important subjects of human inquiry, and quoted, in support of his views, the opinions of leading Arabic writers. He spoke in high terms of the Beidhwai and Jelaladdin as commentators of the Koran.

By that time, the center had "several hundred young men" as students, and also had classes for women. Three of Foday Tarawaly's sons had graduated from the instution he headed to become instructors in the university there.

Disaster struck the institution in 1875 when the Temne of the town of Dixing drove Foday Tarawaly from Gbile and dispersed his students. In 1876, even though he had no center of his own, Foday was important enough to be listed among the chieftains of northern Sierra Leone. He was reportedly a very old man by then, and his death probably came soon after.

FOMGBOE (c. 1830–1900). Fomgboe was an ethnic **Loko** ruler of the town of Tembu in the 1880s and 1890s. He built a reputation as a Loko warrior and gave importance to the town of Tembu, which he ruled in the 1980s. Lower Loko was nominally subject to Upper or Sanda Loko, ruled by Alimamy Samura in the 1880s. Fomgboe tried to build a coalition to rival his overlord, but the complex political situation did not allow this and by the early 1890s even the other rulers of Lower Loko were opposed to him. Because Fomgboe was waging incessant wars on his neighbors, the British, moving into the Sierra Leone interior to effect control, offered a 20 pound (sterling) reward for the capture of Fomgboe. He was finally captured in July 1894 and was deported to the Gambia.

FORAY, CYRIL PATRICK (1934–2003). C. P. Foray, as he was popularly known, was a politician and educator who became foreign minister in the Sierra Leone government and later principal of **Fourah Bay College**. He was born March 16, 1934, and attended the **St. Edwards Secondary School** in **Freetown**. He studied at Fourah Bay College and at Durham University in England where he read history. He returned to Freetown to teach at St. Edwards Secondary School and later worked for British Petroleum (West Africa) Ltd. When **Njala University College** was started in 1964, C. P. Foray was one of the first lecturers at Njala. He then went to the United States for postgraduate studies at UCLA in the United States. Upon his return, Foray immediately entered politics and was detained when a military coup erupted in 1967. After his release, he taught briefly at Fourah Bay College before being elected to Parliament for Bo Town I in 1969. He was appointed minister of external affairs in 1969 and later minister of health. After he left the cabinet in 1971, he returned to Fourah Bay College to teach history and stayed on to become head of the history department, dean of the Faculty of Arts, and later principal of Fourah Bay College in 1985. After he retired from the college faculty, he was appointed Sierra Leone's high commissioner to the United Kingdom for the period of 1993–1994 under the military government of Valentine Strasser. He later held the same position in the government of President Tejan **Kabbah** in 1996. He died in 2003.

FORNAH, JIM (1942–2001). Jim Fornah was an economist who became governor of the Central Bank of Sierra Leone and later minister of finance in the Sierra Leone government. He was trained as an economist in the United States and held positions in United Nations agencies before returning to Sierra Leone in the 1970s to become director of the National Authorizing Office. In 1981, he was appointed governor of the Bank of Sierra Leone. When he left that position in 1985, he was appointed minister of finance in the last government of President Joseph Saidu Momoh in 1990. When that government was overthrown by the military, Jim Fornah was appointed secretary of state, finance in the military Junta of the National Provisional Ruling Council (NPRC). He abandoned the job on a trip to attend a conference in the Ivory Coast. He remained in the United States to work for the World Bank until his death. He died in the United States on October 21, 2001.

FORNA, MOHAMED S. (1935–1975). Mohamed Sorie Forna was a medical doctor who became a politician, eventually was minister of finance, and was executed for treason on July 19, 1975. He was educated in Sierra Leone and trained as a doctor at Aberdeen University in Scotland. When he returned to Sierra Leone in 1966, he enrolled as a medical doctor in the army and later went into private practice. He entered Parliament in 1967 on an All People's Congress (APC) ticket, representing his home constituency of Tonkolili West. He was briefly detained when a military takeover followed the elections. When the APC resumed office under Siaka Stevens, Forna was made minister of finance. He resigned his cabinet post in 1970 to join a newly formed party, the **United Democratic Party (UDP)**. Siaka Stevens quickly moved to detain Forna and others who led the UDP. Freed from detention in 1973, he was again arrested, together with 14 others, charged with treason, convicted, and executed.

FOURAH BAY COLLEGE (FBC). Fourah Bay College began as a Christian Institution founded by the Church Missionary Society (CMS) in 1827 to train future Anglican priests. It came to be located on the east end of Freetown called Fourah Bay, hence the name of the college. In 1876, FBC was given university college status and affiliated to the University of Durham in England, subsequently offering degrees of Durham University. Many leaders from British West Africa and beyond trained at Fourah Bay College. During World War II, FBC was temporarily housed at the Mabang Academy a few miles outside Freetown. After the war, the college was moved to Mount Aureol which became its permanent home. By 1950, the CMS indicated its intention to relinquish responsibility for the college and turned operations over to the Sierra Leone government.

As FBC expanded to offer degrees in engineering, the Teacher Training Department, which had been a popular segment of the college, was discontinued. Soon after independence, moves were made by the Sierra Leone government to develop FBC and a new university college at Njala into the University of Sierra Leone. The University of Sierra Leone Act of 1967 finalized this policy, and the FBC severed its almost century-long relationship with Durham University.

FREETOWN. The largest town in Sierra Leone, Freetown is the capital of the Republic of Sierra Leone. The population of Greater Freetown, including its suburbs, is currently about one million. Freetown was founded in 1792 from land obtained from local Temne rulers at a place the Temne called Romarong. British agents had founded this settlement to resettle freed slaves from England. Soon the population swelled, populated by other freed slaves from the New World and by other African would-be slaves captured by the British Navy and released in Freetown. In 1808, the British government took over control of Freetown and its immediate environs as a crown colony.

Freetown is situated on a good natural harbor on the coast of West Africa, and this made it attractive to the British as a strategic harbor during the two world wars and as a base for administering other British colonies in West Africa, at least temporarily, in the 19th century. State capitals in Africa are inordinately central places, and Freetown is no exception. Thus Freetown character is representative of the entire country in both culture and ethnicity. The original population for which the town was founded—the former slaves and liberated Africans—were integrated with other neighboring peoples. With an overlay of Western values represented by the colonial government, a new culture and language emerged, dominated by the Krio language and culture. The Krio language became the lingua franca in Sierra Leone.

FREETOWN SECONDARY SCHOOL FOR GIRLS (FSSG). Also called Osora School, the name of its British cofounder, the Freetown Secondary School for Girls was founded in 1938 as a female institution in the heart of Freetown. Its founding was chiefly due to the efforts of Mrs. Hannah Benka-Coker, wife of a prominent barrister in Freetown. In 1952, the school moved to Brookfields, to new premises created largely through the efforts of Mrs. Benka-Coker. The FSSG remains one of the leading girls secondary schools in Freetown.

FRONTIER POLICE FORCE. The Frontier Police Force in Sierra Leone was formed in 1890 as the Scramble for Africa heated up and the British needed some semiofficial authority to watch over its interests in the interior of the Sierra Leone colony, particularly in those areas where the French were very active. The first head of the force, the British Colonel Gerald Fairtlough, enlisted recruits from all ethnic communities in Sierra Leone. The standard of training was high, as some of the experienced members of the existing police force in the colony were transferred to the Frontier force.

The Frontier Police was a paramilitary force, and was posted to various areas of the colony's interior where the British felt they needed to protect their interests. This was the source of the term "protectorate" that came to be applied to the interior of Sierra Leone when it was appropriated by the British. The main function of the Frontier Police Force was to project a symbol of British military presence and authority but also to keep order and serve as a representative of British interest in keeping the peace and preventing hostilities in the interior. They were not supposed to interfere in the administration of the local rulers and in their administration of justice.

This, however, is exactly what the Frontier Police did. They set about projecting themselves as untouchable by the local rulers and maltreated those rulers who would not allow them to exercise authority they did not legally possess. Local rulers were sometimes handcuffed, jailed, and abused. One Frontier Police sergeant named Coker was instrumental in installing his lover, Madame Nancy Tucker, as paramount chief in Bagru. The local rulers complained about the excesses of the Frontier Police Force, but the British, who depended on the force for sustaining its authority in the interior, upheld their positions. This became a major source of hostility among the local people and fueled the 1898 rebellion.

After this rebellion the Frontier Force remained in place, but in 1902 it was absorbed into a new Sierra Leone Battalion of the West African Frontier Force, which was a full military establishment.

FULA MANSA. The Fula Mansa is the traditional ruler of the Yoni **Temne**, although this title is no longer in use. Fula migrants had settled in Temne country by the early 18th century and one of their leaders, Masa Keleh, helped the Temne of Yoni repel Kpaa **Mende** attacks on their territory. In gratitude, the Yoni Temne recognized one of Masa Keleh's successors as their ruler and gave him the title of Fula Mansa (Fula king). It was these Fula who introduced the powerful Poro society to the Temne; it ultimately spread to other parts of the interior.

FYLE, CLIFFORD N. (1933–). Clifford Fyle, a writer and linguist, was the composer of the lyrics of Sierra Leone's national anthem. He was born in Freetown and educated at the **Methodist Boys High School** and **Fourah Bay College**. After receiving his bachelor of arts degree from the University of Durham, he taught for a few years at his alma mater, the Methodist Boys High School before going to England to study English at Hatfield College of Durham University. On his return in 1960, he won a competition for the words of the national song for the emerging nation of Sierra Leone. He was appointed education officer with responsibility for textbooks at the Ministry of Education. After leaving the ministry he was among the founding faculty of Njala University College when it opened in 1964. Fyle also studied linguistics at Los Angeles and textbook writing at Indiana University. In 1968, he joined Fourah Bay College as senior lecturer in English and, in 1978, left the service of Sierra Leone for a UNESCO position as language specialist. Fyle retired from UNESCO in 1993 and devoted himself to publishing, producing a series of children's books in the major local languages of Sierra Leone—Mende, Temne, Limba, and Krio. He now lives in the United States, where he heads Lekon Publishers and writes novels.

FYLE, HILTON (1946–). Journalist and broadcaster, Hilton Fyle was one of the pioneers of a private radio station in Sierra Leone. He was convicted of treason during the civil war and was sentenced to die but was saved by the reprieve of the Lomé accord.

Hilton was born in Freetown and was educated at the **Methodist Boys High School**. He took the Advanced Teachers Certificate at the Milton Margai Teachers College in Freetown in 1969 and assumed a position as the Sierra Leone agent for Evans Publishers of London. He was a part-time and later full-time news reader for the Sierra Leone Broadcasting Service. In 1973, he joined the British Broadcasting Corporation (BBC) in England, initially on a training program and began working full time for the BBC soon after. He was well known throughout Africa as he hosted the popular BBC show, "Network Africa," for many years.

In 1993, Hilton Fyle left the BBC and returned to Sierra Leone where he started his own radio station and newspaper known as "1-2-3." At the height of the rebel war, when the RUF ousted President Tejan

Kabbah, he was perceived as a major supporter of the RUF and was the object of hostility in Freetown. When the **Kabbah** government was restored in 1998, Hilton Fyle was arrested, tried, and convicted of treason. He remained in prison until January 1999 when the rebels entered Freetown and broke open the prison, freeing all the inmates. He moved into the interior with the rebels and remained there until a general amnesty was proclaimed with the Lomé accord of 2001. Thereupon, he traveled to the United States, where he now lives.

– G –

GALLINAS. *See* VAI.

GANDA, ALI (1927–1964). Ali Ganda was a popular entertainer and singer whose music blended traditional and Western forms, both in the lyrics and the music.

He was born in the town of Serabu in the Moyamba District, home of the Ganda family. His father was a headmaster of a government-assisted Catholic school. Ali Ganda moved to Freetown where he attended high school at the Saint Edwards Catholic school. He studied briefly at Fourah Bay College but moved on to become a teacher, first at his father's school, later at Moyamba Catholic School.

In 1949, Ali Ganda first heard calypso on a record and was carried away by the rhythm; calypso became his main interest from then on. He became well known for singing calypso songs and in 1956 he received a scholarship to study broadcasting and dramatic art at the Rose Buford Training College of Speech and Drama in Sidcup, Kent, in Britain. He established quite a reputation in England among Africans living there when he composed and sang "The Queen's Visit to Nigeria." By then, he had already sung what became his most popular tune in Freetown, "Poor Little Monkey."

Many more calypso songs followed as Ali Ganda became established in West Africa as a calypso king. His songs were known throughout West Africa and celebrated both Ghana's and Sierra Leone's independence events. He expressed his own idea of calypso as an African beat developed elsewhere by blacks, and his intention was to bring it back to Africa. He became a popular entertainer for the Sierra Leone Broadcasting Service, and his popular variety program became a household feature. He died untimely at the age of 37, a suspected suicide.

GANDA, JOSEPH HENRY (1932–). Bishop Joseph Henry Ganda became the first Catholic bishop among the Mende people and rose to the rank of the first indigenous Catholic archbishop in the newly created diocese in Sierra Leone. He was born at Serabu in the Moyamba District and was schooled at the **St. Edwards Secondary School** in Freetown. His pastoral training was in Nigeria, Britain, and Rome, and he was ordained as a Catholic priest in April 1961.

Bishop Ganda rose through the ranks and was made a Catholic bishop at Kenema in 1971, having worked also in Moyamba and Blama as a priest in the 1960s. In 1980, in a high profile ceremony, Bishop Ganda was installed as the Catholic archbishop of Freetown and Bo.

GBANKA (c. 1840–1898). Gbanka was *Fula Mansa* (ruler) of the Temne of Yoni territory before colonial rule. He fought against the British in a campaign against the Yoni in 1886 for which he was banished by the British for seven years. He was reinstated in 1895 and began cooperating with the British against other local rulers until he was killed in the 1898 uprising.

A Muslim, Fula who lived among the Temne had created the title of **Fula Mansa** (in Mandinka, "mansa" means "ruler"). Gbanka, who had been successful as a trader and had made advantageous marriages with powerful neighboring families, became the last Fula Mansa. Gbanka attained prominence in the eyes of the British when he took control of towns belonging to **Madam Yoko** of Senehun, one of Britain's most loyal allies in the area. A British-led force was sent against Gbanka who was captured and exiled to the Gold Coast (now Ghana) in 1887. In 1895, he was allowed to return and assume his position as Fula Mansa shortly before the British took control of the area. Gbanka then concluded that his best means of survival was to show loyalty to the British. He warned the British of an oath taken by chiefs to oppose the house tax; this led to the arrest of 10 chiefs. On his information, the Bai Sherbro was arrested and jailed for inducing other chiefs not to pay the tax. When the 1898 rebellion broke out,

Gbanka provided more than 1,000 troops to the British forces marching on the resistors. Gbanka was killed May 1, 1898 while leading these forces against the town of Gbonjeima, near Moyamba.

GBANYA LANGO (c. 1818–1878). Ruler of the Kpaa Mende or western Mende people up to 1878 and a leading general among the Mende people, Gbanya Lango had already distinguished himself as a warrior when he was very young. He fought under the command of his uncle, Gbenjei, the Kpaa Mende ruler. In Mende custom, a man normally 'inherits' his father's or uncle's wives. Gbanya thus inherited a wife who ultimately became known as **Madam Yoko**. Succeeding his uncle as Kpaa Mende ruler, Gbanya became allied to the British.

As a great warrior, he helped the British fight some of their wars against the Koya Temne in 1861. He also sent some of his soldiers to join the British force against the Ashanti (in present day Ghana) in 1873. It was probably around this time that he moved the Kpaa Mende capital from Taiama to Senehun, a thriving trading center where a number of Krio traders from the colony had settled. But when, in 1875, Gbanya participated in a war between Sherbro factions of the Caulker family and attacked Bagru, a Sherbro chiefdom considered part of the British colony, a British-led force was sent against him. Although the initial colony force was beaten off by Gbanya's troops, the British governor himself led another force against Gbanya that destroyed many towns suspected of being in league with Gbanya and seized himself. Gbanya pleaded innocent but was ordered flogged, even though he was not under British jurisdiction.

Gbanya agreed to a treaty giving Britain influence over his country, a prelude to the British protectorate. Gbanya continued to be regarded as a loyal supporter of the British until his death. In his later years, he allowed the opening of a Church of God Mission at Senehun. After his death in 1884, the British recognized Madam Yoko as the paramount chief of Kpaa Mende.

GOLA. The ethnic Gola, such as the **Kissi** people, with whom they share many cultural similarities, inhabited much of the eastern and southeastern regions of Sierra Leone before the 16th century. They are today found in the southeastern corner of Sierra Leone in the Pujehun District, in much smaller numbers than previously. Across the border from present Gola territory in Sierra Leone there are much larger communities of Gola in Liberia. The Gola have become strongly influenced by the Mende so that most Gola in Sierra Leone today speak Mende. But the influence is mutual, as many place names in Mende country today are Gola. Today, there is also a forested reserve called the Gola Forest that is a habitat for wildlife.

GOVERNORS OF SIERRA LEONE. First the Sierra Leone Company and then the British government (since 1808), used the title of "governor" for the British representative who ran the colony. This official had extraordinary powers in the colony and could completely disregard the recommendations of the indigenous Executive and Legislative Councils. For brief periods in the 1820s and 1840s, the governor of Sierra Leone was also the governor for the Gold Coast and the Gambia. The position of governor of Sierra Leone was carried over into independent Sierra Leone, with a Sierra Leonean as governor from 1962 until the declaration of a republic removed the position in 1971. See **appendix A** for a list of the governors in Sierra Leone.

GRANT, MARCUS (c. 1909–). Marcus C. Grant was the general secretary of the Artisans and Allied Workers Union when a general strike erupted in Freetown in February 1955, with rioting and looting that is still remembered in Sierra Leone history.

Grant was educated at the **CMS Grammar School** and the **Albert Academy** in Freetown. With the support of political activist **Wallace-Johnson**, Grant became part of the Trade Union Movement and quickly became general secretary of the Workers Union. The union gave notice of a strike in February 1955 in a statement signed by Marcus Grant. In negotiations between the union and the colonial government, the latter would not accede to the workers' call for increases in daily wage to ten pence. The government offered six pence. After talks broke down, the workers' strike started, and for two days, there was massive rioting and looting in Freetown before the army was called in to restore order. At least 18 people lost their lives during the strike, including a British officer, Michael Everitt, who was murdered by the mob. A commission of inquiry held after the strike took evidence from Marcus Grant for 15 hours.

Soon after the strike, Grant and his supporters formed the Sierra Leone Labor Party with Grant as national secretary. Although the party initially gained sympathy and popularity, it lost completely in the 1957 general elections. However, five years later, in 1962, Grant won a parliamentary seat representing his native Waterloo and soon joined the ruling **Sierra Leone People's Party**. He remained secretary of the Workers Union for many years thereafter, becoming president of the amalgamated Sierra Leone Labour Congress in 1973.

GULAMA, ELLA KOBLO (1921–). Madam Ella Koblo Gulama, as she is popularly known, was the first woman to be elected to Parliament. She was born in Moyamba town in 1921, the daughter of a powerful paramount chief, **Julius Gulama** of the Kaiyamba chiefdom, of which Moyamba was the chief town. The young Ella attended the **Harford School for Girls**, then the only women's secondary school in the the provinces. She later attended a Women's Teachers College in Freetown and qualified as a teacher. She married an equally prominent paramount chief, Bai Koblo Pathbana of the Maforki chiefdom, in 1946. This union between the daughter of an ethnic Mende leader and an ethnic Temne paramount chief was viewed as a visible sign of interethnic integration in Sierra Leone. When Madam Ella's father died, she succeeded him as paramount chief of Kaiyamba in 1953.

Ella Koblo was quick to enter national politics. She first became a member of the Moyamba District Council, taking her place among the male leaders in that council. She was the first woman to be elected to the House of Representatives in 1957. After reelection in 1962 she was appointed the first woman cabinet minister. She became a close ally of Prime Minister **Albert Margai** and consequently when he lost his office in 1967 she lost her cabinet position. She was deposed as paramount chief during the era of President **Siaka Stevens** in 1975. But she gradually returned to power, reemerging late in the 1970s as leader of the Moyamba District Women's Organization of the ruling All People's Congress Party, and she ultimately regained her chieftanship. In 1992, under the military rule of the **National Provisional Ruling Council (NPRC)**, she was a candidate in the paramount chieftaincy elections and resoundingly won, to become once again paramount chief of Kaiyamba chiefdom.

GULAMA, JULIUS (1893–1951). One of the most progressive paramount chiefs in the protectorate during the immediate preindependence era, paramount chief Julius Gulama of Kaiyamba chiefdom was prominent in new formations and organizations that matured around the time of his death and were the backbone of Sierra Leone politics leading up to and immediately following independence in 1961.

Born of a Mende father and Temne mother, he was originally known as Julius Foday Cole and went to the EUB school at Rotifunk and the Albert Academy in Freetown. Before becoming paramount chief in 1928, he taught at what later became **Harford School for Girls** in his native Moyamba and served as a ticket examiner for the Sierra Leone Railway Department, a carrier clerk in the Cameroons campaign during World War I, and a clerk in the firm of Paterson Zochonis in its branch in Moyamba.

He was thus well traveled within Sierra Leone before becoming a traditional ruler. He used this background to bring reform to his chiefdom. He cooperated with the colonial government in regularizing the system of tribute to fixed amounts in support of the protectorate Native Law Ordinance enacted in 1905. He banned public gambling and the pollution of streams in his chiefdom.

Julius Gulama was instrumental, along with Dr. **M. A. S. Margai** in organizing regular conferences of chiefs, initially in the Moyamba District, to discuss matters of common concern and to submit recommendations to the colonial administration. This formation soon caught on and became the basis for the establishment of **District Councils** and the **Protectorate Assembly** set up by the colonial government. Gulama was in the forefront in the formation of the **Protectorate Educational Progressive Union (PEPU)**, a body intended to narrow the gap in Western education between the colony and protectorate by providing material support for protectorate youths in education. He was also the first honorary president and only paramount chief member of the **Sierra Leone Organization Society (SOS)** formed in 1946 by the Western trained protectorate elite as a political pressure group in the interest of the protectorate. The political landscape was changing very fast with the introduction and debate over the Stevenson Constitution of 1947. Two protectorate groups, PEPU and SOS, were prominent in these discussions, and Julius Gulama was at the heart of it all. But Julius Gulams died March 8, 1951, a month before these two groups merged with the People's Party to form the **Sierra Leone People's Party**, which was to lead Sierra Leone into independence in 1961.

GUMBAY. A cylindrical drum that has a leather cover at the top. It is beaten with both hands while the musician is seated and the gumbay is placed in a slanting position on the ground. Gumbay is the music of the ethnic Krio people of Freetown and is played to the accompaniment of an ensemble with a metal saw rubbed at the teeth with a long metal pin, and a metal triangle hit alternately on both sides with a metal pin. The gumbay player is usually the lead singer.

– H –

HAIDARA "KONTORFILI" (c. 1885–1931). Haidara "Kontorfili" was a charismatic Islamic militant leader who attempted to transform a popular Islamic movement that he had started into an anticolonial struggle. This move was aborted by the British authorities in Sierra Leone.

He entered the colony of Sierra Leone from across its northeastern borders with the then-French colony of Guinea in May 1930. The area in which he settled in Sierra Leone was dominated by ethnic **Soso** people mixed, in the Sierra Leone part, with ethnic Temne. Haidara traveled and preached through this northeastern part of Sierra Leone and finally settled at a town called Bubuya close to the district headquarters town of Kambia. It was apparently here that he acquired the nickname of "Kontorfili," a Soso term meaning an enigma or a thorn in the flesh. This could have been in relation to his increased popularity as he positioned himself to oppose the colonial government.

By October 1930, less than six months after his arrival, Haidara's influence had become strong and he had attracted a considerable following. His religious zeal and demonstrated ability to perform miracle healing attracted people from Sierra Leone and Guinea who would travel long distances to hear him preach or to receive medical treatment. By the end of 1930, Haidara was more emphatically preaching about the need for Islamic reform. On January 2, 1931, he wrote to the district commissioner in Kambia, threatening death to all those who would not practice Islam in terms of what he defined as the true faith.

The colonial administration, concerned about the impact of a major economic recession and with the possibility of mass action disrupting its rule, took no chances. Haidara was charged with subversion on February 9, 1931, and was served with an expulsion order to leave Sierra Leone. Haidara ignored the order and stepped up his campaign. The following day, he wrote an open letter to the people of Kambia telling them that although the paramount chief of neighboring Mange Bure chiefdom in the Port Loko District had fallen, no one should fear a European, French, or British. More significantly, he urged people in this letter not to pay the hated house tax. These statements, which received widespread circulation in the region, were definitely confrontational. Around this time Haidara declared himself an alimamy, an Islamic title used by local rulers influenced by Islam in this part of Sierra Leone.

The colonial administration was now convinced that something drastic had to be done. On February 16, 1931, troops from the Royal West African Frontier Force were dispatched from Kambia to arrest Haidara at Bubuya. Encouraged by the size of his following, Haidara determined to confront this contingent with his own people who were armed only with swords and machetes. The ensuing clash lasted only a few minutes; Haidara and four of his followers were killed and the British lost their commanding officer, Captain H. J. Holmes, who was killed by Haidara.

HARFORD SCHOOL FOR GIRLS. Harford School for Girls is located in Moyamba town and has a long history of providing Western education for women from the protectorate, now the provinces. The school started as the Mary Sowers Home for Girls, founded at Rotifunk in 1888 by the United Brethren in Christ (UBC) Mission. After the 1898 rebellion, during which the school was closed, it reopened, renamed the Moyamba Girls School. In 1903, the UBC decided to merge its girls' boarding school at Shenge with the Moyamba Girls School. The first buildings at Rotifunk were completed and occupied in 1908. The name of the school was changed in 1921 to the Lilian R. Harford School for Girls and attained secondary school status in 1944. The Harford School buildings were severely damaged during the rebel war of the 1990s and the school is now in the recovery mode.

HAZELEY, PETER PHILIP (1862–1941). Peter Philip Hazeley was a Wesleyan Methodist missionary who headed the mission station at Tonko Limba for many years, earning for himself the nicknames "Limba Hazeley" or "apostle to the Limba." He wrote a Wesleyan catechism in Limba and did much to promote teaching in the Limba language.

Hazeley was a Krio, born in **Freetown** and educated at the Wesleyan Boys High School. He studied at the Theological Institution in Freetown in 1884 and attended lectures at **Fourah Bay College**. He became a local preacher in 1881 and in 1884 was appointed catechist to the Methodist station in Tonko Limba, a posting that amounted to a banishment in those days. Apart from a year's break when he went to Richmond College at Cape Coast in today's Ghana, Peter Hazeley ran the Tonko Limba mission until 1907. There was another break in his service in Tonko Limba when conflict between the Tonko Limba and the Soso forced him to leave his post in 1891 until peace was restored; he returned late in 1892. Taking over from James Booth, a British missionary turned trader, Under him, the mission made consideration progress. He ran both a day and a night school, aware that many children spent the day doing farm work. In the process, Hazeley became an authority on the Limba language and wrote a Wesleyan catechism in that language. He also served on the Limba section of the Board of Examiners for Vernacular Studies, established in 1902 by the Sierra Leone Methodist Mission, following a decision that ordination of new ministers would depend on their knowledge of a native language.

By the 1930s Hazeley was teaching at Wesleyan City Mission School in **Freetown**, a school designed to provide Western education to migrant children from the protectorate. Hazeley gave Limba lessons to children attending the school. He also became secretary of the Limba Literature Committee, which, in 1936, issued two booklets in Limba for the school pupils. He died in Freetown on November 18, 1942.

HEDDLE, CHARLES (1812–c. 1880). Charles Heddle was an outstanding businessman who pioneered the export trade in peanuts from

Sierra Leone and in time became the most prosperous merchant in the colony. He commanded general respect and was entrusted by the governor to negotiate with local rulers in order to protect British trade from French encroachment. A prominent and active public figure, he was appointed first to the Governor's Council and later to the Legislative Council that replaced it. He was also largely instrumental in establishing a mail packet service between Britain and **Freetown**.

Born in Freetown in 1812, Heddle was the son of a British Army doctor and an African mother. After his education (possibly in Britain), he went into business, first at Bathurst, then Banjul in the Gambia in 1834, and a few years later in Freetown, where his European ancestry stood him in good stead in official circles. He was in partnership for a while with J. P. Pellegrin, a merchant from Senegal, and by 1840 he had established his own company of Heddle and Co.

It was Heddle who opened up the peanut trade. Peanuts, together with timber, were among the earliest exports from the Sierra Leone colony. In 1837, 13 pounds sterling worth of peanuts was exported, largely by his firm, and shortly thereafter he went into business on a large scale. He bought up factories from the timber trader, John McCormack, at strategic points on Kikonke Island at the mouth of the Scarcies River, and at Gbinti on the Melacourie River in what is now Guinea. From these points he could tap the peanut production of the interior.

By the mid-1840s, he already owned half a dozen ships transporting peanuts and timber to Freetown, and by 1850 he had become the most important merchant in the colony, having acquired the premises of Macauley and Babington, his predecessors in this position. By 1846, he was also including palm kernels in his exports.

Because of his wealth and far-reaching trade connections, Heddle was well known in Sierra Leone and its surroundings, his reputation as the "groundnut king" extending as far as 300 miles beyond the colony to distant chiefdoms. He also held a prominent position in the colony itself. In 1845, he persuaded Governor William Ferguson to let him lead a mission to negotiate a commercial and antislavery treaty with the king of the Morea in Soso country in order to safeguard British trading interests (in which he largely participated) against French initiatives. Impressed by Heddle's enterprise and success, Fergusson gave him a seat on his advisory council.

In 1851, Heddle became the first chairman of the Mercantile Association, formed in Freetown to articulate the interests of the business community. He also played an important role in the establishment in 1852 of a mail packet service between Britain and Freetown called the African Steamship Company, controlled by Macgregor Laird. By the 1860s, Heddle owned an impressive amount of property both in Freetown and in Bendu, in Bonthe, and on the Rokel River. He put part of his enormous profits into the acquisition of property, whether by purchase or mortgage, from less-successful traders.

In 1863, Heddle was appointed to the newly constituted Legislative Council by Governor Norman Macdonald. But by 1870, he was a sick and crippled man. He left Freetown in that year to settle in Paris, leaving first his nephew and then one of his sons as his agent in Freetown.

HORTON, JAMES AFRICANUS BEALE (1835–1883). James Africanus Beale Horton, a prominent indigenous medical doctor in the British colonial service in Sierra Leone, was best known for his writings on African nationalism.

Horton's parents were Ibo liberated Africans and he was born in the village of Gloucester, near **Freetown** on June 1, 1835. He entered the **CMS Grammar School** in 1847 from where he was transferred to **Fourah Bay College** in 1851 to study theology, like many brilliant youths in the colonial period. The secretary for the CMS in London, Henry Venn, helped secure a scholarship for Horton, who had excelled in science, to study medicine in England. Horton graduated in medicine in 1859 with a thesis titled "The Medical Topography of the West Coast of Africa," which was later published. Horton joined the British Army Medical Service, being one of the first African doctors to serve as a regular officer in the British Army. He spent much of his active service in the Gold Coast but also served in the Gambia.

Horton is well known for his writings on African nationalism. He proposed a university in West Africa as well as a small government medical school in Sierra Leone, which would prepare young Africans, tutored by other Africans, in the preliminaries of medicine before sending them to study medicine in England. He wrote a book entitled *Political Economy of British Western Africa* in 1965 advocating that Fourah Bay College in Sierra Leone be the nucleus of such a university. In 1873, he joined the supporters of **Edward Blyden** in campaigning for a university in West Africa. In his popular book, *West African Countries and Peoples*, Horton called for independence for West African nations in the Gambia, Sierra Leone, and others.

When Horton returned to Freetown upon his retirement a fairly wealthy man, he energetically demonstrated his faith in commerce and education. He established a commercial bank to assist local entrepreneurs who would be the source, he believed, of a vibrant middle class.

Although in many ways he still thought like the Europeans with whom he had worked, Horton coupled those attitudes with a genuine concern for his fellow Africans. He died October 15, 1883, leaving a substantial part of his estate for further scientific education.

HUGHES, WILLIAM (c. 1840–1898). William Hughes was the first African to be appointed as assistant district commissioner when a British protectorate was established over the interior of Sierra Leone in 1896. Hughes was a Krio police clerk who had an unrivaled knowledge of the laws of the colony, and thus the British governor, **Sir Frederic Cardew**, thought it fitting to appoint him as an assistant to Thomas Alldridge, a British trader who was district commissioner in the Bonthe District. Alldridge stayed in Bonthe Island while Hughes was assigned to Imperri on the mainland, a remote post where it was perhaps felt risky to station a British district commissioner.

The declaration of the protectorate was quickly followed by widespread protest by local rulers and people. The Sherbro rulers placed a ban on all trade passing through their country to **Freetown** as a means of expressing resentment at the establishment of the protectorate and the impending house tax. Hughes, realizing that that there was going to be trouble, warned the administration of signs of concerted action toward a resistance, one of the leaders of which was the okong (ruler) of Imperi. His report was not taken seriously by his superiors and, being a loyal servant, Hughes stayed at his post.

When the widespread rebellion broke out in April 1898 in the southern areas, including Imperi, District Commissioner Alldridge was alerted to the seriousness of the situation by the influx of refugees into Bonthe. Alldridge sent five policemen to Imperi as reinforcements for

Hughes. By the time they arrived there, the worst had happened. The Sokong had captured Hughes, his household, and his clerk and had taken them inland where they were tortured and executed at a village called Gbanbaia. When the rebellion was over, Governor Cardew refused to support the rebuilding of Gbanbaia, which had been destroyed in the retaliation by colonial forces because it was there that Hughes had been murdered.

HUMONYA, MADAM (c. 1865–1930). Madam Humonya ruled the Nongowa chiefdom in the Kenema District as paramount chief from 1908 to 1918. Records show that this was a troubled period in the history of that chiefdom, as Madam Humonya was regarded as despotic, a reputation she earned because she had the full support of the colonial government.

She took office in 1918 replacing her mother, Madam Matolo, who had been appointed paramount chief of Nongowa in 1898 after the massive rebellion against colonial rule. Madam Humonya had a strong pedigree. Her mother, Madam Matolo, was the wife of Faba of Dodo, a popular ruler whose even more popular son, **Nyagua**, was accused by the British of having been one of the ringleaders of the rebellion. The British were now looking for more pliable traditional leaders after the rebellion and women seemed a likely possibility. Madam Matolo was then appointed and confirmed, and when she became incapacitated, her daughter Humonya was appointed in her place by the British.

The unwavering support of the British for this chieftaincy encouraged Madam Humonya to literally terrorize her people with excessive executions and punishment of those who opposed her. In fact, the British regarded her as "a sort of paramount chief over the other paramount chiefs of the district." One British district commissioner, W. D. Bowden, attempted to be stern with Madam Humonya. However, she managed to get through to Governor Wilkinson, who imposed his authority on Bowden and transferred him to another district. But the governor's own investigations concluded that Madam Humonya had been oppressing her people. She was found guilty of failing to appoint a speaker (her deputy), of arbitrarily choosing two men as her principal counselors, and of oppressing her subjects with excessive fines and forced labor. It was decided that the people should choose a speaker; two of Madam Humonya's unofficial counselors were to be banished; and all fees and fines were to be recorded. Trouble continued in the chiefdom under the new district commissioner, but Madam Humonya managed to stay ahead of the affray and no proceedings for deposition were brought against her. Even when the "tribal authorities" voted for her resignation, Madam Humonya refused to be deposed. It was not until chiefship elections were allowed in Nongowa in 1919 that she was voted out. She subsequently lived out her remaining life in anonymity.

HYDE-FORSTER, LATI. Lati Hyde-Forster was the first female graduate of **Fourah Bay College**. She later became principal of her alma mater, the **Annie Walsh Memorial School**. She was born Lati Hyde in **Freetown** and after graduating from **Fourah Bay College** in 1938 she married a prominent lawyer, Justice Forster in Freetown. She retained her maiden name and become known as Lati Hyde-Forster. Her entire life was spent teaching and in 1961 becoming principal of the Annie Walsh Memorial School. She retired in 1975, and in 1987 the University of Sierra Leone honored her with a doctor of civil laws degree.

– I –

INTERNATIONAL BANK FOR TRADE AND INDUSTRY. Usually referred to as IBTI for short, the International Bank for Trade and Industry was incorporated in Sierra Leone under the provisions of the banking Act of 1970 as amended by Act No. 10 of 1978. It came into operation in October 1982 with Mohammed Tejan-Cole as its first managing director. By the 1980s, 80 percent of the bank's equity was owned by Sierra Leoneans, and the bank's board of directors was mostly Sierra Leonean.

ISA (c. 1815–1891). Isa was ruler of the town of Kaliere, a province of Solimana, the 19th century state centered on Falaba and dominated by ethnic Yalunka. Presently Kaliere, like Falaba, is in the Sulima chiefdom in the Koinadugu District in northern Sierra Leone. Isa occupied an uncomfortable position between warring states and eventually joined forces with **Samori Toure**, the Mandinka emperor, and his warriors called ***sofas***.

Isa was probably born early in the 19th century. He belonged to the Samura clan of Kabelia, a political unit founded by his grandfather toward the end of the 18th century. About the middle of the 19th century, Isa became ruler of Kaliere, then part of the Solima **Yalunka** state. During the 1860s, conflict erupted between Isa and the rulers of the Solimans state. They believed that Isa was in league with the Fula of adjacent Futa Jalon, a state that was intent on destroying Solimana. When a Fula prince was killed in Falaba, his golden saddle and sword were given to Isa who had no idea where the items came from. Some years later the Fula were searching for the saddle and sword and found the apparently incriminating objects with Isa and attacked his town, causing much destruction. Isa then broke off relations with Solimana, marking the break by changing his last name from Samura (also the name of the Solimana rulers) to his maternal name of Turay.

Isa's son, Sayo, determined to be avenged on the rulers of Solimana. In 1882, Isa sent Sayo to join the forces of Samori and his sofas who were moving southward to gain control of the trade route to **Freetown** on which Falaba was situated. Through Sayo's trickery, the narration goes, the sofa attacked and destroyed Falaba after a nine-month siege. Sayo continued to fight with the sofa thereafter, while Isa remained ruler of Kaliere, now part of Samori's empire.

By 1889, however, Isa had begun to regret his cooperation with Samori's forces. Baba, the sofa general near Kaliere, had captured some of Isa's people without just cause and, disillusioned, Isa began to shift his allegiance back to the rulers of the former Solima state who were hostile to the sofa. By this time, however, he was a very old man and was afraid of angering the sofa and bringing down their wrath on his town.

Meanwhile, Sayo was fighting on the side of the sofas. When he heard of their hostile action toward his father, he broke with them and returned to Kaliere to plan vengeance against his former allies. While Isa lived, he remained a restraining influence on his son. He died in 1891, leaving Sayo as his successor, still determined to be avenged against the sofas.

ISLAM IN SIERRA LEONE. Islam has been a dominant religion in Sierra Leone since before the establishment of a colony there in the late 18th century. By the 1740s, people in large sections of the northern interior had converted to Islam following the jihad in Futa Jalon in 1727–1728. Itinerant Muslim clerics traveled and lived among communities in different parts of the interior, establishing Islamic influence that remains to this day. Christian missionary effort in the northeast of what became the colony had been opposed by proponents of Islam for many years, leading to the Christian European missionaries labeling the Muslims as "heathen," a value that was passed on to the colony inhabitants by the 19th century.

With the invasion of **Samori Toure** in the late 19th century, much of the north of Sierra Leone was converted to Islam. Today, Islam has a strong footing in most parts of Sierra Leone.

In **Freetown**, Christian missionary dominance, supported by the colonial government, sought to limit the spread of Islam—largely unsuccessfully, especially because Islam received strong reinforcement as migrants from the interior moved to the colony on a continuing basis. Many of these migrants were Muslims and settled in the eastern side of the colony, thus Islam was much more prevalent in the east end of Freetown.

By the 20th century, much adjustment had taken place between Muslims and Christians in Freetown as members of one religion joined in celebrating the feast of the other. Deriving their prejudices from the colonial government, however, Christians tended to believe themselves superior to Muslims, identifying their religious persuasion broadly with Westernization as seen in their colonial rulers. For example, for the past half a century or more both religions take part in the lantern parades that accompany the Islamic holy feast of Ramadan, even though leading Islamic clerics in Freetown recently proclaimed this parade as non-Islamic. Muslims formerly attended clearly Christian schools for Western education; however, in the past few decades, Islamic schools at the secondary level have been established to administer that level of education in the Islamic manner.

– J –

JAH, MOMOH (LATE 1840s TO EARLY 1900s). Momoh Jah was a leading general of his brother, **Momoh Kaikai**, who ruled Pujehun at the time of the colonial takeover. While Momah Jah initially opposed the house tax imposed by the British and was imprisoned, he later cooperated with the British, and was recognized as paramount chief of Lower Krim territory in the present Pujehun District.

Momoh Jah was born about 1840 of an ethnic Fula father and a **Mende** mother. He led Momoh Kaikai's forces in domination of the region around Pujehun in the last quarter of the 19th century, subsequently building the town of Sembehun, which he established as his own locus of political power.

In 1886, the governor of the colony of Sierra Leone, Sir James Hay, administered a treaty of friendship with many chiefs in the interior, including Momoh Jah. Jah and others were falsely led to believe that the British did not intend to take over their territory, and Momoh Jah enthusiastically cooperated with Governor Hay's policy of road building and the construction of a block house for the Frontier Police. He even persuaded other skeptical neighboring local rulers in the Bumpe region to sign the treaty of friendship, which the British actually intended to use as a basis for the declaration of a protectorate over the interior of Sierra Leone. Because of this, upon the proclamation of a protectorate in 1896, Momoh Jah and some other rulers called on Governor Cardew to question some of the clauses of the protectorate declaration. After initially refusing to see the rulers, Hay finally gave them audience but Momoh Jah refused to join the party. In 1897, Jah was recognized as paramount chief of Lower Krim country, but when the house tax was imposed, Momoh Jah refused to pay. He was arrested and imprisoned on the orders of the governor until he gave in and paid his tax. Thereafter, Momoh Jah cooperated with the British even to the point of supplying troops to help quell the 1898 uprising. He was given a reward of 10 British pounds for his support. The British even wanted Momoh Jah to succeed the ailing **Momoh Kaikai** as paramount chief of Malene chiefdom, also part of Pujehun District. This did not happen, and little is known of Momoh Jah, who died probably early in the 20th century.

JOHNSON, LEMUEL (1941–2002). Lemuel Johnson was a high-profile Sierra Leonean professor of English at the University of Michigan in the United States who had a significant impact on the Sierra Leone community of scholars in the United States and also in Sierra Leone.

He was born in Nigeria of Sierra Leonean parents. His parents returned to **Freetown** in the 1950s, when Johnson attended the **CMS Grammar School** in Freetown before proceeding to the United States for higher education. He received his Ph.D. in Literature from the University of Michigan and started a long career of teaching in the same university. This was interrupted briefly in 1970 when he returned to Sierra Leone to teach at **Fourah Bay College** for two years. He became professor of English at Michigan and later president of the African Literature Association of the Americas. He was a widely published scholar in African and Latin American Literature, with earlier works such as *Highlife for Caliban* in 1973 and later ones, such as *Carnival of the Old Coast* in 1995. His famous trilogy, *The Sierra Leone Trilogy,* was published in 1995. Johnson kept in close contact with Sierra Leone and the Sierra Leonean community in the United States, contributing for years to the Internet discussion site called "Leonet." He died in 2002.

JOHNSON, OBADIAH ALEXANDER (1849–1920). Obadiah Alexander Johnson spent much of his medical career in Lagos, Nigeria, but his work in Sierra Leone and love of his homeland led him to leave a bequest to establish a chair in science at his alma mater, **Fourah Bay College**.

Johnson was born at Hiasings village near Freetown and was educated at the **CMS Grammar School**, at Fourah Bay College, and studied medicine at King's College in London and at Edinburgh University. He returned to Sierra Leone where he was assistant colonial surgeon 1887–1889 and also served as justice of the peace in the Sherbro District. He transferred his position as assistant colonial surgeon to Lagos thereafter and upon leaving the service established a thriving private practice, coming to be known as one of the most fashionable and successful doctors in Lagos. In 1901, he was appointed a member of the Legislative Council in the Lagos colony, holding that position until 1913.

Though Dr. Johnson had sought his fortune and career along the coast in British West Africa, as did many of his countrymen during the colonial period, he did not forget his native land. When he died in England in 1920, he left 5,000 pounds sterling of his estate to Fourah Bay College for the founding of a science chair. He also bequeathed some of his books to the college. Another Sierra Leonean, Dr. John Randle of Lagos, offered to underwrite the cost of retaining a science master at the college for three years, and this was the beginning of what became the science faculty at Fourah Bay College.

JOHNSON, PHILIP (1853–1903). Philip Johnson was a **Krio** minister of the Wesleyan Methodist Church in Sierra Leone who spent his life leading his religious congregation in Tonko **Limba** country. Although he had little formal education himself, he earned the respect of his peers in the clergy through his devotion to his congregation and his unrivaled knowledge of the Limba language.

Johnson was born at Hastings near Freetown and became a convert to Wesleyan Methodism in 1870. He began as a prayer leader at his Hastings church and subsequently rose to higher positions of increasing responsibility in the church. He continued to seek to improve his education and studied privately with a European missionary in Freetown. In 1880, when a Methodist mission was established in Forecaria in Tonko Limba (Kambia District in Sierra Leone), Johnson was sent there as catechist under James Booth, the pioneer English missionary who later gave up his persuasion and turned trader. Johnson was in charge of the Kathiri village section of the Tonko Limba mission although he was in charge of the entire mission when Booth was on leave in England. Except for a brief interval during armed conflict between the Soso and the Limba in the 1891, Johnson spent his entire mission life at Tonko Limba. Despite the fact that he could not enter the intricate theological discussions necessary for passing the yearly examination for ordination as a minister, Johnson was exempt from this and was accepted by the church and was ordained as native assistant minister in 1895. Realizing that Johnson was determined to work among nonliterate people in Tonko Limba, church officials accepted that a knowledge of intricate theology was not necessary in his case.

At the end of the Soso-Limba wars in 1893, Johnson returned to Tonko Limba, serving under Rev. **Philip Hazeley**. Johnson's knowledge of Limba was very useful to his ministry. He translated the catechisms into Limba and produced a Limba version of the sacramental services. He died on August 21, 1903.

JONAH, JAMES O. (c. 1934–). James Jonah became well known in Sierra Leone when he served as electoral commissioner during the difficult period of the civil war and the transition from military to civilian government from 1994–1996.

James Jonah was born in **Freetown** and attended primary schooling there. He pursued university studies at the Massachusetts Institute of Technology in the United States where he earned a Ph.D. in Political science. He joined the United Nations Secretariat Department of political and Security Affairs in 1963 and remained with the United Nations until 1994, attaining the rank of under-secretary general.

After retiring from the United Nations, Jonah returned home at the time when the **National Provisional Ruling Council (NPRC)** military government was courting international support for its program of transition to civilian rule. Jonah, with his UN experience, appeared to be the best person to oversee the elections. Under threat from the rebels, Jonah performed the task of overseeing the elections in 1996 as chairman of the Interim National Electoral Commission. In that same year, after the elections, he was appointed as the UN secretary-general's special envoy to Liberia and later Sierra Leone's permanent representative to the United Nations with full cabinet rank. In 1998, James Jonah was appointed minister of finance, development and economic planning, a position he held until 2001 before retiring and returning to the United States.

JONES, ELDRED DUROSIMI (1925–). Eldred Durosimi Jones was a popular professor of literature at Fourah Bay College and eventually became principal of that college in 1974. He was born in Freetown January 5, 1925, and attended the **CMS Grammar School** and **Fourah Bay College**, before proceeding to England where he read English at Oxford and Durham Universities in England. He returned to Fourah Bay College and joined the english department, becoming successively professor and head of that department from 1964–1974. In 1974, he was appointed principal of Fourah Bay College, a position he held until 1985 when he retired. In the post reconstruction government of President Tejan Kabbah, Eldred Jones was appointed adviser to the president and held that position for the next two years.

Eldred Jones is best known for his work in African literature. His first major work, *Othello's Countrymen: A Study of Africa in the Elizabethan and Jacobean Drama*, published in 1965, won him accolades and established his reputation in the discipline. Even though he lost his eyesight by the 1980s, he continued as editor of the popular journal, *African Literature Today* until the end of the 20th century, ably assisted by his wife Marjorie. He held many fellowships and visiting appointments in Britain, Canada, and the United States. He was a popular socialite in Freetown in his younger days and was well known for being a well-dressed figure.

JONES, ETHELRED NATHANIAL. *See* SANKOH, LAMINA.

JUSU-SHERIFF, SALIA (1929–). A former vice president of the Republic of Sierra Leone, Salia Jusu-Sheriff was one of the leading politicians of the **Sierra Leone People's Party (SLPP)** in the 1970s and joined the one-party regime of Siaka Stevens to become vice president.

Sheriff was born at Jojoima in the Kailahun District on June 1, 1929, the son of an itinerant Mandingo Islamic cleric and a Mende mother. He got his early education at the Bunumbu Central School and at **Fourah Bay College** and later studied accounting at King's College, Durham University, and at Newcastle-on-Tyne. Salia taught at **Bo Government School** before joining the cooperative department in 1949. He returned to this department after he qualified as a chartered accountant in Britain in 1960. Later, with some partners, Jusu-Sheriff set up what became a successful accounting firm in Freetown, known as Sheriff-Clinton. He subsequently went into politics and was elected member of Parliament for Kenema South constituency as a SLPP candidate in 1962 and was then appointed a cabinet minister. He served in various cabinet positions until the advent of the military government of 1967. When **Siaka Stevens** took office in 1968, he appointed Jusu-Sheriff as minister of health in what promised to be a national government but it soon collapsed, and Jusu-Sheriff resigned his cabinet position. By then, he had lost his seat in Parliament in an election petition but regained it in a bye-election for the same constituency of Kenema South. He returned to parliament this time as leader of the SLPP opposition party. Under allegations of high-handed interference in the runup to the elections of 1973, Salia Jusu-Sheriff withdrew his party from the general elections, making it easier for the All People's Congress (APC) to win the elections. With the declaration of a one-party state, Jusu-Sheriff returned to government as an APC member of Parliament and again became minister and vice president to President **Momoh** after 1986. After the overthrow of Momoh by the military, Jusu-Sheriff retired.

JUXON-SMITH, ANDREW TERRENCE (1931–). Andrew Terrence Juxon-Smith headed the **National Reformation Council (NRC)** military junta in Sierra Leone for one year (1967–1968). That position carried with it the added responsibility as brigadier and force commander of the military. Juxon-Smith was educated at the **Methodist Boys High School** in **Freetown** and then joined the Sierra Leone army. He was further trained at the British Military Academy at Sandhurst, England. While he was in England, senior military officers took over the government (March 1967). The officers first invited Ambrose Genda, another military officer who was also then in England, to become head of state. However, suspicious that Genda intended to hand over the government to the party that had won the elections, the military officers quickly rescinded their invitation to Genda and invited Juxon-Smith to become head of the junta and thus head of state. A year later, junior officers of the army who felt they had been ignored by Juxon-Smith's cabal, overthrew him, and **Siaka Stevens** was subsequently made prime minister. Juxon-Smith was detained and was later charged with treason and convicted in 1969. He was pardoned in 1972 and left Sierra Leone to live in the United States.

– K –

KABBA SEI (c. 1840–1908). Kabba Sei was the ruler of the ethnic Mende country of Mando in the region of the Upper Moa River in the last years before the imposition of colonial rule. He is known for his substantial efforts toward peaceful measures for resolving major conflicts.

He was born at the town of Potolu and became ruler with contemporaries such as **Kai Londo**, **Nyagua**, **Makavoray**, and **Mendegla**. Kabba Sei formed a society called "Tukpei," meaning "push ahead," an alliance of neighboring countries and rulers meant as a defensive alliance to secure his own authority. The greatest thorn in his side at the time was a powerful Gbandi chief named Mbawulomeh who, from his base in the Liberian hinterland, was raiding a number of his neighbors including settlements under **Kai Londo**'s rule. Kabba Sei joined with Kai Londo to ward off this menace, but Mbwalomeh was only put to flight, not eliminated. Kabba Sei used his good offices and the Tukpei foundation to avert a major conflict between Kai Londo and Mendegla. He invited both of these powerful leaders to Potolu and resolved the misunderstanding between them. In 1890, Kabba Sei signed a treaty of friendship for his region with T. J. Alldridge, who was then a traveling commissioner representing the colonial government in Sierra Leone, which was by now interested in controlling the entire Sierra Leone hinterland and was beginning to intervene in conflicts in the interior.

When Mbawulomeh resurfaced in 1896 and raided towns in Luawa under Kai Londo's successor **Fa Bundeh**, the British intervened when Fa Bundeh, who was in treaty with them, protested. Kabba Sei was somehow implicated and the British interpreted Fa Bundeh's report to mean that Kabba Sei was siding with Mbawulomeh.

The British sent a force to the area and attacked and destroyed Kabba Sei's chief town. Kabba Sei fled but was captured and held a political prisoner in **Freetown** in spite of his protestations of innocence. His domain was divided between **Nyagua** and Fa Bundeh. Kabba Sei was released early in 1898 after promising not to be involved in any further troubles in the interior. A few weeks later, the 1898 rebellion broke out through the south of Sierra Leone. Because of his previous experiences, Kabba Sei would not join the other local rulers against the British but helped the British sustain the garrison at Panguma. He was confirmed as paramount chief of Mando after the rebellion as a reward for his help to the British.

KABBAH, AHMED TEJAN (1932–). Ahmed Tejan-Kabbah was president of Sierra Leone during the "rebel war," the civil war that lasted from 1991 to 2001.

Tejan-Kabbah was born in Pendembu February 19, 1932, and was educated at the **St. Edwards Secondary School** before proceeding to Britain where he obtained a B.A. degree and qualified as a lawyer in Grays Inn. He returned to Sierra Leone and joined the colonial civil service in 1959, becoming district commissioner and then permanent secretary in the postindependence government until 1969. After the defeat of the **Sierra Leone People's Party (SLPP)** government, where he was well favored, and the start of the military regime of the (**National Reformation Council** (**NRC**), Tejan-Kabbah spent a year in private law practice before taking the position of deputy chief of the West African Division, UNDP in New York in 1971. He worked with this UN agency until 1992, seeing service in different countries in Africa in the process.

Upon his return to Sierra Leone, Tejan-Kabbah was appointed chairman of the National Advisory Council to the military government of the **National Provisional Ruling Council (NPRC)** in 1992, a position he held until 1994. He went into active politics and was nominated as the SLPP's presidential candidate for the general elections set up by the NPRC in 1996. He was elected president after and was reelected again in 2002, having been popularly credited with bringing peace to Sierra Leone after the civil war.

KABBA, NFAGI OMAR. A Sierra Leonean, Kabba was successively managing director of the, Freetown Travel Agencies, a successful company that he founded, director of Ocean Assurance, chairman of Nationwide Insurance Brokers, and Honorary Consul for Malagassy Republic in Sierra Leone in the 1970s and 1980s.

KAIKAI, MOMOH (c. 1812–c. 1900). Momoh Kaikai was one of the most prominent rulers in the southern interior of Sierra Leone around the present Pujehun district. Although he initially demonstrated dissatisfaction with the protectorate declaration, he later staunchly supported the British, earning a medal and chain from the British, then considered a high honor.

Momoh Kaikai was paternally of Fula extraction and his mother was Mende. He built a strong political system centered on Bandajuma about the mid-19th century and, ably supported by his younger brother, **Momoh Jah**, consolidated his rule, dominating what later became the Pujehun District by the 1870s. By the 1880s, Pujehun town had become his headquarters. From there, Momoh Kaikai signed a treaty of friendship with the British in 1887 and enthusiastically supported British policy of road building and the establishment of the Frontier Police in the interior.

When the protectorate was declared in 1896, Momoh Kaikai and other neighboring rulers expressed dissatisfaction with the loss of sovereignty implied by some of the clauses of the protectorate ordinance. Together they drafted and sent a letter to the British governor. Being further disenchanted by the abrupt verbal reply, Kaikai joined other leaders in a delegation to see the governor. During their meeting, the governor emphasized that dire consequences would result for anyone who refused to pay the house tax, the main source of contention. In fact the colonial government was extremely suspicious of Momoh Kaikai's influence in this matter, and soon afterward, the British district commissioner in Bandajuma seized Momoh Kaikai's cattle. When Momoh Kaikai protested, the governor justified Hood's action on the grounds that Kaikai was suspected of not wanting to pay the house tax.

Weighing his options, Momoh Kaikai then decided to give open support to the British and assisted with local levies in putting down the 1898 rebellion. The British rewarded his loyalty, and his town became the headquarters of the Bandajuma District, later the Pujehun District. He was then about ninety years old; he died about 1900.

KAI LONDO (c. 1845–1896). Kai Londo was a notable ruler who inherited and later created a prominent state centered on Luawa in the Kailahun District in eastern Sierra Leone. His influence extended beyond the area of his authority, and he is remembered with respect in Sierra Leone history.

He was born at Komalu in Luawa to Dowii Komei, a warrior of repute. During the 1880s, Kai Londo was involved in an intricate network of conflicts involving Makavoray, Benya, and the warrior **Ndawa**. In the course of these conflicts, a major test of skill in warfare occurred in a conflict between Kai Londo and Ndawa in which the latter was defeated and promised to trouble Luawa no more. His wars of expansion brought much of the neighboring territories of the ethnic Kissi and Gbandi under Ndawa's control and with it came wealth in terms of booty and prisoners of war.

In 1890, the British traveling commissioner, T. J. Alldridge, signed a treaty of friendship with Kai Londo and was impressed by his qualities of leadership. Alldridge described Kai Londo as "a man of small stature but large intelligence, beloved by the people for miles around who used to speak of him . . . as a father . . . a chief who was never spoken of except in the highest terms."

KAI SAMBA I (1902–1956). Paramount chief of Nongowa chiefdom (1942–56), he was chiefly responsible for founding modern-day Kenema town. Kai Samba was also a member of the Legislative Council from 1948–1951. His original name was Alpha Lalugba Kalei Samba, and he assumed the title of Kai Samba upon election as paramount chief in 1942. Unlike many paramount chiefs of his time, Kai Samba had a high school education at the **Bo Government School** and had worked in the colonial civil service from 1924 to 1942. When **District Councils** were started in 1946, Kai Samba was deputy president of the Kenema District Council and was prominent in **District Council** matters nationally. He was also a member of the **Protectorate Assembly**, which advised the governor on protectorate affairs. He is most remembered for developing Kenema into a thriving town, encouraging cash crop production and pushing for the development of the forest industries, which became prominent in Kenema. He improved the sanitation and road system of Kenema, saw to the building of a park near the railway station and the expansion of the Kenema dispensary into a hospital with a full-time medical officer. Kai Samba also promoted the building of the Kenema government secondary school in 1952 and personally provided building materials to expedite the construction.

KAI SAMBA, KUTUBU, I. (1931–). Kutubu Ibrahim Kai Samba was a lawyer and politician who made history by refusing to be bought by the **Sierra Leone People's Party (SLPP)** after he won the 1967 general elections as an independent candidate for Kenema Central.

Kai Samba was the son of paramount chief **Kai Samba I** and was born at Pendembu in the Kailahun District on March 6, 1931. His early education was at **Bo Government School** and later at **Fourah Bay College** and King's College of Durham University and Newcastle. He was called to the Bar at Gray's Inn. First elected to Parliament in 1962, Kutubu was appointed a cabinet minister of agriculture and natural resources in 1964. In the 1967 elections, the SLPP government of Albert Margai was narrowly defeated. Margai and his supporters delayed the announcement of the final results while putting pressure on four independent candidates, including Kutubu, to declare for the SLPP so that that party could declare a victory. Kutubu Kai Samba, L. A. M. Brewah, J. B. Francis, and **P. J. Williams**, the four independents, wrote a joint letter to the governor general declaring that they wished to remain independent and would only support the SLPP if **Albert Margai** resigned as prime minister and leader of the party.

Kutubu Kai Samba remained in Parliament as a member of the opposition SLPP after the military interregnum and the **All People's Congress (APC)** government of **Siaka Stevens**. When the SLPP withdrew from the general elections in 1973 on charges of illegal practices by the APC government, Kai Samba returned to his private practice.

KALLON, FORAY. *See* VA FORAY SASABLA.

KAMA, MANSA [KING]. Dominant Koranko leader of the 16th century, his real name is believed to be Yira, but because he was a great hunter and killed many elephants, he was called "Kama" meaning "elephant." He belonged to the Kargbo clan, another name for the ruling Keita clan among the Mandinka peoples. Near the end of the 16th century, Mansa Kama moved into the Sierra Leone hinterland from Sankaran country in Guinea in the company of the *alfa* (Islamic religious leader) of the Sesay clan. For the first part of his journey, he was with Mansa Morifing, the leader of the first Koranko migrants, and stayed with him at Morifindugu before moving southward with Morifing's blessings. His next stop was close to the Rokel River where he founded a settlement, Kamadugu, named after him. This is now part of Sengbe chiefdom.

By the end of the 16th century, Mansa Kama had fought his way from Kamadugu to the coast. He established a new base at Rowala, the center of Kholifa country, and became ruler of the territory, which remained in Koranko hands until it was taken over by the Temne probably sometime in the 19th century. He is said to have returned periodically to Kamadugu, his original country, where he had left his son, Momori Kalko, as ruler. The oldest town in Kamadugu was called Kalkoya after Kalko and still bears that name. Mansa Kama, (*mansa* being the title for "king") is still remembered in both Koranko and Temne traditions as the founding father of the Kholifa and Kamadugu countries.

KAMAJOR. The Kamajor was the largest segment of the **Civil Defense Force (CDF)**, a community-based organization of combatants formed with the support of the Sierra Leone government to effectively prosecute the rebel war. The Kamajor were traditional hunters, mostly from the south and east of Sierra Leone who were organized in local militia units. Although the Kamajor helped the regular army prosecute the war, they have been blamed for a number of atrocities throughout the country. When the **Special Court** convened in 2003, one of the first to be indicted and arrested was **Hinga Norman**, the former head of the Civil Defense Force, also regarded as head of the Kamajor. Until his arrest, Hinga Norman was minister of internal affairs in the government of **President Tejan Kabbah**. Also arrested sometime later were Allieu Kondewa, the former 'high priest and initiator' of the Kamajor, and Moinina Fofana, the former director of war of the CDF. These arrests led to rumors reported in the local press of Kamajor mobilization to defend their interests, since these three men, particularly the latter two, were seen as the leaders of the Kamajor. It was reported that around Christmas of 2003, an effort was made by Kamajor elements to assault the Special Court facility where these men were being held without bond.

While President Kabbah reported to the United Nations Security Council in June 2003 that the Kamajor had been disbanded, investigations indicated that, unlike the other CDF units, the Kamajor retained their command structure and continued to regard themselves as a distinct group, offering to help the government with security matters, for example, to search the Gola Forest for the fugitive **Johnny Paul Koroma**. Although the government has not as yet accepted any Kamajor offers for security assistance, the Kamajor, as late as 2004, was still considered a potent force in Sierra Leone. The Kamajor, with their base close to the Liberian border, had, since April 2000, known close links with the well-armed rebel fighters of the movement called LURD (Liberians United for Reconciliation and Democracy) in Liberia and this was a source of concern for the Sierra Leone government. The government initiated a two-phase community arms-collection program, one from December 2001 to March 2002 and another in November, 2002), amid fears that most of the Kamajor arms would remain in civilian hands.

KAMARA, BAMBAY. Bambay Kamara was inspector-general of the Sierra Leone Police Force under President **Joseph Saidu Momoh**. He was reportedly influential and had the ear of the president. After President Momoh was overthrown, Bambay Kamara was arrested and charged with treason for allegedly planning a coup. He was summarily tried and executed in December 1992.

KAMARA-TAYLOR, CHRISTIAN ALUSINE (1917–1985). Kamara-Taylor became prime minister of Sierra Leone in 1975 and was second vice president until his death in 1985. Popularly known as "C. A.," he was born June 3, 1917, at Kafanta in the Tonko-Limba chiefdom of the Kambia District and was educated at the **Methodist Boys High School** and the London School of Accountancy, where he earned a diploma in business methods. He was initially employed at the Sierra Leone Development Company as a clerk and later joined the Sierra Leone regiment, rising to the rank of sergeant and seeing service in Burma during World War II.

C. A. entered politics in the early 1960s, joining with **Siaka Stevens** in forming the **All People's Congress (APC)** party. He became the first secretary general and held that position for 15 years. He was elected to Parliament on an APC ticket to represent the Kambia East Constituency in 1962 and was successively reelected to Parliament until his death. His first cabinet position came when **Siaka Stevens** became prime minister in 1968 when he assumed the portfolio of lands mines and labour. He later became minister of finance and in 1975 became prime minister and minister of the interior. Following the institution of the one-party government, Kamara-Taylor became second vice president and remained so until his death in 1978.

KAMBIA. The Kambia District is named after its chief town of Kambia, located in the Magbema chiefdom. Being close to the Temne-

Soso frontier, identifiable with Sierra Leone's northeastern borders with the Republic of Guinea, Kambia became a battleground for Soso and Temne interests as each attempted to establish control over the town and region during the 18th and 19th centuries. These conflicting interests were reconciled, and **Soso** and **Temne** have lived together in Kambia and surrounding towns and villages and have influenced each other culturally.

KANDE BURE (1908–). Kande Bure was a popular political figure of the 1970s who became a cabinet minister and acted as president on several occasions. He was born Saidu Bai Kamara in 1908 at Mange Bure in what is now the Port Loko District in the Northern Province. While acquiring primary education at the African Methodist Episcopal (AME) school in Mange, he also learned Arabic from an Arabic scholar named Santigi Rembu. On moving to **Freetown** in 1920, he attended the **Methodist Boys High School** and later qualified as a teacher. He taught at several primary schools in Freetown, including the Madrassa Islamia school.

Kande Bure left the teaching vocation in 1945 and was elected "tribal headman" for the Temne community in Freetown, a position recognized by the colonial government. It was apparently at this stage that the name Kande Bure became popular. He became very active in programs and organizations meant to help ethnic Temne people in Freetown. This included setting up friendly societies, such as the *Ambas Geda* and in the building of mosques. His activities led him into national politics, and he joined the **Sierra Leone Organization Society (SOS)** formed by educated protectorate elements and thus became part of the newly formed **Sierra Leone People's Party (SLPP)**. He contested and won a seat in the parliamentary elections in 1957 and was appointed minister of works and housing. After the 1962 elections, Kande Bure became minister of transport and communications and on several occasions acted as prime minister.

KANFORI (14TH CENTURY). Domin Konteh Kanfori was the leader of the earliest wave of **Soso** migrants into the area of present-day Sierra Leone. After the defeat of the Soso by Sundiata in the 13th century, groups of Soso fled eastward toward the coast. One large group, led by Kanfori, eventually reached the coastal area around Sierra Leone and

Guinea, the home of the Baga people. After a series of clashes with the Baga, both groups accommodated to living together. By the time of Kanfori's death, the Soso were firmly established in this area, and he was succeeded by his son, Manga Kombeh Balla, during whose rule the first Portuguese traders came into contact with the Soso.

KAREFA-SMART, JOHN (1915–). John Karefa-Smart is better known in Sierra Leone politics than in medicine, even though he excelled as a medical doctor of international repute. He was born June 17, 1915, at Rotifunk in the Bumpe chiefdom, present Moyamba District. He attended the EUB primary school at Rotifunk, the Albert Academy in **Freetown**, and took a B.A. at Fourah Bay College. His further education in medicine took him to Otterbein College and Harvard University in the United States, and McGill University in Canada. He acquired several medical degrees and certifications. He served as medical officer in the Royal Canadian Army during World War II and later as missionary doctor at Rotifunk hospital. He also saw service as regional medical officer for the World Health Organization West Africa Region from 1951–1954 and served in Monrovia, Lagos, and Brazaville. Karefa-Smart taught briefly at Ibadan University College where he was also dean of the medical school.

However, it was in politics that he blossomed. He was a founding member of the **Sierra Leone Organization Society** and so became a founding member of the **Sierra Leone People's Party (SLPP)**. He was first elected to the Sierra Leone House of Representatives in May 1957 to represent the Tonkolili West Constituency. In the cabinet that followed, he was appointed minister of lands, mines, and labor with special responsibilities for defense. He also became minister of lands and surveys, and later minister of external affairs.

At the death of Prime Minister **Milton Margai** in 1964, Karefa-Smart, who aspired to the position of prime minister, opposed as unconstitutional the appointment of **Albert Margai** to become prime minister. He, along with three others, was thus dropped from Albert Margai's newly appointed cabinet. He then returned to his medical career, serving as assistant director-general of the World Health Organization from 1965–1970. Karefa-Smart returned to Sierra Leone soon after **Siaka Stevens** was made prime minister in 1969, where he teamed up with some members of Siaka Stevens' cabinet who had recently resigned in September 1970 to form a new party, the **United Democratic Party (UDP)**. The party was quickly banned by Siaka Stevens, and its leaders, including Karefa-Smart, were arrested and detained. Upon his release in 1971, Karefa-Smart was appointed visiting professor of international public health at Harvard. He served as medical director of the Roxbury Comprehensive Community Health Center in Boston from 1975–1980 and followed this up with a professorship at the Harvard University medical school from 1980–1983.

His departure from Sierra Leone was, however, not the end of his political career. Karefa-Smart returned to politics in 1996, forming his own political party, the **United National People's Party (UNPP)** to contest the presidency. In the first round election for the presidency, he was the leading contender, polling 23 percent of the votes as against Tejan **Kabbah's** 36 percent. In the run-off a month later, he gained 43 percent of the vote, but his opponent gained 60 percent. Since his UNPP party had gained the second largest number of seats (17) in the elections, Karefa-Smart became the leader of the opposition in the Legislature and remained so until 2002 when he was suspended from Parliament. As leader of the UNPP, he again sought and lost the presidency in the general elections of 2002. He eventually returned to the United States where he continues to live.

KARIMU (c. 1835–1892). Karimu was a powerful **Soso** warrior leader in northwestern Sierra Leone who waged continuous war with the Limba to defend and extend his jurisdiction at the height of the French and British quest to take over this part of Africa. Karimu managed to get support alternately from the British and French until the end of his life. Karimu had been trained as a warrior and had succeeded his father, Sori Gbay, as ruler of Samaya after the latter was captured and killed by Samori's sofas in 1885. Karimu then proceeded to build a large force largely from runaway servile labor and instituted a reign of terror in the region astride the northwestern border between Sierra Leone and Guinea. He conquered and controlled a number of Tonko **Limba** towns and several Soso towns.

Since the British suspected that Karimu had been parleying with the French, a mission headed by **J. C. E. Parkes** was sent to Karimu in 1889. Karimu succeeded in evading Parkes who then used his own forces to burn down a settlement of Kolonkoray, one of Karimu's strongholds. Karimu himself continued to evade British pursuit by moving into French territory across the ill-defined boundary. A coalition of local rulers including **Bai Bureh** of Kasseh, Brima Sanda of Sanda Loko, **Bomboh Lahai** of Tonko Limba, and **Fomgboe** of Lower Loko failed to dislodge Karimu from his fortress of Laminaya in 1890. It took three British expeditions to dislodge Karimu's forces from the towns of Tambi and Kukuna where they had dug in. By 1891, Karimu had moved deeper into French territory and reports indicate that by October of 1892 he was dead.

KARIMU, JOHN AROUNA. John Karimu was lecturer in the geography department of **Fourah Bay College** in the 1980s after receiving his Ph.D. in Britain. He worked with the United Nations until he was invited by the **National Provisional Ruling Council (NPRC)** government to become minister of trade in 1992. He later held the portfolio of finance. When the NPRC decided on elections for 1996, John Karimu formed his own political party, the **National Unity Party**, and became a candidate for the presidency for his party. He lost the bid, but his party won the required 5 percent of the overall vote to qualify him to sit in Parliament as party leader. In the compromise following the elections, John Karimu accepted a cabinet position in the government of **President Ahmad Tejan Kabbah**. In 2003, he was appointed the commissioner-general of the newly established National Revenue Authority.

KAYAMBA (MID-19TH CENTURY). A famous Mende warrior who founded the town of **Moyamba**, which became the center of the Kayamba chiefdom in the Moyamba District. It is said that a soothsayer, Solonto of Gbangbama (Moyamba District), prophesied to Kayamba that he would found a settlement between two hills by a river with many tributaries. There, he was told, his fortune would lie. One day during his wanderings with his warriors and family, some of his men, who had been out hunting, came back to tell him that they had discovered a river with six tributaries between two hills. This is where Kayamba finally settled with his following and this became Moyamba, which was later incorporated into the Kpaa **Mende** state.

KEMOKO BILALI (LATE 19TH CENTURY). Bilali became one of the chief lieutenants of **Samori Toure**, the Mandinka empire builder in Upper Guinea. As governor of Samori's territories in northern Sierra Leone, Bilali played an important part in negotiations with the British over control of trade routes to **Freetown**. Bilali was a **Mandinka** from Torong, now in the Republic of Guinea. He is said to have been captured by Samori in 1875 while still a child and won his master's confidence. During Samori's siege of a fortress town named Sikasso in upper Ivory Coast in the 1880s, Bilali proved himself an outstanding soldier and was made a leading general. Subsequently, a rebellion broke out in the southern area of Samori's empire, including northern Sierra Leone. Abandoning the fruitless siege, Samori set about the reconquest of his empire and early in 1890 sent Kemoko Bilali at the head of a contingent to subdue northern Sierra Leone. Within a few months Bilali had accomplished this mission and became governor of this region, which included parts of Soso country north of Kambia, the former Solima state of Solimana, and of large areas of Koranko country in present-day Koinadugu District.

This was an area of great importance to Samori, as the trade routes to Freetown, his main source of arms, passed through this country. Bilali's major task as governor was to secure these routes, a matter that put him in direct communication with local rulers in the area, as well as with the colonial administration in Sierra Leone. The latter, keenly interested in trade with the north, were also at this point in imperial expansion and were very concerned with the activities of the French, who were progressively annexing parts of Samori's empire and claiming them by right of conquest. This alarmed the British since it meant that the Sierra Leone colony would be hemmed in by French control. Negotiations between the British administration and Bilali were therefore stepped up in a bid to persuade him to give up areas west of the upper Niger, which they wished to claim. Bilali had to walk a tight rope between the British authorities who controlled areas closer to the coast and the local rulers who actually stood along the trade routes he was supposed to protect.

In 1891, hostilities broke out between Sayo, the ruler of Kaliere in northeast Sierra Leone and Bilali. Sayo, who had once been a **sofa** but had broken with these followers of Samori over a dispute involving his father, Isa, attacked his former allies and refused to join Bilali when invited to do so. Bilali declared that he would attack Kaliere to punish Sayo, but the British backed Sayo in his refusal to join Bilali on the strength of an 1885 agreement they had made with Samori. However, Kaliere was within Samori's domain and Bilali stood his ground. When one of Bilali's lieutenants advanced toward Kaliere, threatening to attack, Sayo fled and Bilali ordered his soldiers to pursue him. Bilali apparently called off the pursuit and ordered the detachment to join his master Samori farther in the interior.

Nothing further is known of Bilali after this episode.

KENEMA. The town of Kenema is the headquarters of the Nongowa chiefdom. It is also the chief town in the Kenema District in the Eastern Province of Sierra Leone. The dominant ethnic group in Kenema is **Mende**. Since this town is in the heart of the diamond-mining region, Kenema has seen some of the fastest growth in this region in the past four decades. It is now a thriving town with a cosmopolitan population, including a middle class closely tied to the mining sector. Kenema is among the six largest towns in Sierra Leone. Its expansion was stifled somewhat by the civil war and the imposition of rebel control in the area. Diamond mining has recovered and the diamond buying offices for the region are located in Kenema.

KISIMI KAMARA (c. 1890–1962). Noted for the invention of the Mende writing script, the *KiKaKu,* Kisimi was born about 1890 at Vaama in the Barri chiefdom, Pujehun District. He studied Arabic extensively and is reported to have received the idea of the script for KiKaKu from a dream. The KiKaKu writing has some relationship to Arabic and is written from right to left, as is Arabic. The Mende script gained currency as it was adopted by adults for everyday use and schools were opened to teach KiKaKu. By the 1940s, with colonial education adopting the writing of the **Mende** language in the Latin alphabet, the Mende script began to lose its significance. However, it is still remembered as one of the local inventions of writing in Africa.

KISSI. The Kissi ethnic group is found predominantly in four Kissi chiefdoms in the Kailahun District of eastern Sierra Leone. These are the Kissi Kama, Kissi Teng, Kissi Tongi, and Luawa chiefdoms. The Kissi are bifurcated by the political boundaries where Sierra Leone,

Liberia, and Guinea intersect. There are many more Kissi in Guinea and Liberia. The Kissi are one of the oldest ethnic groups in Sierra Leone, along with the **Bullom**, **Krim**, and **Gola**. Subsequent migrations of numerically more powerful groups have shifted the early groups around so that their current location is not matched by their early history.

One aspect of Kissi culture that became attractive to foreigners was the fertility dolls called "**nomoli**" that the Kissi fashioned out of steatite rocks. This was part of Kissi ritual, and the dolls, buried in the farm fields, were believed to be capable of bringing fertility to the land as well as to humans.

KOINADUGU. Koinadugu used to be a small town in the district of the same name and was the colonial rulers' headquarters town for the extreme northeastern region of Sierra Leone. Thus the region was called the Koinadugu District. The headquarters of that district moved to the town of Falaba and finally to the current town of Kabala. However, the district retained the name of Koinadugu, but the center from which it derived its name is now a miniscule village.

KNIGHT, CHARLES (c. 1799–1879). Charles Knight was an ethnic Ibo liberated African who became the first African to be appointed as general superintendent of the Wesleyan Methodist Mission in Sierra Leone. After being liberated in **Freetown**, Knight was sent to the new recaptive village of Gloucester near Freetown where he attended primary school. He taught primary school and was selected for teacher training in England, sponsored by the English Quakers. After a six-month period in England, cut short by illness, Knight came back to Freetown and served as an assistant missionary for four years before being ordained a full minister in 1848. After serving in a few parishes, he became head of the theological and educational institution that trained people for church work and for teaching in the Wesleyan schools. These were the early beginnings of formal training above the primary level.

Working with **John Ezzidio**, a prominent businessman and churchman, Knight made elaborate plans for the construction of the Wesley Church in **Freetown** and for the renovation of many other churches in the city. He hoped that this building program would draw back the Wesleyan Mission members who had left because of the poor buildings that housed the Wesleyan churches. Knight was made acting general superintendent of the Wesleyan Mission in Sierra Leone in 1861. A stormy decade followed the appointment of Benjamin Tregaskis as head of the mission in Sierra Leone in 1864, and Tregaskis had so much trouble with his African subordinates for whom he showed much contempt that he was prevailed upon to give up the position and return to England. Knight replaced him in 1874.

Knight's tenure was marked by attempts by European clergy in the mission in Sierra Leone, as well as Aku (Yoruba) liberated African clergymen, to discredit him. Tregaskis returned to Sierra Leone and joined in the affray. But Knight was able to weather all of these attacks and sustained his position. He devoted much attention to improving the standard of education in the mission schools as well as in his Christian ministry. A system of school inspection and improved conditions for teachers were implemented during his tenure. He planned to extend the Wesleyan work outside Freetown and sent a catechist to **Bonthe Sherbro**. This work was, however, cut short when Knight became ill late in 1877 and died December 13, 1879.

KONDI. The *kondi* is a musical instrument found among the ethnic **Temne**, **Limba**, and **Loko** in Sierra Leone. Among the Limba, it is also called the *kututen.* It is a metal box with a number of metal strips fixed on top of it, the longest being in the center and the others tapering out on both sides with measured regularity. The box also has an extension piece facing away from the player, and this piece is threaded with small metal wires. The player holds the box between his body and his hands and, with his thumbs, plucks the strips that point away from him. As he does this he shakes the box up and down to obtain a rattle from the threaded wires and small pebbles inside the box. This provides some rhythm for the player/singer.

KONKO GBAKU (c. 1870–1911). Konko Gbaku was probably quite young when he became the *bombo lahai* (sometimes rendered *bombolai*) or ruler of the Tonko **Limba** people. He succeeded Keleha Horo, the former *bombo lahai,* in 1884, at a time when the British in the Sierra Leone colony were beginning to recognize these interior rulers, styling them as paramount chiefs. Much of Konko Gbaku's rule was consumed by a prolonged war with the Soso, and he is therefore best remembered in Tonko Limba history for his efforts to repulse **Karimu** of Samaya, a powerful ruler in the neighboring ethnic Soso kingdom.

Konko Gbaku's rule witnessed an unprecedented spread of European influence among the Tonko Limba. The Wesleyan Methodists established a mission station at Forecaria, then the capital of Tonko Limba. In October 1889, Konko Gbaku signed a treaty with the British who were intent on forestalling expanding French influence in this area that became the boundary between what was the French colony of Guinea and the British holding in Sierra Leone. Konko Gbaku tried to enlist the support of the British in the struggle against Karimu of Samaya. Karimu was seeking revenge in an age-old dispute that had started a generation earlier when a Soso slave named **Bilali** escaped from his territory and took refuge with his followers in Tonko Limba. Bilali's fortress in Tonko Limba thus became a home for displaced persons fleeing Soso territory. Karimu continued the tradition of frequent clashes between the Tonko Limba and the Soso of Samaya over this issue of getting their slaves back. In his attempts to withstand Karimu's onslaughts, Konko Gbaku enlisted the support of neighboring Temne, Loko, and other Limba rulers without scoring any decisive victory against Karimu.

The British colonial authorities in Sierra Leone began to side with Konko Gbaku for fear that the French would use this issue to support the **Soso** and thus expand their influence in the area. Two attempts made by British-led forces to dislodge Karimu from his stronghold at the town of Tambi were unsuccessful. A third and more forceful attempt enlisted the support of Bai Bureh and succeeded in breaking the resistance at Tambi in 1892. Konko Gbaku then turned his attention to the reconstruction of his war-ravaged territory, seeking the assistance of the Wesleyan missions and the British. The British declaration of the protectorate soon followed, and Konko Gbaku, weakened by the Karimu problems, refrained from participating in the ensuing rebellion of the other rulers against the imposition of British colonial rule. He sent statements of support and friendship to the British colonial administration, which, in later years, gave him favorable decisions in many boundary disputes with neighboring rulers.

Though an active supporter of the Wesleyan mission, it is doubtful whether Konko Gbaku ever turned Christian. He had many wives, as tradition demanded, and fulfilled the traditional rituals according to oral sources. He died in 1911 after a 25-year reign.

KONO. The Kono and the **Vai** are believed to be branches of the same splinter group from the main Mande family that moved southward into the interior of Sierra Leone, separated at one point from each other. It is believed that those who stayed in the interior came to be called Kono because those who ventured farther south told those left behind, "ku-kono," which in their language meant "wait for us (here)." By the early 16th century, the Kono were largely in their present location. The Kono people became better known by the 20th century with the discovery of diamonds in the district bearing their name. Part of Kono effort since the mid-20th century has been to secure for the Kono people as much benefit as possible from the diamonds. However, the quest for diamonds led to much devastation of Kono country during the civil war of the 1990s. The main towns of Mortema, Koidu, Yengema were devastated. Much rebuilding is going on at present.

KORANKO. An ethnic group found in northeastern Sierra Leone in the Koinadugu District, Koranko is a branch of the main **Mande** peoples; their language is mutually intelligible with **Mandinka**, nearest to the parent language in the Mande language family. The Koranko represent a breakaway branch of the Mande (**Mali**) empire that migrated southwest from Mande and spread along parts of the Republic of Guinea and across that region into what became Sierra Leone. This movement must have started in the 15th century, as evidence of Koranko presence in the area of present day Sierra Leone dates to the early 16th century.

The dominant Koranko clan historically is the Mara.

KOROMA, ABU AIAH (1928–2005). Prominent lawyer and political luminary in Sierra Leone, Abu Koroma was born in the Kono District November 26, 1928. He was educated at the **Bo Government School**, **Fourah Bay College**, the University of London and New York University where he took the LL.M. degree. He started private practice on his return to Sierra Leone in 1958 and was a police magistrate from

1961–1964. He was personal assistant to the attorney-general from 1965–68 and in the latter year was appointed attorney general. During the 1970s and 1980s, Abu Koroma moved from active politics and became assistant mines general manager in 1971 in the **National Diamond Mining Company (NDMC)**. He became managing director of the National Diamond Mining Company in 1987.

When political party activity was resumed after military rule in the 1990s, Abu Koroma returned to active politics. In 1995, he became interim leader of the **Democratic Center Party (DCP)**. Following the 1996 general elections, leaders of all political parties were wooed by the **Sierra Leone People's Party (LPP)** leader, **President Tejan Kabbah**, and Abu Koroma was given the post of minister of parliamentary and political affairs. He was reappointed to that position for the period 1998–2002.

KOROMA, JOHNNY PAUL (1969–?). Johnny Paul Koroma was a Sandhurst-trained soldier in the Sierra Leone army who rose to the rank of major. He was one of the soldiers in the frontline during the first military incursions of the rebels into Sierra Leone in 1991, commanding the battalion attached to the Rutile Mines at Mokanji. In 1996, Johnny Paul Koroma was jailed for allegedly plotting a military coup against the government of **Ahmed Tejan Kabbah**. In May 1997, soldiers of the Sierra Leone army staged a coup that removed Kabbah from office. The prisons were opened during the coup, and Johnny Paul Koroma was released and was invited to become the new head of the military junta called the **Armed Forces Revolutionary Council (AFRC)**. The AFRC government, which ruled conjointly with the **Revolutionary United Front (RUF)**, was removed by the **Economic Community Cease-Fire Monitoring Group (ECOMOG)** forces led by the Nigerians in February 1998 and the Kabbah government was reinstated. Johnny Paul Koroma then moved into the provinces of Sierra Leone where he spent a year and a half with the RUF forces prosecuting the war against the reinstated Kabbah government.

With the end of the rebel war in 2001, Koroma was incorporated into the Sierra Leone government as chairman of the government's Commission for the Consolidation of Peace. In the gencral elections of 2002, he was an unsuccessful candidate for the presidency as leader of his Peace and Liberation Party. However, he polled three percent of the total votes cast. Accused of an attempted coup later that year, Johnny Paul Koroma was nowhere to be found and rumors suggest he may have been killed by RUF forces.

KOROMA, SALIA (1903–). Salia Koroma was a popular entertainer, playing the accordion, and entertained Sierra Leoneans with his musical compositions for a number of years.

He was born in Segbwema from parents who had settled there from Kpaa **Mende** country. His father was an accomplished traveling musician who played the accordion, and Salia spent his early years with his mother at Segbwema. He discontinued his Western education at the early age of nine, keen on learning to play the accordion. His father had insisted that his son Salia should learn to play this instrument and promised to place a curse on him if he did not. This promise was not taken lightly in Salia's world and so he went in search of his father, locating him at the town of Boajibu in the Sembaru chiefdom. Instead of sending him back to school, which was Salia's desire, his father gave him an accordion and insisted that he learn how to play it. However, he himself did not teach Salia to play the instrument but left this to his apprentices. Salia struggled through on his own and eventually learned to play the accordion. In the process, he destroyed a number of these instruments, which were as frequently replaced by his father.

As Salia perfected his skill with the accordion, he began to gain a reputation first among his own Mende people in whose language he sang and later throughout Sierra Leone. He traveled extensively, entertaining traditional rulers and people with his stories and songs. This made him an honored guest of many paramount chiefs, most notably that of Chief Albert Caulker of Rotifunk. After staying in Rotifunk for a few years, he moved to Moyamba, where he was entertainer for **Julius Gulama**, the chief there.

Salia's travels eventually took him to **Freetown**, where he joined the Sierra Leone Police Force, bearing the number 377, which he remembered well into his old age. This did not interfere with his music, which ultimately led him to leave the police force. Salia composed hundreds of songs in Mende and sang these in varied occasions in different parts of the country. He became a popular fixture with the

Sierra Leone Broadcasting Service and "Salia and his accordion" became a household phrase. His songs were patronized by presidents of Sierra Leone, whom he was always called upon to entertain.

KOROMA, SORIE IBRAHIM (1930–1998?). Born in Port Loko, Maforki chiefdom in the Port **Loko** District, S. I. Koroma rose to become prime minister and first vice president in the 1970s. He attended the **Bo Government School** and worked in the Government Cooperative Department from 1951 to 1958. During that service, he attended a course at the Cooperative College in Ibadan, Nigeria. In 1958, S. I., as he was popularly known, resigned from government service to start private business, becoming also secretary-general to the Sierra Leone Motor Transport Union.

S. I. Koroma entered politics when he became one of the founders of the **All People's Congress (APC)** in 1960. He then assumed the position of the first National Propaganda and Organizing Secretary of the party. He won election to Parliament in 1962 as APC representative for Freetown Central One Constituency and remained in Parliament until 1986. In 1968, he got his first cabinet position in trade and industry and then in 1975 was made vice president and minister of finance. Following the establishment of a one-party state in 1978, he became first vice president.

Often called by the nickname "*agba'satani*" ("the viciously powerful big man"), S. I. Koroma seemed to have acquired a reputation for thuggery as he led the dreaded APC youth wing. When **Siaka Stevens** decided to retire in 1986, S. I. Koroma retired from politics along with his mentor. He lived a private life until his death.

KOSO-THOMAS, KOSONIKE (1932–). Koso-Thomas was a successful businessman and became vice chancellor of the University of Sierra Leone. He was educated at the **Prince of Wales Secondary School** and received his Ph.D. in civil engineering at St. Andrews University in England. He returned to Sierra Leone to teach at **Fourah Bay College**, where he was instrumental in setting up the faculty of engineering and became its first dean. He was well known as a civil engineer and published several papers. He was appointed vice chancellor of the **University of Sierra Leone** in 1984 and retired from that position in 1992. By 1970, Koso-Thomas had set up what became a thriving consultancy firm named Techsult. He continued this company after his retirement from the university, expanding the Techsult agency to other countries in Africa. He also served on several public boards and was chairman of the board of the Aureol tobacco company.

KPAA MENDE. See **Mende** for Kpaa Mende origins. The Kpaa Mende territory marks the frontier between Mendeland and Temne territory. It is centered around the town of Taiama in the Kori chiefdom of the **Bo** District and parts of Moyamba District. The Kpaa Mende developed the **Wunde** society, which became a military as well as a regulatory cultural institution, apparently concerned with defending this frontier.

KPOKPO. Intricately designed cloth woven by **Mende**, **Vai**, and **Gola** weavers. Strips of cloth woven on traditional looms from cotton are sewn together to give the finished product. In one type of kpokpo called *Njawi cloth*, the design is usually made in indigo blue on a white or natural beige background. Other types of kpokpo have different colors from dyed cotton woven together. Apart from clothing, kpokpo is also ornamental, to demonstrate wealth of the owner, expressed in the skill of the weaver. Kpokpo are thus used for display on very important occasions. In contemporary Mende society, kpokpo is made largely from imported cotton thread.

KRIM. Krim is one of the smallest ethnic groups in Sierra Leone, located largely in the Kwamabai Krim chiefdom (**Bonthe** District) and the Yakemo Kpukumu Krim, Panga Krim, and Mano Sakrim chiefdoms in the Pujehun District and other small chiefdoms in the Bonthe District. The Krim represent an almost extinct language grouping, akin to the **Sherbro** language. The Krim are among the oldest of the ethnic groups found in Sierra Leone. Today, most Krim speak the **Mende** language and are culturally influenced by Mende.

KRIO. An ethnic group that emerged by the late 19th century from the interaction between liberated Africans, predominantly Yoruba from Nigeria, returned former slaves from the New World called settlers, and the indigenous peoples in the territory around Freetown. The

Krio language that developed in **Freetown** largely from English derived words became the lingua franca in Sierra Leone. The Krio represent no more than 1 percent of the population of Sierra Leone, but with their early access to Western education and influence, they have exerted a strong influence on other ethnic groups in Sierra Leone and on English-speaking West Africa in general. As with most coastal peoples in African states that had early access to Western influence, the Krio came to believe that this made them superior to other ethnic groups in the country. Much of this attitude has disappeared as the numerically far stronger peoples have asserted their dominance.

– L –

LANSANA, DAVID (1922–1975). David Lansana was the first prominent Sierra Leonean in the Sierra Leonean military forces then under the British. After independence in 1961, he became the first Sierra Leonean brigadier and force commander of what became the Sierra Leone army. He is especially known as the head of the army at the time of the coup d'état of 1967, which was aimed at preventing the appointment of **Siaka Stevens** as prime minister and at reinstating his friend **Albert Margai** who had lost the elections.

Lansana was born at Baiima in the Mandu chiefdom, Kailahun district on March 27, 1922. He attended Union College, Bunumbu in the Kailahun District, which was then the major institution of higher learning in the provinces. After he joined the army, he saw training in England particularly at the Officers' Training School in Chester. He quickly rose through the ranks, having joined the army in 1947 and having become brigadier and force commander in 1965.

When the general elections of March 1967 were held, it became apparent at the counting that the **All People's Congress** had won the elections, and its leader, Siaka Stevens, was called in by the governor general to be sworn in as prime minister. The government-controlled broadcasting service was announcing trumped-up results when David Lansana went on the radio and declared martial law on March 21, placing the governor general and president-elect Siaka Stevens under house arrest. His declared reason for doing so was that the elections were not yet over and the governor general had no basis on which to appoint a prime minister.

Lansana's martial law and control lasted only a few days. He was arrested by his own senior officers who then instituted a military government, the **National Reformation Council (NRC)**. Although the NRC later gave Lansana a diplomatic appointment in New York, that government was overthrown in 1968, and Brigadier Lansana left New York to seek refuge in Liberia. He was later extradited in negotiations between the new government of **Siaka Stevens** in Sierra Leone and the Liberian government. He was tried in **Freetown** and convicted of illegal exercise of power and jailed for five years. After his release in 1973, he was again arrested on a treason charge against him and 14 others. He was found guilty and executed on July 19, 1975.

LAWSON, THOMAS GEORGE (c. 1814–1891). A major institution for brokering relations between the British in the Sierra Leone colony and the local rulers in the interior developed around Thomas George Lawson in 19th century Sierra Leone. Lawson worked in the colonial service for 40 years starting in 1846, and his unrivaled knowledge of local languages and contact with the interior rulers made him an invaluable asset to the colonial government; his memos are a major source for historians of Sierra Leone today.

During his tenure, the "Aborigines Branch" of the colonial government in Sierra Leone was virtually Lawson alone. He was born about 1814 to a local ruler in Little Popo in what is now the Republic of Togo. Some of the coastal rulers having dealings with the British at the time wanted some of their sons to have a British education. Lawson's father therefore decided to send Lawson to England. But Lawson stopped in Freetown en route and stayed on for the rest of his life. He came to live with **John McCormack**, an Irish timber trader in **Temne** country adjacent to the tiny Sierra Leone colony. McCormack's trade in the interior had won him the confidence and contact with interior rulers, and the colony administration often relied on McCormack to go into the interior and settle disputes on behalf of the colony, disputes that had the potential for hampering the trade on which the colony so vitally depended. Lawson began accompanying McCormack on these official missions and learned several languages and the culture and customs of the interior peoples. The extent of his contacts was evident when Lawson married the granddaughter of the Bai Farma or ruler of Koya, a polity not too far from the Sierra Leone colony.

In 1846, Lawson joined the colonial service in a temporary position as government messenger. Appointed "native interpreter and government messenger" in 1952, Lawson held this position until his retirement in 1886. His position also included the functions of a police inspector. For most of his tenure, Lawson wrote virtually all correspondence between the colonial government and the local rulers, who came to have almost a reverence for him. He advised interior rulers about government policy, paid out government stipends to them, entertained their emissaries to **Freetown** in his own home, supervised the education of the sons of various interior rulers in Freetown, and reported to the colonial government on such matters as "natives," "escaped slaves," "political prisoners," "trade caravans from the interior," and a host of other topics having to do with relations between the colonial government and interior rulers and peoples.

As the government became more dependent on Lawson, his annual salary, initially 11 pounds sterling, was progressively raised, and by 1882 he was earning the then princely sum of 350 pounds sterling. The government always accepted Lawson's opinion, and only once, during the crisis over the implementation of a treaty with the Temne of Loko Masama in 1879, did the government question his conclusions. Although he was given different assistants during his tenure, only one, **J. C. E. Parkes**, came to assume a position close enough to Lawson and succeeded him in a revised department. Parkes and Lawson wrote a manuscript titled "Information Regarding the Different Districts and Tribes of Sierra Leone and Its Vicinity," almost entirely the product of Lawson's memory but finished by Parkes. This is a valuable research tool for historians on Sierra Leone. A fitting tribute to Lawson was given by Governor Samuel Rowe, describing Lawson as "alone and without equal in the history of Her Majesty's settlements on this Coast."

LEBANESE IN SIERRA LEONE. The Lebanese started arriving in the Colony of Sierra Leone toward the end of the 19th century, initially from neighboring Guinea and also from Dakar in Senegal. They were identified as Syrians because in the late 19th century, Lebanon was effectively part of Syria and Lebanon only became a separate entity after World War I. Between 1921 and 1923, the number of Syrian migrants to Sierra Leone had risen from 184 to 804. By 1926, there were 1,077 "Syrians" on the Aliens Register in the colony.

The early Lebanese in Freetown lived in abject poverty. They took to petty trading, especially selling coral beads, imitations of the very expensive items valued in Freetown. This item sold readily and the Lebanese became identified with these beads so that the people of Freetown interchangeably used the term "coral" to refer to the Lebanese. But they showed much enterprise, buying goods on credit from the major European merchants in the colony and retailing to the local population. The Lebanese entered the trade in kolanuts and came to dominate it. Kolanuts are a nicotine-laden cultural fruit in many parts of West Africa and, according to the comptroller of customs in Sierra Leone in 1923, kolanuts accounted for about a fifth of the exports from the colony.

Very quickly, the Lebanese broke into large-scale trading, operating very cheaply with tremendous plow back of resources. Although the incipient Krio middle class paid more attention to Western education and "clerkly" employment, the Lebanese concentrated on trade and, within two decades, were firmly established in trade in Freetown. Estimates by 1923 indicated that "not less than a quarter of the total export produce of the colony" passed through the hands of the Lebanese.

The rapid rise of the Lebanese in business earned for them the envy and resentment of the Krio of Freetown. Resentment of Lebanese domination of trade led to accusations that the Lebanese were hoarding essential commodities, such as rice, to hike the price of the foodstuff. Obviously, this resentment had more to do with Lebanese success in trade because the Krio press, dominant in Freetown, was also charging the Lebanese with "seducing decent Krio girls" and that the Lebanese were also threatening that they had the economic power to "make the Creoles eat grass." This hostility fed into a workers' strike that degenerated into rioting in 1919, with mostly the shops of the Lebanese traders being looted. The British colonial government, however, responded by making the Freetown City Council, considered as Krio government, pay compensation to the Lebanese community. Evidence coming from the inquiry into the claims for compensation by the Lebanese showed that there were some reasons for Krio concerns about the Lebanese.

The Lebanese retained their preeminence in trade, moving into the provincial towns as produce trade expanded in Sierra Leone. They became involved in buying rice, cacao, coffee, and other commodities, and making profits as middlemen. Some of them, however, took Sierra Leonean girls as wives and had children who sometimes enjoyed the favor of their Lebanese fathers and exploited this to effect. By the period of independence, the Lebanese became prominent in the diamond trade and in all types of business ventures in Freetown. Prominent names like Mattar, Yazbeck, and others were influential with political leaders and had access to the president and his cabinet. One "Afro-Lebanese," **Jamil Sahid Mohamed**, became one of the most dominant figures in Sierra Leone in the 1970s and 1980s, during the rule of President Siaka Stevens. He was reputed to do business directly with the president and to be able to influence Stevens in favor of cabinet ministers and top civil servants who did his bidding. Jamil identified himself more typically with the Lebanese community, though he had very good relations with the local population. He owned major businesses in Sierra Leone, such as the Sierra Fisheries and dominated diamond buying for a while.

The Lebanese however preferred to remain identified as a separate community and were reputed to be guilty of bribing and corrupting politicians and the civil service. Today, the Lebanese are still very prominent in the local economy, dominating the building construction business and able to win major government contracts.

LIBERATED AFRICANS (RECAPTIVES). Liberated Africans were those Africans who were set free from slave-trading vessels captured by the British navy close to the coast of West Africa in the 19th century and set free in the colony of Sierra Leone. After Britain abolished the slave trade for British citizens, an attempt was made to enforce the antislave trade law by getting ships from the British navy to patrol the West African waters and intercept slave vessels of British provenance that were violating the law. Obvious targets were those vessels that had slaves on board. Because it would have been prohibitively expensive to take every such vessel to England to face the consequences, the British government took over the tiny colony of Sierra Leone to become a Crown Colony in 1808 and a venue where the slaves would be landed and the ship captains tried. Slaves thus set free had been initially captured to be sold into slavery, then recaptured by the British Navy, the source of the term "recaptives," and finally liberated in Sierra Leone and so became also known as "liberated Africans."

The numbers of liberated Africans landed in Sierra Leone in the first two decades of the 19th century quickly changed the fortunes of the struggling colony, vastly increasing its population and providing many industrious elements that were to promote trade and farming in the colony. The liberated Africans came from a variety of ethnic backgrounds all along the coast of West Africa. The majority of them, however, were of Yoruba extraction, following the Yoruba civil wars of the late 18th century that resulted in many prisoners of war being sold into slavery. The medley of different subcultures, predominantly Yoruba, became a strong infusion to the emergence of a new culture, the **Krio** culture, blending elements from all of these sources and the dominant English culture of the colony's rulers.

LIMBA. The Limba is perhaps the third largest ethnic group in Sierra Leone, found predominantly in the Koinadugu, Kambia, and Bombali Districts of Sierra Leone. The Limba count among the earliest inhabitants of present day Sierra Leone, with their earliest settlements dominating the mountainous region of Koinadugu. From there, they spread out to other regions and in time became differentiated into five subgroups, speaking not so easily inter-intelligible dialects of the Limba language. These five groups are the Biriwa **Limba** found around the towns of Kamabai and Bumban in the Bombali District; the Sela Limba found in the Bombali District around Kamakwie; the Tonko Limba around Madina in the Kambia District; the Safroko Limba centered on Binkolo; and the Wara Wara around the towns of Fadugu and Bafodia in the Kasunka chiefdom of Koinadugu District. The main Limba cultural institution is the gbangbani, responsible for regulating rights of puberty and politics in many Limba societies.

LEGISLATIVE COUNCIL. One of the major arms of government in the British colonial system in Africa was the Legislative Council. In Sierra Leone, the Legislative Council was introduced with a new constitution for the colony in 1863. The Legislative Council replaced a former governor's advisory council made up of British officials and the occasional appointed African from the colony. The new Legislative Council included the same white officials in the colony and two Sierra Leoneans. One of these, **John Ezzidio**, was nominated by the Mercantile Association, an interracial group representing business interests. The British government expressly approved of Ezzidio's nomination if it was clear that he owed his position to the British crown, not to the Mercantile Association. The composition of the council was later expanded to include a few more Sierra Leoneans who were accorded the title of "honorable." The Legislative Council "legislated" for the colony. Since the vast majority of its members were white officials of the colonial administration, it simply proclaimed the wishes of the administration

The Legislative Council remained in force until constitutional changes leading to independence in the 1950s. To the people of **Freetown**, membership of the Legislative Council was the highest honor and marked the consummate in achievement for the emergent **Krio** population.

KPANA LEWIS (c. 1840–1912). The last Bai Sherbro, titled ruler of the **Sherbro** state, Kpana Lewis was a leading member of the secret society of Poro, which society he effectively used to bolster his suzerainty in defiance of the colonial administration that exiled him to the Gold Coast in 1899. Kpana Lewis was the grandson of the last holder of the ruling title of Kong Kuba, the supreme ruler who is said to have signed a treaty in 1825 ceding Sherbro country to the British. By the time Kpana became Bai Sherbro in 1879, the Sherbro state was in decline with the former provinces exercising autonomy. As Bai Sherbro, Kpana was determined to sustain control over these provinces, and he used the Poro society to effect this. When the protectorate was declared in 1896 and a house tax was instituted, the Bai Sherbro joined other chiefs and traveled to **Freetown** to protest the provisions of the protectorate ordinance. Kpana was then informed that his territory was part of the colony, based on the 1825 treaty and the stipend he had been receiving from the colonial government. This did not placate the Bai Sherbro for when he returned to his chief town of Yoni, he enlisted the services of the **Poro** to organize a boycott on the participation of **Krios** and Europeans in trade with Sherbro. The colonial administration replied by passing ordinances making it a criminal offense to use the Poro or any similar institution to impose trade embargoes and another to empower the governor to detain Kpana Lewis as he saw fit.

When the 1898 rebellion fell in Sierra Leone, Kpana, as a leading Poro member, was believed to have been instrumental in its organization, even though there was little evidence to support this. The colonial government therefore arrested and deported him to Accra, along with Nyagua and Bai Bureh, other suspected leaders of the rebellion. Despite pleas for his release when Bai Bureh and others were let go, Kpana Lewis remained in exile. Tradition dictated that a new Bai Sherbro could only be appointed on the death of the former. The British feared that the return of Kpana Lewis, still considered as the Bai Sherbro in the minds of his people, would stir up trouble for the substitute whom they had approved to act as chief in place of Lewis. Kpana Lewis died in exile in 1912.

LEWIS, SIR SAMUEL (1843–1903). Samuel Lewis was one of the most prominent legal luminaries of 19th century Sierra Leone. He had a thriving private practice but also served in the colonial establishment as mayor of **Freetown** and member of the **Legislative Council**, then the highest preferment for Africans in the British colonial service.

Lewis was born of Egba recaptive parents and was educated at the **CMS Grammar School**. After assisting his father in his trading business for a few years, he went to study law in England, being called to the bar of Middle Temple in 1871. He was appointed acting Queen's Advocate for 15 months and although he later twice acted in a temporary capacity as chief justice, he eschewed permanent government employment preferring his lucrative private practice. He had a number of high-profile cases in his time, serving both Africans and at one time a British official charged with the murder of his African servant.

In 1882, Lewis became an unofficial member of the Legislative Council and used his legal training to ensure rights of the councilors to receive information, debate legislation, and propose amendments, among other issues. Lewis was bold enough to criticize the governor, Sir Samuel Rowe, in the Legislative Council for his policies for addressing the local rulers in the interior. He even collaborated with other African and European critics of Rowe in the short-lived Sierra Leone Association, a discussion group that sought to exert political pressure on the colonial government. He boldly expressed his views in three published pamphlets in Freetown.

Lewis was also important in the establishment of the Freetown municipality and in 1895 became the first mayor of Freetown; he was reelected in 1896. In that same year, he was knighted by the British monarch, the first African to be so honored. Lewis was noted for seeking greater understanding between the peoples of Freetown and the interior. When the protectorate was established by the British, Lewis welcomed this as a way of improving relations and commerce between the interior peoples and the **Krios**. A devout churchman of the Wesleyan Methodist persuasion, Lewis remained a prominent figure in Freetown until his death on July 9, 1903.

LOKO. The Loko is an ethnic group found chiefly in the Port Loko and Bombali Districts of northern Sierra Leone. From available evidence, the Loko, like the Gbandi of Liberia, were an offshoot of the **Mani** invaders of Sierra Leone in the 15th century. While the Gbandi stayed in the Liberian hinterland, the branch that came to be called **Loko** moved deeper into Sierra Leone roughly to the area of their present location. The Loko have also moved around the interior of Sierra Leone; one of their prominent ancestors, **Gombu Smart**, was responsible for a major Loko settlement in the area around the towns of Rotifunk and Bradford in the Moyamba District.

LOMÉ PEACE AGREEMENT. The Lomé Peace Agreement was signed on July 7, 1999, between the government of Sierra Leone and the leaders of the **Revolutionary United Front (RUF)**, both parties in the rebel war that had raged in Sierra Leone since 1991. This was the final agreement that largely ended the civil war. Apart from the parties in the civil war, the peace was brokered by President Obasanjo of Nigeria, where the leader of the RUF, **Foday Sankoh**, was in custody. Sankoh was allowed to attend the negotiations in Lomé, the capital of

Togo, whose president, Eyadema, was also the president of the Organization of African Unity and so played host to the deliberations. Also in attendance was President Blaise Compaoré of Burkina Faso who had strong links with **Charles Taylor**, the Liberian leader who had instigated and continued to actively support the rebel invasion of Sierra Leone. Together, these parties hammered out an agreement that came to be known as the Lomé Peace Agreement.

The agreement had seven main components. The first dealt with cessation of hostilities, details of a cease-fire and monitoring of the cease-fire. The second, on governance, attempted to map out the integration of the RUF into the political system of Sierra Leone. Thirdly, "other political issues" addressed pardon and amnesty, review of the constitution, elections and creation of a National Electoral Commission. The fourth main clause dealt with postconflict military and security issues while the fifth dwelt on humanitarian, human rights and socioeconomic issues, particularly in relation to former combatants. The sixth and seventh clauses were on details for implementation of the agreement, and moral guarantors and international support.

Prominent in the agreement was the granting of total and unconditional amnesty to all former combatants. One of the rebel leaders, **Johnny Paul Koroma**, was later appointed chairman of the Commission for the Consolidation of Peace. There were a few violations of the Lomé agreement, notably the capture by the rebels of troops of the United Nations Mission in Sierra Leone (UNAMSIL) that had been dispatched to Sierra Leone following the Lomé accord, and the firing on demonstrators in Freetown by Foday Sankoh's guards, which led to the arrest of Foday Sankoh. On the main, however, the Lomé Peace Agreement held and signaled the declared end of the war several months later.

LUKE, DESMOND EDGAR FASHOLE (1935–). Desmond Edgar Fashole Luke was foreign minister for Sierra Leone in the 1970s and became chief justice of Sierra Leone in 1998. He was born October 6, 1935, and attended the **Prince of Wales School** in **Freetown**. He then studied law in England at Oxford and Cambridge Universities. He returned and began private practice in law in Sierra Leone. In 1970, Desmond was appointed Sierra Leone's first ambassador to West Germany and combined this with an ambassadorship to France starting in 1971. At the same time, he was also Sierra Leone's permanent representative to the European Economic Community (EEC). In 1973, Desmond Luke was elected to parliament for Freetown West III constituency. He was appointed foreign minister that same year but resigned his cabinet post in 1975 in a disagreement with the government. In 1977, Desmond Luke was again given a cabinet position as minister of health. Then in 1998, the government of President **Tejan Kabbah** appointed Desmond Luke as chief justice, a seat he occupied until 2002.

– M –

MACFOY, FRANCIS. *See* SCRUBBY, the name by which he was commonly known.

MACCARTHY, CHARLES (1769–1824). Charles MacCarthy's tenure as governor of the colony of Sierra Leone was most noted for his resettlement of the liberated African population in villages around **Freetown** and for his ambitious program of public buildings at the capital. He also tried to centralize all British West African colonies under his rule in Sierra Leone.

MacCarthy was an Irishman who had seen service in both the French and British armies. He commanded the Royal African Corps in Senegal in 1811 and became governor of Sierra Leone in 1814. He fashioned the village settlement of liberated Africans, creating some 10 more new villages, all given names of British heroes or places. MacCarthy got the **Church Missionary Society (CMS)** missionaries in the colony to work in these villages, virtually as agents of the colonial government. MacCarthy also expanded a program of public works buildings, giving the city a more attractive look and attracting more European businessmen.

MacCarthy met his fate in his attempt to unite all of the British West African colonies under his own command. This made him governor-in-chief over all of Sierra Leone, the Gambia and the Gold Coast (Ghana). In an attempt to subdue the Asante of the Gold Coast interior, he led a war against the Asante in which he was killed in 1824.

MACAULEY, JOHN (c. 1800–1867). "King" John Macauley was a wealthy **Freetown** trader and the powerful unofficial leader of the liberated Africans of Aku (Yoruba) extraction. He played an important role in reducing interethnic conflict in the fledgling colony by persuading the various ethnic groups in and around Freetown to form multiethnic councils to arbitrate in disputes.

Macauley was a Hausa **Muslim** who was recaptured between 1815 and 1822 and brought to **Freetown**. Being an enterprising young man, he quickly prospered as a trader. He was also a man of great physical strength, which earned him the nickname of "Atapa" (from the Yoruba word for "kicker") because he was reputed to use both his feet and his hands in fighting.

It seems likely that in the 1820s, he was headman in one of the provident societies started as a means of self-help for settlers and liberated Africans by "king" Abraham Potts, an African ex-soldier who had settled in Freetown. From the late 1830s on Macauley served in a number of minor positions, including that of policeman, with the colonial administration and in 1849 was appointed overseer in the Liberated African Department Yard, where these recaptives were first brought.

More significantly, Macauley succeeded to the position of king of the Aku on the death of their former king, Thomas Will. Although unofficial, this position as head of the largest and most powerful ethnic group among the liberated Africans carried great authority. Even the rich and influential obeyed their leader under threat of severe social sanctions, such as the denial of burial rites. Macauley's success as a trader also contributed to his rise to leadership. By the late 1840s, his business was large enough for him to use his own ship to trade with Badagry, Nigeria, carrying cargoes of tobacco and rum. When he retired from government service in 1853, he invested his profits in property and ran a retail spirit trade from his house.

The colonial government utilized this position of king of the Aku even though it was not officially recognized. When a serious conflict broke out between the Aku and other groups in the village of Waterloo outside Freetown, the governor of the colony sent Macauley to Waterloo to mediate. Macauley persuaded the various groups to form a superethnic council to include one member from each of the 17 major ethnic groups at Waterloo. The function of this council, which became known as the Seventeen Nations, was to settle all petty grievances as well as help maintain law and order. Macauley's Seventeen Nations turned out to be a very manageable form of government, and the organization continued in Waterloo under successive presidents until the end of the 19th century. Macauley was also later called upon to intervene in other local disputes and achieved similar results, setting up a modified version of his Seventeen Nations in Hastings after a dispute there in 1851. As a result of helping the colonial administration in so many ways, Macauley was made overseer in the Liberated African Department Yard in 1849 by Governor N. W. Macdonald. Later, Macauley was instrumental in a petition to recall Governor Macdonald and when Macdonald resumed his post he tried unsuccessfully to remove Macauley from the Liberated African Department Yard. A later governor, Arthur Kennedy, abolished Macauley's post in 1853 but this did not diminish Macauley's hold over the Aku in the colony.

Macauley became a Christian in his old age. He was converted by the Rev. James Johnson of Christ Church in Freetown after becoming ill in 1862. He gave up polygamy and began attending church regularly. His newfound religion did not, however, affect his position with the Aku, many of whom were Muslims, and he remained effectively king Macauley until his death in 1867. Markets and shops in Freetown closed down for his funeral, and large crowds from all of the different ethnic groups, especially his own Aku, turned out to pay him their final respects.

MACFOY, SAMUEL BENJAMIN AUGUSTUS (c. 1843–1893). Samuel Benjamin Augustus Macfoy was a businessman and trader who was dominant in business and farming in the Sherbro region for many years in the late19th century. He originally came from Kent village, south of **Freetown** but found his way as a boy to Sherbro where he stayed and made a fortune. He became an agent for a British export firm in Manchester, receiving goods worth 40,000 pounds sterling from that firm in return for produce. One of his most familiar strategies was to buy up European and Krio trading establishments along the Sherbro rivers. He built his own warehouse in **Bonthe** and commissioned his own cargo steamship, which he named "**Sherbro** Monarch," the pseudonym by which he went.

Macfoy also gained political influence by lending money to some of the rulers in the Sherbro and Imperri areas and taking control of their territory when they could not pay. Some of these rulers complained to the British who turned a blind eye rather than raise the issue of Sherbro being claimed as British territory when it was not. In this way, Macfoy expanded a trading empire that, however, declined by the late 1880s. He survived by using his territorial expanse to convert to farming on Sherbro Island and then in Imperri. The British tried unsuccessfully to stop him. A newly appointed British official, George Garrett, had Macfoy detained as a political prisoner on suspicion of implication in ritual murders in Imperri. Macfoy retained Sir **Samuel Lewis** as his lawyer and was acquitted.

Macfoy died January 16, 1893.

MADDY, YULISA AMADU (1936–). Also known as Pat Maddy, Yulisa was a playwright and novelist popular both in Sierra Leone and internationally. He was born in **Freetown** December 27, 1936, and his high school training was at **St. Edward's Secondary School** in Freetown. He later attended the Rose Buford College of Speech and Drama in Britain. He has worked as an actor and director and as a lecturer, instructor, and professor in Zambia, Nigeria, Great Britain, and the United States. He was artistic director of Pan-African Players at the First World Festival of Negro Arts in Dakar in 1966. He spent much of the 1970s in Sierra Leone, where he was acting director of culture and art in the Ministry of Tourism and Cultural Affairs and later professional head of the Sierra Leone National Dance Troupe in 1975.

Yulisa Maddy is best known for his published plays and performances. His first play was *Obasai and Other Plays,* published in 1971; this was followed by a novel, *No Past, No Present, No Future* (1973). He received the Sierra Leone National Arts Festival Award in 1973 and the Edinburgh Festival Award in 1979. His other plays include *Big Breeze Blow* (1984), *Take Tem Draw Di Rope* (1975), *Naw We Yone Dehn See* (1975), *Big Berrin* (1984), and a play for television, *Yon Kon* (1982). Yulisa Maddy writes mainly for an African audience, which he reaches by using the **Krio** language and African images.

MAKENI. Makeni is a large town in the Bombali Sebora chiefdom in the Bombali District. It is also the capital of the Northern Province of

Sierra Leone. Located some 114 miles north of Freetown, Makeni is among the six largest towns in Sierra Leone. The town is said to have been founded by a man named Keni, and the prefix "ma" is usually added to give the toponymy in the **Temne** language. The dominant ethnic group in **Makeni** is Temne, but because the town is immediately surrounded by the dominant area of other northern ethnic groups, notably the **Limba**, there is a greater cosmopolitan population mostly of northern ethnic groups such as Limba**, Loko**, and **Soso**. Makeni was the headquarters of the **Revolutionary United Front (RUF)** during the civil war and suffered tremendous devastation during the war.

MALI. *See* MANDE.

MANA SIAKA (c. 1800–1872). Mana Siaka was ruler of the **Vai** or **Galinas** state in the middle of the 19th century. He became rich as a slave trader, but the era of partition hit this area very hard and much of Mana's tenure was absorbed with international territorial disputes dominated by competition between Liberia and the British for control of the Vai country.

The Galinas state was founded by Mana's father, King Siaka, creating the Massaquoi crown, the regalia of office of the rulers of the Gallinas. Mana Siaka inherited the Massaquoi crown from his father by the 1840s. Mana had a large army of professional warriors from the sale of slaves to Pedro Blanco, a Spanish slave dealer. He used his wealth and dynastic marriage alliance to dominate all other rulers in the Gallinas. He fortified his capital, Gendama, and built European style houses and furnishings for his extended family.

After Mana Siaka signed antislave trade treaties with the British in 1850, his main source of revenue was cut off and, having neglected food production, he no longer had the means to buy food from Sherbro country. Moreover, Mana had also signed treaties of friendship with the Liberian government, which interpreted these treaties as giving them some suzerainty over Mana's territory. The 1860s witnessed contested claims to Gallinas territory by the Liberian government with the British supporting Mana's sovereignty as a way of keeping off the Liberian government from taking over the area. Mana died in 1872, and the contested claims were only settled with the demarcation of the boundary between Liberia and Sierra Leone in 1917.

MANDE. The term Mande represents a group of West African languages and subcultures with close affinity around the contemporary states of Guinea, Guinea Bissau, Sierra Leone, Mali, Liberia, Cote d'Ivoire, and Burkina Faso. The Mande languages have been shown to have emanated from an original Mande language a couple of thousand years ago, and this original language is believed to have derived from the Mande heartland around the Niger River bend in the present state of Mali. The term "Mali" itself is another name for "Mande." Although Mali is more familiar in the literature recorded largely in European languages, the people themselves refer to the region, their ancestral homeland, as Mande. The Mande languages diverged over a few thousand years as original Mande peoples fanned out to many areas of West Africa. The language in the Mande family that is closest to the original is Mandinka, called Malinke in some areas. The difference again relates to the Mande/Mali appellations, with the suffix "ka" or "ke" meaning "of." In Sierra Leone, the term **Mandingo** is used to refer to this language. Mande languages in Sierra Leone would include also **Koranko**, interintelligible with Mandingo, **Soso**, **Yalunka**, **Mende**, **Kono**, **Vai**, and **Loko**.

MANNAH-KPAKA, JOHN (c. 1865–1945). John Mannah-Kpaka was one of very few paramount chiefs in the 19th century who was Western educated. This stood him in good stead and supported his vying for the chiefship and his being appointed to the Legislative Council in 1934.

He hailed from the Kpaka or Rogers family, which derived from a European trader named Zachary Rogers who came to the Gallinas coast in 1868 and married an African wife from the ruling Massaquoi family there. The name Kpaka comes from the **Mende** word for a chair (*kpakai*), in this case derived from one of its members who liked sitting in a chair, an uncommon act among the Gallinas in those times. King **Mana Siaka**, at the urging of the governor, sent two of his sons to school in **Freetown**, John being one of them. Mannah-Kpaka later became a teacher in the lower school before joining the customs department in 1886; he later became assistant customs clerk for a European company. By the time he returned to the Gallinas in 1895, he had been away for 23 years and many of his relatives had died by then.

Mannah-Kpaka turned to trading at the Mano River estuary in ivory and other commodities. When the protectorate was proclaimed and the 1898 rebellion broke out, he escaped from the region and upon finding his way to Freetown proceeded to assist the colonial authorities to overcome the resistance. In 1913, he was elected paramount chief of the Kpaka chiefdom. Deposed in 1916 for receiving money illegally on behalf of the colonial government, Mannah-Kpaka was pardoned by Governor R. J. Wilkinson. However, by then another person, Momo Rogers, had already been elected as his successor. Momo Rogers, too, was deposed, and John Mannah-Kpaka again contested the chiefship against his uncle, Momo Tibo Rogers. Rogers actually won the elections but agreed to step down in favor of his nephew with the proviso that Momo Tibo would become the paramount chief immediately following John. The colonial government, empowered by the 1924 constitution to appoint three paramount chiefs to represent protectorate interests, appointed John Mannah-Kpaka to the **Legislative Council** in 1934 for his support of the government. He sat on the council until 1939 and remained a paramount chief until his death in 1945. He was succeeded by Momo Tibo Rogers.

MANDINGO (MANDINKA). One of the ethnic groups in Sierra Leone, found chiefly in the Biriwa **Limba** chiefdom of the Bombali District. Mandingo clans are also found in many parts of Sierra Leone where they have largely become integrated into other ethnic groups such as the **Mende** and **Loko**. They are referred to as Mandingo in Sierra Leone while in other areas around Sierra Leone they are better known as Mandinka, a form of the name also recognized in Sierra Leone.

The Mandingo language and culture represent the closest in the language family referred to as the Mande. Mande is the name best known to the indigenous people of that culture, while in Western literature the term "Mali" came to represent that ancient culture. This was because the first Europeans who recorded the term heard "Mali" rather than "Mande" from the first Africans they spoke to on this matter. What the Europeans heard related to the manner of speech of the people they spoke to on the coastal areas of West Africa. By the 14th century, Mande constituted a large empire in the interior of West Africa dominated by Mande language and culture but also including other ethnic groups such as the **Soso**. As that empire expanded and later disintegrated, Mande elements migrated to many parts of West Africa with their culture and language. They have since influenced many among whom they lived and traded, sometimes as discreet Mande communities, such as in the settlements of Kamaworen in Biriwa **Limba**, sometimes also as clans, families, or individual migrants whose clan names (such as the Mansaray, Koroma, Turay of Sierra Leone) remained significant although they were culturally integrated to become Mende, Temne, and so on.

MANDINKA. *See* MANDINGO.

MANI INVASION OF SIERRA LEONE. The Mani invasion of Sierra Leone in the middle of the16th century represented a train of events that came to have a major political and cultural impact on the map of Sierra Leone. Mani influence gave rise to the emergence of new ethnic groups in Sierra Leone, notably the **Mende**, but also the **Sherbro** and **Loko**. The invasion also led to the radical redistribution of other ethnic groups, such as the **Kissi**, **Gola**, and **Bullom**.

The Mani were a group of Mandinka from the Mande empire. Apparently cut off from the Mande heartland, they decided to migrate southward and in the process moved eventually toward what became their heartland in the Cape Mount region of present-day Liberia. From there by the 1540s successive splinters of the Mani moved deeply into the Sierra Leone interior, dominating, sometimes by physical conquest, many of the original inhabitants. In this way, Mani influence on the Bullom gave rise to the Sherbro ethnic group. The Loko, broke away from a Mani subgroup known as the Gbandi, now found in the Liberian interior, and came to settle in Sierra Leone. By far the largest single group to emerge from the Mani invasion was the **Mende**, a product of the Mani influence on a Gola and Kissi substratum. The Mani also came to influence ethnic Temne political institutions as one of their leaders, **Farma Tami** settled among and came to define the ruling group among the **Temne** of Port Loko.

MANO RIVER UNION. On October 3, 1973, **Siaka Stevens**, president of the Republic of Sierra Leone, and William Tolbert, president of the Republic of Liberia, signed the Mano River Declaration at

Malema on the Mano River, the border between Sierra Leone and Liberia, thus setting up the Mano River Union. The description of the objectives of the Union reads: "The objective of the Mano River Union is to intensify economic cooperation and accelerate economic growth, social progress, and cultural advancement between Liberia and Sierra Leone, so as to establish a firm economic foundation for lasting peace, friendship, freedom and social progress between the two countries." On October 25, 1980, the heads of states of Sierra Leone and Liberia were joined by President Ahmed Sekou Toure of the Republic of Guinea, agreeing to Guinea's accession to full membership in the Mano River Union.

The emphasis of the Mano River Union since its inception has been on economic integration and development. A press release marking the eighth anniversary of the Union is 1980 stated, among other things, that:

> The Secretariat has . . . been involved in several areas of development and economic integration: trade, a road project, the (Mano River) Basin Development project, agriculture, industrial development, standardization and quality control, training institutions such as Forestry, Post and Telecommunications, Customs, Marine, Curriculum Planning, Instructional Materials Production and Book Development (CIB) Project.

The foundations of the Mano River Union rested on a recognition of the common cultural and physical character of the region occupied by these three countries with contiguous borders and an attempt to cooperate, not only on the economic matters stipulated but also on political and border issues. Thus, in a 1990 meeting, there was a move toward signing a long sought-after agreement on "peace, nonaggression, and mutual security."

Unfortunately, civil wars had started in both Liberia and Sierra Leone. Both of these wars altered the landscape and the fortunes of the Mano River Union, which virtually ceased to function. There have been recent attempts to revive the role of the Mano River Union.

MARA, BALANSAMA (c. 1750–1835). Balansama Mara was a ruler of Barawa, a chiefdom where ethnic Koranko are found, now part of Nieni chiefdom in the Koinadugu District of northeastern Sierra Leone. He promoted trade with neighboring states as well as with **Freetown**.

He is referred to as Mara Balansama. The name Balansama is common among the **Koranko** and is particularly associated with rulers of the Koranko Mara clan to which he belonged. At the turn of the 19th century, for example, a Balansama Mara ruled the Koranko chiefdom of Sengbe in what is now Koinadugu District. In the 1970s, this same chiefdom had yet another Balansama Mara as paramount chief.

Balansama Mara was born probably in the mid-18th century and was the son of Mansa Sewa of the Koranko of Barawa. By the end of the 19th century, Balansama succeeded his father as ruler of Barawa, having his capital at Kulakonka. He also ruled over the domain of the Koranko of the Koroma clan, then centered at Kamarow, now an abandoned site in the Koranko chiefdom of Diang, Koinadugu District. The British traveler, Alexander Gordon Laing, believed to have been the first European to have visited Timbuctu, visited Kulakonka in 1822 and gave the following description of Balansama and his domain:

> The capital of North Western Koranko is Kulakonko, where Balansama, the present king, resides; he is a man of considerable influence and property and is the most powerful chief between his country and Sierra Leone; his authority extends as far as the banks of the Niger and his capital is visited by the nations of Sangara for the purposes of trade.

In the 18th century, Balansama's father, Sewa, had joined with the Yalunka of the state of Solimana to oppose the jihad launched by the Fula of Futa Jalon. This gave the Solima, the people of Solimana, a dominant influence over the Barawa. Later, when Balansama had consolidated his authority in Barawa, he apparently tried to end Solima influence. In consequence, a Solima force attacked Kamarow, then an important town in Balansama's domain, leading to conflict between Balansama and the *manga* (king) of the Solima. The influence exerted by the Solima did not effectively diminish Balansama's authority, as Gordon Laing attests. Balansama placed his sons as rulers of the major towns in his domain. One son, Kalu, became headman of Kulakonka. By the 1820s, large trading caravans were being organized in Balansama's territory to travel to **Freetown**. Numerous other trade caravans from Sankaran country (a region on the headwaters of the Niger River, northeast of Solimana) traded with Kulakonka or passed through that town en route to Freetown. Balansama assured the safety of the trade route through Barawa, and, in return, levied tolls that provided him with wealth and consequent influence.

Balansama died in the 1830s. He was succeeded by his son Damatibolo.

MARGAI, ALBERT MICHAEL (1910–1980). Albert Margai was the second prime minister of Sierra Leone from 1964–1967. He was born at Gbangbatoke, Banta chiefdom, Moyamba District on October 10, 1910, and attended school at St. Patrick's in **Bonthe** and at the **St. Edwards Secondary School** in **Freetown**. After working as a nurse in the medical service from 1931–1944, he went to England and studied law at the Inner Temple Inns of Courts. He returned home in 1948 and set up private practice.

Margai's return home coincided with the period of political change leading to independence. He took an active part in debates on the Stevenson Constitution, representing protectorate interests. Although he failed in his bid for Freetown City Councilorship in 1950, he was elected to the revised **Legislative Council** as the first protectorate member and became the first minister of education in the new cabinet in 1952. In 1957, he was reelected to parliament representing his Moyamba South Constituency. Shortly after the election he successfully challenged his older brother, Milton, for leadership of the ruling **Sierra Leone People's Party (SLPP)** but was prevailed upon to step down in favor of **Milton Margai**. Soon after this, he refused the cabinet position offered him by his brother, the prime minister. He resigned from the SLPP and formed his own party, the **People's National Party**, together with **Siaka Stevens** and other disgruntled leaders. When Milton Margai put together a United Front coalition to precede independence, Albert Margai was brought into the cabinet as minister of agriculture in 1959. In 1962, he was appointed minister of finance after winning elections. The Central Bank of Sierra Leone and the Leone currency were inaugurated during his tenure as finance minister.

Following the death of the prime minister, Milton Margai, Albert Margai was appointed prime minister on April 29, 1964. Protests by some SLPP leaders over his appointment led Albert Margai to dismiss four ministers, including **Sanusi Mustapha** and **John Karefa-Smart**, from his cabinet. His tenure as prime minister lasted three years. During that period, he increasingly lost popularity. He identified himself too closely with Nkrumah of Ghana and Sekou Toure of Guinea, two leaders whom some influential Sierra Leoneans saw at the time as authoritarian rulers. The Freetown intelligentsia saw this as linked with Albert's desire to set up a one-party state and republican constitution for Sierra Leone. This suspicion of an impeding move toward dictatorship was accompanied by accusations of corruption. Albert Margai had antagonized younger elements in the SLPP party and this, in the end, contributed greatly to his losing the 1967 elections. Margai's hopes that his appointed leaders of the army would intervene and reinstate him as prime minister were dashed when, instead, a military coup led to establishment of a military government. Albert Margai left Sierra Leone for voluntary exile in England, where he died in 1980.

MARGAI, MILTON AUGUSTUS STRIEBY (1895–1964). Milton Margai was the first prime minister of independent Sierra Leone. He was born in Gbangbatoke in the Banta chiefdom, Moyamba District on December 7, 1895, the son of a prominent businessman, M. E. S. Margai. He acquired primary education at the Evangelical United Brethren (EUB) School in **Bonthe** and later at the **Albert Academy** high school in Freetown. In 1921, he took the B.A. degree from **Fourah Bay College**, then under the University of Durham. He later traveled to Britain where he took an M.A. degree and studied medicine at King's College, Durham, graduating in 1926.

Milton Margai had a series of firsts. He was the first protectorate person to graduate from Fourah Bay College and to qualify as a medical doctor; he founded the first protectorate newspaper (the ***Sierra Leone Observer***), and he was Sierra Leone's first chief minister and prime minister. Milton Margai was a distinguished member of the Colonial Medical Service who pioneered social welfare and hygiene education in remote areas of the protectorate. He encouraged leaders of the Mende women's secret society, the ***Sande***, to include training courses in hygiene, literacy, and childcare in their program of initiation for young girls. These courses were taught by qualified instructors, most of whom were trained by Margai himself.

Retiring from the government medical service in 1950, Milton Margai entered private practice, thereby affording himself more time to participate in politics. He was from its inception an active member of the **Protectorate Educational Progressive Union (PEPU)**, which later merged with the **Sierra Leone Organization Society (SOS)** to form the **Sierra Leone People's Party (SLPP)**. He became the first national chairman of that party and after the 1951 elections, he became leader of government business and, in 1954, chief minister.

The process of bringing together Western trained protectorate leaders and paramount chief into a single party and reconciling these with the **Krio** leadership in **Freetown** was an arduous task that demonstrated the consummate leadership skill of Milton Margai. He accomplished this by first forming the SLPP and later, in 1959, the United Front government, which achieved independence for Sierra Leone in 1961.

By the time he died in office in April 1964, he was regarded as a grand old man, blending the traditional respect for age with that of the office he had filled so gracefully, free of the usual accusations of corruption. He is remembered as the architect of Sierra Leone's independence.

MARLAY BOKARI (c. 1800–1900). Marlay Bokari was ruler of the Mara clan of the ethnic **Koranko** in the second half of the 19th century and was a direct descendant of earlier great leaders. Although his authority did not extend over the entire Koranko territory, his influence did extend well beyond his own clan, and he was, in fact, considered ruler of all the Koranko.

He was the great-great-grandson of Mansa Morifing of the Koranko Mara clan, who led the earliest Koranko migrants from Sankaran in the present Republic of Guinea into northeastern Sierra Leone, and after whom the chiefdom, which came to be known as Morifindugu (now part of the Mongo chiefdom), was named. Tinalei, Marlay Bokari's father, to whom he was born about the beginning of the 19th century, is described in Koranko traditions as the first ruler of all *Ferensola* (all territory inhabited by that ethnic group), and his son is described as a ruler who was even greater than his father.

Based in a town called Yindekuma, located in the present Mongo chiefdom, Koinadugu District, Marlay Bokari ruled the Mara of the northern half of Koranko country from about the middle of the 19th century, and his influence reached lower Koranko as well. The Koranko Mara clan of Barawa (now a section of Nieni chiefdom in Koinadugu) and Sengbe (another chiefdom in Koinadugu) continued to accept Marlay Bokari's authority until the early 1890s, just before the British occupation of the Sierra Leone hinterland. Mori Musa (also called Fina Bala), ruler of Kamadugu, is described as the nephew of Marlay Bokari.

When the expansionist campaigns of the Mandinka ruler **Samori** reached the Sierra Leone hinterland in the 1880s, Marlay Bokari's domain at Morifindugu was threatened. In 1890, Bokari was captured by Kemoko Bilali, Samori's general in that region, and was imprisoned at Heremakono in Sankaran country, close to his original homeland. Recognizing Bokari's importance, Kemoko Bilali treated him well.

Meanwhile Bokari's son, Kumba Wulen Lai, was acknowledged as Bokari's deputy over the Koranko, while Mori Musa and Boltamba of the Barawa Koranko around Kabala implored the British to intercede with the *sofa* for Bokari's release. In 1893, Bokari was set free. He founded a new capital at Kombili, but the unsettled state of the country led him to seek temporary refuge with his lieutenant, Boltamba, in the Wara Wara hills.

By 1895, Morifindugu was recovering from the effects of the *sofa* invasion. Under Marlay Bokari's supervision, some 15 new towns were built and although Bokari was by then a very old man, from all reports, his authority was still respected. In 1899, Bokari appeared as the first paramount chief of Morifindugu, but apparently he died the following year and was succeeded by his son, Kumba Wulen Lai, who was also by then an old man.

MASSALLY, ARTHUR JOHN (1915–1969). Arthur John Massally was the first person from the provinces to be appointed a judge in Sierra Leone. He was born in April 20, 1915, and received his early schooling in Bonthe and at the **St. Edwards Secondary School** in **Freetown**. He then studied at the Middle Temple Inns of Court in London, where he was called to the bar. He married Kade Wurie, daughter of the prominent educator, **Amadu Wurie**. After a brief private practice, he was elected to the Sierra Leone parliament in 1957 and was then appointed deputy speaker of Parliament in 1957, a position he held until 1962. In that year, he became magistrate and in 1965 was appointed puisne judge. Arthur Massally was one of the leading political activists in the years leading to independence. He was one of the group of dissidents who broke ranks with the **Sierra Leone People's Party (SLPP)** in 1957 to form the **People's National Party**. He died in Freetown at the early age of 54.

MATTURI (c. 1855–1936). Matturi was the first paramount chief installed by the British over the Kono territory, which became Jaiama Nimikoro chiefdom. Before the British protectorate was established, Matturi had earned a reputation as a valiant warrior, which had led to his acknowledgment as ruler of southern Konoland by the supreme ruler in this area, Nyagua of Panguma.

The part of Kono country, where Matturi was born and raised, was called Nimikoro, and the neighboring **Mende** ruler, Nyagua, had established control over this southern part of Konoland through successive attacks that had sent many of the southern Kono fleeing north to Koranko territory, some hiding in caves in that area. Matturi's prominence emerged by the last quarter of the 19th century when the **Kono** ruler, Faba, deputed him to lead a contingent of warriors to support his overlord, Nyagua, who was facing attacks by another Mende warrior named **Ndawa**. Matturi distinguished himself, leading all of Nyagua's forces into victory against Ndawa. Nyagua was so pleased that he declared Matturi the ruler of southern Kono centered on Matturi's base at the town of Jaiama.

Matturi's reconstruction of southern Kono after he took office was proceeding well when, in 1893, the **sofas**, forces of the Mandinka empire builder, **Samori Toure**, attacked Matturi's domain and occupied the towns of Levuma and Tecuyama. Even before the British, who were in hot pursuit of Samori, could get to **Kono** after being warned of the sofa attack, Matturi's and Nyagua's forces had successfully eliminated the sofa threat from Kono.

Matturi was now a prominent ruler, to be recognized by the British as paramount chief after the colonial takeover. This meant that he was no longer subject to Nyagua, but at the same time he lost control of much of southern Kono, which the British demarcated into separate Kono chiefdoms.

Matturi lived well into the colonial period, although he was senile by the 1920s and, much of his chiefdom administration was subsequently run by a regent. He died in 1936.

MATTURI, SAHR TOM (1925–). Dr. S. T. Matturi was an educator who rose to become vice chancellor of the **University of Sierra Leone** in 1971. He was born October 22, 1925, at Jaiama in the Kono District and educated at **Bo Government School** and the **Prince of Wales School** in **Freetown**. He received higher education at the University of Ibadan in Nigeria and at **Hull University** in Britain, where he obtained a doctorate in the natural sciences. He taught for a while in Nigeria and was the founding principal of **Njala University College** in 1963. He took time off in 1967 to serve as chairman of the National Advisory Committee organized by the military junta of the **National Reformation Council**. In 1971, he was appointed vice chancellor of the University of Sierra Leone. On leaving the university, he assumed an ambassadorial position for Sierra Leone in the United States.

MAY, JOSEPH CLAUDIUS (1845–1902). Joseph Claudius May became a Methodist minister, first principal of the second boys high school founded in Sierra Leone in 1874, and founder of an influential newspaper in colonial West Africa, the ***Sierra Leone Weekly News***.

He was born of liberated African parents, and his father, Joseph May, was also a Methodist clergyman. The younger May received his early education in **Freetown**, and at age 14 he left school to become a clerk in a business owned by his father's friend, James Macfoy. May then traveled to England in 1865 with the help of his father's Methodist friends in England. He excelled in business studies and studied Pitman's shorthand with its inventor, Isaac Pitman. He also took a keen interest in the art of teaching and trained to become a Methodist minister. In 1874, May became the first principal of the newly founded **Methodist Boys High School**. Under May's guidance, the school rapidly developed an impressive reputation, favorably rivaling the long established **CMS Grammar School** in Freetown, which was the most prestigious school in the whole of British West Africa. He remained principal until his death in 1902.

J. C. May, as he was known, was also interested in publishing and ran a newspaper, *The Methodist Herald* between 1882 and 1884. The experience he gained in this led to his launching in 1884 *The Sierra Leone Weekly News* with the help of one of the fathers of Pan-Africanism, Edward Blyden. Edited and printed by his brother Cornelius May, the *Sierra Leone Weekly News* became an important publication throughout colonial West Africa for more than 60 years, well after May's death.

MBRIWA, TAMBA SONGU (1910–1968). Tamba Songu Mbriwa was a paramount chief among the ethnic **Kono** people. He formed a political party to secure the interests of his people and became instrumental in the defeat of the incumbent **Sierra Leone People's Party (SLPP)** government in the 1967 elections.

He was educated at the **Bo Government School** and worked as a government dispenser (also called a druggist) before he became paramount chief. Mbriwa was one of the prime movers in the formation of the Kono Progressive Movement in the 1950s, which sought to interest the ethnic Kono people in the diamond mining taking place in their territory. Mbriwa led the Kono Progressive Movement into a merger with a short-lived party, the Sierra Leone Independence Movement, formed by Edward Blyden III. This union gave rise to the **Sierra Leone Progressive Independence Movement (SLPIM)**. With the formation of the **People's National Party (PNP)** by **Albert Margai**, **Siaka Stevens**, and others, the SLPIM developed close ties with the PNP in 1959.

After the United Front was formed and the PNP faded away, Mbriwa's SLPIM allied with the newly formed **All People's Congress** in 1960. This put Mbriwa in a collision course with the SLPP government led by **Milton Margai**. Mbriwa was suspended from office as paramount chief and banished to Kamakwie in the Bombali District, Northern Province. He was later reinstated and joined forces with the APC. This proved decisive in the APC victory in the 1967 general elections, as the SLPIM won almost all seats in the Kono District, throwing in their support for the All People's Congress.

T. S. Mbriwa died in 1968, a few days after winning the bye-election as paramount chief and member of Parliament for Kono District.

McCORMACK, JOHN (1791–1865). John McCormack was one of the few Europeans in the 19th century who spent almost their entire working lives in West Africa. Starting as a timber trader, he acquired a unique knowledge of the Sierra Leone hinterland and its peoples, especially the **Temne**. He was then employed as a government agent, playing a vital part in negotiations and treaty-making and strongly influencing colonial government policy.

Born in Ireland, McCormack started working in West Africa at about the age of 18 as a trading agent. Around 1814 he settled in Sierra Leone, where he remained almost continuously for the next 52 years. In 1816, he shipped the first batch of African oak from **Freetown** to England, starting a trade that boomed for over a decade. McCormack built himself a house on Tombo Island on the Rokel estuary, complete with wharf and sawpit, and logs from up the Port Loko River were processed there. Other European merchants joined, expanding the trade to neighboring islands such as Tasso and Bunce.

The timber trade was extremely valuable to the new Sierra Leone colony and also to the neighboring Temne. In the pursuit of the trade, McCormack learned the Temne language and customs, which proved invaluable to him and to the colony later. Despite his attempts to expand the trade, as timber was depleted around Port Loko, the trade declined sharply by the 1830s and McCormack was ruined. But his creditors allowed him to keep his beautiful Freetown house, and he began working for the colonial government, his first appointment in 1840 being that of a police magistrate. He then became an unofficial government agent, negotiating in trade disputes at Port Loko. This activity bore even greater fruit as **T. G. Lawson**, who lived in his household and ultimately was appointed by the government as native interpreter and government messenger, learned Temne laws and customs through McCormack.

McCormack signed a number of treaties on behalf of the colonial government with local rulers in **Port Loko**. In 1825, he assisted Governor Sir Charles Turner in settling a disputed succession to the rulership of Port Loko, the first of several similar missions over the next three decades. In 1831, he accompanied the colonial secretary on a mission to mediate in the Temne-Loko wars around Port Loko. McCormack went on several others to Koya and to settle conflict between Mende and Temne of Koya in the 1840s.

As he grew older, McCormack's diplomatic negotiations were increasingly colored by his religion. By the 1850s, he had founded a free-will Baptist Church, a branch of the Church of God, and his congregation met regularly at his house in Freetown. He became increasingly anti-Islamic and began to give opinions against **Muslim** interests in the disputes he was called upon to mediate. In succession disputes at Port Loko throughout the 1840s and 1850s, McCormack influenced the governor's decision against known Muslim candidates. In disputes between the Temne and **Soso** over the succession in Kambia by 1860, McCormack was persuading the Soso to accept the Temne candidate instead of the Muslim Soso aspirant. The Temne had encouraged Christianity, and McCormack hoped that this would be useful in the spread of Christianity.

In 1862, Governor Stephen Hill appointed McCormack as a police magistrate in Freetown, but he was too old for the job to be more than a sinecure. He died in England on March 20, 1865. His grandchildren of African descent on the maternal side survive in the Easmon family of Freetown, which has provided several generations of medical doctors in Freetown and along the coast of West Africa.

MENDE. The Mende, found mostly in the southern and eastern regions of Sierra Leone, are one of the two largest ethnic groups in Sierra Leone, the other being the **Temne**. The Mende emerged as an ethnic group following a major invasion of a group of Mande people called the Mani in the interior region of southwestern Liberia, which is close to the border with eastern Sierra Leone. There the invading parties interacted with the **Gola** and **Vai** people and gave rise to the Mende people. By the 18th century, the Mende began pushing farther inland into the interior of present day Sierra Leone. The **Bullom**, one of the early groups they met there, still refer to the Mende as "Meni," strikingly close to the Mani origin of the Mende.

Subgroups of the Mende are not nearly as significant as they are among the **Limba**. Limba chiefdoms, for example, are named after Limba subgroups. Mende subgroups are hardly known or discussed outside groups with particular interest in them. The Kpaa Mende mark one such group, while there are also the Koh-Mende of the Kenema and Kailahun Districts and the Sewa Mende of the **Bo**, Kenema, and Pujehun Districts. The **Poro** for men and the **Sande** (or Bundo) for women are cultural institutions that dominate social and political life among the Mende.

MENDEGLA (c. 1820–1890). Mendegla, ruler of the Gallinas state centered on Joru (present day Pujehun District), was best known for his establishment of permanent peace in a Gallinas country that had been plagued by wars of succession in the 1880s. Mendegla did this by setting up a "peace Poro," the use of a powerful secret society to mandate peace in a region where this cultural institution was dominant.

Much of the information on Mendegla comes from the writings of **T. J. Alldridge**, who had been designated traveling commissioner by the British from **Freetown** and was eager to sign treaties with local rulers, which would become the claim to territory in this part of Africa. Alldridge traveled extensively in **Mende** and Gallinas countries in 1889 and stated that:

> The names of Mendingrah and **Kai Londo** are passwords . . . in the countries through which I have traveled . . . and from what I have seen myself of the way they govern the extensive territories under their jurisdiction, I gladly endorse the high opinion which I am convinced the masses generally entertain towards these chieftains.

When the Gallinas king, **Mana Siaka**, died in about 1872, his immediate successor, Jaya, was extremely incompetent and senile, and this led to competition between rival factions to accede to Mana Siaka's authority. A famous professional warrior, **Ndawa**, supported Fawundu, one of the main aspirants from Lower Gallinas, while Mendegla backed Boakei Gomna, another claimant. In repeated conflicts between Ndawa and Mendegla, the latter was victorious and Ndawa lost his life in one of the clashes with Mendegla's forces. This was about the time of the Scramble for Africa, and the British were making moves to control this area as a prelude to partition. However, by the time Traveling Commissioner Alldridge reached Joru in 1889, the peace Poro was already in place, and in an area of about 100 miles in radius, the peace Poro held until the colonial takeover in 1896.

Mendegla died six months after successfully effecting the peace **Poro**. Alldridge described him as ". . . a magnificent man, about six feet two in height and of unusual intelligence, a great warrior and beloved by the people."

METHODIST BOYS HIGH SCHOOL (MBHS). The Methodist Boys High School was opened on April 6, 1874, to provide education at a higher level for Wesleyan Methodists. It opened with eight pupils and was at first called the Boys High School and Training Institution. Its first principal was **Joseph Claudius May**, a learned Sierra Leonean. In 1903, the colonial government made an annual grant of thirty pounds sterling to the Wesleyan Boys High School, among others, to support a department formed for the training of teachers for primary schools. At the time of independence, the school moved from the familiar site at Soldier Street in the center of Freetown to new premises at Kissy Mess Mess just outside Freetown.

MILLER, FREDERIC ADOLPHUS (1862–1934). Frederic Adolphus Miller gained a reputation as a prominent African official in the colonial service and also later held leading positions in major organizations of political protest in Sierra Leone. Although he had only a primary education at the first model school set up by the colonial government, Miller educated himself first through menial jobs and then entered the colonial civil service a junior clerk. He eventually rose to become clerk of the Executive and **Legislative Councils**, a position only held by white officials after he retired from the service in 1922.

His position as clerk of the government gave him a thorough knowledge of colonial government practice, knowledge that he used with his characteristic eloquence to gain much attention among the urban elite in colonial **Freetown**. He thus became one of the founders and the first president of the African Civil Service Association, which looked after the interest of Africans in the colonial civil service. Miller also took a keen interest in local politics and was a founding member of the local branch of the National Congress of British West Africa, becoming one of its vice presidents. He was also vice president of a short-lived Sierra Leone Aborigines Society, which brought together educated people from the protectorate and the colony.

Miller supported young and aspiring politicians. He was unique in his support of Wallace Johnson when the latter formed the West African Youth League. This was not typical since the conservative elder elite of Freetown were decidedly snubbing Wallace Johnson. Miller's support encouraged some others of his stature to openly show their support. Miller served as secretary of the Sierra Leone Chamber of Commerce for a few years and worked actively in the

Methodist Church, becoming its representative on the Fourah Bay College Council, its governing body. Miller died at age 72 after a full and active life.

MINAH, FRANCIS MISHECK (1925–1987). Francis Minah was a prominent politician who became vice president of Sierra Leone in the 1980s. He was subsequently convicted of treason and was executed before the end of that decade.

He was born August 19, 1929, and attended the **Methodist Boys High School** before proceeding to England, where he studied at King's College of London University. After working in the civil service as a development officer in the late 1950s, Minah returned to Britain and was called to the bar at Gray's Inn in 1962. He returned to Sierra Leone and set up private practice, entering politics as a member of Parliament for Pujehun South constituency in 1967. Minah refused to declare for the **Sierra Leone People's Party (SLPP)** at the 1967 elections but later joined the government of **Siaka Stevens**, where he became a cabinet minister and ultimately vice president of Sierra Leone. Not long after **President J. S. Momoh** took office, Minah was implicated in a plot to overthrow the government. He was arrested, tried, and convicted of treason and was executed.

MOHAMED, JAMIL SAHID (c. 1930–1995). Jamil Sahid Mohamed was a powerful and influential Afro-Lebanese businessman in Sierra Leone during the rule of **Siaka Stevens** in the 1970s and 1980s. He was born in Sierra Leone of a Lebanese father and a Mandingo mother. He attended school in **Freetown** and went into business, and in the 1960s, he became a prominent figure in the diamond industry in the **Kono** diamond fields and developed a reputation for power and wealth derived from diamonds. When Siaka Stevens became ruler of Sierra Leone in 1969, Jamil became a close confidante of the president, influencing virtually every major government contract that was issued. He dominated and ran the Sierra Fishing Company, controlling Sierra Leone's production of fish and shrimp, which were exported to the Western world. By the end of the 1970s, Jamil was influencing government and ministerial appointments, and he was dreaded, feared, or admired, depending on the perception of the viewer.

When Siaka Stevens handed over the reins of government to **J. S. Momoh** in 1986, some of Momoh's immediate supporters who were dissatisfied with Jamil's dominant influence sought to influence Momoh against Jamil. Not long thereafter, Jamil became implicated in a coup attempt with prominent politicians such as **Francis Minah**, who was sentenced to death for treason and executed. Jamil, however, escaped from Sierra Leone and continued to live outside the country until his death.

MOMOH, ALBERT J. (c. 1908–1968). A. J. Momoh was a popular figure in Sierra Leone politics in the period around independence. He was one of the few politicians from the provinces who was more generally acceptable to virtually all groups in the **Freetown** middle class society. He was born at the town of Serabu in the Southern Province and had his early schooling there. He joined the colonial civil service where he spent most of his working life. He was one of the protectorate elite who founded both the **Protectorate Educational and Progressive Union (PEPU)** and the **Sierra Leone Organization Society (SOS)** in the 1950s. As these groups merged into the **Sierra Leone People's Party (SLPP)** in 1951, A. J. Momoh became the first vice president of that party, holding that position until 1957. Although he did not sit in Parliament, he was always given prominent positions by the SLPP government and served on a number of government boards and commissions. On his retirement from the civil service, he became member and then, until his death, chairman of the Public Service Commission.

MOMOH, JOSEPH SAIDU (1937–2003). Joseph Saidu Momoh held the distinguished positions of president of Sierra Leone and prior to that head of the Sierra Leone army. Born January 26, 1937, he attended the West African Methodist Collegiate School and the Technical Institute in **Freetown**. On joining the army, he saw training at the Nigerian Military Academy in Kaduna, Nigeria, and in England. He was commissioned as a second lieutenant in the Sierra Leone army in 1963. He rose through the ranks quickly to become force commander in 1972. President **Siaka Stevens** who appointed him decided to bring the head of the army into the government and appointed Brigadier Momoh as a cabinet minister of state in 1975.

In 1986, President Stevens singled out Momoh, the head of the army, to succeed him as president, forcing measures through Parliament to allow for the head of the army to become head of state. Momoh thus became president in 1986. Momoh was overthrown as president in a military coup led by **Valentine Strasser** in 1992. During the civil war in Sierra Leone, Momoh, along with others, was accused of treason and was detained. In the general amnesty that followed the end of the war, Momoh was released and temporarily left the country. He returned to Sierra Leone shortly before his death on August 3, 2003.

MORIBA KINDO (17?–1825). Moriba Kindo of the Bangura clan put together a conspiracy in 1817 that ultimately gained him the position of *Alikali* (ruler) of the thriving trading town of Port **Loko**, a major trading station on the way to **Freetown**.

The main thrust of the conspiracy was to eliminate the century-old domination of the ethnic **Soso** as rulers of Port Loko and replace it with the then numerically dominant **Temne**, who considered control of Port Loko as rightfully theirs. Moriba Kindo, who was also part Soso but emphasized his Temne ancestry, plotted primarily with Fatima Brima of the Kamara clan who also considered himself primarily Temne in spite of his additional **Mandinka** descent. The plotters had the tacit support of the Bai Forki, the overall ruler of Maforki within which Port Loko was located. The Bai Forki's position had been eclipsed by the Soso rulers of Port Loko and he wanted revenge.

The plan was to overthrow the current Sankoh ruler of Port Loko, Alimamy Brima Konkori, and eliminate Sankoh rule for good. Moriba Kindo would become the next ruler and at his death Fatima Brima or some other nominee of the Kamara clan would succeed. The rulership would henceforth rotate between the **Kamara** and **Bangura** clans.

To strengthen his claim to rulership, Moriba Kindo visited **Soso** country on the Melacourie River (in present-day Guinea) to collect information about the Soso, but also to acquire Islamic education, one of the pillars of Brima Konkori's hegemony over Port **Loko**. At the Melacourie, Moriba Kindo acquired the title of *Alikali* (from *al quadi*, meaning judge) with a turban in addition, and planned to introduce this title as ruler of Port Loko.

On his return, Kindo was quietly acknowledged as ruler of Port Loko by the Bai Forki and given a drum as the symbol of office, a similar drum being used for the same purpose by Brima Konkori. On the appointed day in 1817, the conspirators beat the drum. The unsuspecting Brima Konkori sent his men to arrest whoever was challenging his authority. The arresting party was successfully ambushed, and the coup plotters quickly moved to Saindugu, the Sankoh stronghold where they executed most of the **Soso** leaders, including Brima Konkori.

Upon the success of the revolution, Moriba Kindo became the next ruler of Port Loko with the title of *Alikali*. This position and the policy of alternation was confirmed in 1825 when Moriba Kindo died and Fatima Brima was installed as the new *Alikali* over the rival claims of a schemer named Kunia Banna (alias Jack Coby). This installation, which was consummated in spite of the threat of war on Port Loko brought by Kunia Bana, was facilitated by British intervention with troops from **Freetown**. The British feared that a war in Port Loko would disrupt trade. The British, however, reaped a reward in the form of a treaty with the *Alikali*, ceding land from Port Loko to the Scarcies to the British.

MORLAI LIMBA (17?–c. 1812). Morlai Limba, of **Limba** ethnicity, was affectionately called Pa Morlai, the term "pa" showing respect to a revered leader. Pa Morlai dominated the political scene north of Port Loko at the beginning of the 19th century by his successful military exploits. He thus incurred the envy and hostility of neighboring rulers who banded together to bring about his downfall.

Pa Morlai, who came from the town of Laia near **Port Loko**, had established control of considerable territory in the area, and, by 1810, he threatened the important political center at Sanda Magbolonto. The two rulers in Sanda Magbolonto, Burema Yarri who represented the Limba, and Yainkain Kamara, the Temne ruler, realized they needed help in stopping Pa Morlai. They turned to an unlikely source—the Bunduka, **Fula** traders from the Senegal region who had settled among the **Temne** around Sanda Magbolonto and taken many Temne wives. While the Temne of Sanda were jealous of these Bunduka Fula, they did not hesitate to call on Bunduka help in this time of crisis. The Bunduka used this opportunity to cement their position in the region by asking for continued future control of the territory of Mafonda near Sanda Magbolonto as compensation.

Even the Bunduka were terrified of Pa Morlai, reported to be bullet proof. They brought this matter before their leading **Islamic** scholar and diviner, Chernor Abbas, asking him to come up with an answer of how to deal with Pa Morlai. Chernor Abbas underwent a period of ritual seclusion following which he divined that Pa Morlai could only be felled by golden bullets. Who then would approach Pa Morlai to do this? Gaining information that Pa Morlai was about to travel to Mabanta in the Bombali District to secure an arms deal, it was decided that he should be ambushed. This plan was successful and the first golden bullet mortally wounded Pa Morlai. His bodyguards were overpowered and his head was cut off and presented to the leading rulers in the area. This ended the short-lived reign of Pa Morlai Limba.

MOYAMBA. The town after which the district of that same name was created, Moyamba, is located in the Kaiyamba Chiefdom. The headquarters town of the Moyamba District, Moyamba is historically important for female education in Sierra Leone, having the **Harford School for Girls**, the earliest high school for women in the Sierra Leone Provinces. Moyamba is ethnically **Mende** dominated, but being at the crossroads for entry into the Southern Province, the district includes different ethnic groups represented at Moyamba town. Moyamba Junction, a thriving stopover for entry into the town, has become a thriving town in itself.

MUSA, SOLOMON ANTHONY JAMES (1968?–1998). Solomon Anthony James Musa was one of the coup plotters in March 1992 who, as young military officers in their twenties, seized control of the government in Freetown and set up the **National Provisional Ruling Council (NPRC)**. Musa, a lieutenant at the time, became deputy chairman of the NPRC. A few months later, as chief secretary of state, he was head of the Council of Secretaries, the cabinet of the NPRC. He was also appointed chairman of the National Rehabilitation Committee (NARECOM) set up by the NPRC in August 1992. Musa is remembered for the strict discipline he maintained in the first few months of the NPRC rule.

In December 1992, some alleged coup plotters were arrested, some at the village of Lumpa and others later. They were tried and quickly sentenced to death and were executed, with Musa participating actively in this event. This execution of former leading lights in the army such as Yaya Kanu and **Bambay Kamara**, former commissioner of police, gave Musa a bad name. Ostensibly for his role in this execution, Musa was removed from the NPRC and was given a scholarship to study law in England. It was soon after he graduated that the **Armed Forces Revolutionary Council (AFRC)** coup took place in May 1997. Musa returned to Sierra Leone and was invited to become a member of the AFRC/**RUF** junta as acting vice chairman in place of **Foday Sankoh**, who was in detention in Nigeria. Musa was made chief secretary. The junta was forcibly removed from Freetown in February 1998 by the **ECOMOG** forces, and what remained of the group, including Musa, moved into the interior and continued the war there, still being accused of extreme brutality. He is reported to have died of an accidental gunshot wound in November 1998. He was mourned by the RUF who by then regarded him as their leader.

MUSLIM. *See* ISLAM.

MUSTAPHA, MOHAMED SANUSI (1903–1998?). Politician, businessman, and civic leader, Mohamed Sanusi Mustapha left an indelible mark on **Freetown** society around the middle of the 20th century. He was born in 1903 in an area of Freetown called "Fulah Town." His ancestral line of traders and Islamic leaders were bound to influence his later career. He attended the **Prince of Wales Secondary School** and was the most prominent student at the school. He worked briefly in the colonial government service starting in 1926 before going to England to read for a law degree at Lincoln's Inn. On his return, he went into business and was instrumental in founding the company of Mustapha Brothers, Importers and Exporters and also dealt in the local foodstuff. His business was prominent in rice milling as well as in buying produce as agents for the **Sierra Leone Produce Marketing Board**.

Like most businessmen in Sierra Leone history, Mustapha began to take an interest in civic affairs, becoming secretary of the East Ward Rate Payers Association in 1935. In that same time frame, he was also assistant secretary of the Sierra Leone chapter of the National Congress of British West Africa (NCBWA). Mustapha was one of the founders of the **Sierra Leone People's Party (SLPP)** and was elected to both the **Legislative Council** for Freetown East and the Executive Council. He became a cabinet minister, serving in the Ministries of Finance, Works, Transport, and Trade and Industry. During the period when Sierra Leone became a one-party state under President **Siaka Stevens**, Mustapha switched allegiance to the **All People's Congress (APC)** and became a member of the Governing Council and Central Committee of the APC.

Akpata was his nickname, and he became a very civic-minded leader, leading a move to save **Fourah Bay College** from colonial attempts to reduce it to a technical college, as well as providing leadership in the Sierra Leone Muslim Congress, particularly to set up the Congress Secondary School at Kissy in the 1960s. In 1987, the **University of Sierra Leone** awarded him an honorary doctor of civil laws (D.C.L.) in recognition of his accomplishments.

– N –

NAIMGBANA (c. 1730–1800). Naimgbana was a coastal subruler among the **Temne** who is said to have signed away part of his territory that was used to found the colony of Sierra Leone. Naimgbana became regent of Koya at the death of the Koya King in 1775. By Koya custom, when the *Obai* (king) died, the leading subrulers became successively rulers as regent in turn until the last of them died, whereupon a new Obai was crowned. Naimgbana was subruler of Rogbane up the Sierra Leone estuary. He was identified in one account as Panaburo, but in all other accounts he is identified as Naimgbana. One account indicates that when Europeans first wanted to record his name and asked for this in English, he replied "name Gbana" (my name is Gbana) and this was recorded as Naimgbana.

Naimgbana is believed to have signed a treaty ceding part of the territory on which the colony of Sierra Leone was founded in 1787, but since he could not read English he might not have known what he was signing. In spite of the disputes over this treaty, Naimgbana was interested in British influence, and he sent two of his sons to be educated in England and another son was sent for Islamic education in northern Sierra Leone. A street in **Freetown** is named after him.

NATIONAL COUNCIL OF THE COLONY OF SIERRA LEONE (NC). The term "colony" in the title of this party indicates clearly that it was limited to what was, at the time of its formation in August 1950, the colony of Sierra Leone. This generally referred to Freetown and the peninsula region. The rest of the country was the protectorate. The National Council represented a number of tiny **Krio** organizations that had coalesced under the leadership of **Dr. Herbert Bankole-Bright** to oppose the dominance of the numerically stronger protectorate people in the new political dispensation brought about by the new constitution. In the 1951 elections, the NC won a couple of seats and became the official opposition in the **Legislative Council**. Much of its opposition in that body seemed to reflect its hostility to the ruling **Sierra Leone People's Party (SLPP)** dominated by protectorate peoples. However, the party became increasingly unpopular as it was deserted by the majority of the ethnic Krio. In the 1957 general elections, the party lost miserably, not even getting enough votes to get back their financial deposits as candidates. Bankole-Bright died in 1958 and the party largely died with him.

NATIONAL DEVELOPMENT BANK LTD (NDB). The National Development Bank was set up by the Sierra Leone government in 1968. The primary focus of the bank was to promote agriculture and agro-based industries, and to provide technical support for agricultural and industrial development. Most of the funding for the work of the bank was expected to come from project funding from international donors.

NATIONAL DIAMOND MINING COMPANY (NDMC). This company was formed in 1970, jointly owned by the Sierra Leone government and the **Sierra Leone Selection Trust (SLST)**, to mine and market diamonds mined in Sierra Leone. In the 1980s, NDMC began to pursue proposals for the exploitation of underground diamond-bearing kimberlite ores. These plans did not reach fruition until the rebel war broke out in 1991. NDMC's activities were suspended in 1992 when the rebels attacked **Kono**.

NATIONAL REFORMATION COUNCIL (NRC). This was the name of the military junta that was formed after the 1967 elections in Sierra Leone. Senior officers of the army intervened when it became clear that the governor general was going to appoint **Siaka Stevens**, leader of the party that won the 1967 elections, as prime minister. The military leaders then invited **Andrew Terrence Juxon-Smith**, one of their number who was away on studies in England, to become the chairman of the new National Reformation Council and thus the head of the government. Junior officers of the army overthrew the NRC government in 1968 and ended NRC rule.

NATIONAL PROVISIONAL RULING COUNCIL (NPRC). The National Provisional Ruling Council was formed in the wake of the April 29, 1992, military putsch that ousted the government of President **Joseph Saidu Momoh**. The young military officers (mostly in their twenties) who had staged the coup d'état chose one of their number, **Valentine Strasser**, to become the head of the NPRC and thus the head of state. Although the NPRC leaders appointed a 21-member cabinet, that body was subordinate to the supreme council, the NPRC, which also included three civilians and the head of police, Joseph Stanley. Like all military governments, the NPRC abandoned the constitution and ruled by decree. That government was to remain in office until 1996, when it was pressured to hold elections and hand over to a newly elected president, **Tejan Kabba**.

The NPRC came into office with a wave of popularity as the urban populace, particularly students, gave it much support. Initial moves to address corruption like the Beccles-Davies, Laura Marcus-Jones, and Lynton Nylander Commissions of Enquiry to investigate allegations of corruption were at first very popular and the results, though controversial, were by and large implemented with some individual assets being confiscated by the government. In the early days of the regime, there was a move to address indiscipline with a popular NPRC member, **S. A. J. Musa**, storming the government offices driving fear of dire consequences into government officials. But as the NPRC became determined to prosecute the rebel war with no sign of success, and to execute and punish those who made them feel threatened, the government began to lose credibility, both within the country and with foreign Western governments, which had not been enthusiastic about a military government. Attempts by the NPRC to ease some of the harsh laws on their opponents and the press did not markedly change the mood of the populace. Internal reorganization within the NPRC leadership—the removal of S. A. J. Musa (he fled to England) and his replacement by **Julius Maada Bio** as the second in command—did not seem to do much good. The government forces did not seem to be faring well on the war front either; there were reports that some government soldiers were defecting to join the rebels (the "sobels" as these soldier/rebels came to be called) and these were wreaking havoc in the provinces. The military government now came to be seen as a corrupt and inept government. The Revolutionary United Front (RUF) was still strong in the interior despite the limited success of a South African mercenary unit named Executive Outcomes, hired by the NPRC. Executive Outcomes had captured some key locations, such as the diamond mines in Kono.

This unpopularity contributed to calls by civil society and international representatives for a return to democratic rule through elections. The National Commission for Democracy, which had been created by the NPRC, gradually became influential given the changing conditions and, together with the Interim National Electoral Commission, set up to make necessary moves toward electoral politics. These two bodies came to be more vocal by 1994. Encouraged by popular calls for democracy, these two bodies held conferences in 1995, which reechoed overwhelming calls for return to elected politics, calling for elections in 1996. These developments were reflected in a palace coup within the NPRC on January 16, 1996, in which the head of state, Captain Strasser, was ousted from office and succeeded by his second in command, Julius Maada Bio. Maada Bio claimed that Strasser's removal occurred because the latter was opposed to a return to electoral politics, but Bio's own subsequent statements and moves suggested the contrary. Mounting pressure from civil society ensured that elections were held in 1996 and the NPRC handed over controls to the elected leader, Ahmed Tejan Kabba.

NATIONAL UNITY PARTY (NUP). The National Unity Party was founded by **Dr. John Karimu** to contest the 1996 general elections. Dr. Karimu had held a cabinet position under the National Provisional Ruling Council (NPRC) government, which was then in office, and many believed that the NUP was closely allied with the military government. In the ensuing elections, the NUP scored 5.3 percent of the presidential votes and won four seats in Parliament. The NUP did not contest the 2002 elections.

NAVO, SYLVESTER T. S. T. Navo was a lawyer and politician from the provinces who later became a puisne judge. His early schooling was at **Bo Government** and **Prince of Wales schools**, and he studied law at the Middle Temple Inns of Court in London. He returned to Sierra Leone and went into private practice and later into politics, being elected to Parliament to represent the Bo North constituency in 1957. In 1958, he joined dissidents from the **Sierra Leone People's Party (SLPP)** to form the **People's National Party** and became its first treasurer. He was part of the delegation to the constitutional talks in London for Sierra Leone's independence in 1960. After Navo returned from the independence talks, a United Front government was set up and he was named parliamentary secretary in that short-lived government. During the military interregnum that followed the 1967 elections, Navo was arrested and detained. As the United Front government became a two-party system, Navo returned to the SLPP ranks. When most SLPP stalwarts faded from the political scene, S. T. Navo remained a member of the opposition in Parliament until 1973, when he decided to take up appointment as a puisne judge.

NDAWA (c. 1850–1888). Ndawa was perhaps the best-known leader in **Mende** country in the second half of the 19th century, known more for his being a warrior than a political leader. He was born about 1850 at Manjoro in the present Kailahun District. He exhibited very early signs of becoming a great warrior but was sold as a slave to one Sellu Tifa on being accused of the very serious crime of having an affair with someone's wife. Sellu Tifa later sold Ndawa to Makavoray, ruler of Tikonko, and Makavoray taught Ndawa many of the fine skills of warfare, including the use of the sword.

Ndawa was known for many exploits, selling the military machine that he developed to whomever he chose. None of his campaigns has lived more in historical memory than the "Kpove War" in Upper Mende country in the 1880s. Ndawa had teamed up with a young promising warrior named **Kai Londo** to defend the territory of Makavoray, his master, against another warrior named Benya whose rulership centered on Blama. Benya had been making incursions into Makavoray's domain, but Ndawa's campaign against Benya was successful and Benya was driven out for good.

Ndawa later built his own military stronghold of about 13 towns centered on Wende. The partnership with Kai Londo made the two famous, both as a result of defeating Benya and in attacking other areas. After one campaign however, Kai Londo suspected Ndawa of cheating him over the spoils of war. Angry, Ndawa threatened to attack Luawa, Kai Londo's center. This led to an equally famous confrontation between the two warriors in which Ndawa was defeated and agreed not to threaten Luawa any further.

By the mid 1880s, Ndawa's exploits were beginning to become a threat to areas of British interest close to the southern coast of Sierra Leone. When in 1886 Ndawa was poised to attack the town of Bandasuma, the governor of Sierra Leone, Sir Samuel Rowe, persuaded Makavoray to stop Ndawa. In 1887, Ndawa lent his services in partnership with Makaya, another famous warrior, to intervene in the Gallinas succession dispute. In the process, they destroyed a British customs post at Sulima and captured the ruler of Bandasuma, Madam Nyaloh. The British mounted an offensive against Ndawa and Makaya, destroying many towns in the area of Wende and freeing some 3,000 captives. In his last campaign in the area of Dama, Ndawa met his end when his Achilles tendon was severed by an unknown soldier. He is reported to have called out to a well-known warrior named Jami Lenga to finish him off so, for the sake of posterity, the great Ndawa's death would not be at the hands of an unknown.

NICOL, DAVIDSON SYLVESTER, HECTOR WILLOUGHBY (1924–1994). Davidson Nicol was a medical doctor, better known in Sierra Leone as the first vice chancellor of the newly constituted University of Sierra Leone in 1963. He later went on to become an undersecretary of the United Nations before his retirement. He was born in **Freetown** and attended schools in Nigeria and the **Prince of Wales School** in Freetown. He earned a degree in natural science at Cambridge University in 1946 and worked as a physician in the United Kingdom after qualifying in medicine. In 1958, he had received his Ph.D. from Cambridge. He taught at the University of Ibadan in

Nigeria and then became the first Sierra Leonean principal of **Fourah Bay College** in 1960. When the new University of Sierra Leone was established, Davidson Nicol became its first head as vice chancellor in 1963. The University of Sierra Leone includes both Fourah Bay College and Njala University College. The executive head of the university is the vice chancellor. He left this position to become Sierra Leone's high commissioner in the United Kingdom (in Great Britain) in 1968 and later permanent representative for Sierra Leone at the United Nations. He then took up a regular appointment in the United Nations Institute for Training and Research (UNITAR) in 1970, spending the next 10 years as a UN official.

Davidson Nicol was the first black person to be elected a Fellow at Cambridge University in England. He wrote poetry and short stories in the 1960s and also more scholarly works such as *Africanus Horton and Black Nationalism* (1969) and the *Future of Africa* (1980).

NJALA UNIVERSITY COLLEGE. What became the Njala University College was started in 1923 as the Njala Agricultural Training Institution for teachers for rural primary schools. It became more of a general training college for teachers, still emphasizing agriculture. In 1940, the Mabang Agricultural Academy was absorbed into the Njala Training College. Njala College remained one of three teacher training colleges in the provinces, the others being the **Union College at Bunumbu** and the Roman Catholic College in **Bo**. In 1964, Njala Training College was reconstituted into a university college as part of the proposed **University of Sierra Leone**. The University Act of 1967 consummated this policy. The Njala University College was predicated on agricultural education, offering degrees in agriculture and education.

NICOL-COLE, SAMUEL B. (1920–). Samuel Nicol-Cole became the first Sierra Leonean governor of the Central Bank of Sierra Leone, two years after its creation in 1964. He was born in Lagos, Nigeria, on August 8, 1920, and attended the **CMS Grammar School** in **Freetown** and King's College of Durham University, and finally Keble College, Oxford, where he studied economics. He taught economics at Fourah Bay College, and when the Central Bank of Sierra Leone was created in 1964, Nicol-Cole was appointed deputy governor; two years later he assumed the position of governor of the Central Bank. In 1970, he became an alternate director of the International Monetary Fund. He returned to Sierra Leone in 1975 where he lives in retirement.

NJIAKUNDOHUN (LATE 18TH TO MID-19TH CENTURY). Njiakundohun is remembered in Sierra Leone history as the leader of the first major wave of **Mende** immigrants who entered deep into the Sierra Leone interior, creating the westernmost frontier of the Mende territory, known as the Kpaa Mende. He was regarded as a great orator and warrior, two qualities of leadership held in great esteem among the Mende people.

This band of Mende migrants led by Njiakundohun in the early 19th century included many names that are still revered in Mende history, such as Kaoleh, Tongovila, Momoh Gete, Vanja Lekepeh, Kambayanga, Vonjo, Gbo, Kamagai, Kowa, Nyawa, and Sei. They encountered resistance from the **Banta**, a section of the ethnic **Temne** that they encountered in the south central area of Sierra Leone. The Banta were mostly defeated, and many fled the area. In the territory surrounding present-day Bo, this group of leaders dispersed with their immediate followers, founding new settlements that collectively came to be regarded as Kpaa Mende land. This became the western frontier of Mende country, guarded closely by the Kpaa Mende, whose martial prowess was closely tied to the **Wunde** Society a more military version of the **Poro**.

Njiakundohun built the town of Senehun, which became a prominent Mende center. One of his daughters, Soma, became the well-known **Madam Yoko**. He died about the middle of the 19th century.

NOMOLI. The *nomoli* were steatite figurines carved broadly in human form by the Kissi and Bullom peoples in the interior of Sierra Leone. Some of the nomoli that have been unearthed date back to the 15th century. They have been more recently discovered by farmers and construction workers. However, nomoli were sometimes carved out of wood instead of steatite and often represented important men who had died; these were kept in small separate houses.

The *nomoli* were basically fertility dolls, believed by these early inhabitants of Sierra Leone to have a potency for fertility for humans or the soil. They could be buried in the fields for a successful harvest or kept in some unobtrusive part of the dwelling as guardian angels. Sacrifices of chickens or goats were made to them annually, a form of ancestor worship. Diviners also used *nomoli* to obtain health and fertility, especially for women who had no children.

NORMAN, SAM HINGA (1940–). While the civil war raged in Sierra Leone, Sam Hinga Norman was deputy defense minister from 1998–2002, and coordinator of the **Civil Defense Forces (CDF)**, a coalescence of volunteer defense forces from different parts of the country. The main arm of the CDF was the **Kamajor** forces from southern Sierra Leone. Norman was known as the head of the Kamajor forces. The defense of the country by the Kamajor gave its leaders a free hand in prosecuting the war. At the end of the war, Hinga Norman was appointed minister of internal affairs. When the Special Court was set up in 2003, one of the first people to be indicted was Hinga Norman, accused of committing crimes against humanity as head of the Kamajor.

NYAGUA (c. 1840–1906). Nyagua was one of the most prominent political leaders among the **Mende** in the second half of the 19th century. He ruled a large Mende state centered in Panguma in present-day Kenema District, which expanded when he inherited the neighboring state of Dodo upon the death of his father, Faba, in 1889. Njyagua's enormous power and influence made it inevitable that the British would seek to eliminate him. This happened with his arrest and banishment in 1898.

Nyagua came to prominence as a warrior, at first apprenticed to a famous Mende leader named Makaya. In the 1870s, he conquered and dominated a huge section of neighboring Kono territory and later, with the support of the Kono leader, **Matturi**, defeated **Ndawa** who had threatened towns ruled by Faba, Nyagua's father. While Nyagua built the town of Panguma and a state surrounding it, his link with Faba and his own prominence made it possible for him to be appointed ruler of Dodo upon Faba's death. Combining rulership of Panguma and Dodo gave Nyagua tremendous power and influence.

By the time Faba died, the British had pushed into the interior and were poised to take over control of the entire area. It was inevitable that they would clash with Nyagua, and it was Travelling Commissioner, **T. J. Alldridge**, who first expressed dislike for Nyagua's authority when Nyagua failed to attend a meeting called by Alldridge in 1889. But Nyagua and the British cooperated for the next few years; Nyagua's son was admitted into high school in Freetown, and Nyagua handed over his former mentor, Makaya, to the British who wanted Makaya for attacking areas then under British control. When the **sofas**, fighters of the Mandinka empire builder, **Samori Toure**, attacked Nyagua's territory in 1893, Nyagua complained to the British who sent troops to expel the sofas.

All of this cooperation did not eliminate the perceived threat that Nyagua posed to British suzerainty, and the British pounced on him at every opportunity. When the protectorate was declared in 1896 and with it the house tax, Panguma, Nyagua's domain, was initially exempt. However based on rumors that Nyagua was holding secret meetings with other local rulers who were planning to resist, Nyagua was arrested in May 1898 and taken to **Freetown**. He was held there for a few months since there was no clear evidence of wrongdoing on his part. Later the British accused him of sending secret messages to his people, criticizing them for not resisting his arrest. Nyagua was banished to the Gold Coast, along with Bai Bureh and Kpana Lewis, where he died in 1906.

– O –

OMAR JAMBOURIA (c. 1850—1931). Omar Jambouria was an ethnic Fula trader in **Freetown** who used his resources to further Islamic education in Freetown at a time when such education was neglected by the colonial government. As his leadership became recognized, he also promoted the observance of **Islam** in the east end of Freetown.

The name Jambouria referred to his town of origin in the Futa Jalon highlands and came to be appended to his name as was a popular custom among ethnic groups in Freetown. Omar was initially a clerk for the French company called Compagnie Française de l'Afrique Occidentale (CFAO), which was a prominent business in Freetown. He later became a factor, trading kolanuts for this company. The CFAO used Omar's services to lead a trade mission to Futa

Jalon, a major source of trade to the colony. Omar's success in this trade brought him wealth and enhanced his leadership potential among the growing **Fula** migrant population in Freetown, whose interests he began to champion.

One major area of this was in promoting Islamic education. He started a *madrassa* (Islamic school) at his house in Jenkins Street in the east end of Freetown. He tenaciously pursued this issue of Islamic education with the colonial government, which later agreed to open a school for the children of Fula residents in Freetown, which incorporated learning in Arabic. This was no mean feat with a government that had shown open hostility to Islam in the colony.

While education was his chief concern, Omar also promoted Islam in general and built a mosque for ethnic Fula in the area where he lived. To consolidate his own leadership position, he made the *hajj* (pilgrimage) to Mecca, according him the use of the title *al hajj*. All expenses for the *hajj* were paid by the CFAO for which he had labored so diligently.

Both the Fula community in Freetown and the colonial government began to regard Omar as a leader of the Fula in Freetown. The government appointed Omar to the short-lived Mohammedan Board of Education in 1906. As the colonial government began to recognize ethnic leadership in the colony, Omar was elected "Fula Chief" in Freetown in 1902 to represent Fula interests and mediate among the Fula in Freetown. The value of this election was seen when the governor of the colony himself attended the installation ceremony at Victoria Park in the center of Freetown. Omar then took the Islamic leadership title of Alimamy and came to be popularly referred to as alimamy among dignitaries of all religious persuasions in Freetown.

– P –

PARKES, JAMES CHARLES ERNEST (1861–1899). In a short life span of 38 years, James Charles Ernest Parkes left a strong impression on the Department of Native Affairs, especially during the establishment of the British protectorate over the interior of the small colony of Sierra Leone in 1896. His knowledge of the interior gained from working with **T. G. Lawson** gave him a decided advantage in his office. Parkes wanted to forge a partnership between the Krios and the colonial government in the administration of the protectorate but the British had other ideas. Parkes was born in **Freetown** and educated at the **CMS Grammar School**. He went to study law in England but illness cut short his studies and he returned home to work in the colonial service as assistant clerk to the commandant at **Sherbro**. In 1884, he moved to the colonial secretary's office where he became increasingly involved in 'native affairs'. His work with Lawson gave him an advantage. Lawson recommended Parkes as his successor as he retired in 1888, and Parkes was appointed superintendent of the Aborigines Department, directly under the governor's office. In 1891, the Aborigines Department was renamed the Department of Native Affairs and Parkes was named its secretary.

In 1890, the Frontier Police Force was created to keep the peace in the interior. It became a strong rival with Parkes' establishment for influence over colonial government policy on the interior. Unfortunately for Parkes, the Frontier Police was always headed by a European, and in the colonial hierarchy Europeans were felt to be superior to Africans. Consequently, the Frontier Police and its European superintendent, E. A. W. Lendy, gradually edged out Parkes' influence in protectorate affairs. When in 1892 Parkes suggested that a protectorate be declared in the interior under Krio "political agents," his aim was partly to reduce the influence of the Frontier Police and its European officers. His views were rejected and the role of the Frontier Police increased.

In the conflict with the forces of **Samori Toure** in the runup to the declaration of the protectorate, Parkes advised maintaining friendly relations with Samori while Lendy advocated military action against him. Lendy, who in the process accused Parkes of taking bribes from Samori, prevailed; in the military action against Samori in December 1893, rampant confusion resulted and Lendy, who led the charge personally, was killed in action. Even though Parkes denied Lendy's accusations of bribery, the secretary of state in the Colonial Office in London ordered an inquiry conducted by the highest body in the colony in 1894, the Executive Council. Parkes was "unanimously and fully acquitted."

Parkes again came in conflict with Sir **Frederic Cardew**, the new governor in 1894, over the method of taxation in the new protectorate. Parkes recommended a poll tax instead of the house tax the governor was in favor of. Of course, the governor's views won the day and the house tax became the last straw, leading to massive rebellion in 1898. This did not endear Parkes to the colonial authorities, and Governor Cardew openly demeaned Parkes at the Commission of Enquiry into the causes of the 1898 rebellion. Parkes became ill and died in 1899. His Native Affairs Department was abolished upon his death.

PEOPLE'S DEMOCRATIC PARTY (PDP). Popularly called "Sorbeh," this party was formed in 1995 to contest the 1996 general elections. Its leader, Thaimu Bangura, was an ethnic **Temne**, and his party had a strong following among urban ethnic Temne in the capital of **Freetown**. In the 1996 elections, the party leader had 16 percent of the votes cast for president—the third highest proportion of the votes. The PDP also won 12 seats, the third highest number. By the agreement for proportional representation in government, the PDP leader was given a cabinet position.

PEOPLE'S NATIONAL PARTY (PNP). The PNP was formed in 1958 due to a split in the leadership ranks of the ruling **Sierra Leone People's Party (SLPP)**. The breakaway group, which formed the PNP, was led by **Albert Margai**, brother of the newly elected prime minister but included such political heavyweights as **S. T. Navo**, **A. J. Massally**, Maigore Kallon, and **Siaka Stevens** and others who were later to become prominent in politics. The PNP had a brief period of success, emphasizing a more aggressive attitude to politics and showing greater interest in creating harmony between the colony and protectorate. However, this success was short-lived. While the party won some seats in the **District Council** and **Freetown** municipality elections in 1959, the SLPP still had a commanding lead. When **Milton Margai** formed a United Front coalition for the constitutional talks in London that were to precede independence, the PNP leadership joined the coalition. Its leaders accepted cabinet positions in 1960 at the end of the talks, and this spelled the demise of the PNP.

PEOPLE'S PROGRESSIVE PARTY (PPP). A political party formed by Dr. **Abass Bundu** to contest the 1996 general elections, the party garnered 2.9 percent of the votes for its leader and presidential candidate. The party apparently disbanded and did not field in candidates for the 2002 elections.

PETERS, THOMAS (c. 1738–1792). Against tremendous odds, Thomas Peters, one of the early settlers in **Freetown**, contributed significantly to the founding of the settlement of Freetown.

He was born a slave in the North American colonies and worked in his master's flour mill in North Carolina. Enticed by the promise of freedom made by the British during the American Revolution, Peters, like a number of other slaves, ran away to join the British soldiers. He rose to the rank of sergeant in a unit called the Black Pioneers. When the British lost the war, they evacuated Peters and other black loyalists to Nova Scotia in Canada. After seven years in Nova Scotia, the former slaves were still living on meager government rations and suffering form the bitter cold, and had not received land that had been promised them.

Although poor and illiterate, Peters found the courage and determination to travel to England to seek help for his people. The voyage was fraught with great risks, for Peters was still legally a slave in the United States and could have been handed over by a ship captain to be sent back to slavery in America. But Peters made it to London and convinced the Sierra Leone Company in charge of the new colony of Sierra Leone to evacuate his people to Sierra Leone. Peters had to return to Nova Scotia to rally his people to join the trip to what was to them an unknown Africa about which they had only heard derogatory things. He succeeded in convincing more than a thousand of the black loyalists to leave Nova Scotia and sail to Sierra Leone on ships provided by the British.

When problems surfaced between the new settlers and the Sierra Leone Company over the pattern of government in the colony, Peters confronted the British governor in the colony and demanded the right of participation in the government for his people. The British never agreed to this, but Peters is remembered for his courage in standing up for his people against seemingly insurmountable odds.

PIEH, SENGBE (c. 1812–1879). In Sierra Leone history, Sengbe Pieh is remembered as the courageous **Mende** youth who was captured and shipped to the Americas as a slave, but whose burning desire for freedom led to his leading a revolt on board the ship *Amistad*. This ultimately resulted in his return to his native home, a free man. American history accounts about the same individual are similar, although he is identified by his given Western name, **Joseph Cinque**.

Sengbe was born about 1812 in the area of Gallinas country near the southern coast of Sierra Leone. He was a young farmer, married with three children, when he was captured in 1839 and sold as a slave. He was then transported across the Atlantic to Havana, Cuba, where, along with 48 others from the same region in Sierra Leone, he was sold to a Spanish sugar planter named Jose Ruiz. It was this Spanish slaver who gave him the name Joseph Cinque, by which he came to be known in American history. Sengbe and other slaves were being taken from Cuba aboard the ship *Amistad* to work in plantations in Port Principe. Three days out at sea, Sengbe pulled a loose spike he had seen on the deck and used it to free himself and his colleagues. Armed with cane knives that they found on board, Sengbe and the other slaves, who were mostly ethnic Mende, attacked the ship's crew. The Mende slaves killed the ship-owner captain and another crew member and drove the others overboard. One of the crew was spared and was ordered to sail the ship back to Sierra Leone. The Spanish crewman tried to trick the slaves by sailing the ship toward Cuba at night when a storm drove the *Amistad* toward the United States coast. There, Sengbe and his men were captured by the United States navy off Long Island, New York, and were charged with murder and piracy.

A group of antislavery Americans found out about the case and came to the rescue of Sengbe and his group. They formed the "*Amistad* Committee," which recruited prominent lawyers to defend the captured Africans who were finally freed after former president John Quincy Adams successfully argued their case in the United States Supreme Court. Sengbe and his Mende compatriots became celebrities in the United States; many people bought his portrait and paid to hear him speak on the evils of slavery.

In January 1842, Sengbe and his group returned to their home in the Sierra Leone region under the auspices of American missionaries who then founded the Mende Mission in the area of Sengbe's home in Mende country. This American Missionary Association began the work of bringing Christianity and Western education to the Mende people. Sengbe is also remembered as having been instrumental in the early spread of Western education to the Mende.

POREKERE FORAY BENIA (18?–1893). Porekere Foray Benia was an able general who became leader of a contingent of the **sofa**, soldiers of *Samori Toure*. His military exploits in the area of northeastern Sierra Leone aroused British interest as it coincided with the Scramble for Africa.

By 1892, when Porekere took control of this area, the French had occupied the town of Heremakono in Guinea, to the northeast of Koranko country. This prevented the *sofa* from using their usual route to Freetown, the source of their arms supply. So **Kemoko Bilali**, the *sofa* general formerly in charge of the Sierra Leone hinterland, sent Porekere to open a more easterly route through **Koranko** and Konike Temne countries to get to Freetown.

Porekere built a number of strongholds in Konike country in eastern Sierra Leone. He started his assignment by making an alliance with the southern Koranko, whom he had apparently subdued, against the Konike **Temne**. A number of towns were attacked and destroyed, but Porekere later fell out with the Koranko over distribution of the spoils, and he attacked his former allies.

At this point the Native Affairs Department in Freetown, wanting to prevent colonial troops being sent against Porekere, intervened. **J. C. E. Parkes**, the head of that department, wrote to Porekere warning him off Konike. Porekere obeyed, retired eastward, and captured the towns of Tecuyama and Levuma, towns claimed by the powerful **Mende** ruler **Nyagua**. It appears that a chief, Tellu of Kuruwa, who had a land dispute with **Nyagua**, had asked Porekere for assistance.

While people such as Parkes had good relations with the **sofa**, particularly with Porekere, they could not suppress the report to the Colonial Office that Porekere had attacked Nyagua, a ruler in treaty with the British. Orders were given for an expedition against Porekere. The French had been fighting **Samori** since 1871 and were also determined to put an end to sofa hegemony and claim former sofa-controlled areas as French by right of conquest. A French military officer, Lieutenant Gaston Maritz, had moved into this area and joined forces with Kono warriors, subjects of Nyagua, to drive Porekere out of Tecuyama. Porekere then retreated farther northwest to Bagbema, from where he joined as a mercenary on one side of a land dispute involving two Mende rulers, Foray and Vonjo. Porekere helped Foray attack Vonjo at the town of Tungea.

Meanwhile the British expedition against Porrekere had set out, led by Captain E. W. Lendy with Captain A. B. Ellis commanding the troops. Hearing of Maritz' activities in the area, Ellis sent an advance warning of their arrival to the French officer. It would appear that this information failed to reach Maritz who was acting on information from his Kono allies that a large sofa force was encamped at Waima in eastern Kono country. This force was, of course, Lendy's. British and French each mistook the other for sofa and attacked each other at Waima, both sides losing a number of soldiers, including both Lendy and Maritz.

A **Krio** sub-inspector, Charles Taylor, was also on his way with earlier orders to join Lendy on the expedition. On learning that Porekere and Foray were marching toward Tungea, Taylor hurried to meet them there. The sofa attacked at Varma, a town subject to Tungea where Taylor was encamped and were badly defeated by Taylor's troops, losing 250 dead and 150 taken prisoner. Porekere was among those killed.

PORO. A prominent secret society found among the **Mende** and **Temne** of Sierra Leone. It is believed to have originated among the **Sherbro** ethnic group and spread first among the Temne. It is basically a male society, although a few women are initiated into it. For example, any female local ruler used to be initiated into the Poro. While there is no overarching organization of the Poro, any Poro member from one community normally enjoys the same privileges if he visits another Poro community. One of the major roles of the Poro is control of the rite of passage of males from childhood to adulthood. Young boys who are to undergo the rite are secluded from the community in a restricted clearing in the forest referred to as the Poro Bush. Noninitiates and women are forbidden to enter the Poro Bush, whether or not the Poro is in session. In the rite of passage, young boys are trained to become men, traditionally over a period of a few years. They are given vocational training and educated regarding their society's values and tradition. On completion of training, they emerge as men with new names. The graduation event was a major festival in traditional society. This training is considerably shorter and more symbolic today.

In precolonial times, Poro also had political, cultural, and religious roles. It dominated certain types of ritual in society and had masked spirits such as the *Gbeni,* which were feared by all in the community, including junior members of the Poro. Its senior members, a position to which only a few members could aspire, made decisions about political issues that the local ruler, also a member of the Poro, had to accept. It was responsible for curing barrenness in women, who were invariably initiated into the Poro. The institution also regulated economic matters, such as putting a ban on trade when necessary.

The Poro is more of a cultural institution today, and many of its functions have been taken over by Western-type institutions.

PORT LOKO. The town of Port Loko is located in the Maforki Chiefdom found in the district named after Port Loko. One of the larger towns in Sierra Leone, Port Loko is today predominantly inhabited by **Temne** peoples. The Temne replaced the **Loko** ethnic group after whom the town, a former port for trade, came to be known. The Loko had earlier come to dominate Baga and **Bulom** peoples at this site. The proximity of **Port Loko** to **Freetown** made it a major stopping point for trade coming to Freetown from the interior of Sierra Leone in the 19th century.

PORTER, ARTHUR THOMAS (1924–). Arthur Porter became the first vice chancellor of the University of Sierra Leone. (From 1968 to 1972, the vice chancellorship was held, for a period of two years, alternately by the principal of Fourah Bay College and the principal of Njala University College. In 1972, the University of Sierra Leone Act, passed by Parliament, made the vice chancellorship into a permanent position, separate from the principalship of its two constituent colleges, and Porter became the first permanent vice chancellor). He was born in **Freetown**, the son of a popular businessman and contractor of the same name. He attended the **CMS Grammar School** and **Fourah Bay College** in Sierra Leone before proceeding to Cambridge University in England, where he took the honors course in history. He returned to Sierra Leone in 1952 and joined the faculty at Fourah Bay College.

Porter later traveled to the United States where he received a Ph.D. in sociology from Boston University. In Sierra Leone, he became director of the Institute of African Studies and professor of history before taking up appointment as principal of Royal College, Nairobi, Kenya. He was invited to return to Sierra Leone in 1973 to head the newly constituted University of Sierra Leone as vice chancellor.

Arthur Porter served on many boards, as chairman of the board of the **National Diamond Mining Company**, and after retirement from the vice chancellorship, as pro chancellor of the same university.

PRATT, ISAAC BENJAMIN (c. 1805–1880). In the 19th century, Isaac Benjamin Pratt was a thriving merchant in the Sierra Leone colony, who became the Aku king and later achieved the coveted position of member of the **Legislative Council**.

Pratt was a Yoruba liberated African from life in Nigeria who set up business and progressed from small beginnings to become one of the most prosperous merchants in the colony. He owned his own ship by the mid-19th century and successfully invested in real estate at the center of **Freetown**. He was acknowledged as a leader among the Aku (Yoruba) community in the colony and was instrumental in founding benefit societies that sought to promote the interests of the Aku in the colony. He was recognized as deputy to the Aku king, John Macauley, who was also head of the Benevolent (Benefit) Society. When Macauley died in 1867, Pratt was his logical successor as Aku king. His leadership position in the colony was formally recognized when the governor of the colony, Samuel Rowe, appointed Pratt to the Legislative Council in 1879.

PRINCE OF WALES SCHOOL. When the Prince of Wales arrived in **Freetown** on a visit in 1925, he formally opened a government secondary school at Kingtom in Freetown. The building housing the new government school was bought by the government from the Wesleyan Mission, which had used it for a training school but had recently closed. The Prince of Wales School represented a move away from the Christian denominational schools. It provided cheaper education to people who were not strongly committed to any one denomination. The government provided free meals and well qualified teachers, ensuring very high standards. The school attracted large numbers of Muslim children. The initial snobbery against the nondenominational bias of the school quickly gave way to stimulated interest as products of the Prince of Wales School had very bright prospects due to the high standard of education provided there. The Prince of Wales School has sustained a reputation for a high standard of secondary education, with a strong emphasis on science education.

PROTECTORATE ASSEMBLY. The Protectorate Assembly was set up in 1946 by the colonial government in an attempt to provide a forum where people from the protectorate could come together to discuss issues relevant to their region and advise the government. The Protectorate Assembly became, in effect, the training ground for prominent elements from the protectorate who assumed the mantle of national politics in subsequent years. It held its first meeting in July 23, 1946.

The Assembly was chaired by the chief commissioner of the protectorate, a British official. The membership included officials from departments relevant to the protectorate such as agriculture, education, forestry, and public works. Of the 32 unofficial members, 26 were chosen by the District Councils, the other 6 Africans being nominated by the governor to represent interests other than traditional leadership. Since the majority of the membership were paramount chiefs drawn from the District Councils, Western trained protectorate elements criticized the Assembly as unrepresentative of the "progressive" elements of the protectorate and likely to be more malleable in the hands of the colonial government. In fact, these Western-educated protectorate leaders found ways of influencing the viewpoints expressed by the chiefs in the Assembly to the point that the most vocal chiefs in the Assembly, such as Kai Tongi and Mana Luseni, were deposed in the first four years of the Assembly.

The nonchiefly members of the Protectorate Assembly included well-known names such as Y. D. Sesay, D. L. Sumner, **Amadu Wurie**, R. B. Kowa, **Milton Margai**, and **Siaka Stevens**. The Assembly remained important as long as protectorate people were poorly represented in prominent institutions such as the **Legislative**

Councils. When this was rectified by the Stevenson Constitution, the Assembly ceased to be important. It held its last meeting in 1955 and was dissolved in 1957.

PROTECTORATE EDUCATIONAL PROGRESSIVE UNION (PEPU). PEPU, as it was called, came to be known as a protectorate organization when it was revived in 1946, even though it had been founded in 1929. Its revival in 1946 represented a coming together of the traditional elite of paramount chiefs and western-trained protectorate leaders, such as **Milton Margai**, **A. J. Momoh**, and **Amadu Wurie.** The purpose of PEPU was to raise funds for scholarships to deserving protectorate pupils to attend secondary schools and to pursue higher education. Thus in 1946 PEPU was instrumental in the granting of 10 scholarships to protectorate students to do teacher training at **Fourah Bay College**. With the introduction of the debate on the 1947 constitution, PEPU began to take on a political color, eventually becoming a major arm of the newly founded **Sierra Leone People's Party** in 1951.

PUJEHUN. The Pujehun District is centered around the town of Pujehun. At the start of the protectorate, what later became the Pujehun District was located around the town of Bandajuma and was then called Bandajuma District. By the 1920s, the chief town of that district had been removed to Pujehun and henceforth became the Pujehun District. Pujehun is ethnically dominated by **Vai** (**Galinas**) and **Mende** peoples. It is historically a prominent center, less so today.

– R –

RAINY, WILLIAM (c. 1819–1878). William Rainy was a well-known lawyer in **Freetown** of Afro West Indian origin who worked hard to fight racism in Sierra Leone and elsewhere. He migrated to Sierra Leone from what became the Dominican Republic and first worked at the customs department in the 1840s. He then studied law at the Inner Temple in England, returning to Sierra Leone to set up private practice in 1950.

Rainy became very popular in Freetown for taking up cases of blatant racism, particularly where it involved European officials of the colonial administration such as the case of the colonial surgeon, Robert Bradshaw, who had to settle out of court with a payment of 30 pounds sterling. He was also known for organizing and signing petitions against the colonial government at a time when this was the only means of protest against unpopular colonial government measures. Rainy dominated several local newspapers in Freetown and used this venue to attack his critics and opponents. He attended a meeting of the Anti-Slavery Conference in Paris in 1867 as first delegate from Sierra Leone. The French government presented him with a medal for his services to French citizens who were his clients in Sierra Leone. He returned to Freetown to set up a local branch of the Anti-Slavery Society. He died in 1878.

RASSIN, ALIMAMY (c. 1825–1890). Alimamy Rassin, who ruled the territory known as Mafonda in the 19th century, came to be well known for his aversion to war and his efforts for peace. He set up a special fund in Mafonda used to negotiate peace in the region.

Rassin was born in Mafonda in the present Sanda Magbolonto chiefdom of Bombali District about 1825. His father. Samba Jombor, was a Bunduka Fula from Futa Toro in Senegal, and his mother was ethnic **Temne**. He lived as a child in the home of his cousin, Alimamy Ahmadu, the ruler of Mafonda after his father had left Mafonda for Futa Toro.

It was Alimamy Ahmadu who raised Rassin to detest war, and he carried this through the rest of his life. He was a gifted pupil in the local Islamic school and word of his excellence spread through Sierra Leone and beyond. Delegations came to Mafonda to take him back to Futa Toro, but Alimamy Ahmadu, whom Rassin now regarded as father, would not give him up.

As Rassin grew in the respect and admiration of his people, he became the logical successor to Alimamy Ahmadu who died about 1845. But Rassin would not accept the position immediately, and 12 years elapsed before he agreed to be installed ruler of Mafonda in about 1857. As ruler of Mafonda, Rassin took the title of alimamy and made clear his aversion for war. He set up a fund directed by Pa

Santigie Bokari Kamara to negotiate peace, and this fund was replenished from fines at the ruler's court. He negotiated peace in political disputes in Sanda Tenraran, Tonko **Limba**, Yoni, and Bombali **Temne**, all polities in the near and distant region of Mafonda.

When the forces of the Mandinka emperor **Samori Toure** invaded northern Sierra Leone, much of the region was captured and brought under Samori's empire. The invaders were so awed by the influence of Islam in the administration of Mafonda, that they withdrew and left Mafonda alone. The colonial administration in **Freetown**, impressed with Rassin's efforts to maintain peace in the interior, offered him an annual payment of 2,000 bars of iron, a form of currency at the time. However, Rassin rejected this, believing that he should not be materially rewarded for making peace.

Rassin died in 1890, and one of his grandsons, **Amadu Wurie** believes that had Rassin not died before the Bai Bureh war of resistance in 1898, he could have averted the war.

RAYMOND, WILLIAM (1815–1847). William Raymond was a determined missionary from the United States whose resilience was responsible for the survival of the Mende Mission, the vehicle for first bringing Western education to the provinces of Sierra Leone.

Raymond's desire to train as a minister was initially thwarted allegedly because he was too close to black students. He was driven from Amherst College in Massachusetts and completed his education at Oberlin College in Ohio. He moved to Canada where he lived among fugitive slaves for several years. His passionate desire to go to West Africa was fulfilled with the *Amistad* Committee, set up to defend the slaves led by **Sengbe Pieh**, who had revolted on the *Amistad* ship, and had been captured and then freed by the United States Supreme Court in 1841. The committee hired Raymond to teach the freed slaves at Farmington, Connecticut. Raymond was one of the three missionaries who accompanied the *Amistad* people back to **Mende** country in Sierra Leone.

It was Raymond who survived to carry on the mission with little support from the *Amistad* Committee, which severely criticized his methods and sent little money for the mission. In addition, Raymond was operating in a hostile environment where the Atlantic slave trade was still raging and the slave traders were encouraging the local rulers to turn against Raymond. With dogged determination, Raymond developed the mission and built a church and mission house and a school. He expanded the mission by using his meager funds to pay for the manumission of slaves who then became servants of the mission. In 1846, the *Amistad* Committee told Raymond to end the mission and if possible close the school. Regarding the pupils he had redeemed from slavery as his own children, Raymond told the committee that he preferred to die with the children rather than discharge them.

Raymond had some relief when in 1846 the American Missionary Association was founded, and this body took over responsibility for the **Mende** Mission. Raymond was recalled in 1847 but died in Freetown on his way back to the United States. His resistance against all odds led to the survival of the mission. When he died, the school, which had opened a year earlier, had more than 100 pupils and the mission establishment had a staff of 15.

RENNER-THOMAS, ADE (1945–). Prominent barrister and educator, Renner-Thomas became chief justice of Sierra Leone in 2005. He was educated at the **Prince of Wales** School and **Fourah Bay College** before studying law in England while employed as a civil servant at the Ministry of Foreign Affairs, attached to the Sierra Leone Embassy in France. When he returned to Sierra Leone in the late 1970s, he set up private practice in Freetown and later took up appointment as lecturer in Law at Fourah Bay College. He became senior lecturer before resigning that position to concentrate on his law firm, Renner-Thomas and Co. His private practice was highly successful and he later owned property in **Freetown** including the Africanus House on Howe Street. He was a law consultant to many businesses in Freetown and sat on several boards. He was also president of the Sierra Leone Bar Association in 1986–1988. In 2005, he was appointed chief justice of Sierra Leone.

Revolutionary United Front (RUF). The Revolutionary United Front was formed in 1991 by dissident rebels from Sierra Leone led by **Foday Sankoh**, in collaboration with **Charles Taylor**, who was leading a rebellion against the government of Liberia. The Sierra Leone government had supported the efforts of the Economic Community of West African states, which had set up the **ECOMOG (Economic**

Community Cease-Fire Monitoring Group) to police the war in Liberia. ECOMOG had set up a base in Sierra Leone and Taylor became determined to extend the war into Sierra Leone.

The RUF invasion started on March 23, 1990, from the eastern province border with Liberia. Within a month, RUF forces controlled the Kailahun District in the eastern province and were making inroads into the Pujehun District. The declared aim of the RUF was to overthrow the corrupt APC government. People in the southern and eastern province who had strong feelings of resentment against the APC were therefore encouraged to join the RUF, whose ranks were consequently swollen particularly with the youth who became young warriors. The RUF movement was also attractive to the poor and underprivileged, who saw little opportunity of improving their situations. Unemployment and the visible elements of corruption provided fodder for the RUF in their recruitment drive particularly outside Freetown.

The Sierra Leone government responded to the first wave of attacks by mobilizing assistance from the neighboring Republic of Guinea and soldiers from Nigeria. These combined forces scored some success, but the RUF were there to stay and changed tactics, using simulators to imitate the sound of machine gun fire, which caused havoc among government troops and the populace in the provinces.

The RUF invasion spurned a military coup d'état that overthrew the government of President **Joseph Saidu Momoh** in 1992. Initial attempts by the new military government to end the war proved abortive and the RUF advance into the heart of Sierra Leone became pervasive by 1994. As their successes became obvious, some of the government troops sent to fight them began to defect to the RUF ranks, attacking and plundering the villages in the interior. The military government again sought outside help from a South African unit called Executive Outcomes, which stalled the RUF advance by 1995. Failure to successfully prosecute the rebel war again led to the demise of the military government as tremendous pressures led to elections in Sierra Leone for a new government. The elections of February 1996 went on successfully in spite of RUF attempts to disrupt it. The new government of President Tejan Kabbah was now faced with the RUF problem.

President Kabbah continued peace negotiations, which had been started by his immediate predecessor, Julius Maada Bio. This led to an accord in Abidjan, the capital of Côte d'Ivoire in November 30, 1996, between Kabbah and the RUF leader, Foday Sankoh. But this did not bring the longed-for end of the war. Foday Sankoh, on a trip to Nigeria purportedly to acquire arms, was arrested and detained by the Nigerian government in March 1997. This did not deter the RUF; in fact, it seemed to have energized the rebels, for under **Sam "Maskita" Bockari**, who assumed command of the RUF, the rebels resumed their offensive.

Intense disagreement between President Kabbah's government and the military led to a military putsch in May 1997, which ousted the Kabbah government. A new military junta, the **Armed Forces Revolutionary Council (AFRC)** was formed in Freetown, led by Johnny Paul Koroma. The AFRC invited the RUF to join them in the government of Sierra Leone and so the RUF rebels entered the capital, Freetown, with accompanying mayhem and plunder. With this new energy, the RUF forces recaptured the diamond-rich Tongo Fields and other important positions in Kenema District from the local traditional force, the **Kamajor** in January 1998.

The rule of the AFRC and their RUF allies was shortlived as the ECOMOG soldiers led by the Nigerians expelled them from Freetown in February. The RUF leadership had, in fact, abandoned Freetown before this event and resumed their offensive toward the capital. They were now joined by the expelled AFRC forces and together, they reentered Freetown on January 6, 1999. For two weeks, they wreaked havoc in Freetown, slaughtering people, looting, and burning down buildings before they were again beaten out of the capital by the ECOMOG forces.

RUF fortunes did not fare well after this last expulsion from Freetown. The RUF/AFRC alliance in the provinces carried on a rampage of terror, hacking off limbs from any segment of the population they could lay their hands on. Negotiations for peace continued by the ECOWAS mediation team and it was possible for the Nigerians to put pressure on Foday Sankoh, who was in their custody. By July 1997, the Lomé Peace Accord was signed between the RUF leadership, including Foday Sankoh and Johnny Paul Koroma, former leader of the AFRC. The RUF leadership and associates were granted a general and unconditional amnesty. The process began of reintegrating the RUF fighters into the population of Sierra Leone and of converting the RUF into a political party. Foday Sankoh, the RUF leader, was given a senior position in government akin to that of vice president. He was soon arrested for instigating violence and was held in custody, where he finally died. The RUF fielded candidates for elections in Sierra Leone a few years after the end of the war, but thereafter not much was heard of the party.

ROGERS, SOULIMAN E. (c. 1928–1994). Souliman E. Rogers, or S. E. as he was known, was a well-known musician in the 1960s, He sang songs in English, Krio, and his native **Mende** and remained popular until his death.

He was born in **Pujehun** and attained popularity in **Freetown** during the period of independence in 1961. His best-known song, "My Lovely Elizabeth" was recorded in the early 1960s. It was sung in English and made Rogers an instant success. He also had other popular songs, such as "*wetin mek you du me so*," sung in **Krio**. Rogie, as he called himself in his songs in which the theme of disappointment in love dominated, left Sierra Leone in the early 1970s, recording and performing mostly in the United States and also in England. He recorded the CD "Dead Men Don't Smoke Marijuana" and "The Palm Wine Sounds of S. E. Rogers." He returned to Sierra Leone in 1993, continuing to perform and win awards. He died in 1994 in London.

ROGERS, ZACHARY (16?–1681). Zachary Rogers was the eponymous ancestor of the Rogers or Kpaka family of the **Galinas** country in southeastern Sierra Leone. He was an Englishman who worked with the Gambia Adventurers Company doing business on the African coast. The company appointed Rogers its chief agent in the **Sherbro** country of Sierra Leone in 1668. The Gambia Adventurers Company was absorbed by another company, the Royal African Company, in 1672. Rogers remained as company agent to the new proprietors. Rogers' wife was Fafua-Lue, a member of the Massaquoi family that ruled the Gallinas country. The name Kpaka arose from one of their family members who loved sitting on a chair (*kpakai* in the Mende language). This was an unusual sight in those days, and the name Kpaka came to be added to the Rogers stock in the Gallinas.

Zachary Rogers and his wife had at least two sons, Zachary and Samuel. They both worked for the Royal African Company in the

1690s but gave up their jobs to start out on their own as travelers in the Gallinas. The Rogers family became dominant in the Gallinas, living in European-style housing and using European furniture and artifacts. One of their descendants, Samuel Siaka Rogers, traded along the northern rivers of Sierra Leone for some 20 years toward the end of the 18th century. Samuel spoke good English and used to sleep under a mosquito net.

The prosperity of the Rogers family effectively ended when the British pressured their leaders to sign antislave trade treaties, ending their main source of wealth. Today, the Rogers family is still prominent in Sierra Leone.

ROGERS-WRIGHT, CYRIL BUNTING (1905–1971). Cyril Bunting Rogers-Wright, was a barrister and solicitor in **Freetown** who was prominent in the preindependence politics of Sierra Leone. He formed a political party, the **United Progressive Party (UPP)** in 1955; the party was the official opposition in Parliament for approximately two years.

Cyril Rogers-Wright was born in **Freetown** and studied law in Britain. He set up private practice in Freetown and quickly took an interest in politics. Following adoption of the new constitution and elections of 1951, which saw the ascendancy of protectorate people in the new government, dissatisfied **Krios** supported the formation of several movements, but they mostly supported Cyril Rogers-Wright and formed the United Progressive Party. The party included protectorate members, such as Valesius Neale Caulker and Tarasid Tarawaly.

The UPP proclaimed an intention to bridge the gap between Krios and the protectorate in the politics of Sierra Leone. In 1956, Rogers-Wright founded a newspaper, *Shekpendeh,* which became an organ of his party as well as a critic of the new dispensation. In the general elections of 1957, Rogers-Wright sought to emphasize the ethnic versatility of his party by standing for election in the Port Loko East constituency. He won his seat, and his party won four other seats to become the most viable opposition in the House of Representatives.

When Prime Minister **Milton Margai** put together a coalition called the United Front, Rogers-Wright took the rump of his disintegrating UPP into the United Front government which emerged after the independence talks. He himself became minister of housing and country planning. He again won elections in 1962, this time for Wilberforce constituency, and became minister of external affairs and later minister of health. As the United Front split up into two parties, Rogers-Wright relinquished his connection with the government and joined the **All People's Congress** before the 1967 elections. He won his Wilberforce constituency seat as an APC candidate in 1967. The military, which took over soon thereafter, detained Rogers-Wright briefly. When the one-year military rule ended in 1968, treason trials were set up by the new government under **Siaka Stevens.** Rogers-Wright led the prosecution during the trials. He died in Ireland in 1971.

ROOT, BARNABAS (1846–1877). Barnabas Root was an ethnic **Sherbro** who received Western education at the **Mende** Mission school, studied divinity in the United States, and spent much of his life doing missionary work among freed men in the United States.

He was born in Sherbro country and was taken at the age of eight into the Mende Mission at his father's request. Barnabas proved to be an exceptional student, and in 1850 he was taken by one of the missionaries, John White, on a visit to the United States. White intended to show off Barnabas as part of the success of his mission and to use him as a resource in his quest to record the **Sherbro** language. Audiences at missionary meetings through the northern states were impressed by the young African's command of the English language and his knowledge of the Bible.

When Barnabas returned with White to Africa in 1860, he continued his studies in the mission school and acted as interpreter for the mission until 1863. He later went to the United States to prepare for the ministry and graduated in 1870 from Knox College at Galesburg, Illinois, with honors. He also received a bachelor of divinity degree from the Chicago Theological Seminary in 1873. Reporting on the commencement exercises for Root's class at the seminary, the newspaper *Advance* mentioned that "The oration which showed the most thought and the finest culture was by a native of Africa, Mr. Barnabas Root."

In 1873, Root was appointed pastor for a Congregational mission church for freedmen in Montgomery, Alabama. He then became one of a very few native Africans who have served as Christian missionaries in the United States. He was the second such missionary commissioned by the American Missionary Association (AMA), the first being Thomas DeSaliere Tucker, also from Sherbro country, who was appointed in 1862 to teach in a school for freedmen in eastern Virginia.

During his time in the United States, Root experienced color prejudice. In 1859, sitting with John White, Lewis Tappan, the treasurer of the AMA, and two white ladies at breakfast in a Chicago hotel, the landlord ordered Barnabas to leave because some of the lady hotel guests refused to enter the dining room "while that black was there."

After his leave in 1874, Root returned to Montgomery with additional duties in a church in Selma. During this time, he also attended a meeting of the Congregational Association of Illinois. At that meeting, the entire membership of the association boycotted a hotel operated by the Illinois Central Railroad because of its refusal to serve Barnabas a meal.

Barnabas longed to return to Sierra Leone. In 1868, he declared that he had given himself to God for the benefit of Africa. Steadfast in this resolution, he returned to his homeland in 1874. But he suffered from frail health and could not adjust well to the climate. Nonetheless, in the last three years of his life, Root established a new station of the Mende Mission, built a school house, revised a Mende dictionary, and began a translation of the Bible into Mende. He died in 1877.

– S –

SANDE. A female secret society among the **Mende**, similar to the **Bundo** found among other ethnic groups. There can be more than one Sande cell in a single community since senior Sande officials normally break off and form their own units. These units compete for membership and for the commitment of girls to be initiated into adulthood within the community. The main role of the Sande is the rite of passage from childhood to adulthood for girls. It involves training to become a good mother, wife, and community member and in the use of herbs to treat illness. Parents are required to pay fees for the trainers and for the upkeep of the initiates during training. The period of training was traditionally less than a year and is currently much shorter. Part of the Sande process of becoming an adult involves the excision of an initiate's clitoris. At the end of the training, there is a graduation ceremony accompanied by performance of the Sande spirit, wearing a carved mask with a body dress made of raffia palm and sack cloth, all dyed black. These young graduates are eligible to, and usually do, get married immediately upon graduation. The Sande spirit sometimes also appears on other occasions, sometimes for entertainment, accompanied by a follower. The Sande also trains initiates to assume higher positions in the organization, since these positions are based on achievement.

SANGBAI. A musical instrument common among many ethnic groups in Sierra Leone, the sangbai is a drum more or less conical in shape with a drumskin at the wider end while the other end is open. The drum is played with the hands, unlike the *bata*, another type of drum played with sticks. The Koranko call it *yimbei,* but the most common name is the *sangbai*.

SANKOH, FODAY (?–2003). Foday Sankoh was the leader of the rebel group, the **Revolutionary United Front (RUF)**, which waged civil war in Sierra Leone for a decade. A former corporal in the Sierra Leone Army, Sankoh was imprisoned for six years in 1971 after being convicted of participating in a failed military putsch. After he was released he opened a photography business at the provincial center of **Bo**. His desire for revenge against the **Siaka Stevens** government, which had imprisoned him, led him to Libya where Colonel Moammar Gadaffi provided training and support in military attacks on various governments. There, Sankoh met **Charles Taylor** who was waging a rebel war against the Liberian government. Taylor teamed up with Sankoh to form the Revolutionary United Front, supported by a few mostly young aggrieved Sierra Leoneans. The RUF launched a rebel war against Sierra Leone in March 1991, largely with Taylor's forces. Sankoh quickly gained a reputation for brutality, reportedly executing those around him who opposed his leadership style as well as leaders of local communities in the eastern Sierra Leone war front. RUF troops captured diamond-rich **Kono** late in 1992, although they were later beaten back. In late 1993, Sankoh was reportedly wounded on the eastern war front.

Foday Sankoh signed a peace accord with President **Tejan Kabbah** in Sierra Leone in November 1996. This did not last long. After a 1997 coup, which ousted President Kabba, the new **Armed Forces Revolutionary Council (AFRC)** government invited Foday Sankoh's RUF to become part of a new government. On a trip to Nigeria in March 1997, Foday Sankoh was detained by the Nigerian government on weapons charges. He was subsequently handed over to the Kabbah government, which had been reinstated by **ECOMOG** forces in February 1998. In October 1998, Foday Sankoh was tried and sentenced to death. In April 1999, the Lomé Peace Accord was signed, with Foday Sankoh, who had been released from prison, as a signatory. The Lomé accord gave a general amnesty to prisoners of war, including Foday Sankoh. It also called for a national unity government headed by President Kabbah and including Foday Sankoh and the AFRC leader, **Johnny Paul Koroma**. Later in 1999, Foday Sankoh and Johnny Paul Koroma reconciled their differences after a meeting with Charles Taylor in Liberia and issued a joint statement that the RUF and AFRC were forming a political alliance.

On May 8, 2002, Foday Sankoh's "security" forces fired into a large crowd of peace demonstrators, killing 20 of them. Sankoh was captured and imprisoned the next day. He was charged with war crimes by the UN-backed **Special Court** in **Freetown** in 2003 and remained in custody until his death in July 2003.

SANKOH, LAMINA (1884–1964). Lamina Sankoh is best known for his courageous fight in the period of heated preindependence politics to bring the leading figures of the colony and the protectorate together. To demonstrate his support for indigenous values, he adopted the name of Lamina Sankoh to replace his Western name of Ethelred Nathaniel Jones.

He was born to a well-to-do merchant in the mountain village of Gloucester near **Freetown** on June 28, 1884. He attended the **Albert Academy** and **CMS Grammar School**, both in **Freetown**. He obtained the B.A. degree from **Fourah Bay College** and later entered Wycliffe College in Oxford, England, where he read theology and philosophy. He was, in these latter studies, trying to fulfill his father's wish that he become a Christian minister. In the process, he experienced racial discrimination firsthand in his bid to become an ordained priest in England. This affected his attitudes for the rest of his life, and he came to adopt a radical pro-African position, which did not sit well with the **Krio** intelligentsia in **Freetown**.

On returning to Freetown in 1924, he served for a while as a priest at Holy Trinity Church and lectured in logic part time at **Fourah Bay College**. Because his views brought him into constant friction with the church elders, Lamina Sankoh resigned his curacy and returned to Britain, where he read education at Oxford. He traveled then to the United States, where he taught at Tuskegee Institute in Alabama, at Lincoln University in Pennsylvania, and at Orangeburg State College in South Carolina. In 1930, he returned to England, where he was active in the West African Students Union, a radical anticolonial organization. He was a regular contributor to the West African Students Union journal, which he later edited.

When he returned to Sierra Leone in the early 1940s, Lamina Sankoh quickly embarked on political and civic activities. This brought him squarely into the political conflict with colony and protectorate. He publicized his views in a newspaper that he started, the *African Vanguard* and founded a People's Forum, a cultural organization intended to examine the values held by Sierra Leoneans. It became so popular with its regular meetings at Memorial Hall that the **Freetown** elite spread the word that Sankoh was a revolutionary.

In the heat of the debate over the Stevenson Constitution, which gave a political majority in the Legislature, to protectorate people, the articulate political groups in the colony formed a political party called the **National Council**, led by **Bankole-Bright**, Hotobah-During, and C. M. A. Thompson. This party was intended to pursue the unrelenting **Krio** stance opposing the constitution. The sole **Krio** group not represented in the National Council was Lamina Sankoh's People's Party, which he had formed in 1948, supported by liberal **Krios** and protectorate leaders. Eight months after the formation of the **National Council**, Lamina Sankoh agreed to merge his People's Party with the **Sierra Leone Organization Society (SOS)** to form the **Sierra Leone People's Party**, and he later transferred ownership of the *African Vanguard* to the new party. In the first national election of officers of the SLPP, Lamina Sankoh was elected one of the vice presidents of the SLPP. Consequently, Sankoh lost the support of conservative **Krios** who were in the majority. In the **Legislative**

Council elections of 1951, he stood as an SLPP candidate for Freetown and was defeated.

Lamina Sankoh was active in other areas not so overtly political. He founded the Sierra Leone Aro Cooperative Society, opposed by the colonial government, which declared that he had no authority to use the word *cooperative*. He taught in the Extra-Mural Department of **Fourah Bay College** and was at one time president of the Freetown Adult Education Society. He set up an African church, where theology and philosophy were discussed free of Western influences.

Lamina Sankoh was considerably ahead of his time. The integration he fought for is much closer to reality today, and a prominent street in Freetown is named after him.

SANKOH, MOMOH (c. 1812–1890). Momoh Sankoh was one of those tireless aspirants for the position of *Alikali* or ruler of the town of Port Loko, a major trading and staging post not too far from **Freetown**. Sankoh was part of an ethnic **Soso** clan of the same name that had migrated to **Port Loko** and had gained prominence through trade, consequently becoming the rulers there. However in 1817, the **Soso** *Alikali* **Alimamy Konkori Sankoh** was captured and beheaded through conspiracy between the local **Temne** and **Mandinka** residents of Port Loko. These two allies made a solemn oath to alternately hold the position of Alikali and thus permanently keep out the Sankoh clan.

Momoh Sankoh never gave up hope of retrieving the position of Alikali for the Sankoh clan each time it became vacant. This happened in 1841when Sankoh even threatened war, and again in 1853. The intervention of the British administration in the Sierra Leone colony, eager to maintain its sway over Port Loko, had always supported the policy of alternating the position of *Alikali* between the ethnic Temne of the Kamara clan and the Bangura clan, which was Mandinka. Momoh Sankoh was an ardent **Muslim** who had received Islamic training in the Melacourie, a major Islamic Soso center in this part of West Africa. He was thus not altogether acceptable to the colony administration. His strong Islamic persuasion and anti-Christian influence in **Port Loko** sealed his inability to gain support from the colony representatives who always turned up each time the *Alikali* seat was vacant.

Momoh Sankoh again sought the *Alikali* crown in 1856 when the reigning *Alikali* died. Sankoh's persistent claim threatened to erupt into hostilities. The colony's mediator, **George Lawson**, sided against Sankoh, and the governor, Stephen Hill, went personally to Port Loko in 1857 to confirm the new Alikali, Yan Koba of the Bangura clan. Sankoh would not give in. With support from the neighboring **Soso** allies, he launched an attack on Port Loko, burning down parts of the town. **Krio** traders living in Port Loko complained to the **Freetown** colonial government of heavy losses in the attack. Colonial forces were hastily sent to Port Loko to keep the peace.

This was reportedly Momoh Sankoh's last attempt at the position of *Alikali.* He emerged again in 1886, supporting local rulers in an ethnic Temne region called Yoni who were fighting against the colonial government interests in Sierra Leone. He was captured and detained in Freetown in 1887. Little is known of him after this.

SARA BAYO. Sara Bayo, who lived from the late 19th to the early 20th century, was ruler of Katimbo in northern Sierra Leone when the ***sofa***, **Samori's** warriors, invaded northern Sierra Leone. By a stroke of fortune, his territories were spared the worst of the invaders' attacks.

Bayo was born at Katimbo in the present Kasunko chiefdom. Katimbo was an important town in territory that later belonged to a long line of rulers who traced their roots to Futa Jalon in what is now the Republic of Guinea. His father, Bayo Seri, sent his son as a youth to Timbo, the capital of the Futa Jalon kingdom, then regarded as an important training ground for future rulers. He may have acquired some Koranic learning there.

After Sara Bayo returned to Katimbo, he became ruler in succession to his father who died shortly after his return. In the 1880s, **Samori Toure's** warriors swept down on northern Sierra Leone, and Sara Bayo's domain was one of those over which the sofas assumed control. But like many northern rulers, Sara Bayo considered it unwise to attempt any military confrontation with a more powerful force such as the sofas. Instead, he and his people took refuge at Kamiliki in the present Koinadugu District, an earlier settlement long since eclipsed by neighboring towns such as Katimbo and Fadugu. There, safely hidden in caves, Sara Bayo and his elders sent out scouts to spy on the movements of the invaders. When their reports suggested that things were quiet, Sara Bayo and his people returned to their hometowns.

The invaders were now stationed at the town of Fadugu, where Sara Bayo, accompanied by two of his elders, met the sofa leader, Lankanfali. To demonstrate recognition of sofa rule, Sara Bayo presented Lankanfali with gifts of a bowl full of kolanuts, three captives, and three cows. Lankanfali accepted the gifts, but noticing that Sara Bayo's fingers were twisted, he declared that his troops had been forewarned by divine authority not to wage war on anyone with such a deformity. Following up on this prophecy, Lankanfali had the gifts offered as a sacrifice. The kolanuts were shared, and everyone ate some of the beef. The captives were beheaded. Some of the invading forces stayed in that area even after **Samori's** empire had been destroyed by the French in the mid-1890s.

The imposition of British rule followed the sofa withdrawal from northern Sierra Leone, and Sara Bayo was recognized as paramount chief. Despite the fact that this put him on an equal footing with his former overlord, Alimamy **Suluku** of Bumban, Sara Bayo continued to refer certain matters to Suluku. Sara Bayo died in the early 20th century and was succeeded by Lamina.

SATTAN LAHAI (c. 1815–c. 1890). The name of Sattan Lahai runs through much of the 19th century in the Scarcies region around the town of **Kambia**, which he dominated for almost half a century. The better part of his political career involved his determination to retain dominance in the area in the face of persistent and expanding British influence, spearheaded by **Krio** traders from the **Freetown** in the colony of Sierra Leone.

We know mostly about Sattan Lahai by his encounter with the British through treaties he signed with them or in his relations with Krio traders settled in Kambia, a thriving trading town linking trade routes in the northwest interior with **Port Loko** and Freetown.

The region Lahai dominated was a meeting point of ethnic **Soso**, spreading into the area from neighboring Morea in Guinea, which was Soso country, and ethnic **Temne** from the Port Loko region. Sattan Lahai himself was of a Soso father and Temne mother. He must have gained control of **Kambia** since the 1840s and his influence, if not control, spread northward to the major **Soso** centers of Morea and Kukuna, and south sometimes as far as Port Loko.

In 1851, Sattan Lahai signed a treaty with the British in Freetown, meant to facilitate trade and good relations with the colony. The colony, however, represented such values as anti-Islam and anti-slavery, while a "free slave" center had been established in Kukuna by **Bilali**, which encouraged runaway slaves. Because the British stood for those values that threatened some of the bases of Sattan Lahai's rule, he openly opposed British interests, represented particularly by the **Krio** traders who settled in Kambia. On two occasions in 1856 and 1879 he expelled all **Krio** traders from his territory. In the latter case, Sattan Lahai joined with other local rulers in the area to disavow treaties of trade that they had signed with the British a couple of years earlier. British and Krio trader activities were encroaching on his control of the trade of the Kambia region. Although the British bombarded Kambia the first time the traders were expelled, on the second occasion negotiations prevailed, and Lahai soon began to cooperate with British interests.

Sattan Lahai also stood firm against political opponents in this troubled region. In 1885, one of his rivals, Tansa Lamina, an ethnic Soso from Morea, who was trying to overthrow him, burned down Kambia, forcing Lahai to flee to Mambolo and seek refuge with Lahai Young, the ruler there. Things were soon sorted out though and Lahai returned to Kambia.

Sattan Lahai's influence seemed to have waned by the 1890s, and little is heard of him thereafter. He was by then an old man and would have died in that decade.

ST. EDWARDS SECONDARY SCHOOL. The St. Edwards Secondary School was founded by the Roman Catholic Mission in Sierra Leone in 1866. It was located at the Mission House at Howe Street and started as a primary school. By 1925, it had achieved secondary school status. In the 1960s, the school moved to new buildings at Kingdom and is now a leading secondary school in **Freetown**. Though it is a boys school, such as other leading secondary schools in Freetown are, it does sixth form work where girls are admitted.

ST. JOSEPH'S CONVENT. The St. Joseph's Convent started off as a primary school for girls at a Catholic house of the Sisters of Mercy at Howe Street in **Freetown** in 1866. By 1900, St. Joseph's Convent had gained secondary school status The school was also training teachers for primary schools by the 1940s with funds provided by the colonial government. In 1943, the St. Joseph's Convent started the first school clinic in Sierra Leone with the support of the colonial education department. For many years, this remained the only school clinic in Freetown. St. Joseph's Convent moved to a new site at Brookfields with new buildings soon after independence and came to be known as St. Joseph's Secondary School.

SAWYERR, HARRY A. E. (1909–1987). Harry Sawyerr spent a half century teaching theology and being a scholar at **Fourah Bay College**. He rose to the rank of principal of the college and vice chancellor of the University of Sierra Leone.

Harry Sawyerr was born October 16, 1909, in **Freetown**; he attended the **Prince of Wales School**, then **Fourah Bay College**, and later St. John's College of Durham University where he read theology. He joined the faculty of Fourah Bay College in 1933 as tutor and became chaplain, dean of faculties of theology and of arts, professor of theology in 1962, principal for five years starting in 1968, and vice chancellor of the University of Sierra Leone in 1970.

Harry Sawyerr was well recognized in scholarship on African religion and published widely in this area. His best-known works were *The Springs of Mende Beliefs and Conduct* (1968) and *God: Ancestor or Creator* (1970). On leaving Fourah Bay College in 1970, Harry Sawyerr held a position at St. John's College in Cutherington, Barbados, where he remained until 1978. He returned to Sierra Leone and was head of the Theological Seminary in Freetown, continuing to teach at Fourah Bay College until his death in 1987.

Harry Sawyerr was also prominent in the Anglican Church in Sierra Leone, becoming a Canon of St. George's Cathedral in Freetown from 1961–1974.

SCOTT, MOSES N. C. O. (1911–). The Right Reverend Moses Scott became Archbishop of West Africa in the 1960s. He was born August 18, 1911, and attended the **CMS Grammar School**. He had higher education at **Fourah Bay College** and, in England, the London School of Divinity. He taught school and also did pastoral service in a number of towns in the provinces of Sierra Leone before being ordained as a priest in 1945. He was well known as a priest in **Bo**, where he was appointed archdeacon. In November 1961, Scott was consecrated bishop of Sierra Leone, the first Sierra Leonean to hold this position in the Anglican Church in that country. He became Archbishop of the Anglican Province of West Africa on July 1, 1969, again the first African to hold that office, which hitherto was always held by Englishmen. He remained in both positions as Bishop of **Freetown** and Archbishop of West Africa until his retirement in 1981.

SCRUBBY (FRANCIS MACAFOY). His name was Francis Macfoy, but he was better known by the pseudonym "Scrubby" as band leader and banjo player of his own band called "Famous Scrubbs and His Band." He lived in the east end of **Freetown** and entertained Freetown with his music in the 1940s and 1950s. He was well known for the many songs he composed and sang dwelling on the theme of poverty and hard times, such as "Cost of Living Killing Us," "Poor Freetown Boy," and "Doti Scrubby."

SEGBUREH. This is a musical instrument played mostly by women. It was most common among the ethnic **Mende**, although it is also played in the north as well. It is called *saka* among the **Temne** around Masingbi in the Tonkolili District. The instrument is made of a stalked gourd surrounded by a network of beads, more recently also of buttons or shells on an intricate spider web of strings. The end of the string is held in one hand and the stalk of the gourd in the other. Rhythmic movements of the gourd produce the desired rattle of the beads (or buttons or shells) against the gourd.

In a typical musical ensemble, there would be more than one segbureh player, the rhythm ones, and the lead player, who is also often the lead singer.

SEWA (c. 1810–1984). *Manga* (king) Sewa was a powerful late-19th-century ruler in northern Sierra Leone where he dominated a prominent polity and coastward trade with the colony of Sierra Leone. In the latter part of his rule, his country was attacked by the sofas, **Samori Toure's** troops, and Sewa lost his life in the siege of Falaba, his capital.

Sewa was a member of the ruling Samura clan of the Solima state that straddled the border along the extreme northeast corner of Sierra Leone. He was born in the early 19th century, the second son of Sori Wuleng (also called Asana Yira), then *manga* (ruler) of Solimana. Sewa became ruler of Solimana in about 1862. He is credited with the extension of the area of influence of Solimana to include numerous small Koranko states in northern Sierra Leone. The **Koranko** of Barawa, around Kabala, southeast of Falaba, and other Koranko of Deldugu (part of present Neya chiefdom) were subjects of the Solima state under Sewa. Manga Sewa maintained strong trade relations with neighboring Futa Jalon to the far north in what is now the Republic of Guinea, with Sankaran country to the northeast, and with the Biriwa Limba state under **Alimamy Suluku**.

In 1869, Sewa was visited by a British explorer and author, Winwood Reade, who was seeking the source of the Niger River. He was received warmly by Sewa but was not permitted to continue his search for the Niger. A decade later, two French explorers, J. Zweifel and M. Moustier, arrived at Falaba in search of new openings for trade. Sewa was described by all three European visitors as one of the greatest kings in the distant interior of the Sierra Leone colony.

Sewa committed suicide in September 1884, following a siege of his capital by the **sofas**, warriors of **Samori Toure**. As Samori's armies moved southward toward Falaba, the sofa general Nfa Ali sent a message to Falaba asking them to surrender. The messenger was Sayo of Kaliere, a town formerly part of the Solima state that had submitted to the sofas. Unfortunately for Sewa, Sayo saw this as an opportunity to take revenge on Falaba for what he considered an act of treachery Falaba had committed against his father, Isa, the former ruler of Kaliere.

When Sayo reached Falaba, Sewa called his council together to discuss whether or not to submit to the sofas, considered a more powerful enemy. The council agreed on submission, and Sewa sent Sayo with this message to Nfa Ali. Sayo, however, on leaving Falaba, took red kolanuts, signifying war, tied them up in a cloth and presented them to Nfa Ali with the message that Falaba had chosen to fight. The fate of Falaba was sealed by this trick. The sofa army surrounded Falaba and launched an abortive attack after which they settled down for a siege. After six months, the people inside Falaba were reduced to eating rats and the soles of shoes. Sewa sent his son and general, Duga, to seek help. Whereas the general convention was that messengers of war were not usually taken prisoner, Duga was captured by the sofa warriors who allowed him to send a message to his beleaguered capital, following which Duga was killed.

After this incident, Sewa decided to accede to the sofa. But his son, Sewa Sayo, insulted him, calling him a coward. This so grieved Sewa that he decided to commit suicide. He called on all those who would die rather than have a **Muslim** sofa lay a finger on them to join him in his armory. There, with his head wife and a few elders, he put a lighted torch to the armory and the whole group was blown to pieces. The sofa then entered Falaba and took control.

SHERBRO. The Sherbro are found in the **Bonthe** District, around the island of Bonthe. The Sherbro emerged from an "invasion" of **Bullom** people by a segment of the **Mani** invaders who came to dominate southern Sierra Leone. The leader of this Mani invasion of the Bullom was called Serabola, and the name Sherbro resulted from a corrupted version of this name. Today, the Sherbro are a minority ethnic group accounting for less than 1 percent of the population of Sierra Leone. Most Sherbro today speak **Mende** as a second language, some even identifying themselves as Mende.

SHORUNKEH-SAWYERR, ALFRED JAMES (c. 1861–1929). Alfred James Shronkeh-Sawyerr was a well-known legal luminary in **Freetown** who was best known for his bold and articulate criticisms of colonial rule and his leanings toward African values in the last years of the 19th century when African voices still mattered in the colonial system. He was known to have joined the **Poro** society, as well as becoming a member of the **Legislative Council**.

Born in Freetown, the son of a bookseller who also became a **Legislative Council** member, A. J. Shorunkeh-Sawyerr attended the **CMS Grammar School** and studied in England for six years. He began working at his father's business. As part of this business, he published a news pamphlet called *The Sierra Leone Ram* and, later in the

1890s, a magazine called *Saturday, Ho!* After working for a few years in his father's business, he qualified in law in England in 1889. He divided his time thereafter between managing his father's business and practicing as a lawyer until his brother returned from England after also becoming a lawyer in 1892. Together, they set up a law firm called "Shorunkeh-Sawyerr and Shorunkeh-Sawyerr," which became a thriving partnership.

The 1870s and 1880s marked a period of intense debate in the colony about the depression that adversely affected the colony. It also brought into sharp focus the issue of the future of the colony in relation to its hinterland from where trade emanated, which sustained the colony. Shorunkeh-Sawyerr was squarely in this debate, trading barbs with Sir **Samuel Lewis** in the Sierra Leone Association, an organization of the **Freetown** elite. Shorunkeh-Sawyerr was opposed to the idea of European annexation of the interior, which Samuel Lewis proposed, and this fueled endless debates on the issue. Shorunkeh-Sawyerr was also influenced by the **Dress Reform Society**, spearheaded by **Edward Blyden**, which impacted the issue of the Africanity of the Westernized elite in Freetown. This led to a flurry of name amendments by the elite in **Freetown**, and it was around this time that "Shorunkeh" was added to "Sawyerr" to form the compound name of Shorunkeh-Sawyerr. Caught up in the colonial indoctrination of the urban elite in Africa, Shorunkeh-Sawyerr, despite his bold anti-imperialistic stand and Africanization of his name, maintained that **Krios** were "black Englishmen" and should behave accordingly.

Alfred Shorunkeh-Sawyerr was appointed a member of the **Legislative Council** in 1911. By then however, colonialism was more firmly entrenched in the protectorate as in the rest of Africa, and the views of Africans mattered little. The Legislative Council was now reduced to a body meant to endorse the policies of the governor and his officials, and Shorunkeh-Sawyerr could not play as prominent a role as he had done earlier. His tenure on the Legislative Council ended in 1924, five years before his death.

SIBTHORPE, AARON BELISARIUS COSIMO (c. 1840–1916). A liberated African from present-day Nigeria, Aaron Belisarius Cosimo Sibthorpe was the first historian of Sierra Leone. Though hardly recognized in his lifetime, his *History of Sierra Leone* remains one of the primary readings on the history of the colony of Sierra Leone during the 19th century.

Brought as a recaptive from Nigeria, Sibthorpe attended the **CMS Grammar School** and in 1865 began teaching at Christ Church primary school in **Freetown**. In that same year, Sibthorpe exhibited some of his drawings and models at the Sierra Leone Exhibition. However, he was much more successful as a writer. He authored two textbooks, a *History of Sierra Leone* and a *Geography of Sierra Leone*. He enlisted the assistance of a visiting school inspector to get them published in London in 1868. These were the first editions, and Sibthorpe continued to produce subsequent editions as he revised both books.

Sibthorpe's writings were pioneer works, written during a period when the only writings about Africa were demeaning, racist comments by Europeans. Sibthorpe sought to write a balanced history of an African people, largely from printed sources but also from contemporary observations and oral tradition. He enriched his history with details of economic and social life, so scanty in even contemporary histories. He also reflected the society of his time, including in his books lists of commodity prices and songs and proverbs. His *Geography of Sierra Leone* also included descriptions of village handicrafts and of prevalent diseases of the time.

By 1869, Sibthorpe was living, teaching, and leading church work at Hastings village near Freetown and in the neighboring village of Grafton. He took a strong interest in natural history, extending this interest into practice as a herbalist, using his own medicinal concoctions. He even tried to include this in a manuscript he called "The Latent Riches of Sierra Leone," but he could not get a publisher for this. Sibthorpe continued to write pieces on history in newspapers in Freetown. He delivered a speech in Freetown in 1907 at a celebration of the centenary of the passing of the Slave Trade Abolition Act in Britain. This was later published as a pamphlet.

Sibthorpe received very little recognition for his writings during his lifetime, in a society where the colonial authorities had no interest in or belief that there was a history of African people, and where his own peers, the Western-trained elite, thought almost exactly like the Europeans who tutored them. He died in 1916, but his *History of Sierra Leone* lives on.

SIERRA LEONE COMMERCIAL BANK. The Sierra Leone Commercial Bank was founded soon after independence as the first government-owned commercial bank in Sierra Leone. It is governed by a board appointed by the government. It has become one of the great success stories, with branches in the major towns in Sierra Leone.

SIERRA LEONE DEVELOPMENT COMPANY (DELCO). More popularly known as DELCO, the Sierra Leone Development Company mined iron ore in Sierra Leone from 1930 to 1975. Iron ore was first discovered in Marampa in the northern province in 1926. A British company, the African and Eastern Trading Corporation Ltd., obtained from the colonial government a 4.5 square mile long concession lease to control mining in this area in 1927. The lease was valid for 99 years at an annual rent of 250 pounds sterling payable to the "tribal authority" in the Marampa chiefdom. To facilitate production, the British Colonial Development Fund (CDF) provided a loan of half a million pounds sterling to the colonial government at 5 percent interest to build a 52-mile railway from Marampa to the port of Pepel. With this loan, the African and Eastern Trading Corporation set up a subsidiary company called the Sierra Leone Development Company (DELCO) in 1930. Iron ore became Sierra Leone's second major export, and the loan to DELCO was paid back within five years. By the early 1970s, the company complained of escalating production costs due to the need to introduce other mining techniques. As export prices began to fall, the company closed its mining operations in November 1975. The Sierra Leone government tried to interest other companies in the mining and succeeded temporarily in 1981 when an Austrian government company, Austromineral Ges MBH started mining, only to cease operations in 1984.

SIERRA LEONE GRAMMAR SCHOOL. The Sierra Leone Grammar School was started by the **Church Missionary Society (CMS)** to bridge the educational gap between the primary schools and the higher institution they had started at Fourah Bay. Thus on March 25, 1845, an initial 14 of the younger students at **Fourah Bay College** were transferred to begin the Grammar School at Regent Square in the center of Freetown. Of the total, five were from the **Galinas** country; three were from Kissy, two were from the seaside village of

Kent, two were from **Freetown**, and one was from the mountain village of Charlotte. The Grammar School maintained high standards from its inception and began preparing students for higher education throughout British West Africa. By 1851 the school had become self-supporting except that the salary of the European principal was paid by the CMS. There was an attempt to introduce industrial education in the 1850s, and a farm was bought for that purpose. However, this part of the curriculum was short-lived, and the school continued teaching only academic subjects. Indeed, the Grammar School achieved its goal so well that the CMS decided in 1858 to close **Fourah Bay College** and did so temporarily in that year. After World War II, the Sierra Leone Grammar School, as it was then called, moved to accommodations at the eastern side of Freetown, next to the residence of the Anglican Bishop at Bishop's Court. In 1962, the Grammar School again moved to new buildings at Murray Town, just outside Freetown's west side.

SIERRA LEONE ORGANIZATION SOCIETY (SOS). The Sierra Leone Organization society formed in 1946 was spearheaded by young professionally trained protectorate people who had been largely excluded from the extant political institutions provided by the colonial government. It was founded at Moyamba, and the founding members were almost all Western trained professionals. One literate paramount chief, **Julius Gulama**, was noticeable among its founders, and was named honorary president. The SOS proclaimed its intentions to improve self-government and development in the colony. One of its main objections at the time was the apparent dependence of the colonial government on the paramount chiefs as speakers on protectorate issues. The SOS was moving to deal with this issue when the debates on the 1947 constitution began. Since the debate seemed to polarize opinions between the colony and the protectorate, the SOS sought rapprochement with the paramount chiefs, leading to a common front and the formation of the **Sierra Leone People's Party** in 1951.

SIERRA LEONE PEOPLE'S PARTY (SLPP). The Sierra Leone People's Party (SLPP) was formed in April 1951 when a couple of organizations decided to come together in a political coalition. These organizations were the **Protectorate Educational Progressive Union (PEPU)**, the **Sierra Leone Organization Society (SOS)**, and the People's Party of **Lamina Sankoh**. PEPU's interest was in promoting the advancement of the protectorate, particularly the education of protectorate people. The SOS was a combination of Western-educated protectorate elements who banded together as a pressure group.

The SOS was formed in 1946 while PEPU, although it had been formed in 1929, had remained dormant and was only revived in 1946. These two groups were thus well placed to join in the political affray following the new constitution for Sierra Leone in 1947. Both groups joined forces with Sankoh's People's Party. A **Krio** priest who had changed his name to emphasize his Africanity, Sankoh represented an advance guard of the Krio people, seeking to harmonize major forces in the country. The SLPP thus came to be more representative of the entire country than any other political party of the time. Its leader, **Milton Margai**, who became the first prime minister, was more inclined to compromise, thus giving the SLPP a major boost. In the first elections following the implementation of the new constitution, the SLPP won with a comfortable majority. The SLPP was disbanded when Sierra Leone became a one-party state in 1978. A constitutional revision in 1992 reinstated multiparty politics, and the SLPP was revived, winning the general elections of 1996 to again become the ruling party.

SIERRA LEONE PRODUCE MARKETING BOARD (SLPMB). The SLPMB was formed in 1949 by the colonial government to take control of the marketing of farm produce of the farmers in Sierra Leone. All former interests buying produce from farmers would then act as buying agents of the SLPMB. One of the expressed intentions in setting up the SLPMB was that it would give a relatively stable price to farmers for their produce irrespective of the fluctuations of the world price of produce. The world market price of produce remained high throughout the rest of the colonial period, so the surplus collected from farmers by the SLPMB was retained by the colonial government and was invested in England. With the coming of independence, these monies were not turned over to the newly independent government of Sierra Leone.

The SLPMB continued its function under the new government of Sierra Leone, and farmers sometimes resisted the low prices offered to them by taking their produce to Liberia to sell for higher prices. There were many allegations of corruption in the SLPMB where the directors of the board were said to enrich themselves out of the revenue collected from farmers.

SIERRA LEONE PROGRESSIVE INDEPENDENCE MOVEMENT (SLPIM). The SLPIM was a political party of the decolonization era. It emerged out of a merger between **Edward Blyden** III's Sierra Leone Independence Movement (SLIM) and a **Kono** Progressive Movement (KPM) led by a druggist turned paramount chief, **Tamba Mbriwa**. The SLIM was a dwindling party while the KPM was seeking to avoid being branded an ethnic party. Mbriwa became president of the SLPIM, and the SLIM was virtually absorbed under the new name. The fortunes of the SLPIM remained at best tenuous when Mbriwa was stripped of his paramount chieftaincy and banished to Kamakwie in the Bombali District in 1964. In March 1965, **Albert Margai**, the new prime minister, reinstated Mbriwa. The SLPIM was shifting alliances between the **People's National Party (PNP)** and the **Sierra Leone People's Party (SLPP)** in the political horse-trading that preceded independence. It eventually joined forces with the **All People's Congress** Party in the 1967 general elections, ensuring the defeat of the SLPP. The SLPIM ceased to exist after Mbriwa died in 1968.

SIERRA LEONE RAILWAY. The Sierra Leone railway was started in 1895 and completed in 1906. It was directed from **Freetown** toward the eastern part of the country, where the colonial government felt it would best serve the exploitation of palm produce, which grew well and naturally in that part of the country. The rail moved from Freetown to the eastern terminus at Pendembu, some 220 miles eastward. A branch line was added by 1916 that left Bauya and went northward to Makeni covering a distance of 83 miles.

The railway revolutionized the transport of produce and manufactured goods to and from Freetown. It improved the administrative processes of the colonial government and became the single most important conduit for the movement of Western goods and ideas from the capital, Freetown, to the protectorate. Railway workers became one of the largest single group of workers in Sierra Leone, and they attempted to unionize and advocate better working conditions. These movements led to two major strikes of railway workers in 1919 and 1926. Complaints that the railway was operating at a loss started with the colonial government in the 1940s and continued into the independent governments of the country. The military government led by **Andrew Terrence Juxon-Smith** phased out the railway in 1968.

SIERRA LEONE SELECTION TRUST (SLST). This company was formed in 1928 as a wholly owned subsidiary of the Consolidated African Selection Trust (CAST), a South African company, to mine diamonds in Sierra Leone. When diamonds were found in the **Kono** District in 1930, CAST negotiated an exclusive prospecting license for the entire country with the colonial government in 1931. Successive agreements with the colonial government up to 1935 gave CAST monopoly rights for 99 years to mine and market all of Sierra Leone's diamonds outside the area operated by DELCO for iron ore mining. CAST agreed to pay a tax of 27.5 percent on net profits plus 7,000 pounds sterling as annual mineral rent.

The monopoly that SLST possessed over the mining of diamonds was threatened with the diamond rush when "illicit" miners, as they were called, began to do alluvial mining with such basic materials as shovels, picks, and sieves. This diamond rush reached a climax in the early 1950s, when **Mandinka** miners, referred to as *Maracas,* dominated the illicit mining. Firm action against these miners was deterred by the thinking that these were indigenous miners working diamonds that, after all, belonged to the country. In 1955, the colonial government renegotiated the concession with SLST, reducing the area under the company's control and modifying the length of the lease. SLST was given a compensation of about 1.5 million pounds sterling and a government commitment to increase security patrols around the new lease. The Alluvial Diamond Mining Ordinance and Rules of 1956, which set these rules, also approved the Alluvial Diamond Mining Scheme, whereby Sierra Leoneans would be licensed to do surface mining.

As licensed miners generalized the mining and marketing of diamonds, further negotiations between the colonial government and the

SLST led to the creation by these dealers of the Diamond Corporation (Sierra Leone) Ltd. to purchase all diamonds mined by these licensed alluvial miners. This arrangement was modified in August 1959 with the creation of the Government Diamond Office (GDO), which became the final and sole exporter of diamonds produced by alluvial diamond mines. The GDO was to be managed by the Diamond Corporation, an arm of the De Beers Mining cartel of South Africa. Various modifications were made by the newly independent government of Sierra Leone, first with the creation of the Diamond Corporation of West Africa (DICORWAF) to replace De Beers control of the GDO, and then (in 1970) with the formation of the **National Diamond Mining Company (NDMC)**, jointly owned by the Sierra Leone Government and the SLST.

SIERRA LEONE TEACHERS UNION. The Sierra Leone Teachers Union was officially registered in 1969. It was formed from an amalgamation of two teachers' unions, one in the colony and the other in the protectorate. The combined union was at first called the Amalgamated Teachers Organization at its inception in 1948. At a conference at the provincial town of **Bo** in 1963, the name was changed to the Sierra Leone Teachers Union. The union has been continuously involved in a running battle with the independent governments of Sierra Leone over the poor wages of teachers. In the government of **Siaka Stevens**, in a move to muffle the union, the union boss was elevated to membership in Parliament.

SIERRA LEONE WEEKLY NEWS. The *Sierra Leone Weekly News* was the longest surviving newspaper in that country. It was founded in 1884 by **Claudius May** with the support of **Edward Blyden**. The *Sierra Leone Weekly News* quickly became the dominant newspaper not just in Sierra Leone but throughout British West African colonies of the Gambia, Gold Coast, and Nigeria. It became the major organ for the expression of the views of the **Freetown** elite and of similar West African elements. It continued publication until 1951.

SIERRA RUTILE. The origins of the Sierra Rutile Mining Company can be traced back to the last years of colonial rule. In 1955, the British Titan Products Company was granted an exclusive prospecting license covering some 2,000 square miles of the **Bonthe** and **Moyamba** Districts.

This company teamed up in 1964 with the Pittsburgh Plate and Glass Company of the United States to form the Sherbro Mineral Rutile Company. The first shipment of rutile—a mineral consisting of titanium dioxide with a little iron, with a brilliant metallic luster—was in May 1967. The Sherbro Minerals temporarily ceased operations in 1971 due to technical problems and was replaced in 1972 by Sierra Rutile Ltd., jointly owned by Bethlehem Steel International and Nord Resources Corporation of Dayton, Ohio. Sierra Rutile signed an agreement with the Sierra Leone government in 1972, whereby Bethlehem Steel acquired rights to 85 percent of the shares. Another agreement of 1976 gave the company the right to prospect for and mine rutile with a grant of a five-year "tax holiday," which ended in November 1981. Bethlehem Steel withdrew a year later, and Nord Resources became the sole owner of Sierra Rutile. A new agreement between Sierra Rutile and the Sierra Leone government of 1989 gave the government increased revenue from the rutile mining. All of the operations of the company, including the export and processing of the rutile, were controlled by the Sierra Rutile Company, leaving the Sierra Leone government little control over this precious resource.

The company ceased operations in January 1995 because of the instability caused by the rebel war. In November 2001, the government of Sierra Leone signed an agreement with Sierra Rutile Company for the takeover of the Mokanji bauxite mines, formerly managed by **SIEROMCO** mines. Sierra Rutile was preparing to resume operations in 2004.

SIERRA LEONE ORE AND METAL COMPANY (SIEROMCO). SIEROMCO is an acronym for the Sierra Leone Ore and Metal Company, a wholly owned subsidiary of Swiss Aluminium Industries (Alusuisse), which controls the mining of bauxite in Sierra Leone. Rich deposits of bauxite are found mainly in the Mokanji Hills in the Moyamba District of Sierra Leone. An agreement between Alusuisse and the Sierra Leone government in 1961 allowed the company to prospect for and mine bauxite in the known prospective sites. The government also granted SIEROMCO a tax-free concession of seven years from the commencement of production in 1963. Production, pricing, marketing, and processing of the bauxite remained under the control of SIEROMCO, leaving the Sierra Leone Government little means of verifying the statements of the company. SIEROMCO temporarily stopped operations in 1995 because of the rebel war. In 2002, a new agreement between the Sierra Leone government and Sierra Rutile company allowed the latter to take over control of the Mokanji bauxite mine from SIEROMCO.

SMART, CHARLES (c. 1850–c. 1910). Charles Smart was an ambitious member of the ethnic **Loko** Smart family, which held a high position in Mahera, near the mouth of the Rokel River close to the Sierra Leone colony. In his determination to be free of the domination of the **Temne** of Koya, Smart threw in his lot with the colonial administration and intrigued ruthlessly and successfully to overthrow his enemies.

Though dominant in Mahera, the famous **Loko** Smart family to which **Gombu Smart** belonged was nevertheless under the overall rule of the Bai Kompa, king of the Koya Temne. The wars between the **Temne** and Loko in the mid-19th century had led to the dispersal of the Loko, some of whom found their way to the Sierra Leone colony. The outcome of these wars was that the Temne now ruled over much of what was formerly Loko country. There still existed a few Loko enclaves however, of which Mahera was one.

Charles Smart was probably born at Mahera about 1850 and was among the many Loko who, wishing for colony protection, had become Christian. He was educated by the **Church Missionary Society** partly in **Freetown**, and, by the 1880s, had returned to Mahera, determined to rule.

In 1892, Smart, now apparently leader of the **Loko** Smart family, asked the Bai Kompa to make him chief of Mahera and allow Mahera to become an independent entity. The Bai Kompa refused, doubtless on account of Smart's colony and Christian affiliations. Smart then collaborated with the colony administration, joined the Frontier Police, and had himself installed and officially recognized by the administration as chief of Mahera.

Bai Kompa and his **Temne** subchiefs were angered by this affront to their sovereignty, an anger that was aggravated by their fears that Smart would encourage the spread of Christianity in their domain. There was by now open enmity between Smart, whose loyalties, willingly enough given, were with the colonial administration, and the Temne.

The conflict between the two groups escalated with the declaration of the protectorate in 1896 and the imposition of a house tax. The Temne were opposed to the provisions of the protectorate administration, as were other rulers, and particularly to the house tax, which they vowed they would not pay. In 1897, when the acting district commissioner of Ronietta District sent a circular to the chiefs of Koya telling them to begin collecting the tax, Charles Smart was one of the few who was ready to comply.

Pa Nemgbana, second in command to the Bai Kompa, is said to have tried to stop Smart from paying the tax by asserting that he would take responsibility if the British came to arrest Smart. Smart immediately reported this to the British authorities, adding that Nemgbana had threatened to kill him if he continued to collect the tax. A British assistant inspector of police was sent to arrest Nemgbana and Bai Kompa, with Smart accompanying them and helping them with information and men. It was on the strength of Smart's evidence that Nemgbana was jailed for 12 months for his defiance of the administration.

Smart continued to exploit opportunities to settle old scores, afforded by the concerted resistance of the Koya chiefs to the house tax. Smart informed the authorities that Serra Bundu of Foredugu, another Koya chiefdom down-river from Mahera, was disloyal and suggested to the district commissioner that Fula Mansa of Yoni, another "loyal" chief, be invited to help subdue Bundu. Smart once more accompanied this expedition through Koya country, provoking many skirmishes in which at least 58 Koya Temne were killed.

Enraged at the activities of Smart and his family, the Temne of Masimera revenged themselves by killing Smart's brother, Pa **Gombu (Smart)**, ruler of the town of Rokon on the Rokel River. Pa Gombu had been collecting tax and blockading the river. The colony later retaliated by burning down some Temne towns.

Having played his part in supporting the administration against his Temne opponents and one-time overlords, Smart continued to enjoy the support of the colonial authorities in his position at Mahera until his death, which occurred probably in the first decade of the 20th century.

SMART, GOMBU (c. 1750s–c. 1820). An enterprising former slave who built up a powerful following through trade and came to rule the thriving town of Rokon in Masimera country. His real name was Koko and he hailed from Kalangba in the current Gbendembu-Gowahun Chiefdom. There, as a boy, he accidentally killed his brother and had to flee as a consequence. He was later sold to British slave traders at the prominent slave trading center at Bunce Island on the Rokel River. He showed much diligence and assiduity there and earned the nickname of "Smart" from his European owners. These owners preferred to keep him as an employee, sending him inland with goods to buy slaves for them. In the process, Gombu Smart bought a lot of his own ethnic **Loko** slaves to become his own followers, which enabled him to become powerful enough to break from his British employers.

Smart joined the **Wunde**, a Kpaa **Mende** secret society, and, as was custom, took a new name, that of Gombu (meaning "fire" in Mende). As a reward for helping the Masimera **Temne** in a civil war, Gombu Smart was given control of the town of Rokon. Smart built a large, well-laid-out town at Rokon. He still retained contact with Europeans at the Sierra Leone colony, and several of them visited Rokon. Smart even allowed Christian missionaries to carry out their mission at Rokon, though with little success. He also supported the Sierra Leone Company ruling the colony in its wars against the Koya Temne under **Tom II** in 1801–1802. In 1806, he was visited by Joseph Corry, an employee of a trading firm at Bunce Island who mentioned Smart in a book he later wrote titled *Observations*. By the 1820s, records show that Smart had died. The prominent Smart family in Sierra Leone is descended from him.

SMART, HENRY MATTHEW JOKO (1934–). Henry Matthew Joko Smart became the dean of the Faculty of Law at **Fourah Bay College**, University of Sierra Leone and ultimately a judge of the High Court of Sierra Leone.

He was born June 15, 1934, in **Bonthe** and attended the **St. Edwards Secondary** School in **Freetown** and Fourah Bay College where he graduated with a B.A. from the University of Durham. He studied law in Britain and was called to the bar at Gray's Inn, proceeding to a doctorate in law at London University. He has taught law at Fourah Bay College since the 1960s while pursuing a lucrative private practice in Freetown. He was one of the organizing figures in the creation of the Faculty of Law at Fourah Bay College and reached the height of his career there as professor of law and dean of the Faculty of Law. At the beginning of the 20th century, he became a judge of the High Court in Sierra Leone.

SOFA. *See* TOURE, SAMORI.

SOLIMANGA SAMURA. Solimanga Samura, who lived during the 17th century, was a warrior who was famous for his enormous stature. He was believed by the ethnic **Yalunka** of the Samura clan in northern Sierra Leone and the Republic of Guinea to be their eponymous ancestor.

Originally called Dantili Samura, he is said to have been a **Mandinka** from the ancient kingdom of Mande in present-day Mali. This huge warrior did not make an impression in Mande and left to seek his fortunes elsewhere. He traveled southward until he reached Firia, the country of the Yalunka of the Kamara clan north of Sierra Leone where he met a Kamara blacksmith, Sa Yere, at work. Tired from his travels, Dantili sat down on a heap of wooden chips that had flown off the hoe handles (*solidagina* in Yalunka) that Sa Yere was carving. Thus he came to be called Solimanga, a fusion of *solidagina* and *manga* (Yalunka for "ruler"). His original name of Dantili soon fell into disuse.

While he was in Firia, the ruler there, Fori Frigi (after whom the country was named), issued a proclamation that four warriors were attacking and robbing people in Firia. They were native Yalunka of the **Kamara** clan but had disguised themselves and taken strange names in order to prevent identification. Frigi announced that he would be indebted to anyone who could rid him of the warriors. Solimanga took up the challenge and killed them all.

It was then that Fori Frigi knew about Solimanga's presence in Firia. In gratitude, Frigi gave Solimanga his daughter Mmame Yeri as his wife. Together with some other relations in the area, Frigi also gave Solimanga a total of 700 males and as many females to form his retinue. These people were of different clans, but none were Samura. Through living with them, Solimanga's Mandinka identity was transformed and he became Yalunka.

While he was in Firia, the Yalunka there were being harassed by the neighboring Fula of Futa Jalon presently in the Republic of Guinea. Solimanga and his warriors drove away the Fula menace, and Fori Frigi was then able to extend his territory over the areas cleaned up by Solimanga. Frigi and Solimanga then agreed that the latter should keep any other territory he might conquer from the Fula. Solimanga thus founded his first town of Kalota in conquered land.

Most of the Yalunka who were given to Solimanga as followers took the clan name of Samura as a mark of honor and association with their leader. Solimanga had four sons—Yirisa Yella, Kumbasa, Yeri Fateh, and Yana Tagesa. They became the rulers of Solimankhori (*khori* is Yalunka for "country"), the area named after Solimanga. Thereafter, the Yalunka of Solimankhori regarded themselves as Solima Yalunka.

Solimanga died, probably in the late 17th century, and was succeeded by his son Yirisa Yella as ruler of Solimankhori. In the 18th century, a state was founded by Yalunka of different clans, led by the Samura, descendants of Solimanga and centered in Solimankhori. This state was called Solimana or the Solima state with the capital at Falaba. Today, Falaba is still the principal town of the Sulima chiefdom in the Koinadugu District, named after Solimanga.

SORI KESSEBEH (c. 1820–1897). Sori Kessebeh was an ethnic **Loko** warrior and leader of the Kanu clan who built the settlement of Rotifunk into a thriving town in the 1870s. He was the son of the mid-18th-century **Loko** king named Sori Kutu and was educated at the Loko military training center at the town of Malal. In the early 18th century, Loko territory spread from **Port Loko** northward to **Kambia**. Loko dominance of this area was eclipsed first by **Soso** migrants who became rulers of Port Loko, and by increasing **Temne** migration into the region. As Temne predominance grew, they staged a revolution, overthrowing **Soso** hegemony in Port Loko in 1817. The next stage was conflict with the Loko for control of major centers and trade, leading to continued warfare between Temne and Loko in the 1820s and 1830s. Ultimately, the Temne were victorious, leading to Loko dispersal, some to **Freetown** and some to Mahera and elsewhere.

Sori Kessebeh, who did not get along with his brother, Gbanga Koba-Wa who was the Loko king, agreed to a request by the ruler of

Bumpe, **R. C. B. Caulker**, to help him in war. Sori's military prowess was remarkable. He always wore Islamic-influenced traditional charms called *sebe,* and this earned him the name of Kessebeh. He fought valiantly for Caulker who rewarded him with the town of Rotifunk, advantageously situated on the Bumpe River, providing a route for commerce with the coast.

Under Sori Kessebeh, Rotifunk became a thriving center by the 1870s. Kessebeh encouraged farming and trade and attracted many of the Loko displaced by the Temne-Loko wars. In spite of his Islamic persuasion, he agreed to the opening of a center at Rotifunk by the Women's Missionary Association, and his son, Santigi Bundu, was educated at the **Church Missionary Society Grammar School** in Freetown.

In the 1880s, Sori Kessebeh was prominent in repelling attacks by the Temne of Yoni country on Bumpe territory. But the Yoni were relentless and continued attacks on areas, such as Bauya and Senehun, that had signed treaties giving the British influence over those areas. The British from Freetown responded by sending an expedition against the Yoni Temne in 1887. Sori Kessebeh and his troops joined the expedition, as did some other neighboring towns. The Yoni Temne were decisively defeated and peace returned.

Sori Kessebeh died in 1897. By then, Christian missions were firmly established in the prosperous town of Rotifunk. He was succeeded by his son, Santigi Bundu.

SORI SESAY, ALIMAMY (c. 1890–1970). Alimamy Sori Sesay was a vigorous and progressive paramount chief of Konike Barina chiefdom in the Tonkolili District of Sierra Leone. One of his main concerns was to persuade the central government to build a road to promote the marketing of rice, which his chiefdom produced in abundance. After many years of campaigning, the road, later to be extended to the Tonkolili-Kono highway, was eventually completed, due largely to his efforts.

He was born at Mayopeh in Konike Barina (one of the two Kunike chiefdoms in the Tonkolili District), a member of the **Muslim** Sesay ruling family in which he grew up. He appears to have begun extensive trading in rice, for which his chiefdom was noted. By 1930 he had become a successful trader at Magburaka, the nearest large town to his chiefdom and a terminus for the northern branch of the **Sierra Leone Railway**.

When the paramount chief of Kunike Barina, Alimamy Kanu, died in 1930, Alimamy Sori stood as candidate in the subsequent elections to succeed him. He was opposed by other candidates, among them Ali Fefegula, son of Mirabong Sesay, the last 19th century ruler of all of Konike **Temne**, who had a reputation as a great warrior. Alimamy Sori won the election, but his opponent could not accept defeat and created trouble in the chiefdom during the first two years of Sori's rule. In 1932, Sori took action and had Fefegula banished to Bo by the colonial authorities. He eventually forgave Fefegula but never allowed him to return to Konike Barina.

Alimamy Sori was a determined and forward-looking ruler. He made the pilgrimage to Mecca twice during his lifetime and was an unofficial member of the colonial **Legislative Council** from 1942 to 1945. He was awarded the Certificate of Honour by the colonial government in 1946 and later the OBE (Order of the British Empire), considered a mark of high recognition by the colonial government.

Successive district commissioners, colonial secretaries, and governors spoke highly of him. E. F. Sayers, a notable provincial commissioner in the north, wrote in 1940 that Alimamy Sori was "an energetic and progressive minded chief who favors common sense when it and old tradition are in conflict." Another district commissioner stated that the paramount chief had "a natural dignity and courtesy . . . (was) very sound and public spirited, (and) . . . was prepared to risk unpopularity" among his subjects for their own benefit. This same district commissioner, however, said on another occasion that Alimamy Sori was "impulsive and hasty, quite ready to forget the native law and quite prepared to be overbearing." Different situations appeared to have brought about different reactions.

One of Alimamy Sori's most significant endeavors was his campaign for a road to link his main town of Makali with Matotoka, a town situated on the major **Bo** to **Makeni** highway. Long before a new highway linking Tonkolili and Kono was constructed at the end of the 1960s decade, Alimamy Sori had seen the need for a main artery of this nature. For more than 13 years he pressured the colonial authorities, even though they kept procrastinating.

He first sent a letter to the district commissioner of Bombali District north of Tonkolili in 1935, requesting the construction of a road whose main purpose would be to assist the marketing of rice, which Konike produced so abundantly. The letter stated in no uncertain terms that the paramount chief wanted his people to "get rest (from) transporting loads by head." He promised labor and financial assistance if only administrative blessing and support were forthcoming.

Colonial government reaction was tardy, but Sori pressed his case again in 1937 with a written appeal this time to the governor, and later in July 1939 by talking personally with Governor J. D. Jardine. Successive letters did not speed up the project and it remained in the feasibility stage for many years. When rice quotas were imposed by the colonial government during World War II, Alimamy Sori reported to the provincial commissioner that transporting rice by headloads made it impossible for his chiefdom to fulfil his quota. In reaction to this, the governor ordered, in November of 1943, that work should start on the Matotoka to Makali road. Only now was the need for a road, expressed by Sori eight years earlier, seen to be urgent.

Work was started in 1944 but was suspended for some practical difficulties; the end of the war also contributed to this development. Work on the road resumed in 1947 and was completed in 1948. Finally, Alimamy Sori's dream became a reality, amid celebrations in Konike. It was this road that was extended and later redone in 1971 to become the Tonkolili-Kono highway.

Alimamy Sori died in 1970 after ruling as paramount chief of Konike Barina for 40 years.

SOSO. Western writers usually called this ethnic group "Susu," arising usually from the misinterpretation of African names by the earliest European visitors to the coastal areas. The people call themselves Soso. They are said to have migrated from the 13th-century kingdom of the same name, which preceded the rise of Sundiata's **Mande** (Mali) kingdom. Over the next two centuries, the Soso moved slowly westward until they reached the coast of West Africa, where Europeans first recorded their presence in the 15th century. Some of the Soso who remained in the mountainous regions of West Africa came to be called Jalunka (variously Yalunka, Dialonke), a term distinguishing them by their mountainous habitat. The Yalunka and Soso languages are mutually understood. Soso are found in larger numbers in the Republic of Guinea from where they spread into much of the **Kambia** District and **Port Loko** Districts of Sierra Leone, which border Soso country in the Republic of Guinea. A struggle for domination of this region of northern Sierra Leone marks the history of Soso expansion and their contact with the **Temne** peoples in the 18th and 19th centuries.

SPECIAL COURT FOR SIERRA LEONE, THE. This court was established by an agreement signed by the United Nations and the government of Sierra Leone in January 2002, following a decision by the UN Security Council in August 2000. Its brief is "prosecute persons who bear the greatest responsibility" for war crimes, crimes against humanity, other serious violations of international humanitarian law, and certain crimes under Sierra Leone national law committed since November 30, 1996. The Special Court is independent of any government or organization, and is funded by 30 contributing states. It has both international and national judges and staff. Based in **Freetown**, it has a mandate of three years. Proceedings started in 2003, and one of the most controversial indictees is **Charles Taylor**, former president of Liberia.

SPENCER, JULIUS SONNY (1955–). Julius Spencer was popularly known as the editor of the *New Breed* newspaper and of an "antirebel" radio station, Radio Democracy, during the height of the rebel war.

He was born in **Freetown** October 18, 1955, and attended the **Prince of Wales Secondary School** and **Njala University College**, where he took the B.A. degree in education. He later studied at the University of Ibadan, Nigeria, where he took an M.A. and Ph.D. in theatre arts in 1987. Spencer returned home and taught drama first at Njala University College and later at Fourah Bay College. He developed a number of popular drama productions in Freetown soon after his return.

In June 1992, Julius started the *New Breed* newspaper, which was extremely critical of the then **National Provisional Ruling Council (NPRC)** military government. The October 13–19, 1992, edition of the *New Breed* carried an article entitled "Redeemers or Villains," which included an excerpt from a Swedish newspaper, *Sunday Ex-*

press, alleging that the chairman of the NPRC had personally traveled to Belgium to sell diamonds. Spencer, his editor, Donald John, and several others were arrested, detained, and later charged with seditious libel. They spent several months in jail before their case was finally settled. Spencer was convicted and fined.

Spencer was undaunted. When the military again took over control of the government during the rebel war in 1997 and set up a junta called the **Armed Forces Revolutionary Council** (AFRC), Spencer founded the antirebel radio station in July 1997. This station was mobile, and the military government made every effort to hunt it down because its broadcasts were directly attacking the AFRC. During that period, if anyone was caught with a radio tuned to the station, that person's personal safety was in serious danger.

When the government of President **Tejan-Kabbah** was reinstated after the AFRC junta was ousted, Spencer was appointed minister of information, communication, tourism, and culture. He resigned the position in May 2001 and returned to mass media productions, starting his own company, the Premier Media Consultancy Limited.

STANDARD CHARTERED BANK OF SIERRA LEONE. This British-run bank has undergone a number of name changes since its inception. It began in 1894 as the Bank of British West Africa Limited, with branches found all over the British colonies in West Africa. In 1957, on the eve of independence, the appellation "British" was dropped, and it was renamed Bank of West Africa. In 1966, a new name, Standard Bank of West Africa, was adopted. However, a few years later, the West African orientation of the bank was discarded and in 1971 The Standard Bank of Sierra Leone Ltd. was born. The name has recently been changed to Standard Chartered Bank, Sierra Leone Limited.

STEVENS, SIAKA PROBYN (1905–1988). Siaka Stevens became prime minister and then president of Sierra Leone. Born August 24, 1905, at **Moyamba** in the Southern Province, he was educated at the **Albert Academy** secondary school and much later took courses at Ruskin College, Oxford, on trade unionism. His early career was in labor union work, which he pursued only after having served on the colonial police force, rising to the rank of first class sergeant. He worked with the foreign company, **Sierra Leone Development Company** (DELCO), which was constructing the railway to exploit iron ore in Sierra Leone. He stayed with DELCO from 1931 to 1946, becoming stenographer and station master at the company's base at the mines of Marampa town in the Northern Province. It was during this period that he cofounded the Sierra Leone United Mine Workers Union. In 1946, when the **Protectorate Assembly** was set up, Stevens was appointed to this body to represent workers' interests. He was elected to the **Legislative Council** as second protectorate member in 1951 and was appointed the first cabinet minister of mines, lands, and labour. He retained his seat in the Legislative Council in the 1957 elections for another five years. However, at this time, he left the **Sierra Leone People's Party (SLPP)** together with **Albert Margai** and others to found the **People's National Party**; he became first secretary-general and later deputy leader.

Siaka Stevens joined the United Front coalition to attend the independence talks in London in 1960. At the talks, he refused to sign the final documents and on his return formed the Elections before Independence Movement, which quickly became the **All People's Congress** political party. Since he was not in Parliament at the time, he apparently realized he could not be made cabinet minister and so struck out on his own. The APC became the main opposition to the ruling SLPP after winning the second-largest number of seats in the 1962 general elections. Stevens himself entered Parliament as leader of the opposition. He also served for a year as mayor of **Freetown**. Stevens' APC won the 1967 elections, but his appointment as prime minister was halted by a military take-over that ushered in a year-long military junta called the National Reformation Council led by **A. T. Juxon-Smith**. In 1968, the NRC was overthrown by junior army officers, and Stevens, who was in self-imposed exile in Guinea, was again named prime minister.

In 1978, following a major student protest that threatened to overthrow his government, Stevens introduced a one-party constitution followed by a referendum recorded as overwhelmingly in favor of the proposed constitution. Sierra Leone then became a one-party state with Stevens as executive president. In 1986, Stevens, then an old man, retired but not before maneuvering to hand over the reins of office to his handpicked head of the army, Major-General **Joseph Saidu Momoh**. He died on May 28, 1988.

STRASSER, VALENTINE (1967–). Valentine Strasser was one of the military officers in the Sierra Leone army at the start of the rebel war who, together, staged a coup d'état that ousted the government of President **Joseph Saidu Momoh** in 1992. A young man in his mid-20s, Strasser was called upon by his peers to become the head of the newly set up military government called the **National Provisional Ruling Council (NPRC)**. He was thus effectively head of state from 1992 to 1996 when he was ousted in a coup by his second in command, **Julius Maada Bio**. He then left the country to study law in England and drifted from there to the Gambia from where he was sent back to Sierra Leone. He was, by then, poor and destitute. He continues to live in **Freetown**.

STRASSER-KING, VICTOR ESEWANU (1942–). Victor Strasser-King was a geologist who became principal of **Fourah Bay College** in 1974. He was educated at the **Sierra Leone Grammar School** and Fourah Bay College where he took a degree in the geological sciences. He proceeded to Britain, where he earned a Ph.D. in geology at Manchester University. He returned to Fourah Bay College in 1974 to teach in the Department of Geology, where he rose to the rank of professor in September 1985 and dean of the Faculty of Pure and Applied Science. In 1993, he was appointed principal of Fourah Bay College, a position he held until his retirement in 2004. He also served as pro-vice chancellor of the **University of Sierra Leone**. Strasser-King served on a number of public committees and boards, including the board of the National Power Authority in Sierra Leone, and was chairman of the board of the **Sierra Leone National Diamond Mining Company**.

SULUKU, ALIMAMY (c. 1820–1906). Alimamy Suluku was a powerful ethnic **Limba** ruler who succeeded in maintaining his independence from the British for some time through brilliant political maneuvering.

Suluku was the son of Sankailay, the ruler of the Biriwa Limba country with its capital at Bumban. There is presently a Biriwa

Limba chiefdom centered on the town of Kamabai near Bumban. Suluku rose to become the leading warrior called the *kurugba*. Even before he became the ruler or *gbaku*, he had expanded the territory under Biriwa control to include Saffroko Limba territory, parts of **Temne**, **Loko**, and **Koranko** territory. Thus, when Sankailay died in 1873, Suluku became the undisputed successor as *gbaku* of the Biriwa state.

As *gbaku*, Suluku markedly improved the agriculture and trade of the Biriwa Limba polity. His progressive rule impressed the British administration in **Freetown**, which sent him annual payments called stipends throughout the 1880s. When **Samori Toure's Mandinka** forces occupied Biriwa in 1884, Suluku skillfully maneuvered to get British support to remove the sofas, Samori's forces, from Biriwa, while ensuring that he did not precipitate a premature confrontation with the sofas.

In the 1890s, as British power over the Sierra Leone interior increased, Suluku remained determined to pursue his own independent policy while making the British believe he was their loyal ally. He sent frequent messages of friendship to the British governor in Sierra Leone and royally entertained every British delegation that arrived at Bumban. But he did exactly as he pleased even in instances where he was obviously working against expressed British interest. Some lower-ranking officers warned of Suluku's deception, but the British administration was convinced of his loyalty. When the 1898 rebellion led by Bai Bureh broke out, Suluku sent warriors and weapons to Bai Bureh. When the British complained, he sent them a letter expressing his support for British position and offered his services as mediator.

After the protectorate became a reality, the British wanted to dismantle Suluku's relatively large domain. Suluku's subjects in what were provinces of the Biriwa Limba state refused to cooperate and elect new chiefs while Suluku was alive. When he was very old, a British official asked Suluku to name his successor to the new dispensation of paramount chief. The *gbaku* replied, "Suluku will never die."

SUMAN, ALIMAMY (c. 1810–1905). Alimamy Suman was ruler of the Wara Wara Limba in the 19th century. Like many northern leaders, he was severely plagued by the aggressive activities of the **sofa**, warriors of the **Mandinka** emperor **Samori Toure**. Despite a treaty of friendship with the British, his area of jurisdiction was much decreased by the turmoil of the *sofa* invasion.

Suman was born in the early 19th century, a member of the **Limba** Mansaray clan, descended from Ba Fofay Mansaray, the founder of Bafodea, at that time the capital of all of Wara Wara Limba. Suman had begun to rule by the middle of the century. In the 1870s, he led his people in collaboration with the Hubu, Fula rebels south of Futa Jalon in the present Republic of Guinea, in conflict against the **Yalunka** state of Solimana in the far northeastern corner of Sierra Leone.

When, in the course of his wars of expansion, Samori's forces reached the Sierra Leone hinterland, Suman prudently submitted to the sofa rather than have his country destroyed. In 1886, he joined another powerful Limba ruler, **Alimamy Suluku**, to petition the British for assistance in securing the trade routes that had been affected by Samori's campaigns. By 1889, the British colonial government was making moves to sign treaties with more distant rulers in the hinterland, and a treaty of friendship was signed with Alimamy Suman as ruler of all the Wara Wara in 1890.

By then, the sofa had recaptured the northeastern part of Sierra Leone, which had rebelled against Samori in 1889, reclaiming that region as part of Samori's empire. Sofa activities in Suman's country made him intensely hostile toward them. When Sayo of Kaliere (formerly in the Solima state) fled from the sofa and took refuge with Suman at Bafodea, Suman closed the trade route to **Freetown** through his country as a way of avenging himself on the invaders.

The aftermath of the sofa invasion created unrest, which greatly reduced the area under Alimamy Suman's rule. Some of his subchiefs sided with the sofa against him in order to secure their independence. The **Limba** of Bongobong and Kakrima are examples. After the sofa had left, the Bongobong Limba, determined to be free of Suman's rule, enlisted the help of mercenaries to fight against Suman.

When the British took over the hinterland as a protectorate in 1896, Bonbong and Kakrima were regarded as independent of Suman and were made separate chiefdoms. Greatly reduced in authority and weakened by the upheavals of the 1880s and 1990s, Alimamy Suman died in 1905.

– T –

TABULAY. Tabulay is a large bowl-shaped laced drum with one skin cover and is beaten by two people hitting it in turn with a short length of tough ropes knotted at the head with leather. The tabulay can be some 60 cm. high with a diameter of some 20–25 cm. The tabulay is used to assemble people for a variety of purposes. It came to be a symbol of authority in traditional society because it was usually the ruler who had the authority to assemble people.

TAQI, IBRAHIM BASH (1931–1975). Ibrahim Bash Taqi was a prominent journalist and politician whose forceful journalism was significantly responsible for the overthrow of the ruling government that had inherited rulership from the colonialists. In the mid-1960s, Taqi was the dominant columnist of the popular newsprint called *We Yone*, the voice of the opposition **All People's Congress (APC)** party. This contributed immensely to the APC winning the elections in 1967.

Taqi came from a well-known family from Ropolo in the Tane chiefdom, Tonkolili District. He was educated at the **Prince of Wales School** in **Freetown** and then at Ibadan University and later at Heidelberg University in Germany.

In March of 1967, Taqi won election to Parliament as a member for Freetown East I constituency and was appointed and sworn in as minister of information in the new APC government led by **Siaka Stevens** before the military cut short this process with a coup. The APC came back in 1968 after the military interregnum, and Taqi became a government back bencher until he was appointed minister of information and broadcasting in April of 1969.

Less than a year after he took office, Taqi resigned from the APC government and joined the newly formed United Democratic Party, which had suddenly emerged with boundless popularity as opposition to the government. In September of 1970, when **Siaka Stevens** banned that party, Taqi was arrested and detained under public emergency regulations. He was released in 1973 only to be rearrested in 1974 and charged with treason. In the celebrated case of **Mohammed Sorie Forna** and 14 others, Taqi was convicted of treason and was executed in July 1975.

TAYLOR, CHARLES (1948–). Charles Taylor was president of Liberia from 1997 to 2003. He started and successfully prosecuted a civil war in Liberia, which ultimately took him to the presidency as the head of the main surviving group at the end of the war. While conducting the Liberian war, Taylor also originated and continued a civil war in Sierra Leone starting in 1991.

Taylor was an Americo-Liberian (descendants of former-slaves, freed blacks who immigrated in the 1800s to Liberia from America), who was born and bred in Monrovia, the capital of Liberia. He was educated in the United States, where he obtained a degree in economics from Bentley College in Massachusetts. While in the United States, Taylor became involved in student politics, strongly advocating Pan-African and Marxist principles. Taylor returned to Liberia after his studies and became a teacher, later taking up appointment in the government of Samuel Doe soon after Doe's successful military coup made him president of Liberia. Under a cloud of accusations for misappropriating Liberian government funds, Taylor fled to the United States, where he was convicted and sent to prison in Massachusetts in 1984 for stealing Liberian government funds. Taylor escaped from prison a year later, and in 1989, he returned to Liberia from the Ivory Coast and launched a war against the government of Samuel Doe, the then-president of Liberia.

In the process of this Liberian war, Taylor decided to punish the Sierra Leone government for, among other grievances, supporting the **Economic Community Cease-Fire Monitoring Group (ECOMOG)** forces against him. He teamed up with Sierra Leonean dissidents, led by Foday Sankoh, and launched an attack on Sierra Leone, which started the civil war there in 1991. In the course of the war, Taylor trained and armed the Sierra Leonean rebels but also sent his own soldiers to fight in Sierra Leone as the civil war died down in Liberia. When the Sierra Leone rebels captured the **Kono** diamond region of Sierra Leone, all of the diamonds were channeled to Charles Taylor in Liberia, who thus enriched himself and used part of the proceeds to continue providing arms for the Sierra Leonean rebels.

At the conclusion of the civil war in Sierra Leone, a **Special Court** was set up with the support of the United Nations to try those guilty of crimes against humanity. One of its first indictees in June 2003 was Charles Taylor. By then, rebels in a group known as Liberians

United for Reconciliation and Democracy (LURD) were fighting a bitter war against Taylor's National Patriotic party in an attempt to overthrow him. When the war reached a stalemate, tremendous international pressure was brought to bear on Taylor to step down. He was granted asylum by the Nigerian government and left office in December 2003.

TAYLOR-CUMMINGS, EUSTACE HENRY (1890–1967). Eustace Taylor-Cummings was a former mayor of **Freetown** and a leading medical doctor in the colonial service in Sierra Leone. He was born in Freetown, the son of a leading merchant and also a former mayor of Freetown, Emmanuel Cummings. He was educated at the Wesleyan Boys High School and **Fourah Bay College** before studying medicine at the University of Liverpool. He then joined the colonial medical service and was attached to the sanitation department where he is remembered as having helped to improve sanitation in both Freetown and the protectorate. By the time he retired in 1947, he had been promoted to senior medical officer.

In the municipal council in Freetown, he became a nominated member in 1936 and held this position until he became mayor in 1948. He was noted for starting the system of municipal primary schools, which is now well known in Freetown. He worked with others such as **Sanusi Mustapha** to form the "Save the Fourah Bay College" committee when there was a threat to reduce the status of that college to a technical college in 1944. From 1950 to 1953, Taylor-Cummings was president of the Fourah Bay College Council, the governing body of the college, being the first Sierra Leonean to hold that position. In 1960, he was awarded the honorary doctor of civil laws by Durham University in England.

TEJAN-SIE, AHMED KONIGBAGBE (1927–1977). Ahmed Tejan-Sie was a popular musician, composer, and singer who put together his own calypso band and rocked **Freetown** in the 1950s.

He was born in Freetown and attended the **Methodist Boys High School**, where he was noted as a singer in a 100-voices choir organized by Professor Greywood, a notable musician at that school. He sang in churches all over Sierra Leone. When he left school, he worked on the Sierra Leone Railway where he formed his calypso band and played the guitar and the ukulele banjo. He was also the lead singer and composed several songs. One popular song carried his name, "Konigbagbe let go-o, I will give you sweet potato." In 1959, he was given a scholarship to study speech and drama in England after he used his band to help the **Sierra Leone People's Party (SLPP)** campaign and win the first general elections in Sierra Leone. He returned to Freetown in 1964 but lost the political influence that had been instrumental in his singing career. He continued to be employed by the Sierra Leone Broadcasting Service, where he sang a number of his compositions. He suffered a stroke and died five years later in 1977.

TEJAN-SIE, BANJA (1917–). Banja Tejan-Sie's claim to fame was as chief justice and later governor general of Sierra Leone in the late 1960s. He was educated at the **Bo Government Secondary School** and the **Prince of Wales School** in **Freetown**. Before proceeding for further studies in England, he worked for a year as a station clerk in the Sierra Leone Railway starting in 1938, and later for six years as a nurse in the medical department, starting in 1940. At the London School of Economics and at Lincoln's Inn, he qualified as a lawyer.

When Banja Tejan-Sie returned to Sierra Leone he began private practice and also became involved in politics. He was a prominent member of the **Sierra Leone People's Party** from its inception and was elected vice president of that party in 1953. In 1958, he was appointed police magistrate but continued to be active in politics, notably as a member of the Independence Constitutional Committee. In 1967, he was appointed chief justice and in April 1968 became an officer performing the functions of the governor general. He was officially appointed governor general in 1971 and held this position until April 1971, when the adoption of a Republican constitution in Sierra Leone abolished the position of governor general. He retired to England in enforced exile.

TEMNE. The Temne constitute one of the largest ethnic groups in Sierra Leone, found chiefly in the Tonkolili, Bombali, **Port Loko**, and **Kambia** Districts. Temne traditions and extant records place Temne migration from the region of Futa Jalon highlands southward into Sierra Leone before the 15th century. As they migrated into

Sierra Leone, the Temne influenced and were influenced by other groups they met in the region. Similarly, groups who came later, such as the **Soso** and other **Mande** elements settled among and came to dominate many ruling houses among the Temne. This helps to explain the predominance of Islam among the Temne.

Major groupings have not produced much distinction among the Temne. There are two major groups, the Sanda of the Bombali District and the Yoni Temne found in the **Moyamba** District. Believed to be the older grouping, the Yoni are credited with the spread of the **Poro** society into most of Sierra Leone. Two other smaller subgroups, the Kholifa and Kunike Temne, in chiefdoms bearing the same names in the Tonkolili District, are more heavily Mande influenced. The Temne ruler is called the *o'bai,* a term that is very well known among most Sierra Leoneans. The **Poro** for men and the **Sande** (or ***Bundo***) for women have significant roles in social, religious, and cultural life.

THOMAS, JOHN HENRY "MALAMAH" (1845–1922). John Henry "Malamah" Thomas, descended from liberated African parents, ran a thriving business in **Freetown** and became a leading figure among the **Krio** people of Freetown. He served several terms as mayor of Freetown.

He was later nicknamed "Malamah" but at birth was named John Henry in the village of Hastings, near Freetown, in February 1845. His parents, John and Beth Thomas, were liberated Africans from Egba country in Yorubaland in Nigeria. Since his parents were poor, he could not attend school regularly, and as a boy he did odd jobs to help with the family's survival. Later, he began working for a family friend, Thomas Macauley, who had a business on the Rio Nunez north of Sierra Leone. When Macauley's business folded, he recommended John for a job with the African Merchants, Ltd., a European company that had recently started trading in Sierra Leone. John Henry worked as a bookkeeper for this company on Sherbro Island, and when that company left Sierra Leone, one of its agents took John into the company's branch at Calabar, Nigeria, as a bookkeeper.

By this time, John had married Christianna Rollings, the sister of T. J. Rollings, a shopkeeper in Freetown. John went with Christianna to Calabar but later decided to return to Freetown and set up on his own business as a trader on the Rokel River. He started with a loan of 100 pounds sterling from a friend, Dr. Robert Smith. John's business thrived, and he built a warehouse at a town named Malamah, which earned him the nickname, Malamah Thomas.

A few years after John had started his own business, Ernest Vohsen, an agent for the Compagnie du Senegal (later the Compagnie Francaise de l'Afrique Occidentale or CFAO) approached John Malamah Thomas about working for that company. Vohsen, who was the company's agent on the Scarcies River, asked whether Thomas would be willing to take over his functions. Thomas agreed and closed his business on the Rokel. Before leaving for the Scarcies, Thomas opened a small shop in Freetown in October 1882 and left his wife in charge.

Thomas held the position with the CFAO agency until June 1888 when he resigned and returned to Freetown to prosecute his own business. His trading efforts thrived and he became one of the foremost merchants in the city. He built a beautiful house in East Street, still retained by his descendants, which became known as Malamah House. It was the first of its kind in Freetown, with decorative carved heads on the stone masonry. Thomas traded chiefly in cotton fabrics. He invented and patented in England his own brand of cotton known as "Malamah baft."

After achieving prosperity, public service logically followed. The elegantly dressed Thomas, smoking cigars and often visiting England, held office in both church and state. He became warden at the Holy Trinity Church in Freetown and later treasurer of the Sierra Leone Native Pastorate Church. In December 1891, he was appointed charity commissioner by Acting Governor J. J. Crooks and became commissioner of the peace in 1894. In municipal elections in Freetown in 1903, Thomas won the contest to represent the East Ward. In 1904, he was elected mayor of Freetown and held that position for eight years thereafter. In 1907, he was appointed an unofficial member of the **Legislative Council** in **Freetown**, then considered one of the highest honors in the colonial system.

His influence extended beyond local politics in Freetown. He became president of the local branch of the National Congress of British West Africa, a body that advocated united political agitation for self-government among the African peoples of the British West African colonies. He supported the Congress with both time and money.

John Henry Malamah Thomas died in Freetown on January 17, 1922.

THOMAS, SAMUEL BENJAMIN (ABUKE) (1833–1901). Samuel Benjamin (Abuke) Thomas was a hardworking businessman who amassed a large fortune by frugal living and calculated investment. At his death, he left a substantial endowment for an agricultural college to be created in Sierra Leone.

Samuel was born in Wellington, a village near **Freetown** that was the home of many other prominent Sierra Leoneans. Not much is known of his early life. He was educated for the Anglican ministry at **Fourah Bay College** but chose instead to turn to business, using as capital the inheritance left by his father who had himself been a prosperous businessman.

Samuel was one of the few educated ethnic **Krio** of Freetown, in the company of people such as J. A. Songo-Davies, **A. J. Shorunkeh-Sawyer**, and **J. Abayomi-Cole**, who took a keen interest in practical agriculture. While others manifested zeal and ideas on the subject, Thomas had the wealth and foresight to give practical expression to his own views. When he died, he left what was then a small fortune of over 54,000 pounds sterling to set up an agricultural college to train his own people not only in the liberal arts and sound Christian teaching but also in the theory and practice of agriculture. The S. B. Thomas Agricultural Academy that was built at Mabang on the Ribi River with his money was completed in 1912. When he died, a plaque was erected at his local church in Wellington testifying to his exemplary contribution.

THOMPSON, BANKOLE (1938–). Bankole Thompson is a lawyer and a scholar in Sierra Leone legal history. He was one of the trial judges at the Special Court for Sierra Leone. He was born and educated in **Freetown** at the **Prince of Wales School**. He took a B.A. degree at **Fourah Bay College** and a master's in philosophy. He assumed appointment as state counsel in Freetown and later joined the **Mano River Union** as legal officer in the 1970s. Thompson served as a judge of the High Court in Sierra Leone before leaving for the United States where he began to teach law at Kent State University. He then proceeded to Eastern Kentucky University where he became a professor and dean of graduate studies. He was invited by the United Nations, with the approval of the Sierra Leone government, to sit as a trial chamber judge in the **Special Court** for Sierra Leone and took up this position in 2002. Bankole Thompson has written widely on legal issues relative to Sierra Leone. His two books, *The Criminal Law of Sierra Leone* (1998) and *The Constitutional History and Law of Sierra Leone: 1961–1995* (1998), were both published by the University Press of America.

TOKBA ASANA (c. 1730–1788). A courageous ruler who lead his Solima **Yalunka** people from under the yoke of oppression of the Fula of Futa Jalon, Tokba Asana is also remembered as the founder of Falaba, the capital of the Solima Yalunka kingdom.

Tokba Asana of the Samura clan was born about 1730, the second son of Yima Yella, the *manga* (ruler) of Solima country. When Asana's older brother, Yella Dansa, became ruler of the Solima in his turn, Asana became his *kurugba* (general). By this time, the Yalunka of Solima country and other Yalunka in the neighborhood had come under the rule of the **Fula** of Futa Jalon in the present Republic of Guinea. The Fula had taken control of the Solima following a jihad starting in 1727, and the Solima subjects were now forced to fight with the Fula against other neighboring peoples. The Solima were also being heavily taxed by the Fula and found Fula overlordship burdensome but could see no way to free themselves.

Tokba Asana rallied the Yalunka into defiance. Sometime during the 1770s, he called together Yalunka elders of Solima, Sinkunia, Dembelia, and Folosaba countries all in what is now the Koinadugu district of Sierra Leone to discuss the odious subject of vassalage to the Fula. He persuaded them all to "eat country bread," (to take a binding oath) and thus swear to free themselves of Fula overrule led by Tokba Asana in this quest.

Under Tokba Asana's leadership, the combined Yalunka force withdrew its support for the Fula in a war against Konde Brima of Sankaran, in what is now the Republic of Guinea. In retaliation, the Fula killed all Solima Yalunka headmen then in Futa Jalon. The

Solima responded by killing all Fula in Solima country, which meant war with Futa Jalon. Tokba Asana then led the Yalunka in an alliance with Konde Brima of Sankaran, and there started a period of Futa-Solima wars.

It was during these wars that Falaba was founded by the combined Yalunka force under Tokba Asana. After three centers of resistance had been destroyed by the Fula, the Yalunka forces moved southward and about 1780 established Falaba in an almost impregnable position. Falaba proved its worth, surviving a number of attacks for over a century until in 1884 the forces of the **Mandinka** conqueror, Samori, destroyed it after a nine-month siege. Under Tokba Asana, Falaba became the capital of the Solima Yalunka state that came to include all those who had sworn the oath to be led by him in war against the Fula. And so Tokba Asana became the first ruler of the greater Solima state.

In 1788, the Yalunka forces, still led by Tokba Asana, decided to strike a final blow against the Fula. The two large armies met on the plains of Herico River close to the Solima territory. Tokba Asana lost his life in the bloody battle that ensued.

TOM II (KING) (LATE 18TH TO EARLY 19TH CENTURY). King Tom was the subruler of the territory around the Rokel River estuary where the Sierra Leone colony was established. He resisted attempts by the Sierra Leone Company rulers of the new colony to claim the land on which the colony stood by claims of cession. However, his resistance failed and the colony rulers then claimed the land by right of conquest.

His actual name was Kokelly but he took the title of King Tom when he assumed rulership of the "watering place" as this area came to be called in the literature because ships docked there frequently and paid to take on fresh water. It was in 1796 that the overall ruler of the region, the Bai Farma, appointed King Tom to succeed King Jimmy to this position. King Tom had been on good terms with the colony settlement before assuming office and his son, Henry, studied in England at the company's expense.

On King Tom's accession, he expected the customary initial payment to a new ruler by the Sierra Leone Company whom he considered his tenants. The company apparently thought it had bought the land from King Jimmy, but King Tom insisted that land could not be alienated in the traditions of his own people.

When King Tom got no satisfactory response from the Sierra Leone Company, he became hostile to the colony settlement and disregarded boundary lines claimed by the colony. In this, he was supported by his overlord, the Bai Farma. Toward the end of 1799, there was an insurrection among the Nova Scotian settlers, one of whose principal grievances was the imposition of quit-rents to be paid to the Company. In their rebellion, they found a ready ally in King Tom. Encouraged by refugee rebels, King Tom's **Temne** forces together with Bai Farma attacked Fort Thornton, the Company's stronghold in Freetown on November 18, 1801. One officer, two soldiers, and a number of people were killed. A few days later, the Company retaliated by burning down King Tom's towns between **Freetown** and Cape Sierra Leone. Subdued by this display of colony force, King Tom retreated to the Northern Rivers where the **Mandinka** chiefs tried to mediate between the Temne and the colony. Nonetheless, Fatima Fodi, the Mandinka Chiefs' envoy, encouraged King Tom to resume fighting. Captain Bullen of HMS *Wasp*, whose sailors had participated in the attack on King Tom's towns, tried unsuccessfully to make peace. No sooner had Bullen sailed away, then the Temne chiefs who had promised peace, found it opportune to strike again. Reinforced by **Soso** and some refugee rebels, they attacked Fort Thornton again but were soon driven back within a half hour and expelled from the colony.

King Tom, supported by a **Bullom** ruler, continued the resistance on the Bullom Shore but his ally was soon overcome and expelled from his territory. Now virtually without any supporter, King Tom returned to his domain east of the colony where he and the Koya Temne remained peacefully. In 1807, a final settlement was negotiated at the town of Robis (between the present Wellington and Hastings) between King Tom and the colony.

The new treaty, signed on July 10, 1807, confirmed the colony's conquest of the lands west of Freetown. The Temne rulers also "ceded" the right to the peninsula to the Company, and cession by means of purchase "was superseded by conquest."

TOM KEBBIE (EARLY 18TH CENTURY–1878). Tom Kebbie came to be known as Tom Kebbie Smith because of a misunderstanding recorded by Europeans. The term *kebi* means "a smith." Family and caste-like attachment to the trade, which was very prominent in precolonial society, meant that families attached the appellation *kebi* to their names. Thus, when Tom Kebbie's name was first mentioned to Europeans, they mistook the interpretation of the term *kebi*, meaning blacksmith, to represent a last name known in their own tradition.

This obviously puts Tom Kebbie into a family of blacksmiths. Little is known of his birth and early life that, from all accounts, seems to have been of the lowest class in society. But by hard work and effort, Tom Kebbie became very wealthy by local standards. He excelled in trade and had control of a lot of land and dependents, two of the most important markers of wealth.

It was this ability to get ahead that Tom Kebbie used, at the death of the ruler of the town of Mongere in the **Sherbro** mainland, to get himself elected to the rulership of that town. Tom Kebbie faced a lot of opposition because people felt he was not eligible for the position. But Kebbie got enough of the leading personalities and chiefs on his side that he was handed the horse tail, the symbol of authority in Mongere.

Opposition to Tom Kebbie was manifested in 1875 when he made a grant of land to one of his dependents. One subchief named Lahai Golay opposed this land grant on the grounds that he had claims to that land. He was supported by Sheriff Golay, son of the previous ruler. Both men created enough trouble to cause a riot in Mongere, but they could not unseat Tom Kebbie, who had a number of the chiefs on his side, including some of the rivals of Sheriff and Lahai Golay.

Tom Kebbie even aspired to the overall rulership of the country around the Jong and Small Bum Rivers. Although he failed in this attempt, he was important enough to be considered for the position. Tom Kebbie died in 1878, and the colony administration in Freetown had to take steps to avert any possible struggle over his enormous property and servile dependents.

TONGO PLAYERS. The Tongo Players were part of a precolonial **Mende** institution that used unscrupulous methods of crime detection, particularly in accusations of "witchcraft." Those so accused by Tongo Players had no recourse and were beaten and burned to death.

In the late 19th century, the Tongo Players were led by Kpowamoh-ei-Nepo who was feared to the extent that if he had to pass through a country where there was a war, hostilities would cease to allow him to pass. The Tongo Players were often called out when there were accusations of "leopard murders," then fairly common in **Sherbro** country. It was believed that the murders were caused by people who used mystical powers to transform themselves into leopards. The victims were murdered and parts of their bodies were used to make medicinal concoctions believed to make humans more powerful. After scouting around to gather information, the Tongo Players would proceed to a settlement where they had been invited and stage a big bonfire at night. They would be specially garbed and the leader would carry a large horn filled with "medicines." Toward the end of a dance around the fire, the leader would strike certain people with the horn and if it stuck to the head or the chest the person was guilty of ritual murder and would be beaten severely and burned to death. The victim's property and that of his relatives would be seized and distributed among the chiefs. This was evidently a means used by local chiefs to regulate the ascendancy of rivals.

When a widespread rash of leopard murders broke out in Imperi in Sherbro country in 1890, the Tongo Players were invited, and among those burned at the event was Gbana Bunje, chief of Gbangbama, one of those who had been instrumental in inviting the Tongo Players. The colonial government eventually passed laws banishing the Tongo Players from the country in 1892 and they faded from the scene.

TOURE, SAMORI (c. 1830–1900). Samori Toure was a **Mandinka** ruler who, in the second half of the 19th century, created a large empire engulfing most of the current states of Guinea, Sierra Leone, and Mali.

He was born about 1830 at the town of Manyambaladugu in present-day Guinea, of **Mande** Muslim traders and Kamara clan traditionalist peasants. He took to trading and came to be counted among the Dyula, that group of Mandinka **Muslim** traders who were to be found generally in this region. Samori's exploits were part of a general pattern of the rise of Dyula operatives in this region of upper Guinea who gradually took advantage of the profits of trade, particularly the acquisition of arms and ammunition, to capture political power in the area. By the

1870s, Samori had built a strong kingdom centered in Balandugu, a new capital that he created. He had adopted Islam and began to use this as a unifying force in his kingdom.

In the course of his military campaigns in the early 1880s, Samori's soldiers, called the **sofa**, launched a major offensive southward toward the Guinea coast, which came to include most of northern Sierra Leone. The Solima Kingdom based in Falaba in northern Sierra Leone was conquered and taken over in 1884. By then, most of **Limba** country north of Biriwa and parts of **Koranko** country had all fallen to the sofa. Samori then began to encounter extreme military opposition by the French who were determined to take over his empire. In fact, by 1887, parts of the empire located in present-day northern Sierra Leone liberated themselves as Samori battled with the French. These areas were later brought again under Samori's control by 1889. The intervention of the British from the Sierra Leone colony saved **Alimamy Suluku's** Biriwa Limba from being occupied by the sofa.

By the 1890s, however, the French had cut Samori's main forces off from this southern part of his empire, which included northern Sierra Leone. British and French forces, struggling to lay claim to areas vacated by Samori's forces, clashed with each other by mistake at the town of Waima in 1898, and the British and French officers leading the affray died in the clash.

The French pursued Samori, destroying his capital at Bisandugu in 1892, slowly but surely destroying his empire. However, Samori fought on and was only captured by the French in 1898.

TRUTH AND RECONCILIATION COMMISSION FOR SIERRA LEONE. The Truth and Reconciliation Commission for Sierra Leone (TRC) is an independent organization created by the **Lomé Peace Agreement** of July 7, 1999. Established by an act of the Sierra Leone Parliament on February 10, 2000, its mandate is to create an impartial historical record of violations and abuses of human rights and international humanitarian law related to the armed conflict in Sierra Leone, from the beginning of the conflict in 1991 to the signing of the Lomé Peace Agreement. It was expected that the TRC would address issues of impunity, respond to the needs of the victims, promote healing and reconciliation, and help to prevent a repetition of the violations and abuses suffered.

The Commission has seven members (commissioners) appointed by the president of Sierra Leone, four of whom are Sierra Leoneans, with the Rt. Rev. Dr. Joseph Christian Humper as chairperson. The commission began public hearings in Freetown April 14, 2003.

TUBOKU-METZGER, ALBERT EMERICK (1856–1950). Albert Emerick Tuboku-Metzger was one of the early promoters of African values, relentlessly striving to defend his countrymen against colonial attitudes of superiority. He was a leading African politician, later becoming president of the National Congress of British West Africa.

He was born at Kissy village east of **Freetown**, the son of an ethnic Egba liberated African from Yorubaland who may well have adopted the last name of a local German missionary. As a young man, Tuboku-Metzger, supporting the nascent African "nationalism" and reacting against racism, added the African name of Tuboku to his German name.

Young Tuboku-Metzger was educated at the **CMS Grammar School** and, in preparation for a career in the church, studied at **Fourah Bay College** from 1877–1881. He received a bachelor of arts degree and then did a licentiate in theology, which he took with first class honors, the only student to achieve this. He later acquired a master of arts degree after teaching at Fourah Bay College from 1881–1885.

Tuboku-Metzger was the first Sierra Leone graduate to enter the colonial service. In 1885, he was taken on as a treasury clerk at the miniscule salary of 45 pounds sterling per year, a position and salary far less than what a graduate in England would receive. He later worked in the registrar-general's office and in the police service in Freetown. As a police clerk, he was requested by the attorney general to draft the Magistrate's Court Ordinance (1905), the Summary Convictions Ordinance (1906), and the Court of Requests Ordinance (1906). Finally, in 1908, he was one of the few Africans ever appointed assistant district commissioner and served in the **Sherbro** District. He retired in 1917. Because of his experience and knowledge of local government, he was often asked for his views, which were always given with precision and confidence and carried considerable weight with his peers.

Albert Tuboku-Metzger was a founding member of the National Congress of British West Africa. Established in 1920, this was the first articulate organization to express open criticism of the colonial government. Tuboku-Metzger thus played a prominent role in the early stages of the development of 20th century African politics. He became one of the Congress' vice presidents and eventually president.

TUBOKU-METZGER, FRED (c. 1928–). Fred Tuboku-Metzger was professor of law and the first dean of the faculty of Law at **Fourah Bay College**. He later became the first director of the Sierra Leone Law School. He did his secondary education at the **Prince of Wales School** in **Freetown** before graduating with an LL.B. from King's College, Durham, in England, being called to the bar at Middle Temple in 1956. On returning to Freetown, Tuboku-Metzger joined the colonial administrative service and was briefly district commissioner at **Pujehun**, **Bonthe**, and **Bo**. In 1958, he was appointed lecturer in law at Fourah Bay College, beginning a long career that would see him become, with the opening of the faculty of law, the first dean. When the Sierra Leone government decided to establish the School of Law to train lawyers, Tuboku-Metzger became the first director of that school. He also served as editor in chief of the *Sierra Leone Law Report* and a member of the Committee on Legal Education in Sierra Leone.

TUCKER, NANCY (c. 1825–1908). Nancy Tucker was a successful trader who eventually became ruler of the Town of Bagru in the Bum chiefdom of the **Bonthe** District in Sierra Leone. Tucker was from Kittam in the same region and after achieving success in trade used her resources to entertain local and European officials. She became the mistress of a Sergeant Coker, an ethnic **Temne** official of the **Frontier Police Force**. Coker used his position to get Nancy Tucker installed as "provisional paramount chief of Bagru" after the death of the incumbent, Humpa Rango of Dodo.

Nancy Tucker was vocal in her support for colonial government policies even when this went against the wishes of her people. After the declaration of the protectorate and the institution of the house tax, she exerted an all-out effort to collect the tax, even paying some of the tax from her own resources in order to present an image of popular support for the tax to the colonial authorities. At the outbreak of the rebellion, she was smuggled under **Frontier Police** escort to safety at the barracks at Kwelu on the Bagru River. From there she was sent to Freetown. At the end of the war, Tucker returned to her position and joined the administration in seeking out and punishing those who had participated in the resistance. In recompense, the governor confirmed her position as paramount chief of Bum and she remained in this position until her death in 1908.

TUCKER, PETER L. Peter Tucker became secretary to the prime minister and head of the civil service in Sierra Leone in 1966. He was born at **Bonthe Sherbro** and was educated in schools in Blama and at the **St. Edward's Secondary School** in **Freetown**. He took a B.A. degree from **Fourah Bay College** and later an M.A. at the University of Cambridge. He became headmaster of the Kenema Government Secondary School and later was an education officer of the Ministry of Education in the 1950s. In 1961, he took up appointment as secretary for training and recruitment in the newly independent Sierra Leone government and two years later became establishment secretary. In 1966, he was appointed secretary to the prime minister and head of the civil service. Two years later, a military coup ushered in a military junta, the **National Reformation Council (NRC)**. Tucker left the civil service and went to England, where he qualified as a barrister of Gray's Inn in 1970. Employed in Britain thereafter, he attained the rank of chief executive of the Commission for Racial Equality. He retired in 1982 and returned to Freetown briefly and took up a position in one of the government parastatals. He has been living in England since the 1990s, and has been writing the history of the **Sierra Leone People's Party** of which he was a founding member.

– U –

UNITED DEMOCRATIC PARTY (UDP). The United Democratic Party was formed in September 1970 following the resignation of two cabinet ministers from **Siaka Stevens' All People's Congress (APC)** government. These two former ministers, **Mohammed Sorie Forna** and M. O. Bash-Taqi then teamed up with other dissidents, former APC strongman **Ibrahim Taqi** and **John Karefa-Smart**, to form the UDP. The party had strong appeal in the Northern Province of Sierra Leone, and its radical approach threatened to undermine the APC government. Siaka Stevens acted quickly, and less than a month after its formation, the **United Democratic Party (UDP)** was proscribed and its leaders and leading sympathizers were detained; some were later tried and executed for treason.

UNITED NATIONAL PEOPLE'S PARTY (UNPP). The UNPP was a political party formed in 1995 by **John Karefa-Smart** to contest the 1996 general elections. The party was registered in September 1995 with the symbol, "Di Lamp" (the lamp). The declared goal of the party was "to unite all the people of Sierra Leone, to organize and lead the mass of our people in their struggle to reverse the current disunity and lay a solid political foundation for economic development." The party contested the 1996 elections and won 17 seats, the second highest number of seats in the Legislature (the SLPP won 36, the largest). The UNPP leader thus became the leader of the opposition in Parliament. The UNPP leader again contested the presidency in 2002, but by then the party had been racked by leadership disputes after its leader had been suspended from Parliament and there was a struggle over who should replace him as interim chairman.

UNITED PROGRESSIVE PARTY (UPP). The United Progressive Party (UPP) was formed in 1954 by **Cyril Rogers-Wright**. He had the support of another radical **Krio** leader, **Wallace Johnson**, who was then a member of the Legislative council. The UPP also included in its leadership people such as Valesius Neale Caulker and Tarasid Tarawaly, and professed that it aimed to unite the country against the polarization of the **Sierra Leone People's Party (SLPP)**, seen as a protectorate party and the **National Council**, almost exclusively a Krio party. Although the party held rallies in the protectorate, it had no branches there probably due to a lack of funds. As if to prove its point of trying to unite the entire country, the party leader, Rogers-Wright, who hailed from **Freetown**, won a bye-election seat in **Port Loko** in 1957 and Valesius Neale Caulker won similarly in his home region of **Moyamba** north. The UPP was, however, a short-lived party since its leading members began to desert the party. The UPP was absorbed by **Milton Margai's** United Front coalition in 1960.

– V –

VA FORAY SASABLA. Also called Foray Kallon, Va Foray Sasabla is reputed to be the ancestor of the Kallons, a prominent clan scattered over many parts of Sierra Leone today.

He is said to have migrated to the northeast of Sierra Leone from his homeland in **Koranko** country probably in the late 17th century. He was an Islamic leader and charm-maker, a practice that blended **Islam** and traditional belief systems. When he first moved into the area of the present day Kailahun District he met ethnic **Gola** people living there, most significantly a Gola hunter named Yarvai who had "wandered" there with his followers. Yarvai had just lost his wife in childbirth and vowed to stay where this had happened, thus giving that place the name of Kambama, meaning "on the grave."

Va Foray and Yarvai became friends and Va Foray decided to stay there after his soothsaying sense had told him that many towns would grow in that heavily forested area. However, he first went back to his Koranko home and returned with presents for Yarvai who gave Va Foray his daughter, Kefuegunde, in marriage. Va Foray had a number of sons by this wife, and he sent all of them to Koranko country for Islamic education except for his youngest son, Borbowa, whom he adored. Va Foray built his own center at Folu (under the *folei* tree) and as he grew old, he convinced Yarvai to agree that Borbowa should succeed him in Folu.

When Va Foray died, Borbowa inherited his position, but his brothers heard of their father's demise and came to Folu to protest Borbowa's succession. To appease them, Yarvai allowed them to settle neighboring places some of which came to be known as Barrie Potoru, Nongowa, and some went as far as Koya country close to **Freetown**.

Thus, most Kallons in all of these places are traced back to their eponymous ancestor, Va Foray Sasabla.

VAI. The Vai were one of the smaller ethnic groups found in the **Pujehun** District in southern Sierra Leone. Vai roots in Sierra Leone can be traced to the **Kono**. Vai country in Sierra Leone came to be called Galhinas because, it is believed, the early Portuguese who visited this area in the 15th century found a lot of chickens there and used the

Portuguese word for hen which sounds like Galhinas. The ruling family among the Vai is the Massaquoi, a term that also refers to the regal symbol, the crown in Galhinas country.

VOUCHERGATE. In the early 1980s, a massive scandal that has come to be termed "vouchergate" erupted over civil servants manipulating vouchers to mulct the government. The vouchers were approved by the top civil servants and the monies were converted to personal use. The government of Siaka Stevens conducted a lackluster investigation and the suspects were finally cleared of wrongdoing.

– W –

WALLACE-JOHNSON, I. T. A. (1894–1965). Wallace-Johnson was one of the foremost political activists in Sierra Leone in the later colonial period, always in the forefront of various anticolonial movements, particularly in defense of workers' rights.

He was born in Wilberforce village, **Freetown,** and educated at Centenary Tabernacle School in Freetown. At age 18, he entered government service as a junior officer in the Customs Department. There and in other employment he was let go because he was leading agitation for better pay for workers. He then became a seafarer, traveling to various European, Asian, and African ports. This broadened his horizon, and during this phase of his exploits, he published a periodical, *The Seafarer*, dedicated to promoting the welfare of seamen.

Using various pseudonyms, Wallace-Johnson traveled to workers' union meetings in Hamburg, Germany, in 1930 and to the International Labor Defense Congress in Moscow in 1931 and enrolled for a course of study at the People's University. He finally settled in Nigeria and became editor of the *Nigerian Daily Telegraph.* He was subsequently driven from Nigeria by the colonial rulers because of his militant journalism and trade union activities. He then moved to the Gold Coast, where he teamed up with local politicians to found the West African Youth League. Wallace-Johnson continued his militant journalism and was convicted of seditious publication in the Gold Coast in 1936.

From the Gold Coast, Wallace Johnson traveled to England where he worked with the Pan-Africanist George Padmore and Jomo Kenyatta. Together, they established the Pan African Federation to promote the cause of African workers. He also started the *African Sentinel* and *Africa and the World*. From England, he returned to Sierra Leone in April 1938 and, on his arrival, 2,000 copies of the *African Sentinel* were seized by the colonial customs authorities in Freetown. He took advantage of this to condemn government attacks on civil liberties at public meetings and in the ***Sierra Leone Weekly News***. He quickly formed the West African Youth League in Sierra Leone and used this platform to attack the colonial government on a number of issues, chiefly the poor condition of workers. In June 1938, the League issued a memorandum on labor conditions, which was forwarded to the Secretary of State for Colonies in London. The League quickly grew in size, and its activities spread to branches in the main towns of **Bo**, Mano, Lunsar, Pepel, **Moyamba**, and **Bonthe**. By June 1938, League membership had increased to 2,000 with seven branches in the protectorate. A year later, there were claims of 25,000 members in the colony and 17,000 in the protectorate. Many lawyers and leading citizens also joined the League.

Wallace-Johnson organized eight trade unions by 1939, one of them in the diamond mining area of Yengema. Pressure from the League also led the Secretary of State for the Colonies in England to instruct the governor of Sierra Leone to examine and report on the labor situation in general in Sierra Leone. All attempts by the enraged colonial administration in **Freetown** to stop Johnson failed until in September 1939 when he was detained by the government using emergency powers that had been put in place at the start of World War II. Johnson was tried and convicted of criminal libel and was sentenced to 12 months in prison.

After he was released from prison in 1944, Wallace-Johnson still carried on his political activism. In England, he participated in the organization of the Pan-African Congress in Manchester in 1945. He subsequently returned to Freetown and won election to the expanded **Legislative Council** in 1951 representing the National Council of Sierra Leone. He joined the **United Progressive Party**, retaining his seat in the 1957 elections, and later formed his own Radical Democratic Party. However, his influence was waning by this time as the predominantly **Krio** parties he had teamed up with had little or no clout. He was killed in an automobile accident in 1965 and his funeral in Freetown drew perhaps the largest crowd of mourners in the country's history.

WILLIAMS, PRINCE J. (c. 1900–1972). Prince J. Williams was one of the four independent candidates in the 1967 general elections who refused to be pressured into declaring for the ruling **Sierra Leone People's Party (SLPP)** government of **Albert Margai** in order to make it possible for Margai to declare a victory in such close elections.

Williams spent most of his life at **Bo** and was the first chairman of the Bo Town Council. He was also one of the founding members of the **Sierra Leone People's Party (SLPP)**, and was its national vice chairman for five years. He first entered Parliament representing Bo Town in 1962 and was elected deputy speaker of the house. In the 1967 elections, he joined four other independent candidates who had also won their seats by resisting the SLPP rulership demands to declare for that party. The SLPP had narrowly lost the elections but was hoping that with the support of those four victors an SLPP victory could be declared. Williams and his three other colleagues wrote a letter to the governor general stating that they wished to remain independent and would only support the SLPP if the prime minister, **Albert Margai**, resigned his position and leadership of the SLPP. Albert Margai and his SLPP consequently lost the elections. After a year's military rule, Williams returned to Parliament and was appointed resident minister for the Southern Province in 1969.

WRIGHT, ERNEST H. (1934–). Better known as Murphy Wright, Dr. Ernest Wright spent most of his life teaching at **Fourah Bay College**, rising to become vice chancellor of the **University of Sierra Leone** in 1998.

Born November 27, 1934, Ernest Wright attended the **Prince of Wales School** before going to England for higher education, culminating in a Ph.D. in chemistry at the University of Hull. He returned to Sierra Leone to teach at **Fourah Bay College** in 1962, becoming professor and head of the Department of Chemistry in 1971. He was dean of the faculty of pure and applied science for four years and held visiting appointments at universities in Nigeria and Ghana. He is a prominent scholar in his discipline, and in 1998 he became vice chancellor of the University of Sierra Leone, carrying that position until his retirement in 2004.

WUNDE. A male secret society among a section of the Mende ethnic group known as the Kpaa Mende. In ritual and function, the Wunde is similar to the **Poro**. It developed on the borders between **Mende** and **Temne** country, emerging from concerns to defend the borders. It thus had a much stronger military role than other societies, emphasizing military training in the rite of passage ceremonies. Like Poro, Wunde does not carry out many of its political functions in contemporary Sierra Leone.

WURIE, AMADU (1898–1977). Amadu Wurie was a prominent educator who spent most of his life in the school system in Sierra Leone. He later became minister of education.

Amadu Wurie was born in Gbinti on August 27, 1898, and was one of the first group of pupils of the **Bo Government School**, which was started in 1906 for educating the sons of chiefs. He became one of the most illustrious alumni of this school, instigating the formation of the Old Bo Boys Association (known as OBBA) of which he became the first general secretary and later president. OBBA became an influential lobbying group in Sierra Leone politics, particularly in the 1960s.

Amadu Wurie saw service as teacher and head of school at Bo School, at Koyeima School, and at Kenema Secondary School in the 1930s, 1940s, and 1950s. He was appointed inspector of schools in 1942, education officer in the Sierra Leone government in 1952, and education secretary for the Northern Province in 1955. In 1962, Amadu Wurie was elected to Parliament to represent **Port Loko** North constituency. He was appointed minister of education (1962–1965) and later minister of the interior. His parliamentary career ended when he lost his seat in the 1967 elections. He retired to private life, making a pilgrimage to Mecca and being honored with the doctor of civil laws degree by the University of Sierra Leone in 1973.

Amadu Wurie took a keen interest in publishing the result of oral histories that he collected about his ethnic Fula ancestors and more particularly about **Alimamy Rassin**, which he coauthored with Elizabeth Hirst.

– Y –

YALUNKA. Also referred to as Djalonké in the Republic of Guinea, this is an ethnic group found in northeastern Sierra Leone in the chiefdoms of Dembelia Sinkunia, Dembelia Musaia, and Sulima in the Koinadugu District. The northern borders of Sierra Leone bifurcates Yalunka territory, with more of this ethnic group found in the Farana region of the Republic of Guinea. The Yalunka have a history similar to the **Soso** and speakers of Soso could converse with Yalunka and vice versa. The dominant clan among the Yalunka in Sierra Leone is the Samura, which dominated this entire region of Yalunka country in the 19th century. Other important Yalunka clans in Sierra Leone are the Jawara of Dembelia and the Mansaray of Sinkunia, all in the Koinadugu District.

YOKO, MADAM (c. 1849–1906). Madam Yoko was a brilliant and ambitious woman who used her friendship with the British to accede to the rulership of the Kpaa **Mende** people. Although she was opposed by some of her subchiefs because of her lack of traditional legitimacy, she ended up with a reputation prominent in Sierra Leone history because of her support for and by the British.

Her childhood name was Soma, but, as was traditional on assuming adulthood after the rite of passage of the Sande society, she assumed the name of Yoko. At her initiation, she attracted admiration for her beauty and graceful dancing. After an unsuccessful first marriage, she became the wife of Gbenjei, ruler of the town of Taiama; and although she was barren, Gbenjei, against tradition, made her his head wife since he was passionately in love with her. When Gbenjei died, Yoko married Gbanya Lango, a prominent warrior, and ruler of the town of Senehun. In 1875, with growing British influence in this area, Yoko saved her husband, Gbanya, from imprisonment by the British by making a personal appeal to the British governor, who was charmed by her beauty and personality. Gbanya then made it a practice of using Yoko in diplomatic missions to the British and to local rulers.

In 1884, at the death of Gbanya, the British recognized Yoko as the paramount chief of Kpaa Mende with the appellation of "Queen of Senehun." Many of the local Kpaa Mende chiefs were disgruntled at this but could not really oppose the powerful British. Yoko, despite some opposition from her subchiefs, was firmly supported by the British. Tradition says that she maintained a prominent Sande unit wherein she trained girls from all over Kpaa Mende, sometimes giving the most beautiful in marriage to sergeants of the **Frontier Police Force**, who were therefore keen in upholding her authority against any refractory subchiefs. It is also maintained in some quarters that Yoko provided mistresses for British personnel when they visited her chiefdom.

When the British declared a protectorate over most of Sierra Leone and imposed a house tax, Yoko ordered her people to pay the tax. Her already-refractory subchiefs joined in opposition to her and to the new tax. They held secret meetings and decided to fight against the British without informing Yoko. At the outbreak of the rebellion, Yoko barely escaped and took refuge at the Frontier Police barracks, which withstood several assaults. After the rebellion, the British awarded her a medal for her loyalty.

Madam Yoko ruled the Kpaa Mende chiefdom until 1906 when she is reported to have committed suicide, apparently because of the loss of support from her people who blamed her for British domination of their lives.

YUSUFU, BOMBOH LAHAI (LATE 19TH CENTURY–c. 1940). Fallout from the rebellion of **Haidara Kontorfili** in the Tonko Limba chiefdom in the Kambia District, Northern Province, led to the deposition of Bomboh Lahai Yusufu, its paramount chief in 1931. *Bomboh Lahai* became the Tonkoh Limba, title for ruler.

Yusufu's Limba father was Dauda and his mother was a Fula. As a descendant of the Kabubuya line of rulers, he was elected paramount chief of Tonko Limba chiefdom in 1922. It was during his rule that a radical **Islamic** leader Haidara Kontorfili appeared in Yusufu's chiefdom, promising to rid the chiefdom of a plague of locusts that was bothering them. These were also difficult economic times in Tonkoh **Limba**, with poor agricultural output, and Haidara's preachings suggested that he could address these issues as well.

Haidara at first preached a general message of return to a virtuous life for all people. But as his following grew rapidly, Haidara became much more forceful, ordering all local diviners to destroy their paraphernalia of worship and their charms and amulets. Many refused, understanding rightly that this spelled doom for their livelihood and way of life. One famous diviner, Nkodi, is remembered as one who successfully evaded these orders. The Bomboh Lahai Yusufu, whose position as traditional ruler was linked with such divination, would definitely not have seriously entertained these orders of Haidara.

As Haidara became more strident, denouncing the colonial government and ordering people not to pay their taxes, the colonial administration called on Yusufu to expel Haidara from Tonko Limba. With Haidara's overwhelming popularity in Tonko Limba and with Yusufu lacking an organized military force, the request to expel Haidara could not readily be carried out. The colonial government had to send a force to Tonko Limba to carry out the expulsion, and Haidara died in the ensuing clash.

The colonial administration then accused Yusufu of complicity in an anti-British uprising. To prove his innocence, Yusufu agreed that he would "eat bread," a solemn oath administered with rice flour and traditional "medicines." If the British had been interested in determining Yusufu's guilt or innocence, they could well have realized that the local people feared the process of "eating bread" wrongfully more than almost anything else. But the British were convinced of Yusufu's guilt and, in any case, disdained African traditions. Yusufu was thus deposed as paramount chief in 1931. He retired into private life and died about a decade later.

– Z –

ZIMMI. A town in the Makpele chiefdom of the Pujehun District in southern Sierra Leone.

Bibliography

This bibliography concentrates on the period from 1970 to the present. However, there are a number of older bibliographic guides that will be listed in the initial section of the collection, irrespective of dates. Some published works of an earlier provenance have had a major impact on research and writing on Sierra Leone, for example, Christopher Fyfe's *Sierra Leone Inheritance* (London: Oxford University Press, 1964). Such works will be included. Noticeably absent will be a listing of articles from the journal *Sierra Leone Studies.* This journal had a long tenure from 1918, as the *Journal of the Sierra Leone Society*, but ceased publication in 1939 and was revived by the Institute of African Studies, Fourah Bay College, as the "new series" in 1953. There are a couple of indexes to *Sierra Leone Studies* found in the general section of this bibliography.

One of the major contributors of documentation in Sierra Leone History is the late Paul Hair. An important portion of his work relates to translation of historical documents from Portuguese to English. He published a series of such translations in the *Africana Research Bulletin* (15 in all) starting with "Sources on Early Sierra Leone: (1) Beaulieu 1619." (6, 4, 1974). While all 15 are not mentioned in this bibliography, other translations by Hair are noted throughout the collection.

Unpublished sources are generally not included in this compilation. An important source is Toma J. Makannah's "A Bibliography of Studies on Population and Development of Sierra Leone." Interested readers can find this on the Internet on http://www.sierra–leone.org/bibliography–population.html.

GENERAL

Avery, Greta. "Bibliography of Literature in Sierra Leone." *Africana Research Bulletin* 1, 1, 1970.

Beoku-Betts, Josephine. "Published and Unpublished Sources on Sierra Leone Women." *Africana Research Bulletin* 6, 4, 1976.

Binns, Margaret, and Tony Binns. *Sierra Leone*. Oxford, England: Clio, 1992.

Blair, J. A. S. "Sierra Leone Studies, 1918–1968 [Bibliography]." *Africana Research Bulletin*, 2, 1, 1971.

Clarke, John I. *Sierra Leone in Maps*. London: University of London Press, 1969

Davies, C. B. *A Bibliography of Education in Sierra Leone*. Freetown: Njala University College Library, 1974.

Davies, Desmond. "Sierra Leone." *New Internationalist* 322 (Apr 2000): 36.

Devis, T. L. F. "A Bibliography of Population Studies in Sierra Leone." *Africana Research Bulletin* 1, 3, 1971.

Fourah Bay College Library. *Catalog of the Sierra Leone Collection, Fourah Bay College Library, University of Sierra Leone*. Boston: G. K. Hall, 1979.

Fyfe, Christopher. "Documents Relating to the Sierra Leone Hut Tax Enquiry in the Sir David Chalmers Collection, University of Edinburgh." *Africana Research Bulletin* 2, 4, 1972.

Gilford, Henry. *Gambia, Ghana, Liberia and Sierra Leone.* New York: F. Watts, 1981.

Hair, Paul E. H. "Contributions to Sierra Leone History." *Journal of the Historical Society of Sierra Leone,* 2, 2, 1978: 61–66.

———. "Early Sources on Religion and Social Values in the Sierra Leone Region: (2) Eustache de la Fosse 1480." *Africana Research Bulletin* 4, 3, 1973.

Jackson, Michael D. "A Short Bibliography of Published Material on the Kuranko." *Africana Research Bulletin* 1, 4, 1971.

Jones, Adam, and Peter K. Mitchell. *Sierra Leone Studies at Birmingham, 1985*. University of Birmingham, Centre for West African Studies, 1987.

———. *Sierra Leone Studies at Birmingham, 1983*. Birmingham: University of Birmingham, Centre for West African Studies, 1984.

Kaplan, Irving. *Area Handbook for Sierra Leone.* Washington, DC: United States Government Printing Office, 1976.

Keane, Christiane. *Ghana, Sierra Leone and the Gambia: A Basic Annotated Bibliography for Students, Librarians and General Readers*. London: Commonwealth Institute, 1977.

Kember, Owen. "Aristotle and Sierra Leone." *Africana Research Bulletin* 1, 3, 1971.

———. "Ancient and Modern Water Needs and Management with Particular Reference to Sierra Leone." *Africana Research Bulletin* 2, 2, 1972.

King, D. "Population Characteristics of Diamond Boom Towns in Kono." *Africana Research Bulletin* 5, 4, 1975.

Lowicki, Jane. *Precious Resources; Adolescents in the Reconstruction of Sierra Leone; Participatory Research Study with Adolescents and Youth in Sierra Leone, April–July 2002*. New York: Women's Commission for Refugee Women and Children, 2002.

Luke, Harry. *A Bibliography of Sierra Leone; Preceded by an Essay on the Origin, Character and Peoples of the Colony and Protectorate*. Oxford: Clarendon, 1884; London: H. Milford, 1925; New York: Negro Universities Press, 1969.

Makannah, T. J. *The Study of Internal Migration in Sierra Leone: A Review and Bibliography of Recent Literature*. Freetown: Central Statistics Office, 1977.

Mitchell, Harry. *Remote Corners: A Sierra Leone Memoir.* London: Radcliffe, 2002.

Ofusu-Appiah, L. H. *Dictionary of African Biography: Sierra Leone/Zaire*. Algonac, MI: Reference Publications, 1979.

Rakita, Sara. *Forgotten Children of War: Sierra Leonean Refugee Children in Guinea*. New York: Human Rights Watch, 1999.
Sheriff, Gladys M. "Sierra Leone Collection: List of New Accessions, January 1971–January 1974." *Africana Research Bulletin* 4, 2, 1974.
Sillinger, Brett. *Sierra Leone: Current Issues and Background.* New York: Nova Science, 2003.
Skinner, David. "The Arabic Letterbooks as a Source for Sierra Leone History." *Africana Research Bulletin* 3, 4, 1973.
Thompson, J. S. T. "Vernacular Publication on Sierra Leone: A Bibliographical Analysis." *Africana Research Bulletin* 6, 3, 1976.
———. "A Bibliographical Analysis of Sierra Leone." *Africana Research Bulletin* 4, 1, 1973.
Turay, A. K. T. "Sierra Leone Studies, 1918–1968: Author Index." *Africana Research Bulletin* 2, 2, 1972.
Williams, Geoffrey J. "*A Note on a Bibliography of Sierra Leone, 1925–1967*." *Africana Research Bulletin* 1, 4, 1971.
———. *A Bibliography of Sierra Leone 1925–1967*. New York: Africana, 1970.
Wylie, Kenneth C. "A Provisional Bibliography for Temne History." *Africana Research Bulletin* 1, 2, 1971.
Zell, Hans M. *A Bibliography of Non-Periodical Literature on Sierra Leone, 1925–1966 (Excluding Sierra Leone Government Publications).* Freetown: University of Sierra Leone, Fourah Bay College Bookshop, 1966.

HISTORY

Abdullah, Ibrahim. "The Colonial State and Wage Labor in Postwar Sierra Leone 1945–1960: Attempts at Remaking the Working Class." *International Labor and Working-Class History* 52, 1997: 87–105.
———. "'Liberty or Death': Working Class Agitation and the Labour Question in Colonial Freetown, 1938–1939." *International Review of Social History* 40, 1995: 195–221.
———. "Rethinking the Freetown Crowd: The Moral Economy of the 1919 Strikes and Riot in Sierra Leone." *Canadian Journal of African Studies* 28, 1994: 197–218.
———. "Profits versus Social Reproduction: Labor Protests in the Sierra Leonean Iron-Ore Mines, 1933–1938." *African Studies Review* 35, 3, 1992: 1–29.
Abraham, Arthur. *An Introduction to the Pre-Colonial History of the Mende of Sierra Leone.* Lewiston, NY: Edwin Mellen, 2003.
———. "Liberia and Sierra Leone: History of Misery and Misery of History." *Sierra Leone Studies and Reviews (SALSAR)* 1, no. 1, 2000.
———. *The Amistad Revolt: An Historical Legacy of Sierra Leone and the United States*. Freetown: U.S. Information Service, 1987.
———. "Cannibalism and African Historiography." *Présence Africaine*, nos. 105/6, 1978.

——. *Mende Government and Politics under Colonial Rule: A Historical Study of Political Change in Sierra Leone 1890–1937*. Oxford: Oxford University Press, 1978.

——. "Sengbe Pieh: A Neglected Hero?" *Journal of the Historical Society of Sierra Leone (JHSSL)* 2, no. 2, 1978: 22–30.

——. *Topics in Sierra Leone History: A Counter-colonial Interpretation*. Freetown: Leone Publishers, 1976.

——. "The Idea of Mende Pre-Colonial Political Leadership." *Africana Research Bulletin* 6, 1, 1975.

——. "A Note on 'Kanre Lahun'." *Liberian Studies Journal* VI, 1, 1975.

——. "The Pattern of Warfare and Settlement among the Mende of Sierra Leone in the Second Half of the Nineteenth Century: *Kroniek van Afrika* 2, 1975: 121–39.

——. "Colonial Rule in Southern Sierra Leone: A Theoretical Conclusion on Political Change." *Africana Research Bulletin* IV, 2, 1974.

——. "Mende Chieftaincy in the Nineteenth Century: A Rejoinder." *Africana Research Bulletin* V, 1, 1974.

——. "Women Chiefs in Southern Sierra Leone: A Rejoinder." *Africana Research Bulletin* 5, 1, 1974.

——. "Mende Influence on the Kono." *Africana Research Bulletin* III, 2, 1973.

——. "Nyagua, the British and the Hut Tax War." *International Journal of African Historical Studies* V, 1, 1972.

——. "Some Suggestions on the Origins of Mende Chiefdoms." *Sierra Leone Studies*, n.s., 25, 1969.

Abraham, Arthur, and B. Isaac."A Further Note on the History of Luawa Chiefdom." *Sierra Leone Studies*, n.s., 24, 1969.

Abraham, Arthur, and E. D. A. Turay. *The Sierra Leone Army: A Century of History.* London: Macmillan, 1987.

Akpan, M. K. "The Return to Africa–Sierra Leone and Liberia." *Tarikh* 5, 4 1978: 92–116.

Alie, Joe A. D. *A New History of Sierra Leone*. London: Macmillan, 1990.

Almada, Andre Alvares de. *Brief Treatise on the Rivers of Guinea (c. 1594).* P. E. H. Hair trans. Liverpool: University of Liverpool, Department of History, 1984.

Asante, S. K. B. "I.T.A. Wallace-Johnson and the Italo-Ethiopian Crisis." *Journal of the Historical Society of Nigeria* 7, no. 4, 1975.

Atherton, John. "Early Economies of Sierra Leone and Liberia: Archaeological and Historical Reflections." In *Themes in the Economic Anthropology of Liberia and Sierra Leone*, ed. V. Dorjahn and B. Isaac. Philadelphia: Institute for Liberian Studies, 1979: 27–44.

Atherton, John. "Excavations at Kamabai and Yagala Rock Shelters, Sierra Leone." *West African Journal of Archaeology* 2, 1972: 39–74.

Atherton, John. "Protohistoric Habitation Sites in Northeastern Sierra Leone." *Bulletin de la Société Royale Belge d'Anthropologie et de Préhistoire* 83, 1972: 5–17.

Atherton, John H., and M. Kalous. "Nomoli." *Journal of African History* 11, 1970: 303–317.

Bah, M. Alpha. *Fulbe Presence in Sierra Leone. A Case History of Twentieth-Century Migration and Settlement among the Kissi of Koindu*. New York: Peter Lang, 1998.

Blyden, Nemata. *West Indians in West Africa 1808–1880*. Rochester, NY: University of Rochester Press, 2000.

Braidwood, Stephen J. *Black Poor and White Philanthropists: London's Blacks and the Foundation of the Sierra Leone Settlement 1789–1971*. Liverpool: University of Liverpool Press, 1994.

Brooks, George. *Landlords and Strangers: Ecology, Society and Trade in Western Africa, 1000–1630*. Boulder, CO: Westview Press, 1993.

Buhnen, Stephen. "In Quest of Susu." *History in Africa* 21, 1994: 1–47.

Campbell, Mavis. *Back to Africa: George Ross and the Maroons: From Nova Scotia to Sierra Leone*. Trenton, NJ: Africa World Press, 1993.

Clifford, Mary Louise. *From Slavery to Freetown: Black Loyalists after the American Revolution*. Jefferson, NC: McFarland, 1999.

Corby, Richard. "The Mende Uprising of 1898 as It Affected the United Brethren in Christ Mission at Rotifunk." *Africana Research Bulletin* 5, 2, 1975.

———. "Early Years at Bo School." *Africana Research Bulletin* 5, 3, 1975.

De Faro, Andre. *Andre de Faro's Missionary Journey to Sierra Leone in 1663–1664* [a shortened version in English translation of "Relação historica da missao ao Reyno da Guiné]. P. E. H. Hair (Ed.). Freetown: Fourah Bay College, Institute of African Studies, 1982.

Denzer, LaRay. *The Autobiography of Constance A. Cummings-John*. Ibadan: Sam Bookman, 2002.

———. "Reflections on the Role of the Military in Civilian Politics: The Case of Sierra Leone." *Australian Journal of Politics and History* 35, no. 2, 1989.

———. "Women in Freetown Politics, 1914–1961: A Preliminary Study." In *Sierra Leone, 1787–1987*. London: International African Institute, 1987.

———. "The Influence of Pan-Africanism in the Career of Constance A. Cummings-John." In *Pan-African Biography*, ed. R. A. Hill. Los Angeles: Crossroads, 1987.

———. "Constance A. Cummings-John: Her Early Political Career in Sierra Leone." *Tarikh* 7, no. 1, 1981.

———. "Bai Bureh." In *West African Resistance*, M. Crowder (Ed.). London, Hutchinson, 1972.

———. "Bai Bureh and the Sierra Leone Hut Tax War of 1898." In *Protest and Power in Black Africa*, ed. R. I. Rotberg and A. Mazrui. London: Oxford University Press, 1970.

———. "A Diary of Bai Bureh's War." *Sierra Leone Studies (new series)* 23, 1968 and 24, 1969.

Encyclopaedia Africana–Dictionary of African Biography. Vol. 2, Sierra Leone–Zaire. MI: Reference Publications, 1979.

Deveneaux, Gustav. "Sierra Leone and South Africa." *Africa* 57, 4 1987: 572–575.
———. *Power Politics in Sierra Leone*. Ibadan, Nigeria: African Universities Press, 1982.
———. "Trade Routes and Colonial Policy in Nineteenth Century Sierra Leone." *JHSSL* 3, nos. 1 & 2, 1979.
———. "The Frontier in Recent African History." *IJAHS* 11, no. 1, 1978: 63–85.
———. "Some Historical Considerations Concerning Elites in Africa." *Journal of the Historical Society of Sierra Leone.* 2, 1 1978: 33–56.
———. "Public Opinion and Colonial Policy in Nineteenth Century Sierra Leone." *International Journal of African Historical Studies I, 2, 1976.*
Dixon-Fyle, Mac. "The Saro in the Political Life of Early Port Harcourt, 1913–1949." *Journal of African History* 30, 1, 1989.
Donelha, André. *Descrição da Serra Leoa e dos rios de Guiné do Cabo Verde, 1625 (An Account of Sierra Leone and the Rivers of Guinea of Cape Verde, 1625).* Lisbon: Portugal, Junta de Investigações Cientificas do Ultramar, 1977.
Fitzjohn, Willie. *Chief Gbondo: A Sierra Leone Story*. Ibadan, Nigeria: Daystar Press, 1974.
Foray, Cyril P. *The Road to the One-Party State: The Sierra Leone Experience*. (Africanus Horton Memorial Lecture, 1988). Edinburgh: University of Edinburgh, Centre of African Studies, 1988.
———. *A History of Fourah Bay College*. Freetown, Fourah Bay College Bookshop, 1987.
———. *Historical Dictionary of Sierra Leone*. Metuchen, NJ: Scarecrow Press, 1977.
Fyfe, Christopher. *Africanus Horton, 1835–1883: West African Scientist and Patriot*. Hampshire: Aldershot, 1992.
———. "1787–1887–1987: Reflections on a Sierra Leone Bicentenary." *Africa* 57, 4: 1987: 411–421.
———. "The Sierra Leone Press in the Nineteenth Century–A Revision." *Journal of the Historical Society of Sierra Leone* 2, 1, 1978: 62–64.
———. "Contrasting Themes in the Writings of Africanus Horton, James Johnson and Edward Blyden." *Africana Research Bulletin* 1, 3, 1971.
———. *Sierra Leone Inheritance*. London: Oxford University Press, 1964.
———. *A History of Sierra Leone*. London: Oxford University Press, 1962.
Fyle, C. Magbaily. *The History of Sierra Leone: A Concise Introduction*. London: Evans, 1981.
———. *The Solima Yalunka Kingdom: Pre-colonial Politics, Economics and Society.* Freetown: Nyakon, 1979.
———. *Oral Traditions of Sierra Leone.* Niamey, Niger: Centre for Linguistic and Historical Studies by Oral Tradition (CELHTO), 1979.
———. *Almamy Suluku of Sierra Leone: The Dynamics of Political Leadership in Pre-colonial Sierra Leone.* London: Evans, 1979.
———. "Oral Traditions and Sierra Leone History." *History in Africa* 5, 12, 1985.

———. "Northeast Sierra Leone in the Nineteenth and Twentieth Centuries: Reconstruction and Population Distribution in a Devastated Area." In *African Historical Demography II*, ed. C. Fyfe and D. MacMaster. Edinburgh: Edinburgh University Press, 1981.

———. *Precolonial Commerce in Northeastern Sierra Leone*. Boston: Boston University, African Studies Center, Working Paper no. 10, 1979.

———. "The Idea of Slavery in Nineteenth Century Sierra Leone: The Career of Bilali." *Journal of the Historical Society of Sierra Leone* 2, 2, 1978.

Fyle, C. Magbaily, and A. Abraham. "Sierra Leone: A Historical Introduction." In *Encyclopaedia Africana: Dictionary of African Biography. Volume II, Sierra Leone–Zaire*, ed. H. Ofusu-Appiah. Algonac, MI: Reference Publications, 1979.

———. "Almamy Suluku of Biriwa Limba: Political and Economic Organization in a Limba Kingdom." *Afrika Zamani* 8 & 9, December 1978.

———. "Collaboration, Cooperation and Resistance: The Case of Almamy Suluku of Biriwa Limba." *Journal of the Historical Society of Sierra Leone* 1,1, 1977.

———. *Commerce and Entrepreneurship: The Sierra Leone Hinterland in the Nineteenth Century.* Freetown: University of Sierra Lone, Institute of African Studies, Occasional Paper No. 2, 1977.

———. "A Propos of Loko History: The Career of Fomgboe of Lower Loko." *Africana Research Bulletin* 6, 2, 1977.

———. "The Kabala Complex: Koranko-Limba Relations in Nineteenth and Twentieth Century Sierra Leone." In *Topics in Sierra Leone History*, ed. A. Abraham. Freetown: Leone Publishers, 1976.

———. "The Origin and Integration of the Solima Yalunka State." *Africana Research Bulletin* 6, 1, 1976.

Fyle, C. Magbaily, and A. Abraham. "The Country Cloth Culture in Sierra Leone." *Odu, Journal of West African Studies, University of Ife, Nigeria* 13, 1976.

Fyle, C. Magbaily, and Akintola Wyse. "Kriodom: A Maligned Culture." *Journal of the Historical Society of Sierra Leone* 3, 1 & 2, 1979.

Gale, Tom. "The Disbarment of African Medical Officers by the West African Medical Staff: A Study in Prejudice." *Journal of the Historical Society of Sierra Leone* 2, 2, 1978: 33–44.

Grace, John. *Domestic Slavery in West Africa with Particular Reference to the Sierra Leone Protectorate 1896–1927*. London: Frederick Muller, 1975.

Grace, John. "Slavery and Emancipation among the Mende in Sierra Leone, 1896–1928." In *Slavery in Africa, Historical and Anthropological Perspectives*, ed. S. Miers and I. Kopytoff. Madison, WI: University of Wisconsin Press, 1977: 415–431.

Hair, P. E. H. "Aspects of the Prehistory of Freetown and Creoledom." *History in Africa* 25, 1998.

———. "Colonial Freetown and the Study of African Languages." *Africa* 57, 1987: 560–65.

——. "Sierra Leone in the Earliest Global Strategy: A Spanish Pamphlet of c. 1590." In *Sierra Leone Studies at Birmingham*, 1985, ed. Adam Jones and Peter Mitchell. Birmingham: University of Birmingham, Centre of West African Studies, 1987.

——. "An Ethnolinguistic Inventory of the Lower Guinea Coast before 1700: Part 1." *African Language Review* 7, 1968: 47–73.

——. "'Africanism': Freetown's Contribution." *Journal of Modern African Studies* 5 no. 4, 1967.

——. "Ethnolinguistic Continuity on the Guinea Coast." *Journal of African History* 8, no. 2, 1967: 247–268.

Hargreaves, J. D. "The Changing Face of Samuel Lewis: A Personal Memoir." *Africa* 57, 4 1987: 576–578.

Harrell-Bond, Barbara, Allen M. Howard, and David E. Skinner. *Community Leadership and the Transformation of Freetown (1801–1976)*. The Hague, Mouton, 1978.

Harrison, James, and K. C. Wylie. "Initiative and Response in the Sierra Leone Hinterland, 1885–1898: The Chiefs and British Intervention." *Africana Research Bulletin* 3, 1, 1972.

Howard, A. M. "Mande Identity Formation in the Economic and Political Content of North–West Sierra Leone 1750–1900." *Paideuma* 46, 2000: 13–35.

——. "Mande and Fulbe Interaction and Identity in Northwestern Sierra Leone, Late Eighteenth through Early Twentieth Centuries." *Mande Studies* 1, 1999, 13–39.

——. "Trade and Islam in Sierra Leone, 18th to 20th Centuries." In *Islam and Trade in Sierra Leone*, ed. A. Jalloh and D. Skinner. Trenton, NJ: Africa World Press, 1997: 21–64.

——. "Trade without Marketplaces: The Spatial Organization of Exchange in Northwestern Sierra Leone to 1930." *African Urban Studies* 11, 1981: 1–22.

——. "Pawning in Coastal Northwest Sierra Leone, 1870–1910." In *Pawnship in Africa: Debt Bondage in Historical Perspective*, ed. Toyin Falola and Paul E. Lovejoy. Boulder, Westview Press, 1994: 267–284.

——. "Production, Exchange, and Society in Northern Coastal Sierra Leone during the 19th Century." In *Essays on the Economic Anthropology of Liberia and Sierra Leone*, ed. Vernon R. Dorjahn and Barry L. Isaac. Philadelphia: Institute for Liberian Studies, 1979: 45–62.

——. "The Relevance of Spatial Analysis for African Economic History: The Sierra Leone–Guinea System." *Journal of African History* 17, 1976: 365–388.

Howard, A. M, and David Skinner. "Ethnic Leadership and Class Formation in Freetown, Sierra Leone." In *New Perspectives on Social Class and Socioeconomic Development in the Periphery*, ed. N.W. and N.Z. Keith. Westport, CT: Greenwood, 1988.

——. "Network Building and Political Power in North-Western Sierra Leone, 1800–1865." *Africa* 54, 1984: 2–28.

Ijagbemi, E. A. "Gumbu Smart: Slave Turned Abolitionist." *Journal of the Historical Society of Sierra Leone* 2, 2, 1978: 45–60.

——. "'Rothoron' (The North-East) in Temne Tradition and Culture: An Essay in Ethno-History." *Journal of the Historical Society of Sierra Leone (JHSSL)* 2, 1 1978.

——. "The Mende of Sierra Leone." *Tarikh* 5, no. 1, 1977: 46–56.

——. "Oral Tradition and the Emergence of Temne Chiefdoms." *Africana Research Bulletin (ARB)* 7, 2, 1977.

——. *Naimbana of Sierra Leone*. London: Heinemann, 1976.

——. *Gbanka of Yoni*. Freetown, Sierra Leone University Press, 1973.

Jalloh, Alusine. *African Entrepreneurship: Muslim Fula Merchants in Sierra Leone*. Athens, OH: Ohio University Press 1999.

——. "The Fula and Motor Transport Business in Freetown, Sierra Leone." *African Economic History* 26, 1998: 63–81.

——. "Alhaji Momodu Allie: Muslim Fula Entrepreneur in Colonial Sierra Leone." In *Islam and Trade in Sierra Leone*, ed. A. Jalloh and D. Skinner. Trenton, NJ, Africa World Press, 1997: 65–86.

——. "The Fula and Islamic Education in Freetown, Sierra Leone." *American Journal of Islamic Social Science* 14, 1997: 51–68.

——. "Muslim Fula Merchants and the Motor Transport Business in Freetown, 1961–1978." In *Islam and Trade in Sierra Leone*, ed. A. Jalloh and D. Skinner. Trenton, NJ: Africa World Press, 1997: 119–136.

——. "The Fula Trading Diaspora in Colonial Sierra Leone." In *The African Diaspora*, ed. A. Jalloh and S. E. Maizlish. College Station: Texas A & M University Press, 1996: 22–38.

Jalloh, Alusine, and David E. Skinner, eds. *Islam and Trade in Sierra Leone*. Trenton, NJ: Africa World Press, 1999.

Jones, Adam. *From Slaves to Palm Kernels: A History of the Galinhas Country (West Africa) 1730–1890*. Wiesbaden: Franz Steiner Verlag GMBH, 1983.

——. "Who Were the Vai?" *Journal of African History* 22, no. 2, 1981: 159–178.

Kalous, M. *Cannibals and Tongo Players of Sierra Leone.* Auckland, New Zealand, privately printed.

Kaniki, M. Y. H. "Attitudes and Reaction toward the Lebanese in Sierra Leone during the Colonial Period." *Canadian Journal of African Studies* 7, no. 1, 1973.

——. "Economic Change in Sierra Leone during the 1930s." *TransAfrican Journal of History* 3, nos. 1 & 2, 1973.

Kohn, Bernice. *The Amistad Mutiny*. New York: Dutton, 1971.

Kromer, Helen. *The Amistad Revolt, 1839: The Slave Uprising Aboard the Spanish Schooner.* New York: Franklin Watts, 1973.

Kup, P. A. *Sierra Leone: A Concise History*. Newton Abbot, England: David & Charles, 1975.

——. *A History of Sierra Leone 1400–1787*. Cambridge: Cambridge University Press, 1961.

Martin, Christopher. *The Amistad Affair*. New York: Abelard-Schuman, 1970.

Matturi, Sahr. "A Brief History of Nimikoro Chiefdom, Kono District." *Africana Research Bulletin* 3, 2, 1973.

McGarry, Georgia. *Reaction and Protest in the West African Press*. Leiden, Holland: Afrika-Studiecentrum, 1978.

McGowan, W. "African Resistance to the Atlantic Slave Trade in West Africa." *Slavery and Abolition* 2, 1 1990.

———. "The Establishment of Long-Distance Trade between Sierra Leone and Its Hinterland, 1787–1821." *Journal of African History* 31, 1, 1990: 25–41.

Mouser, B. L. *Guinea Journals: Journeys into Guinea-Conakry during the Sierra Leone Phase, 1800–1821*. Lanham, MD: University Press of America, 1979.

Ojukutu-Macauley, Sylvia. "Religion, Gender and Education in Northern Sierra Leone, 1896–1992." In *Islam and Trade in Sierra Leone*, ed. A. Jalloh and D. Skinner. Trenton, NJ. Africa World Press, 1997: 87–118.

Okonkwo, Rina. "Adelaide Casely Hayford: Cultural Nationalist and Feminist." *Journal of the Historical Society of Sierra Leone* 2, 2, 1978: 10–21.

Osagie, Iyunolu F. *The Amistad Revolt: Memory, Slavery, and the Politics of Identity in the United States and Sierra Leone*. Athens, Georgia: University of Georgia Press, 2000.

Person, Yves. "Ethnic Movements and Acculturation in Upper Guinea since the Fifteenth Century." *International Journal of African Historical Studies (IJAHS)* 4, 3, 1971.

———. "Samori et La Sierra Leone." *Cahiers d'études africains* 29, 1967: 5–26.

———. *Samori, Une Revolution Dyula* (3 vols) Dakar, IFAN, 1968–75.

Peterson, John. *Province of Freedom: A History of Sierra Leone 1787–1870*. Evanston, IL: Northwestern University Press, 1969.

———. "The Study of African History: The Sierra Leonc Scene." *Africana Research Bulletin* 3, 3, 1973.

Rashid, Ismail. "'*Do Dady nor Lef me Make dem Carry me*': Slave Resistance and Emancipation in Sierra Leone, 1894–1928." *Slavery and Abolition* 19, 1998: 208–231.

Rodney, Walter A. "A Reconsideration of the Mane Invasions of Sierra Leone." *Journal of African History* 8, 1967: 219–246.

———. *A History of the Upper Guinea Coast, 1545–1870*. Oxford: Clarendon, 1970.

Sanneh, L. "Historical Source Materials on Islam in Sierra Leone." *JHSSL* 1, no. 2, 1977.

———. "Christian–Muslim Encounter in Freetown in the Nineteenth Century and the Implications for Mission Today." *Bulletin of the Secretariat for Non-Christian Religions* (Rome) 12, nos. 1–2, 1977: 13–21.

———. "Modern Education among Freetown Muslims and the Christian Stimulus." In *Christianity in Independent Africa*, ed. Edward Fashole-Luke, Richard Gray, Adrian Hastings and Godwin Tasie. Bloomington, IN: Indiana University Press, 1978.

———. "The Origins of Clericalism in West African Islam." *Journal of African History* VII, 1976.

Skinner, David E. "Islam and Education in the Colony and Hinterland of Sierra Leone 1750–1914." *Canadian Journal of African Studies* 10, 1976: 499–520.

——. "Islamic Organization and Influence in Sierra Leone, 1930–1990." In *Islam and Trade in Sierra Leone*, ed. A. Jalloh and D. Skinner. Trenton, NJ: Africa World Press, 1997: 137–161.

——. *Thomas George Lawson, African Historian and Administrator in Sierra Leone*.
Stanford, CA: Hoover Institution Press, 1980.

——. "Mande Settlement and the Development of Islamic Institutions in Sierra Leone." *IJAHS* 2, no. 1, 1978.

——. "Sierra Leone Relations with the Northern Rivers and the Influence of Islam in Sierra Leone." *International Journal of Sierra Leone Studies* 1, 1988: 64–90.

——. "Thomas George Lawson: Government Interpreter and Historical Resource." *Africana Research Bulletin* 4, 4, 1974.

Skinner, David. "Islam in the Northern Hinterland and Its Influence on the Development of the Sierra Leone Colony." In *Islam and Trade in Sierra Leone*, ed. A. Jalloh and D. Skinner. Trenton, NJ: Africa World Press, 1997: 1–20.

Skinner, David, and B. Harrell-Bond. "Misunderstandings Arising from the Use of the Term 'Creole' in the Literature of Sierra Leone." *Africa* 47, 1977.

Spitzer, Leo, and LaRay Denzer. "I.T.A. Wallace Johnson and the West African Youth League." *IJAHS* 6, nos. 3 & 4, 1973.

——. *The Creoles of Sierra Leone: Responses to Colonialism 1870–1945*. Madison, WI: University of Wisconsin Press, 1974.

Steady, Filomena. *Women and the Amistad Connection. Sierra Leone Krio Society.* Rochester, VT: Schenkman Books, 2001.

Turay, E. D. A., and A. Abraham. *The Sierra Leone Army: A Century of History*. London: Macmillan, 1987.

Walker, James W. *The Black Loyalists: The Search for a Promised Land in Nova Scotia and Sierra Leone, 1783–1870*. New York: Africana Publishing, 1976.

West, Richard. *Back to Africa: A History of Sierra Leone and Liberia.* New York: Holt, Rinehart and Winston, 1970.

White, E. Frances. *Sierra Leone's Settler Women Traders: Women on the Afro-European Frontier.* Ann Arbor: University of Michigan Press, 1987.

——. "The Big Market in Freetown: A Case Study of a Women's Workplace." *Journal of the Historical Society of Sierra Leone* 2, 2, 1978:19–32.

Wilson, Ellen G. *John Clarkson and the African Adventure*. London: Macmillan, 1980.

——. *The Loyal Blacks*. New York: Putnam, 1976.

Wurie, A., and E. Hirst. *Rassin.* London: University of London Press, 1968.

Wylie, K. *The Political Kingdoms of the Temne: Temne Government in Sierra Leone, 1825–1910*. New York: Africana, 1977.

——. "Innovation and Change in Mende Chieftaincy, 1880–1896." *Journal of African History* 2, 1969: 295–308.

Wyse, Akintola, J.G. *H. C. Bankole-Bright and Politics in Colonial Sierra Leone, 1919–1958*. Cambridge: Cambridge University Press, 1990.

——. *The Krio of Sierra Leone*. London: C. Hurst, 1989.

———. "The 1919 Strike and Anti-Syrian Riots: A Krio Plot?" *JHSSL* 3, nos. 1 and 2, 1979.

Wyse, Akintola. "The Dissolution of Freetown City Council in 1926: A Negative Example of Political Apprenticeship in Colonial Sierra Leone." *Africa* 57, 4: 1987: 422–438.

———. "The 1926 Railway Strike and Anglo-Krio Relations: An Interpretation." *IJAHS* 4, no. 1, 1981.

———. *Searchlight on the Krio of Sierra Leone: An Ethnographical Study of a West African People*. Institute of African Studies, University of Sierra Leone. Occasional Paper no. 3, 1980.

———. "Some Thoughts on Themes in Sierra Leone History." *Journal of the Historical Society of Sierra Leone* 2, 1, 1978: 65–73.

———. "The Sierra Leone/Liberia Boundary: A Case of Frontier Imperialism." *Odu*, n.s., 15, 1977: 5–18.

———. "Research Notes on Dr. Bankole-Bright (1883–1958): His Life to 1939." *Africana Research Bulletin* 5, 1, 1974.

POLITICS

Abdullah, Ibrahim, "Bush Path to Destruction: The Origin and Character of the Revolutionary United Front/Sierra Leone." *Journal of Modern African Studies* 36, 2, 1998: 203–235.

———. "War and Transition to Peace: State Conspiracy in Perpetuating Armed Conflict." *Africa Development* 22, nos. 3 & 4, 1997.

Abraham, A. "Dancing with the Chameleon: Sierra Leone and the Elusive Quest for Peace." *Journal of Contemporary African Studies* 19, (July 2001); 205–228.

Adeshina, R. A. *The Reversed Victory (The Story of Nigerian Military Intervention in Sierra Leone)*. Ibadan, Nigeria: Heinemann Educational Books, 2002.

Amnesty International. *Ending Impunity–An Opportunity Not to be Missed*. New York: Amnesty International, 2000.

———. *Sierra Leone: Political Detainees at the Central Prison, Pademba Road, Freetown*. New York: Amnesty International, 1993.

———. *Sierra Leone: The Extrajudicial Execution of Suspected Rebels and Collaborators*. New York, Amnesty International U.S.A., 1992.

Ayissi, Anatole, and Poulton Robin-Edward, eds. *Bound to Cooperate: Conflict, Peace and People in Sierra Leone*. Geneva: UN Institute for Disarmament Research, 2000.

Bangura, Y. "Reflections on the Abidjan Peace Accord." *Africa Development* 22, 3 & 4, 1997.

Barrows, W. *Grassroots Politics in an African State: Integration and Development in Sierra Leone*. New York: Africana Publishing, 1976.

Bebler, Anton (ed.). *Military Rule in Africa: Dahomey, Ghana, Sierra Leone and Mali*. New York: Praeger, 1973.

Bergner, Daniel. *In the Land of Magic Soldiers: A Story of White and Black in West Africa*. New York: Farrar, Straus and Girou, 2003.

Bones, Alan. "Case Study: Peacekeeping in Sierra Leone." In *Human Security and the New Diplomacy: Protecting People, Promoting Peace,* Rob McRae and Don Hubert (eds.). Montreal: McGill-Queens University Press, 2001.

Bundu, Abass, and J. Karefa–Smart. *Democracy by Force? A Study of International Military Intervention in the Conflict in Sierra Leone from 1991–2001*. Universal Publishers, 2002.

Cartwright, John R. *Political Leadership in Sierra Leone*. Toronto: University of Toronto Press, 1978.

——. *Politics in Sierra Leone 1949–1967*. Toronto: University of Toronto Press, 1970.

Chege, M. "Sierra Leone: The State That Came Back from the Dead." *The Washington Quarterly* 25, 3 (June 2002): 147–160.

Clapham, Christopher S. *Liberia and Sierra Leone: An Essay in Comparative Politics*. Cambridge: Cambridge University Press, 1976.

Collier, Gershon. *Sierra Leone: Experiment in Democracy in an African Nation*. New York: New York University Press, 1970.

Conteh-Morgan, Earl, and Mac Dixon-Fyle. *Sierra Leone at the End of the Twentieth Century*. New York: Peter Lang, 1999.

Conteh-Morgan, Earl, and Shireen Khadivar. "Sierra Leone's Response to ECOMOG: The Imperative to Geographic Proximity." In *Peacekeeping in Africa*, ed. Karl P. Magyar and Earl Conteh-Morgan. London: Macmillan, 1997.

Cox, Thomas. *Civil/Military Relations in Sierra Leone: A Case Study of African Soldiers in Politics.* Cambridge, Mass.: Harvard University Press, 1976.

Dalby, David. "The Military Take-Over in Sierra Leone." *The World Today* 23 (Jan.–Dec. 1967).

Daramy, S. B. *Constitutional Development in the Post-Colonial State of Sierra Leone*. New York: Edwin Mellen Press, 1993.

Douma, P. S. *The Political Economy of Internal Conflict: A Comparative Analysis of Angola, Colombia, Sierra Leone and Sri Lanka*. The Hague: Netherlands Institute of International Relations. Clingendael, 2003.

Dumbuya, Ahmed. "Emergence and Development of the PDG and the SLPP: A Comparative Study of the Differential Development of Political Parties in Guinea and Sierra Leone." *Journal of the Historical Society of Sierra Leone* 1, 1, 1977: 16–34.

Fanthorpe, Richard. "Locating the Politics of a Sierra Leonean Chiefdom." *Africa* 68, 4, 1998.

——. "Neither Citizen nor Subject? 'Lumpen' Agency and the Legacy of Native Administration in Sierra Leone." *African Affairs* 100, 400, 2001: 363–386.

——. "Continuity in Sierra Leone: From Stevens to Momoh." *Third World Quarterly* 10, no. 1, 1988.

Fisher, H.J. "Elections and Coups in Sierra Leone." *Journal of Modern African Studies* 8, 1969.

Francis, Dana. *Mediating Deadly Conflict: Lessons from Afghanistan, Burundi, Cyprus, Ethiopia, Haiti, Israel/Palestine, Liberia, Sierra Leone, & Sri Lanka.* Cambridge, Mass: World Peace Foundation, 1998.

Funke, N., and Hussein Solomon. *Towards Sustainable Peace in Sierra Leone*. Pretoria: African Institute of South Africa, 2002.

Fyle, C. Magbaily. "Indigenous Political Culture and Democratization in Upper Guinea." *Afrika Zamani,* New Series, 2, July 1994.

———. "The Military and Civil Society in Sierra Leone: The 1992 Military Coup d'Etat. *Africa Development* xviii, 2, 1994: 127–146.

———. "The Political and Economic Scene in Three Decades of Independence, 1961–1991." In *The State and the Provision of Social Services in Sierra Leone since Independence*, ed. C. Magbaily Fyle. Dakar: Codesria, 1993: 1–19.

Ganga, Raymond. "Mende Chieftaincy in Nineteenth Century Taiama." *Africana Research Bulletin* 3, 4, 1973.

Gberie, L. "The May 25 Coup d'etat in Sierra Leone: A Militariat Revolt?" *Africa Development* 22, 3 & 4, 1997.

Gershoni, Y. "War without End and an End to a War: The Prolonged Wars in Liberia and Sierra Leone." *African Studies Review* 40, 3, 1997.

Hayward, Fred. "Sierra Leone, State Consolidation, Fragmentation and Decay." In *Contemporary West African States*, ed. D.B. Cruise O'Brien, J. Dunn, and R. Rathbone. London: Cambridge University Press, 1989.

Hayward, Fred, and Jimmy Kandeh. "Perspectives on Twenty-Five Years of Elections in Sierra Leone." In *Elections in Independent Africa*, ed. Fred Hayward. Boulder, CO: Westview Press, 1987.

Hirsch, John L. *Sierra Leone: Diamonds and the Struggle for Democracy*. International Peace Academy Occasional Paper Series. Boulder, CO: Lynne Rienner, 2001.

Kandeh, Jimmy. "Sierra Leone's Post-Conflict Elections of 2002." *Journal of Modern African Studies* 41, 2, 2003: 189–217.

———."Politicization of Ethnic Identities in Sierra Leone." *African Studies Review* 35, 1, 1992, pp. 81–89.

Kilson, Martin. *Political Change in a West African State: A Study of the Modernization Process in Sierra Leone*. Cambridge: Harvard University Press, 1966.

Koroma, Abdul K. *Sierra Leone: The Agony of a Nation*. Freetown: Andromeda Publications, 1996.

Kpundeh, Sahr. *Politics and Corruption in Africa: A Case Study of Sierra Leone*. Lanham, MD: University Press of America, 1995.

Kpundeh, Sahr. "Prospects of Contemporary Sierra Leone." *Journal of Corruption and Reform* 7, no. 3, 1993: 237–247.

———. "Limiting Administrative Corruption in Sierra Leone." *Journal of Modern African Studies* 32, no. 1, 1994.

Laggah, J. B., J. A. D. Alie, and R. S. V. Wright. "Countries in Conflict: Sierra Leone." In *Comprehending and Mastering African Conflicts: The Search for Sus-*

tainable Peace and Good Governance, ed. Adebayo Adedeji. London: Zed Books, 1999.

Lansana, Musa S., and Musa J. Lansana. *The Invasion of Sierra Leone: A Chronicle of Events of a Nation under Siege.* Washington, DC: Sierra Leone Institute for Policy Studies, 1993.

Lavalie, Alpha M. "Government and Opposition in Sierra Leone, 1968–1978." In *Sierra Leone Studies at Birmingham*, 1985, ed. Adam Jones and Peter K. Mitchell. Birmingham: University of Birmingham, Centre of West African Studies, 1987.

Manby, Bronwen. "'*We'll Kill You if You Cry': Sexual Violence in the Sierra Leone Conflict.*" New York: Human Rights Watch, 2003.

Marcus-Jones, W. M. *Legal Developments and Constitutional Change in Sierra Leone*. Ilfracombe, England: Stockwell, 1988.

Reno, William. *Corruption and State Politics in Sierra Leone*. Cambridge: Cambridge University Press, 1995.

Reno, Will. "No Peace for Sierra Leone" *Review of African Political Economy* 27, 84, 2000: 325–329.

Richards, Paul. *Fighting for the Rain Forest: War, Youth and Resources in Sierra Leone.* London: James Currey, 1996.

———. "Rebellion in Liberia and Sierra Leone: A Crisis of Youth." In *Conflict in Africa*, ed. O. W. Furley. London: Tauris, 1995.

———. "Videos and Violence on the Periphery: Rambo and War in the Forests of the Sierra Leone-Liberia Border." *IDS Bulletin*, special issue, *Knowledge is Power? The Use and Abuse of Information in Development*, Susana Davies, ed., 1994.

Riley, S. "Sierra Leone: The Militeriat Strikes Again." *Review of African Political Economy* 24, 72, 1997: 287–292.

———. "Liberia and Sierra Leone: Anarchy or Peace in West Africa." *Conflict Studies* 287. London: Research Institute for the Study of Conflict and Terrorism, 1996.

Riley, S., and Max Sesay. "Sierra Leone: The Coming Anarchy." *Review of African Political Economy* 22, 63, 1995.

Roberts, George O. *The Anguish of Third World Independence. The Sierra Leone Experience.* Lanham, MD: University Press of America, 1982.

Sesay, Amadu. "The Travails of Democracy in Sierra Leone." In *Governance and Democratisation in West Africa*, ed. Dele Olowu, Adebayo Williams, and Kayode Soremekun. Dakar: Codesria, 1999.

———. "Sierra Leone's Foreign Policy: The Era of Independence." *Africana Research Bulletin* 9, 3, 1979.

Smart, H. M. Joko. *Sierra Leone Customary Family Law*. Freetown: F. B. C. Bookshop, 1983.

Smith, Robert. *The All Peoples Congress: A Contemporary Political History of Sierra Leone*. Monrovia, Liberia: Providence Publications, 1972.

Squire, Chris. *Agony in Sierra Leone*. Freetown: Ro-Marong Industries Ltd. 1996.

——. *Ill-Fated Nation*. Freetown: Ro-Marong Industries Ltd. 1995.

Steady, Filomena C. *Female Power in African Politics: The National Congress of Sierra Leone.* Pasadena, CA: California Institute of Technology, 1975.

Tangri, Roger. "Servir ou se server? A propos du Sierra Leone." *Politique Africaine* 6, 1982: 5–18.

——. "Paramount Chiefs and Central Governments in Sierra Leone." *African Studies* 39, 2, 1980: 183–195.

——. "Central–Local Politics in Contemporary Sierra Leone." *African Affairs* 77, 307, 1978: 165–173.

——. "Local Government Institutions in Sierra Leone: Part One. District Councils 1951–1972." *Journal of Administration Overseas* 17, 1, 1978: 17–27.

——. "Local Government Institutions in Sierra Leone. Part Two. Contemporary Chiefdom Administration." *Journal of Administration Overseas* 12, 2, 1978: 118–128.

——. "Conflict and Violence in Contemporary Sierra Leone Chiefdom." *Journal of Modern African Studies* 14, 2 1976: 311–321.

Thompson, Bankole. *The Criminal Law of Sierra Leone*. Lanham, MD: University Press of America, 1998.

——. *The Constitutional History and Law of Sierra Leone, 1961–1995*. Lanham, MD: University Press of America, 1996.

Tuboku-Metzger, F. C., and H. L. van der Laan. *Land Leases in Sierra Leone*. Leiden, Holland: African Studies Centre. 1981.

Tucker, Peter. *Origin and Philosophy of the Sierra Leone People's Party*. London, privately printed, 2001.

Waldie, Kevin. "'Cattle and Concrete': Changing Property Rights and Property Interests among the Fula Cattle Herders around Kabala, North East Sierra Leone." In *Property, Poverty and People: Changing Rights in Property and Problems of Pastoral Development*, ed. P. T. W. Bater and R. Hogg. Manchester, University of Manchester, Department of Social Anthropology and International Development Centre, 1989: 229–39.

Yekutiel, Gershoni. "War without End and an End to a War: The Prolonged Wars in Liberia and Sierra Leone." *African Studies Review* 40, no. 3, 1997: 55–76.

Zack-Williams, A. "Kamajors, 'Sobels' and the Militariat: Civil Society and the Return of the Military in Sierra Leonean Politics. *Review of African Political Economy* 24, 73, 2001: 373–380.

——. "Child Soldiers in the Civil War in Sierra Leone." *Review of African Political Economy* 28, 87: 2001: 73–82.

——. "Sierra Leone 1968–1985: The Decline of Politics and the Politics of Decline." *International Journal of Sierra Leone Studies* 1, 1989: 122–30.

——. "The Ekutay: Ethnic Cabal and Politics in Sierra Leone." In *The Issue of Political Ethnicity in Africa*, ed. E. Ike Udogu. Brookfield, VT: Ashgate, 2001.

Zack-Williams, A., and S. P. Riley. "Sierra Leone: The Coup and Its Consequences." *Review of African Political Economy* 56, no. 2, 1993.

ECONOMY

Agbonyitor, Alberto K. "The Informal Money Market in Rural Sierra Leone." *Africana Research Bulletin* 3, 1, 1976.

Airey, A., J. A. Binns, and P. K. Mitchell. "To Integrate or . . . ? Agricultural Development in Sierra Leone." *Institute of Development Studies Bulletin* 10, no. 4, 1979: 20–7.

Bah, D. M. "Community Participation and Rural Water Supply Development in Sierra Leone." *Community Development Journal* 27, 1, 1992: 30–41.

———. "Improving Rural Watcr Supply in Sierra Leone." *Waterlines* 6, (July 1987): 30–31.

Bangura, Abdul Karim. "The Effects of Arab Foreign Aid on Sierra Leone's Economic Growth: A Quantitative Analysis." In *Islam and Trade in Sierra Leone*, ed. Alusine Jalloh and David E. Skinner. Trenton, NJ: Africa World Press, 1997: 179–196.

———. "The effects of Total Foreign Aid on Sierra Leone's Economic Growth, 1961–1987: A Multiple Time–Series Analysis Using Ordinary Least Squares and Maximum Likelihood Estimates." *The Sierra Leone Review* 1, 1992.

Bangura, Abdul Karim, and Mohamed S. Dumbuya. "The Political Economy of Sierra Leone's Mineral Industry since Independence." *The Sierra Leone Review* 2, 1993.

Blair, James A. S. "Migration of Agricultural Manpower in Sierra Leone." *Tijdschrift voor Economishe en Sociale Geografie* 68, 4, 1977: 198–210.

———. "Some Aspects of Labour Turnover in Sierra Leone." *Africana Research Bulletin* 1, 4, 1971.

Büscher, Ludger. *Kabdkucge Gewerbeentwicklung in Sierra Leone.* Hamburg: Verlag Weltarchiv, 1985.

———. *Integrated Rural Development: The Case of Southern Sierra Leone*. Hamburg: Verlag Weltarchiv, 1984.

Chuta, Enyinna. *Employment and Growth in Small-Scale Industry: Empirical Evidence and Policy Assessment from Sierra Leone*. New York: St. Martin's Press, 1985.

———. "The Economics of Gara (Tie-Dye) Cloth Industry in Sierra Leone." *African Rural Economy Program Working Paper* no. 25, 1978. East Lansing: Michigan State University.

Chuta, Enyinna, and Carl Liedholm. *The Role of Small Scale Industry in Employment Generation and Rural Development: Initial Research Results from Sierra Leone.* Njala, Sierra Leone: Njala University College, Dept. of Agricultural Economics; East Lansing, MI: Dept. of Agricultural Economics, 1975.

Cleeve, Emmanuel. *Multinational Enterprises in Development: The Mining Industry of Sierra Leone*. Brookfield, VT: S. I. Ashgage Publishing Company, 1997.

Davies, Victor. *Ajustement Structurel en Sierra Leone: Analyse des Mesures Portant sur les PME*. Dakar: Codesria, 1998.

Dorjahn, V., and B. Isaac. *Themes in the Economic Anthropology of Liberia and Sierra Leone*. Philadelphia: Institute for Liberian Studies, 1979.

Dorjahn, V. "The Economies of Sierra Leone and Liberia." In *Themes in the Economic Anthropology of Liberia and Sierra Leone*, ed. V. Dorjahn and B. Isaac. Philadelphia: Institute for Liberian Studies, 1979: 1–26.

Eliott, J. W., and E. A. Webber. *Income Distribution and the Poverty Line in Sierra Leone*. Freetown: Central Statistics Office, 1992.

Fashole-Luke, David. "The Development of Trade Unionism in Sierra Leone." *IJAHS* 18, no. 3, 1985.

———. *Labour and Parastatals Politics in Sierra Leone: A Study of African Working-Class Ambivalence.* Lanham, MD: University Press of America, 1984.

Fowler, D. A. L. "The Informal Sector in Freetown: An Opportunity for Self-Employment." In *The Informal Sector in Developing Countries: Employment, Poverty and Environment*. Geneva: ILO, 1981: 51–69.

———. "The Urban Informal Sector in Sierra Leone: Some Conceptual and Policy Issues." *Africana Research Bulletin* 6, 3, 1976.

Francis, David J. *Politics of Economic Regionalism: Sierra Leone in ECOWAS*. London, Ashgate Publishers, 2001.

Funna, Soule. "Structure and Performance of the Sierra Leone Economy, 1971–81." In *Sierra Leone Studies at Birmingham, 1983,* ed. Adam Jones and Peter Mitchell. Birmingham: University of Birmingham, Centre of West African Studies, 1984.

Fyle, C. Magbaily. "Indigenous Values and the Organization of Informal Sector Business in West Africa." In *Black Business and Economic Power in Africa and the US,* ed. T. Falola and A. Jalloh. Rochester, NY: University of Rochester Press, 2002.

Haas, Andy W. "Communication of Agricultural Innovation in Alikalia, Koinadugu District." *Africana Research Bulletin* 6, 2, 1976.

Harvey, M. E. "Economic Development and Migration in Sierra Leone." In *Population Growth and Economic Development in Africa*, ed. S. H. Ominde and C. N. London: Heinemann, 1972: 167–72.

Hoogevelt, Ankie M., and Anthony M. Tinker. "The Rise of Colonial and Post-Colonial Studies in Imperialism: A Case-Study of the Sierra Leone Development Company." *Journal of Modern African Studies* 16, no. 1, 1978.

ILO. *Ensuring Equitable Growth: A Strategy for Increasing Employment, Equity and Basic Needs Satisfaction in Sierra Leone*. Addis Ababa: ILO Jobs and Skills Programme for Africa, 1981.

Isaac, B. L. "Economic Development and Subsistence Farming: The Case of the Mende of Upper Bambara Chiefdom, Sierra Leone." *Central Issues in Anthropology* 4, 1982: 1–20.

———. "The Economic, Ethnic, and Sexual Parameters of Petty Trading in Pendembu, Sierra Leone." In *Themes in the Economic Anthropology of Liberia and Sierra Leone*, ed V. Dorjahn and B. Isaac. Philadelphia: Institute for Liberian Studies, 1979: 173–196.

———. "The National and International Content of Economic Anthropology in Liberia and Sierra Leone." In *Themes in the Economic Anthropology of Liberia and Sierra Leone*, ed. V. Dorjahn and B. Isaac. Philadelphia: Institute for Liberian Studies, 1979: 225–245.

———. "European, Lebanese and African Traders in Pendembu, Sierra Leone, 1908–1968." *Human Organization*, 33, 1974: 111–121.

———. "Business Failure in a Developing Town: Pendembu, Sierra Leone." *Human Organization* 30, 1971: 288–294.

Iyanda, Olukunle. *Multinationals and Employment in a West African Sub-Region: Liberia and Sierra Leone (Working Paper No. 29).* Geneva: International Labor Office, 1984.

Jabati, Sallu. *An Assessment of the Rural Bank Credit Sector in Sierra Leone*. Boulder, Westview Press, 1995.

Johnny, M. *Informal Credit for Integrated Rural Development in Sierra Leone*. Hamburg: Verlag Weltarchiv, 1985.

———. "Agricultural Change and Peasant Farmer Resistance: The Case of the Traditional Upland Rice Farmer in Sierra Leone" *Rural Africana* 10, 1981: 9–17.

Johnny, M., J. Karimu, and P. Richards. "Upland and Swamp Rice Farming Systems in Sierra Leone: The Social Content of Technological Change." *Africa* 51, no. 2, 1981: 596–620.

Johnny, M., J. Lappia, and S. Nankumba. *Project Performance of IRD–Programmes in Sierra Leone and Malawi.* Hamburg: Verlag Weltarchiv, 1984.

Jordan, H. D. "Rice in the Economy of Sierra Leone." *World Crops* 17, 1965: 68–74.

Kai-Kai, Francis M. *Public Expenditure and Sustainability of the Regional Agricultural Project Strategy: Analysis of Policy in Sierra Leone*. Boulder, CO: Westview Press, 1995.

———. *Public Expenditure and Sustainability of the Regional Agriculture Project Strategy: Analysis of Policy in Sierra Leone*. Munster: Lit. Verlag, 1994.

Kallon, Kelfala. *The Economics of Sierra Leonean Entrepreneurship*. Lanham, MD: University Press of America, 1990.

———. "An Econometric Analysis of Inflation in Sierra Leone." *Journal of African Economies* 3, 2, 1994.

Kamara, Umar I. *Sustainable Rural Development: Semantics or Substance?: The Study of Rural Projects in North Western Sierra Leone (1985–1995)*." Lanham MD: University Press of America, 2001.

Karimu, J. A., and P. Richards. *The Northern Area Integrated Agricultural Development Project: Social and Economic Impact of Planning for Rural Change in Northern Sierra Leone*. Occasional Papers (New Series), no. 3, Department of Geography, School of Oriental and African Studies, 1981.

Karr, G. L., A. O. Njoku, and M. F. Kalon. "Economics of Upland and Inland Valley Swamp Rice Production Systems in Sierra Leone." *Illinois Agricultural Economics* 12, 1972: 12–17.

Ketkar, S. L. "The Economics of Education in Sierra Leone." *Journal of Modern African Studies* 15, 1977: 310–15.

Kireta-Katewu, Patrick, and H.U. Thimm. *Economic Analyses of the Farmer Cropping System under Risks and Uncertainties in Sierra Leone*. Hamburg: Verlag Weltarchiv, 1985.

Lappia, J. N. L. *The Economics of Swamp Rice Cultivation in the Integrated Agricultural Development Project, Eastern Region, Sierra Leone*. Department of Agricultural Economics and Extension, Njala University College.

Leighton, Neil O. "The Lebanese in Sierra Leone." *Transition* 9, 1974: 23–29.

Levi, John. *African Agriculture: Economic Action and Reaction in Sierra Leone*. Slough: Commonwealth Agricultural Bureau, 1976.

———. "Migration from the Land and Urban Unemployment in Sierra Leone." *Oxford Bulletin of Economics and Statistics* 35, 4, 1973: 309–26.

———. "Migration and Unemployment in Sierra Leone." In *Manpower and Unemployment Research in Africa*. 4, 2, 1971: 20–25.

———. "Labour Migration and Unemployment." *Bank of Sierra Leone Economic Review* 4, 5, 1969–70:1–10.

Liedholm, C., O. Roberts, and J. Tommy. "Employment Growth and Changes in Sierra Leone's Small-Scale Industry: 1974–1980." East Lansing: Michigan State University, *African Rural Economy Program Working Paper* no. 37, 1978.

Lisk, F., and G. Van der Hoeven. "Measurement of Poverty in Sierra Leone." *International Labour Review* 118, no. 6, 1979: 771–82.

Lisk, F., and Y. Stevens. "Government Policy and Rural Women's Work in Sierra Leone." In *Sex Roles, Population and Development in West Africa. Policy-Related Studies on Work and Demographic Issues*, ed. Christine Oppong. Portsmouth, NH: Heinemann, 1987: 182–202.

Longhurst, R., S. Kamara, and J. Mensurah. "Structural Adjustment and Vulnerable Groups in Sierra Leone." University of Sussex, Institute of Development Studies, *IDS Bulletin* 19, 1, 1988.

Luke, D. F., and S. Riley. "The Politics of Economic Decline in Sierra Leone." *Journal of Modern African Studies*, 1989.

MacCormack, Carol. "Control of Land, Labor and Capital in Rural Southern Sierra Leone." In *Women and Work in Africa*, ed. Edna G. Bay. Boulder: Westview Press, 1982.

Makannah, T. J. "The Components of Urban Population Growth: Ghana and Sierra Leone." *African Urban Quarterly* 3, 3 & 4, 1988: 78–94.

———. "Remittances and Rural Development in Sierra Leone." *Peasant Studies* 16, 1, 1988: 53–62.

———. "Growth without Development: An Economic History of the Sierra Leone Palm Kernel Export Sector." *Africana Research Bulletin* 6, 1, 1975.

Manley-Spain, P. F. V. "Urbanization and Regional Development in Sierra Leone." In *Regional Planning and National Development in Tropical Africa*, ed. A. L. Mabogunje and A. Faniran. Ibadan, Nigeria: Ibadan University Press, 1977.

Merani, H. V., and H. L. Van der Laan. "The Indian Traders in Sierra Leone."

Mills, L. R. "Migration into a Small Temne Town in Central Sierra Leone." *Africana Research Bulletin* 3, 2, 1973.

Moseley, K. P. "Land, Labour and Migration: The Saffroko Limba Case." *Africana Research Bulletin* 8, 2 & 3, 1977.

Mukonowesuro, E. *Colonialism, Class Formation and Underdevelopment in Sierra Leone*. Lanham, MD: University Press of America, 1985.

Njoku, A. O. "The Economics of Mende Upland Rice Farming." In *Essays on the Economic Anthropology of Liberia and Sierra Leone*, ed. V. Dorjahn and B. Isaac. Philadelphia: Institute of Liberian Studies, 1979: 103–120.

Reno, William. *Humanitarian Emergencies and Warlord Economies in Liberia and Sierra Leone*. Helsinki: World Institute for Development Economics Research, 1997.

———. "Ironies of Post–Cold War Structural Adjustment in Sierra Leone." *Review of African Political Economy* 23, 67: 1996: 7–18.

Richards, Paul. "The Versatility of the Poor: Wetland Rice Farming Systems in Sierra Leone." *Geoforum* 35, no. 2, 1995: 197–203.

———. "Rural Development and Local Knowledge: The Case of Rice in Central Sierra Leone." *Entwicklungsethnologie* 1, 1992: 33–42.

———. *Indigenous Agricultural Revolution: Ecology and Food Production in West Africa.* London: Hutchinson, 1985.

———. *Coping with Hunger: Hazard and Experiment in an African Rice Farming System.* London: Allen and Unwin, 1986.

Ringrose, S. M. "Swamps and Rice Cultivation in Sierra Leone: Digital Landsat Techniques." In *Remote Sensing and Tropical Land Management*, ed. M. J. Eden and J. T. Parry. Chichester, England: Wiley, 1986.

Rogers, J. D. *Patterns of Rural Development and Impact on Employment and Incomes: A Comparative Sub-Regional Study; The Case of Sierra Leone*. Durham, NC: Duke University Press, 1967.

Siddle, D. J. "Location Theory and the Subsistence Economy: The Spacing of Rural Settlements in Sierra Leone." *Journal of Tropical Geography* 31, 1970: 79–90.

Smith, Victor E., Sarah Lynch, William Whelan, John Strauss, and Doyle Baker. *Household Food Consumption in Rural Sierra Leone.* East Lansing: Michigan State University, Department of Agricultural Economics. Working Paper no. 7, 1979.

Snyder, D. W. "Economic Determinants of Family Size in West Africa." *Demography* 11, 4, 1974: 613–627.

Spencer, C. R. "Politics, Public Administration and Agricultural Plantation Development Program, 1964–1967." *Journal of Developing Areas* 12, 1978: 69–86.

Spencer, Dunstan S. C. "Rice Policy in Sierra Leone. Rice Production in Sierra Leone." In *Rice in West Africa: Policy and Economics*, ed. S. R. Pearson, J. D. Stryker, and C. P. Humphreys. Palo Alto, CA: Stanford University Press, 1981.

———. *African Women in Agricultural Development: A Case Study in Sierra Leone*. Washington, DC: Overseas Liaison Committee, American Council on Education, 1976.

——. *The Economics of Rice Production in Sierra Leone*. Sierra Leone: Department of Agricultural Economics and Extension, Njala University College, 1975.

——. *Micro–level Farm Management and Production Economics Research among Traditional African Farmers: Lessons from Sierra Leone*. East Lansing: Michigan State University, Dept. of Agricultural Economics, 1972.

——. *Women in a Developing Economy: A West African Case Study*. East Lansing: Michigan State University Press, 1979.

Stanley, W. R. "The Lebanese in Sierra Leone: Entrepreneurs Extraordinary." *African Urban Notes* 5, 1970: 159–74.

Surr, M. A. *Care International in Sierra Leone: Moyamba Rural Water Supply and Sanitation Project, Sierra Leone Evaluation*. London: Overseas Development Administration, 1993.

Taylor, A. T. B. *Money and Banking in Sierra Leone*. Milan: Finafrica, Cassa di Risparmio delle Provincie Lombarde, 1980.

Van der Laan, L. *European Commercial Enterprise in Colonial Sierra Leone 1896–1961*. Leiden, Holland: Afrika Studiecentrum, 1978.

——. *The Lebanese Traders of Sierra Leone*. The Hague, Mouton, 1975.

Wapensky, Basil A. "Banking and Finance in Sierra Leone: A Developing Economy." Atlanta: Bureau of Business and Economic Research, Georgia State College, 1968.

Weeks, John. *Development Strategy and the Economy of Sierra Leone*. London: Macmillan, 1992.

——. *Structural Adjustment and Rural Labour Markets in Sierra Leone.* Geneva: International Labour Office, 1990.

Williams, Olu. *Formal Credit and Default Problems in IRD-Programmes in Sierra Leone.* Hamburg: Verlag Weltarchiv, 1985.

World Bank. "Sierra Leone: Public Expenditure Policies for Sustained Growth and Poverty Alleviation." *World Bank Report no. 12618–SL* (Feb. 16, 1994).

Zack-Williams, Alfred. *Tributors, Supporters and Merchant Capital: Mining and Underdevelopment in Sierra Leone*. Aldershot, England, 1995.

——. "Sierra Leone: The Deepening Crisis and Survival Strategies." *In Beyond Structural Adjustment in Africa*, ed. J. Nyang'oro and Tim Shaw. New York: Praeger, 1993.

——. "Diamond Mining in Sierra Leone, 1930–80." In *Science and Technology in African History*, ed. G. Thomas–Emeagweli. London: The Edwin Mellen Press, 1992.

——. "Sierra Leone: Crisis and Despair." *Review of African Political Economy* 17, 49, 1990: 22–33.

——. "Some Comments on the Manufacturing Sector in Sierra Leone." *Africa Development* 10, no. 4, 1985.

——. "Merchant Capital and Underdevelopment in Sierra Leone." *Review of African Political Economy* 9, 25: 1982: 74–82.

Zurek, E., ed. *Integrated Rural Development—Research Results and Programme Implementation,* Bonn Conference 1986. Hamburg: Verlag Weltarchiv, 1987.

SOCIETY AND CULTURE

Abraham, Arthur. "Local Government and the Provision of Social Services in Sierra Leone." In *The State and the Provision of Social Services in Sierra Leone Since Independence*, ed. Magbaily Fyle. Dakar: Codesria, 1993: 83–98.

———. *Cultural Policy in Sierra Leone*. Paris: UNESCO, 1978.

Abraham, Arthur, and E. A. R. Gaima. "Ethnographic Survey of the Kalantuba Limba of Kalansogoia Chiefdom, Tonkolili District, Northern Province, Sierra Leone." Freetown: Fourah Bay College, University of Sierra Leone, Institute of African Studies, 1995.

Abraham, Arthur, and Habib Sesay, "Regional Politics and Social Services Provision since Independence." In *The State and the Provision of Social Services in Sierra Leone since Independence*, ed. C. Magbaily Fyle. Dakar: Codesria, 1993: 113–126.

Adeokun, L. A. "Creole and Yoruba Households and Family Size." *In Sex Roles, Population and Development in West Africa*, ed. C. Oppong. London: John Currey, 1987: 91–100.

Amnesty International. Sierra Leone: *Rape and Other Forms of Sexual Violence against Girls and Women*. London: International Secretariat, 2000.

Angoff, Charles, and John Povey, eds. *African Writing Today: Ethiopia, Ghana, Kenya, Nigeria, Sierra Leone, Uganda, Zambia*. New York: Manyland Books, c. 1969.

Asiedu, Deward S. *Research Project on African Government Documents: The Case of West African English-Speaking Countries, the Gambia, Ghana, Liberia, Nigeria and Sierra Leone*. Tangier, Morocco: African Training and Research Centre in Administration for Development, 1978.

Bailey, M. "The Population of Sierra Leone: Growth and Distribution, 1963–1985." *African Urban Quarterly* 8, 3–4, 1993: 239–51.

Bailey, M., and T. Makannah. "An Evaluation of Age and Sex Data of the Population Censuses of Sierra Leone: 1963–85." *Genus* 52, 1 & 2 1996: 191–99.

Bai-Sharka, Abou. *Temne Names and Proverbs*. Freetown: People's Educational Association, 1986.

Bakarr, Frances K. "Educational Development of Girls and Women in Post-War Sierra Leone." *Sierra Leone Studies and Review* 1, no. 1, 2000.

Baksh-Soodeen, Rawwida, and Linda Etchart. *Women and Men in Partnership for Post-Conflict Reconstruction. National Consultative Conference, Freetown, 21–24 May, 2001*. London: Commonwealth Secretariat, 2002.

Bangura, Abdul Karim. "Divisive Barbarity on National Civilization: Linguistic Presuppositions of the Sierra Leone National Anthem as a Tool for Teaching Peaceful Behavior." *Sierra Leone Studies and Review* 1, no. 1, 2000.

———. *Multilingualism and Diglossia in Sierra Leone*. Lawrenceville, VA: Brunswick, 1991.

Bangura, Ibrahim "The State of Adult Education in Sierra Leone." *Pen and Hoe, A Journal of the PEA of Sierra Leone* 2, 1985: 67–71.

Bangura, Ibrahim, Lansana Kamara, and H. Hinzen. *Amump yi malen ma ro Themne*. Freetown: People's Educational Association, 1986.

Bangura, M. S. "Traditional Education among the Limba." *Pen and Hoe, A Journal of the PEA of Sierra Leon.* 4, 1987: 52–61.

Banton, M. "Adaptation and Integration in the Social System of Temne Immigrants in Freetown." In *Black Africa: Its Peoples and Cultures Today*, ed. J. Middleton. Toronto: Macmillan, 1970.

Beckley, Staneala. "State Sponsored Educational Services in Sierra Leone." In *The State and the Provision of Social Services in Sierra Leone since Independence*, ed. C. Magbaily Fyle. Dakar: Codesria, 1993: 62–82.

Benjamin, E., and T. E. Dow. "Demographic Trends and Implications [in Sierra Leone]." In *Population Growth and Socio-economic Change in West Africa*, ed. J.C. Caldwell. New York: Columbia University Press, 1975.

Biddle, Keith. "Acting Inspector General of the Sierra Leone Police." *Bulletin of the Conflict, Security and Development Group.* London: King's College, 5 March–April 2000.

Binns, M., and T. Binns. *Sierra Leone*. Vol. 148, World Bibliographical Series. Oxford: Clio Press, 1992.

Bledsoe, Caroline. "Differential Care of Children of Previous Unions within Mende Households in Sierra Leone." In *What We Know about Health Transition: The Cultural, Social and Behavioural Determinants of Health*, ed. John C. Caldwell. Canberra, Australia: National University Press, 2001: 561–584.

——. "The Cultural Transformation of Western Education in Sierra Leone." In *Schooling the Symbolic Animal: Social and Cultural Dimensions of Education*, ed. Bradley A. U. Levinson. Lanham, MD: Rowman and Littlefield, 2000.

——. "Marginal Members: Children of Previous Unions in Mende Households in Sierra Leone." In *Situating Fertility Anthropology and Demography Inquiry*, ed. Susan Greenhalgh. New York: Cambridge University Press, 1995: 130–53.

——. "The Politics of Polygyny in Mende Child Fosterage Transactions." In *Sex and Gender Hierarchies*, ed. Barbara Diane Miller. Cambridge: Cambridge University Press: 170–92, 1995.

——. "'Met-in-Hand' Children: The Problem of Children of Previous Unions among the Mende in Sierra Leone." *The Cultural Construction of Fertility: Anthropological Contributions to Demographic Theory*, ed. Susan Greenhalgh. Cambridge: Cambridge University Press, 1994.

——. "'No Success without Struggle': Social Mobility and Hardship for Sierra Leone Children." *Man*, n.s., 25, 1990: 70–88.

——. "The Politics of Children: Fosterage and the Social Management of Fertility among the Mende of Sierra Leone." In *Births and Power: The Politics of Reproduction*, ed. W. Penn Handwerker. Boulder, CO: Westview Press, 1990: 81–100.

——. "Side-Stepping the Postpartum Sex Taboo: Mende Cultural Perceptions of Tinned Milk in Sierra Leone." *Fertility Determinants Research Notes* 24, 1988. NY: The Population Council, 1988.

———. "The Political Use of Sande Ideology and Symbolism." *American Ethnologist* 11, 1984: 455–72.

Bledsoe C., and Monica F. Goubaud. "The Reinterpretation of Western Pharmaceuticals among the Mende of Sierra Leone." *Social Science and Medicine* 21, 3, 1985: 275–282.

Bledsoe, Caroline, and Uche C. Isiugo-Abanihe. "Strategies of Child Fosterage among Mende 'Grannies' in Sierra Leone." In *African Reproduction and Social Organization*, ed. R. Lesthaeghe. Berkeley: University of California Press: 442–474.

Bledsoe, Caroline, and Kenneth Robey. "Arabic Literacy and Secrecy among the Mende of Sierra Leone." *Man*, n.s., 21, 1986: 202–226.

Bledsoe, Caroline, D.C. Ewbank, and Uche C. Isiugo-Abanihe. "The Effect of Child Fostering on Feeding Practices and Access to Health Services in Rural Sierra Leone." *Social Science and Medicine* 27, 6, 1988: 627–636.

Boone, Sylvia Ardyn. *Radiance from the Waters: Ideals of Feminine Beauty in Mende Art*. New Haven: Yale University Press, 1986.

Boy, Chopping. *Aw Fish Kam na dis Wol.* Freetown: People's Educational Association, 1986.

Bretherton, D., J. Weston, and V. Zbar. "Peace Education in a Post-Conflict Environment: The Case of Sierra Leone." *Prospects* 33, 2, (June 2003): 219–230.

Calender, Ebenezer, *Krio Songs*. Freetown, People's Educational Association, 1985.

Campbell, E. K. "Internal Migration in the Western Area of Sierra Leone: An Exercise for Policy Formulation." *African Urban Quarterly* 1, 2, 1986: 86–101.

———. "Some Aspects of Migration in the Western Area of Sierra Leone." In *Demographic Aspects of Migration in West Africa*, vol. 1, ed. K. C. Zacharian and J. Conde. Washington DC: World Bank, Staff Working Paper, no. 414, Sept. 1980.

Cannizzo, Jeanne. "The Alikali Devils of Sierra Leone." *African Arts* 12, no. 4, 1979: 64–70.

Carpenter, Allan, and Susan L. Eckert. *Sierra Leone*. Chicago: Children's Press, 1974.

Clarke, John I. "Population Distribution in Sierra Leone." In *The Population of Tropical Africa*, ed. J.C. Caldwell and C. Okonjo. New York: Columbia University Press, 1968: 270–277.

Clifford, Mary Louise. *The Land and People of Sierra Leone.* Philadelphia: Lippincott, 1974.

Cline-Cole, R. Akindele. "The Socio-Ecology of Firewood and Charcoal on the Freetown Peninsula." *In Sierra Leone 1787–1987*. London: International African Institute, 1987: 457–497.

Cole, Bernadette. *Mass Media, Freedom and Democracy in Sierra Leone*. Freetown: Premier Publishing House, 1995.

Cole, B. "Sierra Leone and the International Women's Decade." *PopLeone* 2, 32, 1985: 3–6.

Cole, C. R. A., and B. Singh. *A Study of the Social, Economic and Demographic Characteristics of Leicester Village.* Freetown: Fourah Bay College, University of Sierra Leone. Extra Mural Department Publication 5, 1: 1973.

Coomber, Ajayi. "Form, Distribution and Function/Meaning of the Krio Particle Den." *Africana Research Bulletin* 8, 2 & 3, 1978.

Corby, Richard. "Progressive Chieftaincy in Sierra Leone: Kenewa Gamanga of Simbaru." *Tarikh* 7, no. 1, 1981: 57–64.

Cosentino, D. *Defiant Maids and Stubborn Farmers: Tradition and Invention in Mende Performance*. Cambridge: Cambridge University Press, 1982.

——. "Midnight Charters: Musa Wo and the Mende Myths of Chaos." In *The Creativity of Power*, ed. W. Arens and I. Karp. Washington, DC: Smithsonian Institution Press, 1989.

Dalby, David. "A Survey of the Indigenous Scripts of Liberia and Sierra Leone: Vai, Mende, Loma, Kpelle, and Bassa." *African Language Studies* 8, 1967: 1–51.

Dalby, David, and Abdul Kamara. "Vocabulary of the Temne Ragbenle Society." *Sierra Leone Language Review* 3, 1964: 35–41.

D'Alisera, JoAnn. *An Imagined Geography: Sierra Leone Muslims in America.* Philadelphia: University of Pennsylvania Press, 2004.

——. "Icons of Longing: Homeland and Memory in the Sierra Leonean Diaspora." *Polar: The Political and Legal Anthropology Review* 25, no. 2, 2002: 73–89.

——. "Born in the USA: Naming Ceremonies of Infants among Sierra Leoneans in the American Capital." *Anthropology Today* 14, 1998: 16–18.

Davies, A. Glyn. *The Gola Forest Reserves, Sierra Leone: Wildlife Conservation and Forest Management.* Cambridge, U.K.: International Union for Conservation of Nature and Natural Resources, 1987.

Davies, Glyn, and Paul Richards. *Rain Forest in Mende Life: Resources and Subsistence Strategies in Rural Communities around the Gola North Forest Reserve (Sierra Leone).* London: Overseas Development Administration 1991.

Davies, Clarice, Amy Davies, Anna Gyorgy, and Christiane Kayser. *Women of Sierra Leone: Traditional Voices*. Freetown: Partners in Adult Education Women's Commission, 1992.

Devis, T. L. F. "First Report on a Demographic Sample Survey in Sierra Leone." *Africana Research Bulletin*, 1975.

——. "Household Size and Composition in Sierra Leone." *Africana Research Bulletin* 2, 3, 1972.

Doherty, H. "Housing and Development in Freetown, Sierra Leone." *Cities* 2, 2, 1985: 149–64.

Donald, Leland. "Ethnicity and the Occupational Structure of a Yalunka Town." In *Themes in the Economic Anthropology of Liberia and Sierra Leone*, ed. V. Dorjahn V. and B. Issac. Philadelphia: Institute for Liberian Studies, 1979: 157–172.

Dorjahn, V. R. "The Changing Political System of the Temne." *Africa* 30, 1966.

——. "The Organization and Function of the Ragbenle Society of the Temne." *Africa* 29, 1959: 156–170.

Dorjahn, V. "Temne Household Size and Composition: Rural Changes over Time and Rural–Urban Differences." *Ethnology* 16: 105–127.

Dow, T. E. "Population Growth and Primary Education in Sierra Leone." In *Population Growth and Economic Development in* Africa, ed. S. H. Ominde and C. N. Ejiogu. London: Heinemann, 1972.

Dumbuya, M. B. "Folk Media as Information Supports for Adult Education in Sierra Leone." *Pen and Hoe, A Journal of the PEA of Sierra Leone* 4, 1987.

———. "Social Effects of Industrialization and Urbanization in Sierra Leone." *Africana Research Bulletin* 3, 3, 1973.

During, Chris. *Kapu Sens, No Kapu Wod.* Freetown: People's Educational Association, 1986.

———. *Krio Adages and Fables*. Freetown: Peoples Educational Association of Sierra Leone, 1986.

Edwards, S. Kpanga, trans. *Refund of Dowry in Sierra Leone*. Bo, Sierra Leone: Provincial Literature Bureau, 1966.

Ehret, Rebecca. "Language Attitudes and the Linguistic Construction of Ethnic Identity: The Case of Krio in Sierra Leone." In *Language Choices: Conditions, Constraints and* Consequences, ed. Martin Pütz. Amsterdam, Philadelphia: J. Benjamins, 1997.

Fanthorpe, Richard. "Limba 'Deep Rural' Strategies." *Journal of African History* 39, 1998: 15–38.

Ferme, Marian. *The Underneath of Things. Violence, History and the Everyday in Sierra Leone.* Berkeley, CA: University of California Press, 2001.

Field, G. D. *Birds of the Freetown Area.* Freetown: Fourah Bay College Bookshop, 1974.

Finnegan, Ruth. *Survey of the Limba People of Northern Sierra Leone*. London: H. M. Stationery Office, 1962.

———. The Traditional Concept of Chiefship among the Limba." *Sierra Leone Studies*, n.s., 17, 1963: 241–53.

Forde, E. R. A. "Why People Move from the Rural Areas to the Urban Areas: Some Pertinent Issues." *PopLeone* 1, 1 1984: 9–10.

———."Implications of Rapid Population Growth on Employment in Sierra Leone." In *Population Growth and Economic Development in Africa*, ed. S. H. Ominde and C.N. Ejiogu. London: Heinemann, 1972: 321–328.

Forde, E. R. A., and M. Harvey. "Graphical Analysis of Migration to Freetown." *Sierra Leone Geographical Journal* 13, 1969: 13–27.

Forde, Teddy. "Indigenous Education in Sierra Leone." In *Conflict and Harmony in African Education in Tropical Africa*, ed. Godfrey Brown and Marvin Hiskett. London: Allen and Unwin, 1975: 65–75.

Forna, Aminata. *The Devil That Danced on the Water: A Daughter's Quest*. New York: Grove Atlantic, 2002.

Foston, Mike. *The Animal Story*, Books 1 and 2. Freetown: People's Educational Association of Sierra Leone, 1985.

Frey-Nakonz, Regula. "Women's Programme in Bo-Pujehun Rural Development Project." *Pen and Hoe, A Journal of the PEA of Sierra Leone* 2, 1985: 86–94.

Fyle, C. Magbaily. "Conflict and Population Dispersal: The Refugee Crisis in the Upper Guinea Region of West Africa." *The International Journal of African Studies* 2, 1 (Spring 1998): 1–26.

———."Popular Islam and Political Expression in Sierra Leone." In *Islam and Trade in Sierra Leone*, ed. A. Jalloh and D. Skinner. Trenton, NJ: Africa World Press, 1997: 161–178.

———. "Official and Unofficial Attitudes and Policy towards Krio as the Main Lingua Franca in Sierra Leone." In *African Languages, Development and the State*, ed. R. Fardon and G. Furniss. London: Routledge, 1994.

———, ed. *The State and the Provision of Social Services since Independence*. Dakar: Codesria, 1993.

———. "The State, Culture and Social Services Provision since Independence." In *The State and the Provision of Social Services in Sierra Leone since Independence*, ed. C. Magbaily Fyle. Dakar: Codesria, 1993: 99–112.

———. "The Informal Sector Metal Working Industry." In *Training Opportunities in the Informal Sector of Freetown in Sierra Leone*. Adult Education and Development (Supplement). Bonn, 237, 1991: 27–48.

———. "Learning for Earning: The Training of Blacksmiths in Rural Sierra Leone." Adult Education and Development, Bonn, 32 (March 1989): 71–86.

———. "African Culture and Higher Education: The Sierra Leone Experience." In *Educafrica: Case Studies on Higher Education in Africa.* Dakar: UNESCO, 1987: 237–244.

———. "Crisis of Relevance: Cultural Studies and Development in Sierra Leone." *Pen and Hoe, A Journal of the PEA of Sierra Leone* 4, 1987: 22–37.

———. "Culture, Technology and Policy in the Informal Sector: Attention to Endogenous Development." *In Sierra Leone, 1787–1987*. London: International African Institute 1987: 498–509.

———. *Tradition, Song and Chant of the Yalunka.* People's Educational Association of Sierra Leone, 1986.

———. "The Limba." In *Muslim Peoples: A World Ethnographic Survey*, ed. R. V. Weeks. Westport, CT: Greenwood Press, 1985.

———. "The Soso." In *Muslim Peoples: A World Ethnographic Survey*, ed. R. V. Weeks. Westport, CT: Greenwood, 1985.

———. "The West Atlantic Coast: Cultural Convergence and Diversity in Sierra Leone and Liberia." In *Distinctive Characteristics and Common Features of African Cultural Areas South of the Sahara*. Paris: UNESCO, 1985.

———. "Fula Diaspora: The Sierra Leone Experience." *Africana Research Bulletin* 13, 3, 1984.

———. *Traditional Technology, Rural Development and the Cultural Matrix: The Case of Sierra Leone. The Africanus Horton Memorial Lecture, University of Edinburgh.* Edinburgh: University of Edinburgh, African Studies Centre, 1981.

———. "The Economic and Social Content of Some Traditional Technological Activities in Sierra Leone." In *Traditional Technology and Modern West Africa*, ed. Arthur Abraham. Freetown: Proceedings of the West African Aggrey Society Conference, 1979.

———. "Segmentation and Succession in Upper Guinea." *Africana Research Bulletin* 4, 1, 1974.

———. "A Note on 'Country' in Political Anthropology." *Africana Research Bulletin* 3, 1, 1972.

Fyle, Clifford. "Krio Ways of Thought and Expression." *Africana Research Bulletin* 2, 4, 1972.

———. "Beginning and Final Themes in the Krio Sentence." *Africana Research Bulletin* 1, 1, 1970.

Fyle, Clifford, and E. D. Jones. *Krio–English Dictionary*. Oxford: Oxford University Press, 1980.

Gage, Anastasia J., and Caroline Bledsoe. "The Effects of Education and Social Stratification on Marriage and the Transition to Parenthood in Freetown, Sierra Leone." In *Nuptiality in Sub-Saharan Africa: Contemporary Anthropological and Demographic Perspectives*, ed. C. Bledsoe and G. Pison. Oxford: Clarendon Press, 1994.

Gbakima, Aiah A. "How Can the Educational Services in Sierra Leone be Rescued?" *Sierra Leone Studies and Review* 1, no. 1, 2000.

Gbomba, Lele. *The Bossy Wife*. Freetown: People's Educational Association, 1987.

German Adult Education, Sierra Leone and University Research and Development Services Bureau, University of Sierra Leone. *Training Opportunities in the Informal Sector of Freetown in Sierra Leone*. Supplement to *Adult Education and Development* 37, 1991.

Gervis, G. "Koidu, Sierra Leone's Second City." In *Shelter in Africa*, ed. P. Oliver. London: Barrie and Jenkins, 1971.

Giorgi, Gello. *La Societa Segreta del Poro: Sierra Leone. (The Secret Society of the Poro: Sierra Leon)*. Bologna: EMI, 1977.

Gleave, M. B. "Population Redistribution in Sierra Leone." In *Redistribution of Population in Africa*, ed. J. I. Clarke and L. A. Kosinski. London: Heinemann, 1982: 79–84.

———. "Changing Population Distribution in Sierra Leone, 1974–85." *Geography* 188 (Oct. 1973): 351–4.

Government of Sierra Leone. *Sierra Leonean Heroes: Fifty Great Men and Women Who Helped to Build Our Nation*. London: Commonwealth Printers, 1988.

Gower, Tess. *Art of the Mende from Sierra Leone: The Guy Massie–Taylor Collection*. Glasgow: Glasgow Museums and Art Galleries, 1980.

Gwebu, T. D. "Population Change Determinants in an Early Transitional Society: The Western Area Sierra Leone Example." *Geografiska Annaler* 61, 1979: 91–102.

Gwynne-Jones, D. R. G., P. K. Mitchell, M. E. Harvey, and K. Swindell. *A New Geography of Sierra Leone.* London, Longman, 1978.

Hancock, I. "Manding Lexical Behavior in Sierra Leone Krio." In *Current Approaches to African Linguistics*, ed. I. R. Dihoff. Dordrecht: Foris Publications, 1983.

Harbach, Heinz. "Occupational Stratification in Freetown." *Africana Research Bulletin* 4, 1, 1973.

Hardin, Kris L. *The Aesthetics of Action: Continuity and Change in a West African Town*. Washington, DC: Smithsonian Institution Press, 1992.

Harrel-Bond, Barbara. *"Morality," Class Interests and the Population Dilemma: The Sierra Leone Case.* Warwick: University of Warwick, Legal Research Institute of the School of Law, 1981.

——. *Modern Marriage in Sierra Leone. A Study of the Professional Group*. The Hague: Mouton, 1975.

Harrel-Bond, B., and U. Rijnsdorp. "The Emergence of the 'Stranger-Permit Marriage' and Other Forms of Conjugal Union in Rural Sierra Leone." *Africana Research Bulletin* 6, 4, 1976.

——. *Family Law in Sierra Leone: A Research Report*. Leiden, Holland: Afrika Studiecentrum, 1975.

Hart, W. A. "Woodcarving of the Limba of Sierra Leone." *African Arts* 23, no. 1, 1989: 44–53.

Harvey, M. E. "The Nature and Movement of the Population [in Sierra Leone]." In *Population Growth and Socioeconomic Change in West Africa,* ed. J. C. Caldwell. New York: Columbia University Press, 1975.

——."Social Change and Ethnic Relocation in Developing Africa: The Sierra Leone Example." *Geografiska annaler, ser. B. Human geography* 53, 2, 1971: 94–106.

Harvey, M. E., and J. B. Riddell. "The Urban System in the Migration Process: An Evaluation of Step-Wise Migration in Sierra Leone." *Economic Geography* 48, 3, 1972: 270–283.

Hill, M. H. "Where to Begin? The Place of the Hunter Founder in Mende Histories." *Anthropos* 79: 653–6.

——. "Towards a Cultural Sequence for Southern Sierra Leone." *Africana Research Bulletin* 1, 2, 1971.

Hinzen, Heribert. *Salia Koroma: My Life Story*. Freetown: People's Educational Association, 1985.

——. "African Traditional Pedagogy and Adult Education: A Plea for Reconciliation and Integration in Sierra Leone." *Pen and Hoe, A Journal of the PEA of Sierra Leone* 3, 1986: 17–29.

Hinzen, Heribert, ed. *Fishing in the Rivers of Sierra Leone: Oral Literature*. Freetown: People's Educational Association of Sierra Leone, 1987.

Hoffer, Carol. "Mende and Sherbro Women in High Office." *Canadian Journal of African Studies* 6, no. 2, 1972.

Holmes, Patricia. *Broadcasting in Sierra Leone*. Lanham, MD. University Press of America, 1999.

Innes, G. *A Mende–English Dictionary*. Cambridge: Cambridge University Press, 1969. Institut Fondamental d'Afrique Noire. *Le Massif des monts Loma (Sierra*

Leone). Dakar: Memoires de l'Institut Fondamental d'Afrique Noire, no. 86, 1971.

Jackson, M. *In Sierra Leone.* Durham, NC: Duke University Press, 2004.

——. *Paths Towards a Clearing: Radical Empiricism and Ethnographic Enquiry.* Bloomington, IN: Indiana University Press, 1989.

——. *Barawa and the Ways Birds Fly in the Sky: An Ethnographic Novel.* Washington, DC: Smithsonian Institution Press, 1986.

——. *Allegories of the Wilderness: Ethics and Ambiguity in Kuranko Narratives.* Bloomington: Indiana University Press, 1982.

——. *The Kuranko: Dimensions of Social Reality in a West African Tribe.* New York: St. Martins, 1977.

James, Frederic Bobor. *The Weaver Birds.* Freetown: People's Educational Association, 1986.

James, Frederic Bobor, and S. A. T. Tamu. *A Biography of P. C. B. A. Foday-Kai.* Freetown: People's Educational Association, 1992.

James, F. B. "Traditional Education among the Mende in Sierra Leone: Oral Tradition." *Pen and Hoe, A Journal of the PEA of Sierra Leone* 3, 1986: 30–37.

Jarrett, A. A. "The Encroachment of Rural–Urban Migration in Sierra Leone." *International Social Work* 33, 1 (Jan. 1990): 49–73.

Jedrej, M. C. Structural Aspects of a West African Secret Society. *Ethnologie Zeitschrift* 1, 1980: 133–142.

John, G. J. "Sierra Leone Population Policy—Status Report." *PopLeone* 1, 1, 1984: 2–4.

John, J. T. "Village Music in Sierra Leone." *West African Review* 23, 1952: 1043, 1045, 1071.

Jones, Eldred D., ed. *Reading and Writing Krio.* Proceedings of a workshop held at the Institute of Public Administration and Management, University of Sierra Leone. Stockholm, Sweden: Uppsala, 1992.

Jusufu, Abu. *Love, Women and Men in Stories from Mendeland.* Freetown: People's Educational Association, 1986.

Kaindaneh, Peter. "State Provision of Transport and Communication Services in Sierra Leone." In *The State and the Provision of Social Services in Sierra Leone since Independence*, ed. C. Magbaily Fyle. Dakar: Codesria, 1993: 20–43.

Kallon Abdulai, Heribert Hinzen, and A. Tamu. *Manday Faborie and other Mandingo Stories and Songs.* Freetown: People's Educational Association, 1988.

Kalous, Milan. *Cannibals and Tongo Players of Sierra Leone.* Auckland: Milan Kalous, 1975.

Kamara Iyesha. "The Education of Chiefs and Traditional Birth Attendants in the Magbema Chiefdom, Kambia District." *Pen and Hoe, A Journal of the PEA of Sierra Leone* 3, 1986.

Kamara, James N. *Firewood Energy in Sierra Leone: Production, Marketing and Household Use Patterns.* Hamburg: Verlag Weltarchiv, 1986.

Kamara, Sheikh Gibril. *The Spirit of Badenia.* London: Minerva Press, 1996.

Kamarah, Sheik Umarr. "The Individual and Society: Political Philosophy in the Themne Proverb." *SALSAR* 1, no. 1, 2000.

Kande, Sylvie. *Terres, Urbanisme et Architecture 'Creoles' en Sierra Leone, VIIIe–Ie Siècles.* Paris: L'Harmattan, 1998.

Kandeh, H. B. "Population Growth in Sierra Leone during the Intercensal Period (1974–1985)." *PopLeone (Freetown)* 3, 5, 1986: 4–8.

Kannisto, V., T. Makannah, D. C. Mehta, and J. McWilliam. *Civil Registration and Vital Statistics in the Africa Region: Lessons Learned from the Evaluation of UNFPA-Assisted Projects,* 1984.

Kaplan, Robert D. *The Ends of the Earth: A Journey to the Frontiers of Anarchy.* New York: Vintage Books, 1997.

Kargbo, Thomas K. "Traditional Midwifery in Sierra Leone." In *African Medicine in the Modern World*, ed. Una Maclean and Christopher Fyfe. Edinburgh: Center of African Studies, University of Edinburgh, 1987: 87–113.

Kastenholz, Raimund. *Materialien zum Koranko: (Sierra Leone, Zentral–Mande): Glossar Koranko-Deutsch.* Köln: Institut für Afrikanistik, Universität zu Köln, 1987.

Ketkar, S. L. "Socioeconomic Determinants of Family Size in Sierra Leone." *Rural Africana* 6, 1979: 25–45.

Kilson, Marion. *Royal Antelope and Spider: West African Mende Tales*. Cambridge, Mass: Press of the Langdon Associates, 1976.

Kline, P. M., and E. Mone. "Coping with War: Three Strategies Employed by Adolescent Citizens of Sierra Leone." *Child and Adolescent Social Work Journal* 20, 5 (Oct. 2003): 321–333.

Knoerr, Jacqueline. "Female Secret Societies and Their Impact on Ethnic and Trans-Ethnic Identities among Migrant Women in Freetown, Sierra Leone." In *Women and Migration: Anthropological Perspectives*, ed. Jacqueline Knorr and Barbara Meier. New York: St. Martin's, 2000.

———. "Freetown." In *Encyclopedia of Urban Cultures, Cities and Cultures around the World*, ed. M. Danbury and C. R. Ember. Danbury, CT: Published under the Auspices of the Human Relations Area Files at Yale University, 2002.

Koroma, B. M. "Inferiority Complex: A Deterrence to Development in Sierra Leone and Sub-Saharan Africa." *SALSAR* 1, no. 1, 2000.

Koroma, Salia. *The Spider's Web*. Freetown: People's Educational Association 1986.

Koroma, Salia. *Kasilo Landoi (Haala Bukui)*. Freetown: People's Educational Association, 1986.

Kposowa, A. J. "The Effects of Opportunities and Cultural Difference on Interregional Migration in Sierra Leone." *African Urban Quarterly* 2, 4, 1987: 378–397.

Lamb, Venice, and Alistair Lamb. *Sierra Leone Weaving*. Hertsfordshire: Roford Books, 1984.

Lamp, Fred. "Frogs into Princes: The Temne Rabai Initiation." *African Arts* 9, no. 2, 1978.

———. "Cosmos, Cosmetics and the Spirit of Bondo." *African Arts* 18, no. 3, 1985.

Last, Murray, ed. *Sierra Leone 1787–1987: Two Centuries of Intellectual Life*. Manchester: Manchester University Press in association with *Africa*, Journal of the International African Institute, 1987.

Leach, Melissa A. *Rainforest Relations: Gender and Resource Use among the Mende of Gola, Sierra Leone*. IAI, International African Library, Edinburgh: Edinburgh University Press, 1994.

———. *Dealing with Displacement: Refugee-Host Relations, Food and Forest Resources in Sierra Leonean Mende Communities during the Liberian Influx, 1990–1991*. Brighton, Susse: University of Sussex, Institute of Development Studies, 1992.

———. "Environmental Impacts of Refugees: Liberians in Sierra Leone." *Refugee Studies Programme Newsletter*, Oxford: Queen Elizabeth House, 1992.

Leach, Melissa. "Shifting Social and Ecological Mosaics in Mende Upland Farming." In *The Ecology of Practice: Food Production Systems in West Africa*, ed. E. Nyerges. New York: Lynne Reiner, 1997.

———. "Women's Crops in Women's Spaces: Gender Relations in Mende Rice Farming." In *Bush, Base, Forest, Farm: Culture Environment and Development*, ed. E. Croll and D. Parkin. London: Routledge, 1992.

———. "Delta and Village Level Planning in Sierra Leone: Possibilities and Pitfalls." *RRA Notes* 11, London: IIED, 1991.

———. "Social Organization and Agricultural Innovation: Women's Vegetable Production in Eastern Sierra Leone." In *Peasant Household Systems: Partners in the Process of Development*, ed. H. de Haen. Germany: DSE, 1991.

———. "Women's Use of Forest Resources in Sierra Leone." In *Women and the Environment*, ed. A. Rodda. London: Zed Press, 1991.

———. "Locating Gendered Experience: An Anthropologist's View from a Sierra Leonean Village." Sussex, Institute of Development Studies. *IDS Bulletin* 22, no. 1, 1991.

———. "The Politics of Palm Oil in a Mende village." Freetown, Fourah Bay College, *ARB* 14, nos. 1 & 2, 1989.

Leach, M., and J. Fairhead. "Culturing Trees: The Political Ecology of Kissi and Kuranko Forest Islands." *In Nature is Culture: Indigenous Knowledge and Socio-Cultural Aspects of Trees and Forests in Non-European Cultures*, ed. K. Seeland. London: IT Publications, 1998.

Lebbie, Alpha. "Traditional Methods of Fishing among the Mendes of Sierra Leone in Pre–Colonial Times." *Pen and Hoe, A Journal of the PEA of Sierra Leone* 4, 1987.

Lucan, Talabi Aisie. *The Life and Times of Paramount Chief Madam Ella Koblo Gulama.* Freetown: Sierra Leone Association of Writers and Illustrators, 2003.

———. "Population Education in Sierra Leone." *Educafrica: Bulletin of the UNESCO Regional Office for Education in Africa (BREDA)* 12 1985: 99–110.

MacCormack, Carol. "Sande: The Public Face of a Secret Society." In *The New Religions of Africa*, ed. N. Jules-Rosette. Norwood, NJ: Able Publishing, 1979.

———. "The Compound Head: Structure and Strategies." *Africana Research Bulletin* 6, 4, 1976.

Makannah, Toma J. "Some Aspects of the Methodology of the 1974 Population Census of Sierra Leone." *Africana Research Bulletin* 7, 1, 1976.

Makannah, T. J. *Handbook of the population of Sierra Leone.* Freetown: Toma Enterprises, 1996.

Makannah, T. J., and M. Bailey. "Sierra Leone." In *Urbanization in Africa: A Handbook*, ed. J. D. Tarver. Westport, CT: Greenwood Press, 1994: 298–314.

Margai, Milton. "Welfare Work in a Secret Society." *African Affairs* 47, 1948: 227–230.

May-Parker, Judith. *Out-of-School Programmes for Girls and Young Women in Sierra Leone.* New York: United Nations Economic and Social Council, 1981.

M'bayo, Richard T., and Matt Mogekwu. "Political Authority and the Transformation of the Sierra Leone Press." In *Press and Politics in Africa*, ed. Richard Tamby Mbayo. Lewiston, NY: Edwin Mellen, 2000.

Milburn, S. "Kisimi Kamara and the Mende Script." *Sierra Leone Language Review* 3, 1964.

Minikin, A. V., and P. K. Mitchell. "Demography and Politics in Kenema and Makeni, Sierra Leone." *Pan-African Journal* 4, 1, 1971: 22–34.

Muana, J. L. "The Implicatons of Migration." *PopLeone (Freetown)* 3, 5, 1986: 4–7.

Muana, J. L., and I. S. Njai. "Sierra Leone." In *Urban and Regional Planning and Development in the Commonwealth.* Sleaford, Lincolnshire: Howell Publications, 1988: 68–74.

Ndedewai, S., Ernest Bombor, and S. A. Temu. *Klo Klo Lo a Njave* (Little Drops of Water Flood the River). Freetown: People's Educational Association, 1990.

Ngaboh-Smart, Francis. *Mende Story Telling*. Freetown: People's Educational Association, 1986.

Nicol, E. P. *A Brief History of St. Mark's Church (Countess of Huntingdon's Connexion), Waterloo, Sierra Leone*. Aberdeen, Scotland: University of Aberdeen, Dept. of Church History, 1970.

Nunley, John. *Moving with the Face of the Devil: Art and Politics in Urban West Africa*. Urbana: University of Illinois Press, 1987.

Nyankume, Manty. *The Hunter*. Freetown: People's Educational Association, 1987.

Odile, Georg. "Sierra Leonais, Creoles, Krio. La dialèctique de l'identité." *Africa*, International African Institute. 65, no. 1, 1995.

Okoye, C. S. *An Analysis of the Sierra Leone 1974 Population Census Data.* Vol. 4. Freetown: Central Statistics Office, 1981.

———. "Migration in Sierra Leone." In *Demographic Aspects of Migration in West Africa,* vol. 1, ed. K. C. Zachariah and J. Conde. Washington, DC: World Bank 1980.

Opala, Joseph A. *Ecstatic Renovation: Street Art Celebrating Sierra Leone's 1992 Revolution.* Freetown: Sierra Leone: Adult Education Association, 1992.

——. *The Gullah: Rice, Slavery and the Sierra Leone–American Connection*. Freetown: Sierra Leone, USIS, 1986.

Organization of African Unity. *Some Names and Place Names in Mende Society (Sierra Leone).* Niamey, Niger: Centre for Linguistic and Historical Studies by Oral Tradition, 1980.

——. *Echoes from Sierra Leone*. Addis Ababa: Organization of Africa Unity Political Department, 1997.

Ottenberg, Simon. *Seeing with Music: The Lives of Three Blind Musicians*. Seattle: University of Washington Press, 1996.

——. "Artistic and Sex Roles in a Limba Chiefdom." In *Female and Male in West Africa*, ed. Christine Oppong, 76–90. London, Allen and Unwin, 1983.

——. "The Bride Comes to the Groom: Ritual and Drama in Limba Weddings." *The Drama Review* 32, no. 2, 1988: 42–62.

——. *Boyhood Rituals in an African Society: An Interpretation*. Seattle: University of Washington Press, 1989.

——. "The Dancing Bride: Art and Indigenous Psychology in Limba Weddings." *Man* 24, 1989: 57–78.

——. "The Beaded Bands of Bafodea." *African Arts* 25, no. 2, 1992: 98–99.

——. "One Face of a Culture: Two Musical Ensembles in a Limba Chiefdom, Sierra Leone." In *Carrefour de cultures: Mélanges offerts à Jacqueline Leiner*, ed. Regis Antoine, 57–75. Études Littéraires Françaises, no. 55. Tubingen: Éditions Gunter Narr.

——. "Male and Female Secret Societies among the Bafodea Limba of Northern Sierra Leone." In *Religion in Africa: Experience and Expression*, ed. Thomas D. Blakely, Walter van Beek and Dennis L. Thomson. London: James Curry, 1994: 363–87.

——. "Religion and Ethnicity in the Arts of a Limba Chiefdom." *Africa* 58, 4, 1988: 437–465.

Oyelude, Dosu. *The Press in West-Africa: Ghana, Liberia, Nigeria, Sierra Leone, The Gambia.* Brussels: International Federation of Journalists, 1974.

Pemagbie, J. *Guide to Mende Orthography*. Freetown: Sierra Leone Adult Education Association, 1991.

Peoples Educational Association of Sierra Leone. *Bras, Grens and Ballheads: Interviews with Freetown 'Street Boys.'* Freetown: People's Educational Association of Sierra Leone (PEA), 1989.

Phillips, R. B. "Masking in Mende Sande Society Initiation Rituals." *Africa* 48, 1978: 265–277.

Reeck, Darrell L. "Education and National Development: Church, Schools or Christian Teachers in Sierra Leone." *Africana Research Bulletin* 1, 4, 1971.

Reinhardt, Loretta. *Mrs. Kadiatu Kamaran: An Expert Dyer in Sierra Leone*. Chicago: Field Museum of Natural History, 1976.

Richards, Josephus V. O. *Factors of Limitation in the Art Forms of the Bundu Society of the Mende in Sierra Leone*. Evanston, IL: Northwestern University Press, 1970.

Richards, J. V. O. "The Sande: A Socio-Cultural Organization in the Mende Community in Sierra Leone." *Baessler-Archiv* 22, 1974: 265–81.

Richards, Paul. "Soccer and Violence in War-Torn Africa: Soccer and Social Rehabilitation in Sierra Leone." In *Entering the Field: New Perspectives on World Football*, ed. Gary Armstrong and Richard Giulianotti. Oxford, England: Berg, 1997.

———. "Chimpanzees, Diamonds and War: The Discourses of Global Environmental Change and Local Violence on the Liberia–Sierra Leone Border." In *The Changing Nature of Anthropological Knowledge*, ed. H. Moore. London, Routledge, 1996.

———. "Local Understandings of Primates and Evolution: Some Mende Beliefs Concerning Chimpanzees." In *Ape, Man, Apeman: Changing Views Since 1600*, ed. R. Corbey and B. Theunissen. Leiden: Department of Prehistory, Leiden University, 1995.

———. "Natural Symbols and Natural History: Chimpanzees, Elephants and Experiments in Mende Thought." In *Environmentalism: The View from Anthropology*, ed. K. Milton. London: Routledge, 1993.

———. "Africa in the Music of Samuel Coleridge-Taylor," In *Sierra Leone 1787–1987*. London, International African Institute, 1987: 566–571.

Riddell, J. Barry. *The Spatial Dynamics of Modernization in Sierra Leone: Structure, Diffusion and Response*. Evanston, IL: Northwestern University Press, 1970.

Riddell, J. B., and M. E. Harvey. "The Urban System in the Migration Process: An Evaluation of Step-Wise Migration in Sierra Leone." *Economic Geography* 48, 3, 1972: 270–83.

Rogers, Braima. *Love without Questions*. Freetown: People's Educational Association, 1986.

Rosen, David M. "Some Aspects of the Status of Women in Kono Society." *Africana Research Bulletin* 2, 1, 1971.

Safilios-Rothschild, Constantina. *The Persistence of Women's Invisibility in Agriculture: Theoretical and Policy Lessons from Lesotho and Sierra Leone*. New York, Population Council, Working Paper no. 88, 1982.

Samura, Bokarie, and Heribert Hinzen. *Ngbanni Mene na Kukuna Ka Hulimba Han*. Freetown: People's Educational Association, 1986.

Sarif, Brigitte B. *Educational Efficiency Demonstrated on the GCE 'O' Level Examination Results in Sierra Leone.* Frankfurt: Verlag für Interkuturelle Kommunikattion, 1989.

Sarif, G. J. *Population Development in Sierra Leone.* Frankfurt, Germany: Verlag fur Interkuturelle Kommunikation, 1989.

Sawyerr, Harry. *God, Ancestor or Creator? Aspects of Traditional Belief in Ghana, Nigeria and Sierra Leone.* Harlow: Longmans, 1970.

Selected Women's Programmes in Sierra Leone: A Handbook. Prepared by the Women's Commission in Adult Education. Freetown: A SLADEA Publication, 1989?

Sengova, J. "The National Languages of Sierra Leone: A Decade of Policy Experimentation." *Africa* 57, 1987: 519–530.

——. "The National Languages of Sierra Leone: A Decade of Policy Experimentation." In *Sierra Leone 1787–1987.* London, International African Institute, 1987: 519–530.

Sesay, Bai Bai. "From Guns to Mobile Phones: Calling for Change in Sierra Leone." *Review of African Political Economy* 3, 99, 2004: 128–130.

Sesay, I. M. "Migration and Urban Growth in Sierra Leone and Policy Options for the 1990s." *Nairobi, Kenya: Union of African Population, Spontaneous Papers of the Conference on the Role of Migration in African Development*. 24–28, February, 1990. Dakra: AUPS, 1991.

Shaw, Rosalind. *Memories of the Slave Trade: Ritual and Historical Imagination in Sierra Leone.* Chicago: University of Chicago Press, 2002.

——. "'Tok Af, lef Af': A Political Economy of Temne Techniques of Secrecy and Self." In *African Philosophy as Cultural Inquiry*, ed. Ivan Karp and D. Masolo. Bloomington: Indiana University Press, 2000.

Shawcross, William. *Deliver Us from Evil. Warlords and Peacekeepers in a World of Endless Conflict*. London: Bloomsbury, 2000.

Showers, Charles. *Wildlife and Nature Reserves of Sierra Leone*. Freetown: Conservation Society of Sierra Leone, 1993.

Shrimpton, Neville. "Thomas Decker and the Death of Boss Coker." Africa 57, no. 4, 1987: 531–45.

Siegmann, William. "Women's Hair and Sowei Masks in Southern Sierra Leone and Western Liberia." In *Hair in African Art and Culture,* ed. Roy Siber and Frank Herreman. New York: Museum for African Art, 2000.

Sievers, Bernhard. *Musik in Sierra Leone: Tradition, Wandel und Identitäts–verlust einer Musikkultur in West-Afrika*. Münster: Lit Verlag, Musikm-ethnologie Band I, 1992.

Simpson, D. "A Reply to Minikin and Mitchell: The Kenema and Makeni Discussion." *Pan African Journal* 4, 1, 1971: 22–34.

Smillie, Ian, Lansana Gberie, and Ralph Hazleton. *The Heart of the Matter: Sierra Leone, Diamonds and Human Security*. Ontario: Partnership Africa/Canada Publication, 2000.

Stevens, Siaka P. *What Life Has Taught Me.* London: Kensal Press, 1984.

Stuart, L., Palmer E. J., and E. Holt, eds. *Sierra Leone Education Review; All Our Future: Final Report*. Freetown: University of Sierra Leone, 1976.

Sumner, D. T. *Education in Sierra Leone*. Freetown: Sierra Leone: Government Printer, 1963.

Swindell, K. "The Distribution of Age and Sex Characteristics in Sierra Leone and Their Relevance to a Study of Internal Migration." *Tijdschrift voor Economische en Social Geografie* 41, 6, 1970: 366–73.

——. "The Provision of Secondary Education and Migration to School in Sierra Leone." *Sierra Leone Geographical Journal* 14, 1970: 10–19.

Tagliaferri, Aldo, and A. Hammacher. *Fabulous Ancestors: Stone Carvings from Sierra Leone & Guinea.* New York: Africana, 1974.

Tamu, Ahmed T. *Folk Media, Theatre for Development and Non-Formal Education: A Case Study of CARE's Project 'Learn' in the Pujehun District*. Freetown: People's Educational Association, 1985.

Taussig, Louis. "Milton Margai and Adult Education in Sierra Leone." *Africana Research Bulletin* 8, 2 & 3, 1978.

Thayer, James S. "Some Remarks on Informal Social Networks among the Soso of Sierra Leone." *Africana Research Bulletin* 9, 1 & 2, 1978.

Thomas, Armand C. *The Population of Sierra Leone: An Analysis of Population Census Data*. Freetown: Demographic Research and Training Unit, Fourah Bay College, 1983.

Toure, Masee. *Bai Bureh's Countrymen*. London: Janus, 1995.

Turay, A. K. *Temne Stories*. Trans. Wilhelm J. G. Möhlig. Köln, Rudiger Köppe Verlag, 1989.

——. "Nigerian Pidgin and Sierra Leone Krio: Part I, Leical." *Africana Research Bulletin* 9, 3, 1979.

——. "A Vocabulary of Temne Musical Instruments." *Sierra Leone Language Review* 5, 1966: 27–33.

Turay, E. D. A. *Adult Education in Sierra Leone c. 1870–1939*. Freetown: Institute of Adult Education and Extra-Mural Studies, Fourah Bay College, 1986.

——. "Missionary Work and African Society: James Booth in Tonko Limba." *Africana Research Bulletin* 8, 2 & 3, 1978.

Van Oven, Cootje. *An Introduction to the Music of Sierra Leone*. Self published. Freetown: Government Printer, 1981.

——. "Sierra Leone." In *The New Grove Dictionary of Music and Musicians*, ed. Stanley Sadie. London: Macmillan, 1980: 302–304.

——. "The Kondi of Sierra Leone." *African Music* 5, no. 3, 1973–74: 77–85.

——. "Music of Sierra Leone." *African Arts* 3, no. 4, 1970: 20–27.

Viditz-Ward, Vera. *Paramount Chiefs of Sierra Leone: Photographic Portraits by Vera Viditz–Ward.* Washington, DC: Museum of African Art, 1990.

——. "Photography in Sierra Leone, 1850–1918." *Africa,* 57, 4: 1987: 510–518.

Walton, M. "Introduction to 'History of Bo School'." *Africana Research Bulletin* 5, 3, 1975.

Williams, Raymond R. "Send Me a Love Sign" and Nineteen Other Love Poems." Peoples Educational Association of Sierra Leone, 1986.

Wilson, Richard. "Children and War in Sierra Leone: A West African Diary." *Anthropology Today,* 17, 5 (Oct. 2001): 20–22.

Women of Sierra Leone: Traditional Voices. Freetown: A Publication of the Partners in Adult Education Women's Commission, sponsored by DVV, January, 1992.

Women's Commission in Adult Education. *Selected Women's Programmes in Sierra Leone: A Handbook*. Freetown: SLADEA, 1991.

Wright, S. V. *Foundations of Parliamentary Democracy in Sierra Leone: My Memories of Parliament*. Redi Publications, 2000.

Wurie, A. "A History of Bo School." *Africana Research Bulletin* 5, 3, 1975.

Young, W. C. E. "Highlights of the 1964/65 Statistics of Education." *Sierra Leone Journal of Education* 2, no. 1, 1967.

RELIGION

Avery, W. L. "Christianity in Sierra Leone." *Africana Research Bulletin* 2, 2, 1972.

Cox, Emmett D. *The Church of the United Brethren in Christ in Sierra Leone*. Pasadena, CA: William Carey Library, 1970.

D'Alisera, JoAnn "I Love Islam: Popular Religious Commodities, Sites of Inscription and Transnational Sierra Leonean Identity." *Journal of Material Culture* 6, no. 1, 2001: 89–108.

Fisher, H. J. "The Modernization of Islamic Education in Sierra Leone, Gambia and Liberia: Religion and Language." In *Conflict and Harmony in African Education in Tropical Africa*, ed. G.N. Brown and M. Hiskett, London: Allen and Unwin, 1975.

Foss, David B. "The Task of the Church Missionary Society in Post-Colonial Sierra Leone." *Africana Research Bulletin* 4, 2, 1974.

Fyle, C. Magbaily, and I. Heroe. "Krio Traditional Beliefs." *Africana Research Bulletin* 7, 3, 1977.

Gamble, David P. "Temne Witchcraft Beliefs in Rural and Urban Settings in Sierra Leone." *Africana Research Bulletin* 6, 4, 1974.

———. "Traditional Temne Beliefs and the Introduction of New Rice Varieties in Sierra Leone." *Africana Research Bulletin* 6, 3, 1973.

Gittins, Anthony J. *Mende Religion: Aspects of Belief and Thought in Sierra Leone*. Nettetal, Germany: Steyler Verlag-Wort und Werk, 1987.

Jackson, M. "Structure and Event: Witchcraft Confession among the Kuranko." *Man*, n.s., 10, 1975: 387–403.

Jackson, M. "Sacrifice and Social Structure among the Kuranko," Parts 1, 2, and 3. *Africa* 47, 1977: 41–49, 123–139.

Jackson, M. "An Approach to Kuranko Divination." *Human Relations* 31, 1978: 117–138.

Jedrej, M. C. "Medicine, Fetish and Secret Society in a West African Culture." *Africa* 46, 1976: 247–257.

Parsons, R. T. *Religion in an African Society*. Leiden, Holland: E. J. Brill, 1964.

Reeck, Darrell L. "Innovators in Religion and Politics in Sierra Leone, 1875–1896." *International Journal of African Historical Studies* 4, 1972.

Sawyerr, H. A. E. *God: Ancestor or Creator? Aspects of Belief in Ghana, Nigeria and Sierra Leone*. London: Longmans, 1970.

Shaw, Rosalind. "Dreaming as Accomplishment: Power, the Individual and Temne Divination." In *Dreaming, Religion and Society in Africa*, ed. M.C. Jedrej and Rosalind Shaw. New York: E. J. Brill, 1992.

———. "Splitting Truths from Darkness: Epistemological Aspects of Temne Divination." In *African Divination Systems: Ways of Knowing*, ed. P. Peek. Bloomington: Indiana University Press, 1991.

———. "Gender and Structuring of Reality in Temne Divination." *Africa* 55, 1985.

———. "*An bere*: A Traditional Form of Temne Divination." *Africana Research Bulletin* 9, 1 & 2, 1978.

Steady, Filomena. "Protestant Women's Associations in Freetown Sierra Leone." In *Women in Africa: Studies in Social and Economic Change*, ed. J. Hafkin and Edna Bay. Palo Alto, CA: Stanford University Press, 1976: 213–37.

Thayer, J. S. "Nature, Culture and the Supernatural among the Susu." *American Ethnologist* 10, 1983: 116–132.

Thomas, A. C. "Sierra Leone." In *Population Size in African Countries: An Evaluation.* Vol. 1. Paris: Groupe de Demographie Africaine 1986.

———. The *Population of Sierra Leone: An Analysis of Population Census Data*. Freetown: Fourah Bay College, Demographic Research and Training Unit, 1983.

Whitby, P. *Demographic Characteristics and Population Projections*. Freetown: FAO, 1968.

Winch, Julian M. " Religious Attitudes of the Mende Towards Land." *Africana Research Bulletin* 2, 1, 1971.

SCIENCE AND MEDICINE

Adegbola, Olukunle. *Issues in Population and Development in Sierra Leone. Ministry of National Development and Economic Planning, Freetown*. Geneva: International Labour Office, 1990.

Adegbola, O., O Babatola, and J. Oni. "Sexual Networking in Freetown against the Background of the AIDS Epidemic." *Health Transition Review* 1995: 81–112.

Aitken, I. W. "Determinants of Low Birth Weight among the Mendi of Sierra Leone: Implications for Medical and Socioeconomic Strategies." *International Journal of Gynaecology and Obstetrics* 33, 2, 1990: 103–9.

Aitken, I. W., T. K. Kargbo, and A. M. Gba-Kamara. "Planning a Community-Oriented Midwifery Service for Sierra Leone." *World Health Forum* 6, 2, 1985: 110–114.

Amin, R. "Contraceptive Use and Desire for More Children in Two Rural Districts of Sierra Leone." *Journal of Biosocial Science* 30, 3, 1998: 287–296.

———. "Immunization Coverage and Child Mortality in Two Districts of Sierra Leone." *Social Science and Medicine* 11, 1996: 1599–1604.

Amin R., R. B. Hill, S. A. T. Horton, C. Kamara, and C. Chowdhury. "Immunization Coverage, Infant Morbidity and Infant Mortality in Freetown, Sierra Leone." *Social Science and Medicine* 35, 7, 1992: 851–6.

Amin R., J. Chowdhury, and R. B. Hill. "Socioeconomic Differentials in Contraceptive Use and Desire for More Children in Greater Freetown, Sierra Leone." *International Family Planning Perspectives* 18, 1, 1992: 24–6.

Anonymous. *Sierra Leone, International Digest of Health Legislation* 30, 2, 1979: 359–60.

Awooner-Renner, Marilyn. *A Visual Geography of Sierra Leone*. London: Evans, 1987.

Bailey, M. "Determinants of Fertility in a Rural Society: Some Evidence from Sierra Leone." *Social Science and Medicine* 28, 3, 1989: 285–92.

———. "Female Education and Fertility in Rural Sierra Leone: A Test of the Threshold Hypothesis." *Canadian Studies in Population* 16, 1, 1989: 87–112.

———. "Individual and Environmental Influence on Infant and Child Mortality in Rural Sierra Leone: A Multivariate Analysis." *Journal of Population Studies* (Taiwan) 12, (June 1989): 155–85.

———. "Factors Affecting Infant and Child Mortality in Rural Sierra Leone." *Journal of Tropical Paediatrics* 34, 4, 1988: 165–8.

———. "Differential Fertility by Religious Group in Rural Sierra Leone." *Journal of Biosocial Science* 18, (Jan. 1986): 75–85.

Bailey, M., and W. J. Serow. "Fertility Differentials in Rural Sierra Leone: Demographic and Socioeconomic Effects." *Genus* LVII, no. 3, 1991: 171–82.

Bailey, M., and R. H. Weller. "Fertility Differentials in Rural Sierra Leone: A Path Analysis." *Journal of Developing Areas* 21, (Jan. 1987): 191–207.

Bell, Leland B. *Mental and Social Disorder in Sub-Saharan Africa: The Case of Sierra Leone, 1987–1990*. New York: Greenwood Press, 1991.

Boillot, F., M. Peters, A. Kosia, and E. Delaporte. "Prevalence of the Human Immunodeficiency Virus among Patients with Tuberculosis in Sierra Leone, Established From Dried Bloodspots on Filter Paper." *International Journal of Tuberculosis and Lung Disease* 6, 1997: 493–7.

Campbell, E. K. "A Note on the Fertility-Migration Interrelationship: The Case of the Western Area, Sierra Leone." *Demography–India*,18, 1–2 (Jan.–Dec. 1989): 103–114.

Caponera, Dante A., ed. *Water Law in Selected African Countries.* Rome: United Nations Food and Agriculture Organization, 1979.

Carney, D. "The Economics of Health in Conditions of Low Population Growth: The Example of Sierra Leone." *International Social Science Journal* 17, 1996: 277–283.

Cole, N. H. A. *The Vegetation of Sierra Leone*. Njala: Njala University College, 1968.

Cummings, E. C. "The Development of Health Services in Sierra Leone." In *The Demographic Transition in Tropical Africa*. Proceedings of an Expert Group Meeting, Paris, Nov. 1970. Paris: Development Centre of the O. E. C. D., 1971.

Dahniya, M. T. *Linking Science and the Farmer: Pillars of the National Agricultural Research System in Sierra Leone.* The Hague, Netherlands: International Service for the National Agricultural Research, 1993.

Devis, T. L. F. "Fertility Differentials among the Tribal Groups of Sierra Leone." *Population Studies* 27, 2, 1973: 501–14.

Dorjahn, V. R. "Temne Fertility, Rural Continuity, Urban Change, Rural-Urban Differences and Public Policy Problems." In *Culture and Reproduction: An Anthropological Critique of Demographic Transition Theory*, ed. W. Penn Handwerker. Boulder, CO: Westview Press, 1986.

Dow, T. E. "Some Observations on Family Planning Prospects in Sierra Leone." In *Population in African development*, vol. 2, ed. P. Cantrelle. Liege, Belgium: International Union for the Scientific Study of Population, 1974: 21–32.

——."Family Planning Patterns in Sierra Leone." *Studies in Family Planning* 2, 10, 1971: 211–222.

Dzegede, S. A. "Urbanization and Fertility Decline in West Africa: Ghana, Sierra Leone and Liberia." *Journal of Comparative Family Studies* 12, 2, 1981: 133–44.

Edwards, N. C., J. J. Birkett, and P. A. Sengeh. "Payment for Deliveries in Sierra Leone." *Bulletin of the World Health Organization* 67, 2, 1989: 163–9.

Edwards, N., and M. Lyons. "Community Assessment: A Tool for Motivation and Evaluation in Primary Health Care in Sierra Leone." In *Practising Health Care for All*, ed. D. Morley, J. E. Rohde, and G. Williams. Oxford: Oxford University Press, 1983: 101–13.

Fyle, C. Magbaily. "The State and Health Services in Sierra Leone" In *The State and the Provision of Social Services in Sierra Leone since Independence*, ed. C. Magbaily Fyle. Dakar: Codesria, 1993: 44–61.

Gale, Tom. "The Struggle against Disease in Sierra Leone: Early Sanitary Reform in Freetown." *Africana Research Bulletin* 6, 2, 1976.

Gbakima, Aiah A. "Strengthening Health and Medical Research Capacity in Sierra Leone." *Sierra Leone Studies and Review* 1, no. 1, 2000.

Gooding, E. C. "Infertility and Sexually Transmitted Diseases, Sierra Leone's Experience." *PopLeone* (Freetown) 1, 1, 1984: 16–19.

Gyepi-Garbrah, B. *Adolescent Fertility in Sierra Leone.* Boston, MA: Pathfinder Fund, 1985.

Hardiman, M., and J. Midley. "Social Planning and Access to Social Services in Developing Countries: The Case of Sierra Leone." *Third World Planning Review* 4, 1, 1982.

Harrell-Bond, B. "Some Influential Attitudes about Family Limitation and the Use of Contraceptives among the Professional Groups in Sierra Leone." In *Population Growth and Socioeconomic Change in West Africa*, ed. J.C. Caldwell. New York: Columbia University Press, 1975: 473–489.

Isaac, B. L. "Female Fertility and Marital Form among the Mende of Rural Upper Bambara Chiefdom, Sierra Leone." *Ethnology* 19, 5, 1980: 297–313.

Isaac B. L., and W. E. Feinberg. "Marital Form and Infant Survival among the Mende of Rural Upper Bambara Chiefdom, Sierra Leone." *Human Biology* 54, 3, 1982: 627–634.

Jambai, Amara, and Carol MacCormack. "Maternal Health, War and Religious Tradition: Authoritative Knowledge in Pujehun, Sierra Leone." In *Childbirth and Authoritative Knowledge: Cross-Cultural Perspectives*, ed. Robbie E. Davil-Floyd and Carolyn F. Sargent. Berkeley, CA: University of California Press, 1997.

Kandeh, H. B. S. "Spatial Variations in Infant and Child Mortality in Sierra Leone." *African Population Studies* 2, (March 1989): 18–36.

———. "Causes of Infant and Early Childhood Deaths in Sierra Leone." *Social Science and Medicine* 23, 3, 1986: 297–303.

———. "Some Aspects of Mortality in Sierra Leone." *PopLeone (Freetown)* 1, 1, 1984: 19–21.

Kandeh, H. B., B. Leigh, M. Kanu, J. Bangura, and A. L. Seisay. "Community Motivators Promote Use of Emergency Obstetric Services in Rural Sierra Leone." *International Journal of Gynecology and Obstetrics* 59, suppl. 2, (Nov. 1997): 209–218.

Ketkar, S. L. "Determinants of Fertility in a Developing Society: The Case of Sierra Leone." *Population Studies* 33, 3, 1979: 479–88.

———. "Female Education and Fertility in Sierra Leone: The Moving Target." In *Marriage, Fertility and Parenthood in West Africa*, ed. G. C. Oppong, G. Addis, M. Bekombo-Prinso, and J. Mogey. Canberra, Australia: Australian National University, 1978: 641–653.

———. "Female Education and Fertility: Some Evidence from Sierra Leone." *Journal of Developing Areas* 13, 1, 1978: 23–33.

Ketkar, S. L., and B. Singh. "Fertility and Household Characteristics: Some Evidence from Sierra Leone." *Journal of African Studies* 7, 4, 1980: 204–12.

Konteh, R. "Socio-economic and Other Variables Affecting Maternal Mortality in Sierra Leone." *Community Development Journal* 32, 1, 1997: 49–64.

Kruger, N. "Perinatal and Infant Mortality in Eastern Sierra Leone." *Offentliche Gesundheitswesen* 46, 1984: 504–6.

Lahai, F. S. "The Impact of Rapid Population Growth on the Nutrition Situation of the Populace." *PopLeone (Freetown)* 3, 5, 1986: 9–10.

Lahai-Momoh, J.C., and M. W. Ross. "HIV/AIDS Prevention–Related Social Skills and Knowledge among Adolescents in Sierra Leone, West Africa." *Journal of Reproductive Health* 1, 1, 1997: 37–44.

Lamin, M. M., and A. Singleton. "Adolescent Fertility Management: The Sierra Leone Experience." *Journal of Family Health Training* 1, 2, 1982: 22–5.

Leigh, B., H. B. Kandeh, M. S. Kanu, J. Kuteh, I. S. Palmer, K. S. Daoh, and F. Moseray. "Improving Emergency Obstetrics Care at a District Hospital Makeni, Sierra Leone." *International Journal of Gynecology and Obstetrics* 59, suppl, 2, 1997: 55–65.

Macauley, T. E. "Health Education Strategies for Sierra Leone." *PopLeone* 2, 3, 1985: 11–14.

MacCormack, C. P. "Primary Health Care in Sierra Leone." *Social Science and Medicine* 19, 3, 1984: 199–208.

MacCormack, C.P. "Health, Fertility and Birth in Moyamba District, Sierra Leone." In *Ethnography of Fertility and Birth*, ed. C.P. MacCormack. New York: Academic Press, 1982.

Makannah, T. J. "The Determinants of Infant Mortality in Sierra Leone." *In Sierra Leone Studies at Birmingham, 1988*, ed. P. Mitchell and A. Jones. Birmingham: University of Birmingham, Centre of West African Studies, 1990.

Marie Stopes International. *Emergency MCH and Reproductive Health Relief Services for Displaced People in Freetown, Sierra Leone.* London: Marie Stopes International, 1995.

Marshall, M., M. M. Hung, T. Johnson, and R. Monteith. *Evaluation of Training Component of Family Health Initiatives I Subproject in Sierra Leone: 1983–1986*. Arlington, VA: International Science and Technology Institute, Population Technical Assistance Project, 1987.

Massaquoi, J. G. M. "Salt-From-Silt in Sierra Leone." *Appropriate Technology* 16 no, 3, 1989.

——. *Salt Production and Trade in Sierra Leone*. UNICEF Consultancy Report. Freetown: UNICEF, 1939.

May, J. M., and D. L. McLellan. "Sierra Leone." In *The Ecology of Malnutrition in Eastern Africa and Four Countries of Western Africa*, ed. J. M. May and D. L. McLellan. New York: Hafner, 1970.

Morel, Stephen W. *The Geology and Minerals of Sierra Leone*. Freetown: Fourah Bay College Bookshop, 1976.

Moses, P. "HIV/AIDS in Sierra Leone." *AIDS Analysis Africa* 11, 3, (Oct.–Nov. 2000): 8–9.

Pathfinder Fund. *Adolescent Fertility in Sierra Leone: Health and Social Implications*. Boston, MA: The Pathfinder Fund, 1988.

Prudhon, C., A. Briend, D. Laurier, M. H. Golden, and J. Y. Mary. "Comparison of Weight and Height Based Indices for Assessing the Risk of Death in Severely Malnourished Children" [In Sierra Leone, Rwanda and Madagascar]. *American Journal of Epidemiology* 144, no. 2, 1966: 116–123.

Richter, D. L., R. W. Strack, M. L. Vincent, B. Barnes, and R. Rao. "Sexual and HIV/AIDS Related Knowledge Attitudes and Behaviours of Adolescents in Sierra Leone, West Africa." *International Quarterly of Community Health Education* 16, 4, 1997: 371–81.

Robbin Coker, D. J. Jalloh, and M. A. Jalloh. "Infant Feeding and Protein—Calorie Malnutrition in Freetown." *Journal of Tropical Paediatrics and Environmental Child Health* 21 (1B), 1975: 14–15.

Samai, O., and P. Sengeh. "Facilitating Emergency Obstetrics Care through Transportation and Communication, Bo, Sierra Leone." *International Journal of Gynecology and Obstetrics* Nov. 59, suppl. 2, 1997: 157–64.

Siegel, Bruce. *Health Reform in Africa: Lessons from Sierra Leone*. Washington, DC: World Bank, 1996.

Singh, B. "Estimation of Fertility Measures for the Western Area of Sierra Leone." In *Population Dynamics Research in Africa*, ed. F.O.Okediji. Washington, DC:

Smithsonian Institution, Interdisciplinary Communications Program, 1974; 145–68.

Stevenson, D. "Inequalities in the Distribution of Health Care Facilities in Sierra Leone." In *Health and Disease in Tropical Africa: Geographical and Medical Viewpoints*, ed. R Atkar. Chur, Switzerland: Harwood, 1987.

Stewart, T. J., and D. L. Richter. "Perceived Barriers to HIV Prevention among University Students in Sierra Leone, West Africa." *International Quarterly of Community Health Education* 15, 3, 1995: 253–265.

Tangemann, R. H., H. F. Hull, H. Jafari, B. Nkowane, H. Everts, and R. B. Aylward. "Eradication of Poliomyelitis in Countries Affected by Conflict [Angola, Democratic Republic of Congo, Liberia, Sierra Leone, Somalia, and Sudan]." *Bulletin of the World Health Organization* 78, 3, 2000: 330–8.

Tekse, K. "Some Estimates of Vital Rates for Sierra Leone." Brazzaville, Congo: *World Health Organization, AFRO Technical Papers*, 1975: 7–39.

Thomas-Emeagwali, Gloria, ed. *Science and Technology in African History with Case Studies from Nigeria, Sierra Leone, Zimbabwe and Zambia*. Lewton, NY: E. Mellen Press, 1992.

Weyr, R. *Fertility and Attitudes in Sierra Leone*. Geneva, International Labour Office, Nov. 1977.

Williams, L. O. "1986 Universal Child Immunization for Sierra Leone 1986–89." *PopLeone* 3, 5, 1986: 13–15.

Williams, B., and F. Yumkella. "An Evaluation of the Training of Traditional Birth Attendants in Sierra Leone and Their Performance after Training." In *The Potential of the Traditional Birth Attendants*, ed. A. Mangay Maglacas and John Simons. Geneva, Switzerland: World Health Organization, 1986: 35–50.

World Health Organization. *Some Estimates of Vital Rates for Sierra Leone; Kenya National Tuberculosis Programme: Evaluation of a Test-Run; Migration of Health Personnel of the African Region.* Brazzaville: World Health Organization Regional Office for Africa, 1975.

Yumkella, F. "The Incidence of Pregnancy, Abortion and Sexually Transmitted Diseases in School Children in the Western Area." *PopLeone (Freetown)* July, 1984: 9–10.

CURRENT NEWSPAPERS IN FREETOWN, SIERRA LEONE

The newspaper publication scene in Sierra Leone is very volatile and involves a brisk turnover of newsprints. Papers appear and last sometimes a few months and then disappear, to be replaced by new ones. Some papers appear twice weekly while others have no specific frequency. Papers published in Freetown are not necessarily representative of the entire country because papers sometimes spring up in places like Bo and Kenema or some of the larger towns. A website on Sierra Leone details the Sierra Leone media project, funded by the Ford Foundation to support the media in Sierra Leone. The papers listed there are generally Freetown papers where by far the greatest concentration of newsprint exists.

This web site (www.cmetfreetown.org/Media/default.stm) lists 35 newspapers in Freetown for the period December 2000 to October 2001. In May 2003, the author of this dictionary was able to purchase in Freetown 27 newspapers. Fifteen of the tabloids listed in the website do not appear among the 27 that were bought in 2003, while four of the latter (the *News*, the *Watch*, *Christian Monitor*, and the *Focus*) are not listed on the website. There is a possibility of error because not all of the existing papers might have been collected in 2003; there also is the possibility of errors in the presentation of names. One particular tabloid, listed in the website as *Unity Now*, is a case in point. The bold title on a newspaper recorded in May 2003 as the *News* carries a subtopic "Motto: Unity Now." It is not clear whether the listing of a tabloid as "*Unity Now*" is an error in listing *The News*.

The website noted above carries lists of articles from the 35 papers mentioned. While some of the tabloids have a long list of quoted articles, three of them—*Epo Times*, the *Redeemer* and *Shaft*—have only one article mentioned. Three others have no more than three articles quoted. It is not clear whether this represents the frequency of these papers. The following list includes those papers purchased in April and May 2003.

TABLOID EDITOR ADDRESS AND TELEPHONE

The African Champion, Jacob J. Koroma1, Short Street, Freetown, 076 61-08-70
Analysis, Thomas V., Gbow, 11 Regent Road, Freetown, 229531
Awoko, Kelvin Lewis, 15 Lamina Sankoh Street, Freetown, 224927
Christian Monitor, Charles N. Davies, 8 Howe Street, Freetown, 221295
Concord Times, Alpha R. Jalloh, 9 Bathurst Street, Freetown, 229199
The Democrat, Abu Bakarr Joe Sesay, 14A George Street, Freetown, 228103
The Exclusive, Sheik Sesay, 1 Short Street, Freetown, 229331
The Focus, Alusine M. Fofanah, 29 Rawdon Street, Freetown (none given)
For Di People, Harry H. Yansaneh, 1 Short Street, Freetown, 228071, 228062
The Herald Guardian, Eric Lahai, 12 Bathurst Street, Freetown, 076-60-75-68
Independent Observer, Jonathan Leigh, 1 Short Street, Freetown, 229531, 227053
Midweek Spark, Philip Neville, 7 Lamina Sankoh Street, Freetown, 229634
New Citizen, I. B. Kargbo, 7 Wellington Street, Freetown, 228693
New Frontline, Augustine A. Garmoh, 1 Short Street, Freetown (not given)
The News, Mani N. Sorie, 29 Rawdon Street, Freetown, 227466
The New Storm, Mohammed S. Massaquoi, 1 Sani Abacha St., Freetown, 228811
New Vision, A.B.S. Massaquoi, 29 Rawdon Street, Freetown, 229845
Peep, O. R. Awunoor-Gordon, 28 Savage Street, Freetown, 240066
The Policy, Joseph Mboka, 8 Liverpool Street, Freetown, 030-80-02-39
Salone Times, Prince Kamara, 16 Upper Brook Street, Freetown, 226800

Sierra News, Augustine J. Alliew, 15 Wallace Johnson Street, Freetown, 224965, 223127

Standard Times, Augustine Beecher, 2A Ascension Town Road, Kingtom Bridge, Freetown, 229634

Unity, Franklyn Bunting-Davies, 60 Old Railway Line, Brookfields, Freetown, 240916

The Watch, Momodu Adanis, 1 Short Street, Freetown, 229531

Weekend Spark, Philip Neville, 7 Lamina Sankoh Street, Freetown, 229634

Wisdom, John Koroma, 17 Liverpool Street, Freetown, 220448

APPENDIX A
GOVERNORS OF SIERRA LEONE

1792	Lieutenant John Clarkson
1792–1793, 1795–1796	Lieutenant William Dawes
1794–1795, 1796–1799	Zachary Macaulay
1799, 1800	John Gray
1799–1800, 1803–1805, 1806–1808	Thomas Ludlam
1801–1803	Captain William Dawes
1803, 1805	William Day
1808–1810	Lieutenant T. P. Thompson
1810–1811	Captain E. H. Columbine
1811–1814	Lieutenant Colonel C. W. Maxwell
1814–1824	Colonel Charles MacCarthy
1825–1826	Major General Charles Turner
1826–1827	Sir Neil Campbell
1828	Lieutenant Colonel Dixon Denam
1828–1834	Colonel A. Findlay
1833–1834	Major O. Temple
1835–1837	Major H. D. Campbell
1837–1840	Lieutenant Colonel R. Doherty
1840–1841	Sir John Jeremie
1842–1844	Colonel G. Macdonald
1844–1845	Staff Surgeon W. Fergusson
1846–1852	N. W. Macdonald
1852–1854	Captain A. E. Kennedy
1854–1862	Colonel J. S. Hill
1862–1868	Major S. W. Blackall
1872–1873	J. P. Hennessy
1873	R. W. Keate
1873–1874	G. Berkeley

1875–1877	C. H. Kortright
1877–1881, 1985–1888	Sir Samuel Rowe
1981–1884	Captain A. E. Havelock
1888–1891	Captain Sir James Hay
1892–1894	Sir Francis Flemming
1894–1900	Colonel Sir Frederic Cardew
1900–1904	Sir C. A. Kingharman
1904–1911	Sir Leslie Probyn
1911–1916	Sir Edward Mereweather
1916–1922	R. J. Wilkinson
1922–1927	Sir Ransford Slater
1927–1931	Brigadier General J. A. Byrne
1931–1934	Sir Arnold Hodson
1934–1937	Sir Henry Moore
1937–1941	Sir Henry Moore
1941–1948	Sir Hubert Stevenson
1948–1953	Sir George Beresford-Stooke
1953–1956	Sir Robert de Zouche Hall
1956–1962	Sir Maurice Dorman
1962–1967	Sir Henry Josiah Lightfoot-Boiston
1968–1971	Sir Banja Tejan-Sie

Appendix B
Heads of State of Sierra Leone

1961–1964	Milton Margai
1964–1967	Albert Michael Margai
1967–1968	Andrew Terrence Juxon-Smith
1968–1985	Siaka Probyn Stevens
1985–1992	Joseph Saidu Momoh
1992–1996	Valentine Strasser
1996	Julius Maada Bio
1996–to date	Ahmed Tejan Kabbah

Appendix C
Chiefdoms and Paramount Chiefs

Chiefdom	*Headquarters*	*Paramount Chief*	*Date of Election*
EASTERN PROVINCE			
Kailahun District			
Dea	Baiwala	Augustine A. Jibao Gaima	2 January 2003
Jaluahun	Segbwema	M.B. Jimmy–Jajua	27 April 1984
Jawei	Daru	Musa Ngombu-Kla Kallon	23 December 2002
Kissi Kama	Dea	Tamba Okeke Jabba	15 January 2003
Kissi Teng	Kangama	Tamba J. Ganawa II	19 March 1976
Kissi Tongi	Buedu	Nyuma S. Sahr Kallon	21 November 1987
Luawa	Kailahun	Mohamed Kailondo Banya	17 January 2003
Malema	Jojoima	Joseph Lamin Ngevao	8 January 2003
Mandu	Mobai	Nai Samuel Coomber	27 December 2002
Peje Bongre	Manowa	Charles Lamin Ngebeh	26 March 1976
Peje West	Bunumbu	Mustapha Ngebeh	7 September 1971
Penguia	Sandaru	F.S. Kabba-Sei	22 January 1973
Upper Bambara	Pendembu	Cyril Foray Gondor	10 January 2003
Yawei	Bandajuma	Joseph Kormeh Braima	20 December 2002
Kenema District			
Dama	Giema	Sandy Momoh Fowai	2 December 2002
Dodo	Dodo	Steven F.S. Sam Kpakra	N.A.
Gaura	Joru	Alhaji B.M.Gbatekaka	8 September 1964
Gorama Mende (nee Kanja)	Tungie	Haja Mariama M. Gassama	11 December 2002
Kandu Leppiama	Gbado	Theresa Vibbi	28 October 1969
Koya	Baoma	Al-Ameen Mustapha Kanneh	19 January 2003

Langrama	Ya Baima	Prince Mambu Pewa	4 December 2002
Lower Bambara	Panguma	Alimamy Moiwo Farma	4 January 2003
Malegohun	Sembehun	Sally S. Lamin Gendemeh	20 June 1973
Niawa	Sundumei	Joe Amara Tiameh I	9 December 2002
Nomo	Faama	Bockarie Kowa Kabba	9 December 2002
Nongowa	Kenema	Amara J. Vangahun	9 November 1968
Simbaru	Boajibu	Mamie G. Gamanga	21 January 1983
Small Bo	Blama	Mohamed Dhaffie Benya	16 December 2002
Tunkia	Gorahun	Amara Ngoway Sama	7 October 1988
Wando	Faala	Kenewa Henry Fangawa	31 May 1974
Kono District			
Fiama	Njagbwema	Sahr Yongai K. Mbriwa	18 December 2003
Gbane	Ngandorhun	Sam Nyandemo Quee III	29 November 1962
Gbane-Kandor	Koardu	Tamba Fea Mbawa II	30 November 1971
Gbense	Koidu	Sahr Fengai Kaimachende	13 January 2003
Gorama Kono	Kangama	S.C.N. Kono Bundor II	4 March 1985
Kamara	Tombodu	Aiah Melvin Ngekia	30 December 2002
Lei	Siama	Tamba Alpha Fengai Mani	6 January 2003
Mafindor	Kamiendor	Abu Mbawa Kongoba II	28 April 1986
Nimikoro	Njaiama	S. L. Foamansa Matturi II	27 November 1981
Nimiyama	Sewafe	M.N. Torto	16 May 1966
Sandor	Kayima	Alhaji T.K. S. Sonsiama III	2 November 1981
Soa	Kainkordu	S.E.K. Foyoh III	28 November 1980
Tankoro	New Sembehun	F.J.M. Saquee IV	6 November 1981
Toli	Kondewakor	Samuel M. Soloku III	2 February 1979

(*continued*)

Chiefdom	*Headquarters*	*Paramount Chief*	*Date of Election*
NORTHERN PROVINCE			
Bombali District			
Biriwa	Kamabai	Alimamy Kalawa	(not given)
Bombali Sebora	Makeni	Bai Sebora Kasanga II	30 January 1993
Gbanti Kamaranka	Kamaranka	Kandeh Bangura II	22 November 1959
Gbendembu Ngowahun	Kalangba	Kandeh Saio III	9 April 1964
Libeisaygahun	Batkanu	Bai Yankay Kargbo II	14 December 2002
Makari Gbanti	Masongbon	Massa Yeli N'Tham III	5 December 1972
Paki Masabong	Mapaki	Masapaki Kabombor II	2 December 2002
Magbaimba Ndowahun	Hunduwa	Kande Finoh II	19 December 1958
Sanda Loko	Kamalo	Samura Sanu III	(not given)
Safroko Limba	Binkolo	Alimamy Dura II	11 July 1947
Sanda Tendaren	Mateboi	Hamidu Sesay	30 December 2002
Sella Limba	Kamakwie	Kandeh Luseni	(not given)
Tambakha	Fintonia	Alhaji Kandeh Kolleh	27 February 1968
Kambia District			
Bramaia	Kukuna	Yiki Arafan Dumbuya	13 January 2003
Gbinle Dixing	Tawaya	Kandeh Lansana II	(not given)
Masungbala	Kawulia	Bai Kelfa Sankoh	(not given)
Magbema	Kambia	Bai Farama Bubu Ngbak	2 May 1980
Mambolo	Mambolo	Bai Sebora Somano Kapen III	31 March 1989
Samu	Kychum	Bai Sebora Tonico Ansarr III	(not given)
Tonko Limba	Madina	Alfred Momoh Bangura	20 December 2002

Koinadugu District			
Dembelia Sinkunia	Sinkunia	Alimamy Lahai V	10 March 1989
Diang	Kondembaia	Sheku Magba II	28 June 1996
Folosaba Dembeila	Musaia	Alimamy Amadu Jawara III	28 April 1986
Kasunko	Fadugu	Alfred B.S. Kamara	18 December 2002
Mongo	Bendugu	Foday Saio Marah	8 January 2003
Neya	Kurubonla	Gbondo Madusilai	(not given)
Nieni	Yifin	Balla Kali Koroma	22 January 1964
Sengbe	Yogomaia	Alie Marah	4 January 2003
Sulima	Falaba	Bomba Sana Samura	23 December 2002
Wara Wara Bafodea	Bafodea	Alimamy Hamidu I	14 February 1992
Wara Wara Yagala	Gbawuria	Manso Yembeh Mansaray	28 February 2003
Port Loko District			
Bure Kasse Makonte	Mange	Alimamy Mani Bangura	27 December 2002
Buya Romende	Foredugu	Bai Banta Kennedy II	22 September 1998
Dibia	Gbinti	Alhaji Bai Sheka Bundu	5 March 1973
Kaffu Bullom	Mahera	Bai Sebora Komkanda	20 June 1990
Koya	Songo	Bai Kompa Bomboli II	18 September 1973
Loko Masama	Petifu	Bai Sama Lamina Sam	27 September 1974
Maforki	Port Loko	Bai Forki Sonkoi	2 January 2003
Marampa	Lunsar	Bai Koblo Queen II	9 December 2002
Masimera	Masimera	Alhaji Lamin Bangura	6 December 2002
Sanda Magbolontor	Sendugu	Brima Sanda Sorie	9 December 1977
Tinkatupa Masama Safroko	Miraykulay	Alhaji Musa Conteh	16 December 2002

(continued)

Chiefdom	*Headquarters*	*Paramount Chief*	*Date of Election*
Tonkolili District			
Gbonkolenken	Yele	Bai Suntuba Osarr III	10 March 1989
Kafe Simiria	Mabonto	Alimamy Bangura II	22 February 1978
Kalansogoia	Bumbuna	Bockarie Koroma	24 January 2003
Kholifa	Magburaka	Bai Yossoh Kholifa II	7 October 1974
Kholifa Mabang	Mabang	Alfred Bai Carew	11 December 2002
Kunike	Masingbi	Bai Kurr Kanagbara Sanka III	27 October 1988
Kunike Barina	Makali	Alimamy Kanu II	12 November 1971
Malal-Mara	Rochin	Bai Lal N'Soila II	10 February 1978
Sambaia	Bendugu	Almamy Kulio Jalloh II	31 August 1973
Tane	Matotoka	Bai Kafari Ropolor III	9 June 1971
Yoni	Yonibana	Bai Sebora Kondor III	26 January 1990
SOUTHERN PROVINCE			
Bo District			
Badjia	Ngelehun	S.B. Hindowa	10 March 1989
Bagbwe	Ngarlu	M.M. Gbenga III	22 February 1978
Bagbo	Jimmi	Dauda Alphan Kawa Jah	20 December 2002
Baoma	Baoma	Joseph Nabieu Demby	4 April 2003
Bumpe-Gao	Bumpeh	Joseph Tommy Kposowa	18 December 2002
Gbo	Gbo	A.L. Foray Lamboi IV	29 April 1975
Jaiama Bongor	Telu	Mohamed Kama Gbao	8 Jaunary 2003
Kakua	Bo	Rashid Kamanda Bongay	13 January 2003
Komboya	Njala	Albert Moinina Lebbie	4 December 2002
Lugbu	Sumbuya	A.J. Nallo	7 January 1984
Niawa Lenga	Nengbema	George Gbaniey Njiabo	6 December 2002
Selenga	Dambala	Madam HawaY. Ngokowa II	11 September 1968

Tikonko	Tikonko	Joe Kangbai Makavoray	30 December 2002
Valunia	Mongere	James Bobor Vonjoe	17 January 2003
Wunde	Gboyama	Mohamed Tshombe Kargoi	15 January 2003
Bonthe District			
Bendu Cha	Bendu	Samuel M. Koroma	23 March 1984
Bum Sebureh IV	Madina	Madam Margaret Jami	17 June 1988
Dema	Tisana	S.G.K. Ngabay	26 June 1987
Imperri Sokan IV	Gbangbama	Madam Hawa Kpanabon	22 July 1983
Jong	Mattru	Allieu Sheriff	16 December 2002
Kpanda Kemo	Motuo	Jonathan B. Lebbie	12 February 1994
Kwamabai Krim	Benduma	Janet Elizabeth Bio Tiffa	20 January 2003
Nongoba Bullom	Gbap	C.W. Tucker III	27 April 1979
Sittia	Yonni	Jibrilla Ansumana Fai	20 January 2003
Songbini	Tihun	Steven Woni Bio IV	21 January 1993
Yawbeko	Talia	Joe Jamgba	(not given)
Moyamba District			
Bagruwa	Sembehun	V.K.K. Thaiimu Bakortu II	(not given)
Lower Banta	Gbangbatoke	Edgar Strieby Margai	23 December 2002
Upper Banta	Mokelle	Tommy Maulaylay Jombla	6 January 2003
Bumpeh	Rotifunk	Charles B. Caulker	26 October 1984
Dasse Meama-Kajue	Mano	Haja Fatmata B.K.	2 December 2002
Fakunya	Gandohun	Joseph Kavura Kongomoh	1996
Kagboro	Shenge	Segismond O. Caulker	9 December 2002
Kaiyamba	Moyamba	Madam Ella Koblo Gulama	20 November 1992
Kamajei	Senehun	J.K. Martin Mbayenge	30 September 1988

(*continued*)

Chiefdom	*Headquarters*	*Paramount Chief*	*Date of Election*
Kongbora	Bauya	Alfred S. Banya III	25 May 1991
Kori	Taiama	Thomas B. Gbappi IV	8 August 1975
Kowa	Njama	J. W. Quee	28 November 1952
Ribbi	Bradford	Foday Raka Mahoi	17 January 2003
Timdale	Bomotoke	Mattu Kaikai Yimbo I	27 November 1981
Pujehun District			
Barri	Potoru	Vandi Kong Magona Jr.	2 January 2003
Gallinas Perri	Blama	Issa Baimba Kamara	10 January 2003
Kpaka	Massam	Alhaji M. Rogers	(not given)
Malen	Sahn	B.V.S. Kebbie III	13 October 1980
Makpele	Zimmi	Prince M.B. Konneh	13 December 2002
Mano Sakrim Fawundu	Gbonjema	Madam Edna Gamanga	27 November 1982
Kpanga Kabonde	Pujehun	Alimamy Jaia Kaikai IV	15 January 2003
Panga Krim	Gobaru	S.A.S. Gbonda II	9 February 1979
Pejeh	Futta	Haja Miatta Sogual Koroma	20 January 2003
Soro Gbema Zembo	Fairo	Alhaji Bockarie Vanjawa	11 December 2002
Sowa	Bandajuma	Lahai A.K. Sowa II	27 December 2002
Yakemo Kpukumu Krim	Karlu	Madam Matilda Y. Lansina Minah	17 January 1986

About the Author

Magbaily Fyle was born in Freetown, Sierra Leone, in 1944 and was educated at the Sierra Leone Grammar School and Fourah Bay College, where he took the bachelor of arts with honors in history in 1968. He spent another year obtaining the diploma in education and taught for a year at the Bishop Johnson Memorial School before proceeding for further studies in the United States. He qualified with a certificate in African Studies in 1972 and in 1976 received a Ph.D., both from Northwestern University in Evanston, Illinois.

Magbaily Fyle has been a professor in the African American and African Studies Department of Ohio State University since 1991. Prior to this, he was the first African with a Ph.D. in history to become professor of history at Fourah Bay College, University of Sierra Leone. He was also the first professor to hold the chair of African Studies at Fourah Bay College in 1990. At Fourah Bay College, he was dean of the Faculty of Arts (1986–1988) and was University Public Orator. He served on many boards in Sierra Leone and was a nonexecutive director of the Central Bank of Sierra Leone (1980–1986).

Magbaily Fyle is enthusiastic about publishing information in Africa. He has written eight books and many articles, a number of them published in Africa. These include *The Solima Yalunka Kingdom* (Freetown: Nyakon, 1979); *Oral Traditions of Sierra Leone* (Niamey: Centre for the Study of Languages and History by Oral Tradition, 1979); *History and Soicioeconomic Development in Sierra Leone* (Freetown: Sierra Leone Adult Education Association, 1986), and edited *The State and Social Services in Sierra Leone since Independence 1961–1991* (Dakar: Council for the Development of Social Science Research in Africa, 1993). Dr. Fyle also worked extensively with the German Adult Education Association in Sierra Leone to promote local publishing in the well-known "Peoples Education Association Stories and Songs from Sierra Leone" series, in which he also published, in 1986, *Yalunkayan, Nnamungne enung a siginne, enung a taaline (Traditions, Song and Chant of the Yalunka)*. The best known of his books on Sierra Leone are *The History of Sierra Leone: A Concise Introduction* published by Evans of London in 1981 and *Almany Suluku of Sierra Leone* (London: Evans, 1979). More recently, he authored the two-volume *Introduction to the History of African Civilization* (Lanham, Md.: University Press of America, 1999 and 2002).